BLACK TO MOVE AND DRAW

A literary romp through the chess world of Washington Square Park

KEVIN STOKKER

Butch Press

A BUTCH PRESS CHESS BOOK
Published by
Butch Press Chess

Copyright © 2020 by Kevin Stokker

All rights reserved. No part of this book may be reproduced or transmitted in any form or by any electronic or mechanical means, including photocopying, recording, or by any information storage and retrieval system, without the written permission of the publisher, except where permitted by law.

This book is a work of fiction. Names, characters, places, and incidents either are the products of the author's imagination or are used fictitiously, and any resemblance to actual events or persons, living or dead, is entirely coincidental.

ISBN: 978-0-9965077-0-7

Front and back cover design by damonza.com
Formatting design by Damonza
Illustrations by David Craig
Photograph by Laura G. Stokker

ALSO BY
KEVIN STOKKER

White to Move and Lose
Public & Private Space

For Laura and Mallory,
always

BLACK TO MOVE AND DRAW

They say the entire operation has been jeopardized. They tell me you are the cause of it. I fear for you. I fear for your life. Already, he has killed those who stand in his way.

And yet, I play their game. And I wait…

						"	N
		E		W	Y		O
		R			K	C	
I	T		Y	I	S		
			M	Y			C
		H	E		S		
S	B				O	A	
R			D			"	

Chapter 1
"NEW YORK CITY IS MY CHESSBOARD"

♞ al ♘
ASCENDING & DESCENDING. A BRICK IN THE DOOR. SNOW.

DANTE MENTIONS IT not. The Greeks are silent on the matter. And Jonathan Edwards is clueless. Nevertheless, the fact remains: cellular reception in hell is abysmal. Consider it one of the Underworld's less-documented chastisements.

Not that my office is a literal Hell. The complex of dingy rooms that lies deep within a sub-basement of my university library and is referred to by my Comp Lit students as the Ninth Circle is just too damn far beneath the nearest cell tower for anyone to be able to call or text.

My officemate spoke. "Having troubles with your cell phone, there, Marty?"

"I'm trying to text Monika," I said, pocketing my phone in frustration. "I'll have to go upstairs."

Postdoc swiveled in his chair. His pale grey eyes were lit, and a toothy grin pulled his sideburns and bushy moustache into a wide, sandy W. A purple cardigan hugged his lanky frame. "Woohoo! Mo-ni-*ka*! Marty with his red-hot hottie on Valentine's!" He stood up and started gyrating his narrow hips. He chucked me on my chin, pulled his cardigan tighter around himself, and sat back down at his desk.

Chapter 1

I first met Pat "Postdoc" MacGroddy at a professional conference in Chicago. He was delivering a lecture: "The Effect of Memes on Postracial Discourse and Documentary Cinema." Where most of the attendees had been attired in business casual, he'd sported a pair of factory-ripped jeans made to look like they should have been thrown out with last week's garbage, and his T-shirt had read, "FISCHER SAID IT. I BELIEVE IT. THAT SETTLES IT!"

That had been six years ago. Since then, America had survived a second Bush term; our nation's first Black president was taking on healthcare; a Tea Party movement had begun, advocating for the fundamental principle that that government governs best which governs worst; New Yorkers *still* stared at a gap in the skyline around our financial district; and I had been promoted to assistant professor at NYU. And Postdoc? Postdoc was pretty much the same nudge as ever.

Still, I liked the guy. He was the sort who could do just about anything he put his mind to, provided it didn't require a great deal of common sense. Besides, Monika was always sweet to him, and if Monika likes someone, well, that's good enough for me.

Postdoc's smile was infectious, and soon I was smiling, too. "Well, Postdoc," I said, opening the door to the hall, "I appreciate your enthusiasm for my evening's plans, but it's getting pretty late." I glanced at the wall clock. 10:25. "I'm sure by now Monika has eaten dinner."

"Dinner? Who said anything about *dinner*?" He winked. "As long as you're going up to the outside, how about you take the Brick with you? All this talk about food is making me hungry. What do you say we order from Antonio's. Halvesies?"

"Sure." I wasn't really interested in eating—or, anyway, not with Postdoc. But I knew he was cheap, and if I didn't go in with him on the pizza, he might not eat at all. From a bookcase I grabbed the Brick: a beat-up, mass-market copy of *Atlas Shrugged* we used as a doorstop to let pizza and Chinese food delivery into the building after hours. "Oh, and Postdoc—when you go online to order, don't forget the pepperoni this time, huh?"

"Wouldn't dream of it, sir." He spoke this in a truly miserable Cockney accent—his idea of chuckles, given my British origin. Even threw in a mock salute.

Hilarious. A real screamer.

For a second time I attempted to leave, but he called me back in again. "Hup! Don't go just yet!"

"What is it now?"

He slapped a graded essay on his Done pile and went to our filing cabinet, where we had a chess game in progress. It's our way of keeping things going: you don't get to move until you've graded a paper. "Just graded another one!" he said. "And now I think… my bishop… will make a go at your lady." Postdoc slid his bishop to d5. "Ha! Be careful, Marty! Things are about to get dangerous."

I hovered over the board for a minute, noting a couple of moves I would consider in greater depth when I returned. Then I left, yelling from the hall that I'd make him sorry for that move. I climbed nine flights of stairs, heading for the outside and cell coverage. If Monika wasn't too far, maybe there was still time to have a drink with her before the whole day was shot.

Like Dante the Pilgrim came forth from Hell "to rebehold the stars," I ascended from the Ninth Circle *inferni*, emerging from the concrete bowels of NYU's Bobst Library to rebehold the bright world of the building's main level. If you ever get a chance to visit, it is wonderful: a vast atrium, layer upon layer of glass and light—a vault of knowledge and literature reaching toward the heavens. An Escher-inspired pattern fills the floor with geometrical delight; purple banners hang in mid-air over the circulation desks. *Vexilla Regis prodeunt.* The banners of the king issue forth.

I approached the line of glass doors that exit onto 4th Street. At this time on a Sunday night, just before closing, the odds of someone catching me shoving Ayn Rand into the frame of one of those doors was low. Still, I looked around, and good thing, too.

"Hey, Dr. Malloy!" I heard.

I recognized one of my students. Hipster-looking lad, a couple of lip piercings, a no-doubt-ironic fedora. Name might have been Phil. I'll give the kid credit, he identified the book I was carrying. "Oh, no!" he said. "Don't tell me you're going all Tea Party on us, Doc!"

"Not a chance," I replied. "Good night." Phil headed out to the street.

Instead of following him toward the main entrance, I took a hall branching off to a row of side doors that allow faculty entrance to the basement after library closing hours. I looked around again. This time the coast was clear. Going to the door farthest to the right, I lodged the Brick into the jamb just enough for the door to almost close, yet still fail to latch. Then I stepped outside. Despite near-freezing temperatures, it somehow seemed warmer than my under-heated office. I took out my cell and texted my girlfriend.

At the Ninth. Almost done. Sorry so late. Still good for plans?

While I awaited Monika's response, I took in the Greenwich Village night. Up and down 4th Street, the headlights of the occasional car or delivery truck illuminated streaks of falling snow. Pedestrians were few. Across the street I could discern the black, wrought-iron fence that edges Washington Square Park. The snowfall was topping the fence with a cap of fine, white fluff.

The Square is more of a rectangle, really: a four-block by two-block urban haven of trees, green lawns, walking paths, benches. From my position at its southeast corner I couldn't tell whether a splotch of light that bled through a clump of tall, bare trees to the north indicated the famous Washington Square Arch or if I was seeing the distant buildings that line Waverly Place along the park's northern border. To the south of the Arch, at the park's exact center, a large fountain awaited summer and the kids that splash around its shallow, circular basin.

Most significant, for here was a plausible guess concerning Monika's whereabouts, was the park's southwest corner. There, under the ancient English elms, a circle of twenty marble tables and green wooden benches forms the heart of the downtown chess scene. Chess hustlers can be found playing their game at most hours of nearly any day: the world's smartest homeless, taking on anyone willing to sit down long enough to lose five dollars. A few minutes is all it takes—chess in the park is not like it is in tournament halls. These guys all play fast; a few of them play dirty. As for being homeless, well, that's what I'd read. I had also heard it said that many of them are on drugs. But that's more than I know.

Clarification: it was more than I knew then.

At four blocks, it was impossible to tell if anyone was still playing chess under the trees. If Monika *were* there, it would be because Butch was there. By the time those doleful, blackening months of winter had come, she no longer bothered with anyone else in the park. During the sixteen months we had been dating, Monika's chess had soared from C-class to Master level. She competed almost every week at the Marshall and took lessons on her laptop from distant grandmasters with exotic names. I, of course, remained the hopeless fish I always shall be.

As I stood shivering outside the library, I figured I could guess at the lay of the land. Monica and Butch would be having one of their series of epic battles, and time had stopped for them both. It would be two o'clock in the morning before she noticed my text. When they finally finished, regardless of the score between them, Monika would slip Butch what she called an L-note (that would be fifty bucks to you or me), or a C-note, or even *two* of the Franklin boys. The amount would depend partly on how much of Butch's time she had used, but mostly on how much compassion she couldn't keep from pouring out of her heart. Early on in their friendship, Butch had resigned himself to her generosity.

Butch. Now there was one chess hustler who was definitely not on drugs. And he was certainly not homeless. Over the dozen years I had known him, I had been to his Harlem apartment many times. Fourteen years my senior, he has a capacity for knowledge that is exceeded only by his thirst for it. An eclectic with an internal library of facts, Butch on occasion descends into the Ninth, where he gleefully engages my colleagues in debate and cross-examination over whatever point, usually arcane, embodies his present fixation. A man of both knowledge and action, he avidly follows local crime, and it is usually some self-assigned, Sherlock Holmesian errand that pulls us back into each other's orbits, sometimes after long periods of scarcity.

Butch's one intellectual shortcoming—literature—happens to be my profession; his vast collection of books, magazines, and newspapers is almost entirely nonfiction. Only in the past few months had he suddenly turned his attention to novels, short stories, and even poetry.

A chime from my phone alerted me to a text:

Hi! Stopped by for chess with B. Wasn't there

Odd, I thought. Why would Butch have left the Square so early? Surely not for dinner. Each minute spent away from the board was a minute not making five dollars. Butch always carried food with him in his olive-drab duffel bag—

A second text came.

Shopping with F. On my way. Plans = ♥♥♥

Chapter 1

Forgetting for the moment about Butch and alight with a fresh helping of Monika, I descended the nine flights of white-painted cinderblock stairs (elevator, you ask? sorry, closed after 10:00) to the bottom-most circle of the underworld. I thought about that propped-open outer side door with Ayn Rand jammed into it. Who would be first to enter? Monika? Or the pizza guy from Antonio's? I figured it had to be one or the other.

But on this point, as things turned out, I was wrong.

♘ b1 ♘
AN UNEXPECTED PARTY. A LONG-EXPECTED PARTY.

From a secure and undisclosed location somewhere within the heart of Bobst Library, a furnace pumps heat like blood through the building's ductwork arteries into its most distant extremities. Descending the basement stairwell, you can feel the heat weaken, the pulse of air become more thready. At L4—the fourth level below ground—the building becomes a patient with chronic cardiac arrhythmia. Space heaters begin to appear in some of the halls. By the time you hit L6, those heaters are year-round fixtures.

L-918, a.k.a. the Ninth, sits off a corridor lit only by a bank of underpowered fluorescent tubes and a single space heater, at the far end of the hall. Several of the bulbs, including the one directly outside my office, flicker. Postdoc and I liked to keep our door shut.

Reflecting happily on Monika's eventual arrival, I came to the closed door of my office. A series of sharp thwacks was coming from inside. I cracked the door open. Postdoc had a 16-oz. bottle of Mountain Dew in one hand, while with the other he was helping himself to my darts, throwing them at the corkboard above my desk. The presumed target was a printout of an archery bullseye pattern thumb-tacked into the cork. None of the darts had hit it. One stuck out of a coupon for $3 off a large Antonio's pizza and another had impaled a memo announcing university deadlines for course drops, while a third had tried to score points from an invitation to Adarsh Jayaramana's doctoral defense. Adarsh now had a dart protruding from his forehead. I also spotted a lone dart that had landed on the stack of papers I needed to finish grading.

I entered our office. "How's that work coming along, Postdoc?"

He sighed, handed me the rest of the darts, and flopped down at his desk. "Marty, how long do you think it will take my students to finally get the difference between stream of consciousness and interior monologue?"

I chuckled. "You know most of these papers were probably written by students all stoked up on Adderall, right?"

Ignoring this, Postdoc pulled the next paper off his stack. Then I let out a sigh of my own, recalling my undergraduate days at Oxford, when no one had heard of Adderall and when the cognitive-enhancing drug of choice was a good, strong cup of black coffee.

I walked over to our chess game on top of the filing cabinet. "Hey," I said. "I told you I would make you sorry for moving that bishop."

Without missing a beat, Postdoc swiveled around in his chair. "Marty, haven't you heard? Checkmate—" from the pocket of his cardigan he pulled one last dart and threw it across the room, directly into the bullseye, "means never having to say you're sorry."

"Postdoc," I said, "you're such a—"

Bump, came a thud at the door. A pause lingered between us, like he was expecting me to get the door for Monika, and I just wanted him to get the damn pizza already. Funny how the brain doesn't work correctly around women or food. Even in their absence. That single thud wasn't how people knock. Yet it wouldn't be for another hour, as I sat in the hospital, that that thought would occur to me.

I went to the door and opened it to find neither Monika nor pizza, but Butch.

He didn't fall at once. I had time to stammer, "My God! *Butch!*" before the strength left his legs.

"Jubuwusuff—" he said, perhaps an attempt to eke out his hallmark response, *Just Butch will suffice*, and down he went.

Butch hit the floor with a crack: the sound of cranium meeting linoleum with nothing between but a crust of kinked grey hair. Blood splattered from his head, and a reeking suspension of body odor and cigar filled the room.

I gagged on the acridness; Postdoc pranced about in a tizzy. I think he was trying to move around the body to get to the door and failing for lack of space.

Chapter 1

"Butch hit the floor with a crack."

I knelt next to Butch. He was still conscious, his eyes open but dull. I said something to the effect of *take it easy*, and I touched his arm.

He was freezing. His left hand was clenched into a fist that he held tight against his heaving abdomen. A sticky slather of blood covered this hand; against the black of his skin it looked like oil—a gusher, welling up and over his hand in time with his pulse. Something that looked like a bloody stub of a stick peeked out from his fist. I looked back to his face. The blood around his head had clearly come from his mouth when he fell. At least that blood wasn't flowing.

"Butch," I said, "we're getting help."

His lips started to move, but I couldn't understand.

"*Dufff...*"

I put my head closer.

"*Dufbaghgh...*"

"Postdoc?" I said. "Can you make this out?"

"He's talking about his duffle bag," came her voice—soft, feminine, full of Slavic vowels, crunchy with consonants. I looked up to behold Monika. Her hair flowed red down the sides of her ivory face onto the deep-blue down-filled coat she had given me a week after we had first started dating, when the weather had first turned cold.

"At least this explains the blood spatters all down the stairs," she said.

♞ c1 ♞
BLOOD AND LEATHER. A WALK IN THE PARK.

Monika dropped to her knees and slid off her coat. She pillowed it under Butch's head, crossing its blue sleeves over his chest. Trying to anchor the sleeves tight, she partially unzipped his New York Jets hoodie, stuffed the sleeves inside, and zipped it back up. Under the hoodie was the kelly-green woolen sweater we had given Butch for Christmas. It had gained a certain lived-in appearance.

While Monika worked, Butch's eyes followed her sharply. His lips parted, revealing an incomplete set of crooked, stained teeth. He moved his mouth to speak; I saw Monika flinch away from the sudden stench of his breath. "He's going to lose consciousness," she said. Gathering Butch's right hand in hers, she sandwiched it between the smooth black leather of her blood-soiled gloves. His skin was cracked, his knuckles pink, raw ovals peeking out from between the gloves' gold-plated letters spelling PRADA.

"How much longer?" she asked.

Postdoc and I looked at each other, then back to her.

"Wait. Don't tell me you haven't—"

"Calling 911!" said Postdoc. He went to his desk and grabbed the land line.

Monika rolled her eyes but otherwise didn't say a word as her glance darted across Butch's torso. Calm and detached, she was the seasoned chess master, not particularly liking her position but scanning the board for some salvaging move. Sometimes all you need is a draw.

"We're going to need pressure," she said. "Deep abdominal wound. Probably been stabbed. He's going to be out soon. One of us has to hold that spot." Tenderly, she set Butch's right hand down on the floor next to my knee. When she reached for Butch's left, though, he resisted. "It's okay," she whispered. "I'm going to hold the wound." Butch's hand still held tight. "You're going to be okay." Then to me, with urgency: "Get something soft. Something I can make a bandage with."

I started to look around for something to use when Butch grabbed my hand. His sharp eyes looked right at me, and his right hand pulsed with some desperate imperative—whether to draw strength from me or to impart it I have never been able to decide.

"Read my thoughts!" These, his last words before unconsciousness took him, came as foul air over dried lips. His right hand went limp, and I set it down. His left hand, still clenched tight, smacked the floor. I heard a faint click, and blood spat from his wound.

Postdoc had reached a 911 operator. "Hey, we've got a man down here! On our floor! Bleeding!"

While he spoke, I found what was needed: Postdoc's cardigan.

While Postdoc talked to the police on the phone, Monika made a compress out of Postdoc's sweater. She was on her knees again, holding the purple wool against Butch's stomach. Her long, copper hair grazed his bloody skin. Postdoc hung up and, apparently at a loss for how to occupy himself, grabbed a copy of *Dubliners*. He pretended to page through it, but glanced at the door every few seconds, whether in anticipation of paramedics or pizza I couldn't say.

For the first time since entering the room, Monika looked at me and smiled, and for one moment the world was just us two. "Hey, Martin," she said. She had lips the color of mischief, and her playful eyeshadow almost, but not quite, matched her emerald eyes. Around the neckline of her heather-grey turtleneck, a choker sparkled in brilliant diamonds. I adore how she rolls the *r* in my name.

"Hey," I said.

Her brows came together, and the moment faded into an exquisite and beguiling sternness. "Now what is this? Two academics, but the diplomat's daughter is the only one smart enough to call 911?" Her words held the hard edge of a half-decent paring knife, but her eyes were green satin. She was happy to see me.

I blushed and looked down to where Butch's hand had hit the floor. As if on cue, it opened. A black chess king dropped out. Perhaps owing to the sticky blood, the king—a larger-sized piece than usual, I noticed—balanced improbably on edge, then, in resignation, toppled over and lolled around in a circle.

"Look at that," I said. "Shouldn't all his pieces be—" And then I remembered Butch's words. "His duffel bag! It's not here."

Monika had me take over maintaining the pressure on Butch while she produced some Kleenex out of somewhere. She wiped the king clean and dropped it in her purse. "His duffel bag," she repeated. "He's never without it. And yet—"

"—he is without it," I finished.

"You think he walked here from chess?" she asked.

"He couldn't have made it far like this."

Monika considered this. "If someone tried to rob him, Butch would have fought. But he wouldn't have just dropped his bag."

"Never," I agreed. "So he didn't have the bag on him when he was stabbed."

"Right. And when does he not have his bag physically on him?"

We said it together. "When he's playing chess."

"It's probably still under his usual bench. You should get it before someone else finds it. I'll text you when the ambulance comes."

Chapter 1

Within five minutes I had crossed 4th Street and was entering the park. I was glad to be outside. Back in the library, red drippings from Butch's gut had turned nine flights of white-painted stairs into a trail of pain. Now the crisp smell of freshly falling snow was erasing the tangy, ferric scent of blood from my nose.

Leaving the street din behind me, I gazed across the silent width of Washington Square. The white stone arch was lit from below, its marble abutments disappearing behind a copse of trees that made a jumble of angles against the corona of distant light. I turned left and directed myself along a path that led toward the park's southwest corner. This close to midnight, my four-block trek would be lonely: not many people to hinder my way. That was one way of looking at things. Not so long ago, someone had knifed my friend in this deserted part of town. That was another.

I walked on past tall black metal streetlamps, the snow crunching loudly beneath my boots. I approached a line of benches. Snow had sunk down between the slats, leaving dark grooves and white stripes—a musical staff. A band, I recalled, had played bebop here last summer. Monika had bought a pastrami sandwich from a street vendor and used it as a bribe to get Butch to stop playing chess long enough to join us for a walk. She taught him the Czech for various chess terms; he got her to smoke one of his Swisher Sweets. We had laughed.

I was getting closer to the chess circle. Silhouettes of tables appeared ahead. Far off, but not too far, a siren screamed. Maybe it was the ambulance, come to help Butch, I thought. I wondered if the pizza had ever arrived. I imagined Postdoc scrubbing around in his pocket for a tip and reaching over Butch's unconscious body to hand two crumpled bucks to some guy in a stained green, white, and red Antonio's shirt. ("Here's for climbing all those stairs, pal. You be careful going up now, okay?")

I reached the chess tables. I shuddered—was it the cold? Possibly. An alternative theory might be the darkness all around me, where anyone— say, a man with a big, sharp knife—could be creeping.

The tables were all empty. No, not true. Across the way, two figures sat playing chess in the falling snow. The one smoked a pipe, the other drank from what appeared to be a coffee cup. From this distance the pieces looked strange and unlikely, as if the accumulation of snow had enlarged them, mushing their shapes into one another, the pieces barely fitting inside their squares. And what was I to do? Go over there, ask them about a stabbing? What if one of them was the assailant? Sounded like a great way to get killed.

I went to Butch's accustomed seat to look for his duffel but found nothing. No, again not true. I found a dark splash. I got out my phone and turned on the flashlight. The splashes—there were many of them—were blood.

Butch had been attacked here. He would have had his duffel on him, or at least near him. Somewhere between here and the Bobst, he had dropped it. How would he have gone? Would he have ambled through the park? Not likely. He would have sought safety, and that would mean a dash to the street.

From Butch's bench, I walked a direct line to 4th Street. For all the feeling of seclusion, the chess circle abuts the very edge of Washington Square. Rather than go around a bordered off area of lawn, I walked directly over it, where the untrodden snow was somewhat deeper than it was on the paths. No, not completely untrodden. They were already mostly obscured, filling in fast, but I soon found what surely had been Butch's footprints. Within moments, I discovered a dark indentation in the white. Butch's duffel sat where he had dropped it, not ten feet from the sidewalk.

I walked back along 4th to the Bobst and found a small collection of flashing rescue vehicles parked in a jumble somewhat on, mostly off, the sidewalk in front of the library. Of course. The cell reception. Monika wouldn't have been able to text the arrival of the ambulance. A gentleman in a red, white, and green Antonio's shirt was shoving two dollars into his pocket while he exited a door that, earlier that evening, I had propped open with a dreadful novel.

♞ d1 ♞
CUSHY AND PLUSH. A LONG NIGHT. BREAKING NEWS.

We had taken a cab back to our Upper West Side two-bedroom. I sat on the edge of our bed, chin in hand, watching as Monika prepped for a shower. Sweater and jeans came off, revealing matching bra and panties. Red, for you inquiring minds that need to know. But Valentine's Day had

Chapter 1

ended, I thought to myself; the panties were coming off in the bathroom, and that would be that. Not that there was any other choice, really. The sweater, the jeans, the hair—all were crusty with Butch's blood. Not exactly conducive to Valentine's plans.

As she padded about our room, gathering up supplies, Monika's feet made soft dimples in the deep nap of the carpet, mottling the crisp Vs left behind by our housekeeper's vacuum cleaner. It was always easy to know when she had come around: the room's pieces were in perfect harmony; there was a place for everything, and everything was in its place.

Tonight, there was an item without a place: one olive-drab duffel.

Like an intruder from a lesser world—a world with fewer things and fewer places for those things to be—Butch's bag sat on our floor. Its flap gaped open, and the bag leaned a little, like it was woozy, threatening to vomit its innards over the white carpet.

Stripping off the last of her clothes, Monika disappeared into the bathroom. She turned on the water and started to sing as the steam permeated our bedroom. I caught a few words of Daryl Hall and John Oates's "Rich Girl."

For all her compassion, it's Monika's ability to detach that impresses me more. I brooded, she sang in the shower—and why not? We had done all we could for poor Butch. It occurred to me that a great deal of Monika's chess improvement those days probably owed to that particular skill: detachment. The ability to refocus after a painful event without abandoning the lessons learned from the loss. Most serious chess players hate to lose, and when they do, it's like one of those scribbled clouds that Charles Schulz draws over Charlie Brown's head when Lucy pulls the football out from under his kick and he goes flying through the air and lands on his back, practically kills himself. I know that cloud, how it settles over a head like so much mental rain. But when Monika loses a game, she figures out what went wrong and then forgets all about it. And when a friend lands on his back and gets himself practically killed, she does what she can for him and sings in the shower afterward.

The cloud that was hanging over *my* head, you ask? Well, that would be the flurry and confusion of the night's events, the blood spattering over Postdoc's collection of Mountain Dew bottles in our office, the damp red splotch in the dark and empty place where my friend had been attacked, the useless visit to the ER waiting room. And here I was, living in a cushy apartment with a plush girlfriend, holding down a cushy job at a plush university (my office maybe not so cushy and plush), while Butch—every bit as deserving as me and twice as smart—rented life in pieces, day to day, five bucks at a time, cushy was a side of fries with that dollar-menu burger, plush was when it didn't rain on your chessboard, home was silent hours in a hardscrabble Harlem apartment. Yes. That was *my* cloud.

The flurry and confusion of the night's events...

I had run from the park all the way back to the Bobst, Butch's duffel bouncing against the small of my back the whole way. Outside the library, a pair of ambulances and something from the fire department straddled the sidewalk; a man, probably one of the drivers, sat on a tailgate in dark blue work clothes and thick rubber-soled black boots. He spoke into a mic strapped to his chest, its curled cord leading to a transmitter belted at his waist. One ambulance was painted in school colors. Its rear double doors were open; its insides, stacked with medical equipment, had space enough for a stretcher and maybe two people.

The doors to the Bobst were all locked. Outside the leftmost door, as if fallen from a student's backpack, the Brick lay on the ground. Four times that night—first for Butch, then for Monika, a third time for the pizza man, and most recently for the emergency responders, who must have pushed the thing aside without bothering to replace it—that stupid paperback had allowed everyone and anyone into the library. Its only stipulation seemed to have been that you didn't belong there. Atlas shrugged, indeed. I was picking the book up when Monika came to the door.

"Hey," she said. "You're panting. Everything okay?"

My report could wait. "Sure. What's going on? Are they down there?"

"Yeah. They've got him stable enough to move. Should be up soon." Monika shot a glance at the ambulance and then looked back to me. "What do you want to do?"

I looked again at the driver. He was having a smoke and had walked off a bit from the medical equipment. "These guys are probably from Langone. NYU. In Midtown. Too far to walk." I looked again toward the back doors of the ambulance. "I doubt if all of us could fit in there. See if the driver will let you go with them. If you're calm, they'll probably take you. I'll call a cab and catch up with you."

"If I'm *calm*?" The hands on her hips suggested I was being scolded, but her eyes and her tone let me know I was one funny boy. "Do I look hysterical to you?"

Never.

"Look," she said, "you need to eat. This might be a long night." She bobbed her head toward the library. "The pizza came. I had a couple slices, but if you go quick you might still get some before Postdoc snarfs the rest."

She rolled the *r* in *snarf*, adorably. As for the pizza, I really didn't feel hungry. That was nerves, of course, but I needed to eat. Monika was right. She almost always was, if you insist.

"Okay," I said, "I'll—"

"You found it!" She meant the bag hanging from my shoulder.

"Yeah," I said, remembering myself, "would you mind taking it?" As I swung it off my shoulder, she stepped forward and caught the strap neatly, giving me a soft kiss on the cheek as she brushed past me and walked toward the ambulance.

I watched while she talked with the driver. When she turned to me and signaled the thumbs up, I gave her a wave and for the third time that night hoofed it down to the Ninth.

I made it as far as L4 before I encountered the emergency responders—two of them, grunting directions to each other as they struggled up the stairs with Butch strapped to a stretcher. On the landing, I stepped aside. As the stretcher passed, I felt an urge to reach out and touch Butch's hand. I remember thinking how grey it looked. A mask with some kind of balloon attached was strapped to his face. He was unconscious. Then they were gone. I rushed down five more flights of stairs and entered my office just as Postdoc was lifting the last slice of pizza to his face. I shot him a look that ought to have melted the cheese right off the slice, then decided I just didn't have the energy to scold him. Anyway, he'd probably figured I wouldn't return tonight. "Aw, go ahead and have the feckin' slice," I ended up saying.

What a nudge.

The shower turned off. Monika called out to me from the bathroom. "Martin, you're not still brooding out there, are you?"

"No!" I called back.

The elderly nurse's nameplate had said HELGA.

"I need to know ze patient's full name, honey, you see?" she'd asked. Helga was certainly kind enough. Anyone could hear the forbearance, cultivated over years of working the triage desk in an inner-city ER, pushing through her lingering accent. But if I wanted to know Butch's status, then she needed to know Butch's full name. She drew the white paste of her face close behind the semi-open sliding window until, like those of Dr. T.J. Eckleburg, her spectacled eyes floated, not over a billboard, but just above a sticker that spelled out terms of payment in bright yellow capital letters.

Funny, isn't it? How things never occur to you until, all at once, they do? And what occurred to me just then was that, for over fifteen years, I'd gone without knowing the last name of my good friend Butch.

I started explaining the evening's entertainment. "I was— That is to say, *we* were—" I pointed vaguely across the long and harried waiting room to indicate the *we* aspect of my story. Monika sat on a floral-print couch under a wall-mounted TV that was broadcasting a news station. She had curled her legs up beneath her, and her head was bent down, as if she was studying something on her lap. Butch's duffel was slung open at her side.

I returned my attention to Helga. She was peering at me through watery eyes that matched her uniform's cornflower blue. "Monika came with him—Butch, I mean—in the ambulance. I called a cab, because there wasn't room, you zee—" I paused only a split second before correcting the *zee* to *see*, which Helga accepted with pursed lips and tolerant eyes. "And the ambulance, it must have brought Butch directly—"

"You have no surname for zis patient? Butch, you say?"

An idea popped into my head. Butch's bag! There might be a clue in there—an ID of some sort. I told Helga I would be right back.

The room was busy: a bald priest in a dust mask; a Vietnamese mother sitting beside her boy, who lay in Pokémon pajamas at her side; a woman who read *Good Housekeeping* with a vacant face. A huge man, shiny like a polished bowling ball, held one hand submerged in a bowl of what appeared to be ice water. "That was 500-degree steel, by god! 500-degree steel!"

he bellowed to the elderly man who sat across from him. Suddenly, the TV revved up a tremendous, nerve-throbbing bass beat. Breaking News. Everyone looked up at the screen, and together we learned that Estonia had officially adopted the Euro as its currency.

I sat down next to Monika. Dried blood smudged her jeans and sweater. Her head was still bent down, and I saw that she was studying a hardbound journal. The page she was reading had a chess diagram and some notations on it. I recognized Butch's mechanical handwriting.

"Hello?" I said. No response, try again. "Hello?"

Monika lifted her head. "Oh. Hi, Martin. These positions I found in Butch's duffel are very interesting." Her head went back down.

"Can we talk about our friend?"

That worked. Like a mother laying down her infant child, Monika placed the journal on top of Butch's bag.

"Listen," she said. "We're both worried about Butch. They'll take him to surgery, to the ICU, and they'll treat him. There's nothing more we can do at this point. Let's go back home, and we'll come by tomorrow and check on him. Okay?"

No, this *wasn't* okay. I made a vexed sound and set my chin in my hand. It was the same pose that I would adopt about 45 minutes later, sitting on our bed, watching Monika undress. To be frank, I was sulking. And how was that fair? Monika had arrived before me and had been sitting in this room this whole time. The blood in her hair and on her clothes was Butch's blood.

I sighed and looked around. Helga called out an Italian-sounding name, and the guy with the bowl got up and walked through a swinging door marked CLINIC B. On the TV, the news had moved on to a police drug raid that had happened earlier that afternoon in Union Square Park.

What *were* we doing here, exactly? I remembered my idea about the bag, that it might have some kind of ID in it, something I could use to provide the front desk with Butch's name.

"What about his name?" I said.

"I'm sorry?"

Instantly and without thought, I found myself holding up a hand to Monika's lips. "Checkmate means never having to say you're sorry." And then I broke down giggling, tears streaming from eyes.

Poor Monika. She was utterly perplexed. "What's so funny? Wait. Are you crying?"

"I'll explain it in the cab," I said, regaining control of myself. "But you're right. We should go. Listen, about the surname. They'll probably assign him one. It doesn't matter right now." I wiped my eyes with the back of my hand, leaned in, stole a kiss. "We'll come back tomorrow. Now let's get out of here."

Monika grabbed Butch's duffel bag. As we exited the ER, the TV announced that Kim Kardashian would be holding a kitten in one of her upcoming internet advertisements.

♞ e1 ♞
"WHO SAID ANYTHING ABOUT DINNER?"

Monika Perfilieva is a helpmate in six played out on a board of sandalwood and pink ivory: she wants to be mated, but she requires precise technique. She had just gotten out of the shower. A thin silk robe clung to her damp body; my eyes skimmed her creamy décolletage. By the warmth of her skin, summer lilacs filled our room and my mind; through the violence of her hair—sweet, wet, and red—my blood surged. She leaned back on our bed, and the hem of her china-white robe ran a long diagonal that crossed the open file of her thigh, pointing to an exposed and unguarded center. What followed was a game far older than chess and twice as cunning. Two sets of pieces and two players, both playing a single side; the king and his queen, each reaching across the board to develop the other's pieces. The only rule, written on the heart, is that both players win. Once the opening lines have given way to the middle game, it's the art of positional play, and all flank operations are met by a thrust in the center. And through the action of a thousand and one winning combinations, a key, a battery, a satisfying endgame... a back-rank mate with queen and heavy pieces, and a soft whisper in her ear—it's corny, it's obvious, it's stupid, and I say it every time, loving it because *she* loves it:

"I love you, my Czech mate..."

CHAPTER 1

♘ f1 ♟
FROM A BAG

Monika breathed softly in sleep, may Morpheus bless and keep her. There was that detachment again. But for me, the mind was full and the body empty, and that is no condition in which to seek the blessing of the ancient god of dreams.

I fumbled around in my nightstand, found a pair of plaid flannel pajamas, pulled them on, and stood—right on top of Butch's duffel. It's like the thing was just sitting there, waiting for everything to be finished. I picked it up and padded across the floor.

In the living room, I tossed Butch's bag onto the couch. Then it was into our galley kitchen for some Saltines and warm milk. I gave the crackers a generous smear of peanut butter and arranged them on a heavy, gold-rimmed porcelain plate; the milk went into a huge mug Monika had given me for Christmas. DEFINE NAUGHTY, it said in red-and-white striped candy canes against a green background. I returned to the living room, put the plate and mug on the end table, settled myself on the couch, and began takings things out of Butch's bag.

On top was the hardbound journal Monika had been studying in the ER. This I laid carefully aside, next to the mug of milk, for later investigation. As interesting as I was sure those chess positions were, I was looking for something that would help me understand what had happened to Butch.

Then out from the bag came a half-empty pack of Swisher Sweets cigars; numerous food stamps (all of them thoroughly expired—food stamps had transitioned to EBT cards in all fifty states by 2004) held in a tight roll by a dirty rubber band; a yellow highlighter; a green zippered bag that Butch kept his chess pieces in, except that all the pieces were now missing; a hardbound Barnes & Noble special edition of *The Art of War* with gilded pages and embossed artwork on the cover (Butch's retention of the food stamps was now clear—he used them for bookmarks; I read briefly about when to flee and when to fight; I discovered some of the qualities that determine a good general); an empty water bottle; a Bic lighter that didn't work; a second one that did; an invoice for a new chess set, dated the previous December; a takeout menu from The Great Wall of China restaurant (Butch had circled some of the numbers preceding various entrees and appetizers); a cloth chess board, rolled into a tube and folded in half; a second pack of Swisher Sweets, nearly empty; the 15th edition of Modern Chess Openings, Completely Revised and Updated by 3-Time United States Chess Champion Nick de Firmian (and now I knew what the highlighter was for—I spent at least ten minutes poring over this nearly 750-page tome, shaking my head in admiration at Butch's depth of commitment to this game, as nearly every page had at least some markings on it, and many of the pages had copious notes scribbled in the margins, where Butch had apparently found his own private improvements to modern opening theory); a second highlighter, its faded lettering on the side suggesting age (I went back to the MCO-15 and tried to highlight the passage "Today the opening sees regular use from club players and fair use from grandmasters," but the marker made only a faint smudge over the words, and I felt bad that I had marred the page); a chess clock; a book of matches down to its last match; $252 in cash (this, along with several Metro coins, from an inside pocket); a Chinese newspaper; two granola bars still in their wrappers, possibly edible; a blank chess scorepad; the most recent issue of *The New York Review of Books* ("Paul Krugman & Robin Wells: WHERE DO WE GO FROM HERE?"); and finally, at the bottom, all the chess pieces that were missing from his zippered bag and lots of green felt circles that must have fallen off the bottoms of those pieces.

I stood up and surveyed my work. The sundry items of Butch's life littered the coffee table, the loveseat, and half the couch. For all their plurality, I struggled to see anything that would provide insight into why someone had attacked my friend.

I got out my favorite meerschaum pipe, lit it, and paced around a bit as I smoked. I was trying to induce thought. I looked out through a pair of sliding glass doors that let onto a small balcony. From sixteen floors up, I considered the glittering midnight face of Manhattan. I paced some more, surveying the mute witnesses that sat on my furniture. What would Sherlock observe? What would Poirot's little grey cells tell him? Then there was the journal. I turned my attention to the faux-wood cover with the words MY THOUGHTS etched in gold. It had been lying patiently on the end table beside a half-eaten plate of crackers and a half-cooled mug of milk.

I picked it up. Riffled its pages with my thumb. There wasn't much—eight pages of writing, mostly chess diagrams. I took it into the second bedroom, where we keep a small correspondence desk and a green leather Queen Anne–style chair. I sat down and started reading. In less than a minute I had a pen in my hand, and, just like Butch with his MCO-15 (or was it more like me with a paper to grade?), I found myself scribbling notes in the margins.

♗ g1 ♘
PUZZLES IN THE DARK

Butch, it seemed, had added haiku to his repertoire of exotic fascinations, which now included, to my knowledge, kung fu, a contestable knowledge of Mandarin, and the feeding and care of bonsai trees. For on the first page of his journal he had composed six poems, one for each type of chess piece:

Pawn
Outside passer, run.
Resurrection on the eighth:
Philidor's soul[1] reborn.

Knight
Ripples on square pond—
Eight-fold sphere of influence.
Watch out! You are forked.

Bishop
Clear lines rake the field;
Bishop sees rocks of one hue,
Turns into big pawn.

Rook
From the King's fortress,
Peer into enemy camp:
Success is likely.

---

1   A clever reference to Philidor's famous quote, "Pawns are the soul of chess." —Martin

Queen

Queen! You are my heart,
Cut from my chest—powerful.
Go fight. I'll stay here.

King

So many pieces;
Pieces of wood from a bag.
You and I are one.[2]

Not bad! The next two pages in the notebook were exposition.
Butch's journal continued:

All warfare is based on deception. "Hold out baits to entice the enemy," writes the general in his book. "Feign disorder and crush him."[3]

All warfare is based on deception, yes. But who is presently being deceived? Who is taking what bait, and who is at war with whom? Yin and yang; light and darkness; the black king, the white knight.

I have taken the bait. In remittance to the karmic forces, I am reduced to holding out bait. Not in these last days, so as to lure my opponent into the dark recesses of defeat, but rather to effect my own escape from these same shadows. My escape, into the twilit wasteland of the draw.[4]

And yet in my weakened state[5] I find light—even here I find it. For I discover that if one holds out bait to the destruction of his opponent, the opponent notices: his suspicions are aroused, he senses doom. But if the bait does not lead to destruction, but only to dry stalemate, his suspicions lie dormant. The bait is taken, defeat is defeated.

I will write it plainly: An opponent will be far more likely to capture tainted

---

2   I am reminded of *Searching for Bobby Fischer*, when Lawrence Fishburne tells a young Josh Waitzkin, "This is you." Nice set of haikus!
3   "The general" is surely a reference to Sun Tzu; "his book" refers to *The Art of War*.
4   This sounds ominous.
5   More perilous talk! Has Butch contracted a disease?

pieces when the result is not a loss, but a draw.⁶ According to this principle, I have cheated defeat over fifty times in the last two months alone.⁷

How shall I partition my fifty puzzles? Writes the general: "There are not more than five musical notes, yet the combination of these five give rise to more melodies than can ever be heard." As it is ever my intention to profit from infirmity and gain from iniquity, so, too, will I come to the aid of my students. Pawn, knight, bishop, rook, queen. Five pieces to aid the king. And how many melodies can be composed from these five musical notes? Some say there are more games of chess than there are electrons in the universe. (Note to self: fact-check this.)⁸

I therefore provide five examples of such swindles: positions in which pieces are offered with bad intention. Not to win, should the bait be taken, but to *draw*, and so to evade a loss in what was otherwise a hopelessly losing position.

As for the other fifty positions, I have divided them into five different notebooks according to the piece that is offered as bait.

> *"There are not more than five musical notes, yet the combinations of these five give rise to more melodies than can ever be heard.*
>
> *There are not more than five primary colors, yet in combination they produce more hues than can ever been seen.*
>
> *There are not more than five cardinal tastes, yet combinations of them yield more flavors than can ever be tasted."*
>
> —Sun Tzu, *The Art of War*

Like the first page of poetry and the five pages of chess analysis that followed, the text was written in Butch's methodical, almost dot-matrix-like print. I felt that this ability to keep a smooth, trained hand under the emotional strain hinted at by these pages revealed an extraordinary amount of self-possession. I attributed this capacity to Butch's countless hours spent

---

6 A fascinating conjecture on the psychology of chess. Butch is claiming that an opponent will be more likely to fall into a baited trap if the result is a draw, rather than a loss. I wonder.

7 Poor Butch! I wonder what effect all these draws have had on his income?

8 I have heard this as well.

performing *against*, rather than working *for*, his employer, and his daily staking of his very subsistence on this minute-by-minute labor, where underperformance is paid at a negative hourly rate.

After the quotation from *The Art of War*, which I took as a kind of signature, there followed the five promised chess puzzles, each on its own page. Butch included the solution to each puzzle directly below the diagram. I found it helpful to cover these solutions with a slip of paper while I studied the positions.

CHAPTER 1

I Swindle with a Pawn

In the position below, I was playing the white pieces. It was the endgame, I was down the exchange, and my opponent could make an easy outside passer. My situation was desperate.

Find a way for me to swindle my opponent by offering him a pawn such that, if he takes the bait, I will draw by means of stalemate.

Solution

I played **1 e6+** hoping for 1… Kxe6?, when 2 Nd4+ cxd4 would produce a stalemate.[9]

It is important to emphasize, both here and in all the other positions I will be recording in my notebooks, that I am losing. Black needn't have captured my offered pawn. Almost any other legal move would have retained the advantage. If the capture of the bait would have produced a *loss* for my opponent, rather than a draw, it is my belief that the offer, as if triggering some silent alarm, would have been met with greater suspicion and a proportionally smaller chance of being accepted. If the student wishes, they may choose to interpret this as another manifestation of the oft-observed interconnection between reward and risk.

---

9   Brilliant! I have never seen this type of chess problem before. Someone should write a book.

I Swindle with a Knight

Again I was playing the white pieces, and again I was losing badly. Black had just swept my back rank clear of rooks, and the mating attack I'd hoped for had come up empty.

Happily, I was able to feed my opponent's greed with a knight. Upon his acceptance, I force-fed him a second piece and then demonstrated the draw.

Can you find the drawing knight offer and the subsequent perpetual check?

Solution

I played **1 Nxf7**, baiting Black to fall for the amusing 1... Kxf7?, when 2 Qxe6+! Kxe6 3 Bc4+ Kf5 4 Bd3+ Kg4 5 Be2+ etc. draws by perpetual check.

If Black hadn't taken the bait, his huge material advantage would have allowed him to win with 1... Nf8, safeguarding e6. He would then have had to extricate his queen quickly, before Bf1 arrived.

CHAPTER 1

I Swindle with a Bishop

I was playing the black pieces and down the exchange. Find a way that I can offer a bishop such that if my opponent takes it, he will be forced to put me in stalemate.

Solution

1... Bf1+ was my best try, hoping for 2 Kxf1? Qc1+!, forcing 3 Qxc1 and draw by stalemate.

Correct was 2 Kg1, when White would have been unstoppable.

I Swindle with a Rook

Playing as Black, I had badly miscalculated a rook sacrifice. I proceeded to offer my other rook and was gifted the draw in return, courtesy of my opponent's aggression.

Solution

The key was **1... Ra4**. After 2 Qxa4? I drew by means of perpetual check: 2... Qb6+ 3 Kh1 Ng3+! 4 hxg3 Qh6+ etc.

White should have declined my sacrifice with 2 Rb4. (2... Rxb4 would fail to 3 Rxb4 Qb6+ 4 Qc5.)

CHAPTER 1

I Swindle with a Queen

Another bad rook sacrifice left me at a severe material disadvantage. Find a way for me, as Black, to tempt White into accepting my offer of a queen. A draw at the very least shall unfold.

Solution

I played **1... Qf3**. Then 2 gxf3? Rh5+ draws by perpetual check: 3 Kg2 Rg5+ 4 Kh3 Rh5+ 5 Kg4 Rg5+ etc. (Not 6 Kf4?? Ne6#.)

White's surest path to victory was 2 Qxb5.

♞ h1 ♝
PARTING INSTRUCTION. SUMMER LILAC REPRISE.

I laid down the journal in amazement. Five positions, each asking me to put up a piece of bait that, if taken, would steal a draw from the gaping maw of defeat. I understood Monika's fascination earlier that evening with these positions. I had seen many different types of chess puzzles over the years—helpmates, selfmates, retrograde analyses—but never ones like these. But despite gaining a few insights into my friend's psychology and reading some ominous hints, I still didn't feel that I was any closer to—

And then it came to me. Butch's last words before he sank into oblivion: "Read my thoughts." I had taken this parting instruction as something more mysterious than it was. My Thoughts—it was the title of his journal. Butch was asking me to look deep into these pages.

On the last page, I found the clue I had been waiting for all night. It was another note from Butch: a direct appeal for aid, calm at first (though surely written amid peril, with compromised grammar and improper punctuation), and three postscripts, each more dire and hastily scrawled than the last. Following the postscripts, on the reverse side of the page (and given the steady hand with which they were penned, clearly written *before* the letter), Butch had composed another series of poems.

The note read:

> Martin—
>
> I would liked to have explained everything in person but I hid it from them and now if you're reading this then things went wrong and I was right to have taken measures. Begin at the home of the black king, then pace off the keys. The key you need from each notebook is the one I give back to you. New York City is my chessboard, Check the legend.
>
> Have fun,
> Butch

Chapter 1

> P.S. The poems I composed on the next page will help you on your quest.
>
> P.P.S. Where the queen lays down her crown, seek the King in Yellow.
>
> P.P.P.S. STAY OUT OF THE SQUARE AT NIGHT!

The poems, on the opposite side of this last page, read:

> At the end of the day
> Should you come to a wall,
> Order these numbers
> And order them all:
> 18, 13, 3, 24,
> 7, 9, 16, 1, and no more.
>
> Little Jack Horner
> The King's in his Corner,
> Eating his curds and whey.
> If you want to play with him
> He'll charge you by the day.
>
> Some students are new,
> Some students are old;
> A hat's as good as a hanky,
> As long as it pays in gold.
> What would you say to a brother-in-law
> Who is five plus four all told?
>
> The king was in his master's hall,
> The queen was yet a pawn;
> In honor's case does fortune rest
> For all to look upon.

> Nestled in the twists and turns
> Of proud Vienna,
> You'll find this game close to home.

My previous amazement had been nothing compared to what it was now. In the midst of so much, it was the word *fun* that got me. Have *fun?* There you have it again, chess fans: the detachment of the masters. Leave it to Butch to elevate the present intellectual pursuit to a level almost of giddiness while his surroundings were closing in on him.

Butch's psychological eccentricities aside, at least I *had* something. Now, perhaps, things would begin to line up. To be sure, I understood almost nothing of what I had read. Yet, there were some elements I could guess at. Butch's reference to the keys, for example, was not entirely opaque. In a chess puzzle, the key is the first move, unlocking the mysteries of the position. Apparently, each of these five notebooks held a single key. But that couldn't be right. Butch had talked about putting *multiple* puzzles in each notebook. Yet, in each collection, one puzzle had been given back to me? Butch had hidden something. Something from "them."

He was in trouble, no doubt of that. I suppose I may have bloody well suspected this when he fell to the floor of my office with a knife wound in his gut.

I returned to the journal. The first poem had a sequence of numbers to place in order. This at least looked tangible! Maybe it would be like that old game, Mastermind. I envisioned digging up a briefcase with a combination lock on it. Then again, eight numbers would be one hell of a combination.

"New York City is my chessboard. Check the legend." I tried to think of legends that involved New York City and chess. Was he talking about Bobby Fischer?

The crackers were gone, the naughty mug empty. I returned to the kitchen, put the dishes in the sink, and headed to the bedroom. Along the way I paused by the balcony doors and gazed again through the cold glass to the crystals of white that dotted Manhattan. The red running lights of an airliner flickered across the belt of Orion; destination unknown. In search of sleep, I willed my feet to the bedroom and my mind to follow those red blinking lights into the black void.

Chapter 1

Lying on her side, Monika slept. I slipped into the warmth of our bed, drew her hair over my face, and let the aroma of summer lilacs transport me to that form of detachment called oblivion. As my mind hovered on the edge of consciousness, I heard Butch say: *New York City is my chessboard.*

Butch was playing a game.

The game was afoot, and it was my move.

			Q			U	
	E						E
						N	
A			C		T		
I		V					
	A						T
	I						
					O	N	

Chapter 2
QUEEN ACTIVATION

♞ a2 ♞
THE BLESSINGS OF MORPHEUS

MARTIN STOOD IN a field. The pipe he smoked was not his pipe, for the head of Sir Arthur Conan Doyle had been replaced by a simple bowl at the end of a deep, U-shaped neck. Nor was it his own plaid greatcoat that he pulled tightly against a cold wind that soundlessly whipped at his skin. Then Martin became aware of the checkered deerstalker cap that sat atop his head, and with a certainty reserved for dreams and religious ecstasy, he understood his identity.

Sherlock Holmes turned in search of Watson and found her dangling upside-down from the limb of a leafless tree that a moment ago had been a fountain. Her hair was a shimmering curtain of red, her body clothed in lilacs. She said, "Ecstasy."

"Ecstasy," recited Holmes. "From the Greek *eck*, meaning 'outside of,' and *stasis*, meaning 'to stand.' Literally, 'to stand outside oneself.'"

"Bravo, Sherlock!" Watson said, lightly rolling the *r* in *Sherlock*. She dropped from the tree and landed noiselessly on a black-and-white checkered ground. "Holmes, we are in Washington Square Park."

"That is elementary, my dear. I deduced this at once from the chess tables." Holmes pointed, and a circle of marble tables came into existence some distance to the west, beneath a copse of tall elms and copper beeches.

"What shall we find there?"

"Follow me."

Holmes hopped across the field in the direction of the tables: two hops in a straight line, then a turn of ninety degrees and one hop more. Over and over Holmes did this, each time stopping to see if Watson was following. And how they would laugh, according to a sense of humor that exists only in dreams and never in religious ecstasy. In this fashion they reached the chess tables.

The area around the tables was filthy, with matchbooks, highlighters, newspapers, and empty cigar packages littering the ground. Holmes looked for Butch, and Butch was there. He sat at one of the tables, his back to Holmes. Opposite Butch was a man whose face was little more than a deep shadow. Deep Shadow kept lifting Butch's olive duffel and turning it upside down. "Here goes nothin'," he would say as a torrent of green felt circles fell from the bag onto the table, where they turned into Metro coins.

Then Deep Shadow was gone, replaced by Watson. She was playing chess with Butch. Every time Butch captured one of her pieces, a green circle would fall from the bottom of the piece and onto the ground with the rest of the litter.

"Holmes." Watson had stood up and was tugging a pair of black leather gloves over her hands. "Butch is playing some kind of game." With her gloved hand, she indicated the bench where she had been sitting. "He needs you."

Holmes took Watson's place while Watson stood under one of the elms, smoking a cigar. "I like to have a smoke afterward," she said. "Don't you?" Ashes from the cigar fell onto the lilacs that clung to her otherwise naked breasts.

Ignoring this as best he could, Holmes looked across the table at Butch, who had buried his face in his hands. In the middle of the table, a lone black king lolled around and around. Its green felt circle was missing, and a hollow cavity was visible at its center.

Butch drew his face up from his hands. From behind a pair of old spectacles he peered at Martin through cornflower blue eyes that matched the color of his nurse's uniform. "As your health professional," he said, "I strongly disapprove of your habit."

But that was wrong. It sounded like something Watson should have said. Holmes looked toward the elm trees, expecting to see her, but Watson had gone, and in her place stood Monika.

Where did you come from? Martin spoke the question without saying a word.

I told you once. I was shopping with—

Yes. Martin remembered now. She had been shopping with F.

F…

The walk back home along Central Park to 221B Baker Street, Upper West Side, New York City, was the only part of the dream Martin would later recall. The Park, he would say, was full of police.

Then he was home. Into a syringe that he kept in the back of a silverware drawer, he drew a 7 percent solution of cocaine. He shot up, crawled into bed, and fell asleep in his dreams to the high, tinny pitch of falling coins.

♘ b2 ♞
PERFILIEV, PARTY OF THREE?

I woke to the sounds of clinking dishes and muted voices. I slid out of bed and started across the living room. Like guests sleeping off a late-night party, Butch's belongings were still here, scattered across the furniture. The indistinct murmurs coming from the kitchen resolved into Monika's buttery alto and the woody tenor of her father, Tomas. The conversation was in Czech, and I caught the occasional reference to Butch (*Bootch*). I was halfway to the kitchen when I saw my reflection in the glass of the balcony door: my plaid pajama bottoms hovered over Central Park; a shock of uncombed hair made an indistinct smudge against the sky. I wasn't up for a conversation with Tomas. Not first thing in the morning, not looking like this. Let them have their breakfast.

I slipped back into the bedroom to get showered and dressed. Turning on the water, waiting for it to get hot, I thought to myself that *of course* Tomas had popped by. Half the time I was with Monika, I had the pleasure of sharing her with the man. A date night at the movies? Perhaps one of Monika's romantic selections: *Inglourious Basterds*? *Killshot*? Here's Tomas, showing up toward the end of the trailers, huge bucket of popcorn in hand,

Chapter 2

plops himself down beside Monika. Candlelight dinner at our favorite restaurant? Here comes the maître d'. He's got a third chair in one hand and in the other is his very best bottle of Bordeaux, compliments of the house, and "No, no, please," he says in his very best accent, designed to be served on a cracker beside his very best wedge of Brie de Meaux, "it is the least we can do for our patron saint, Tomas." And we stay for Tomas's life story over dessert.

At this point, it's a story I could tell a great deal of by myself.

If, as Postdoc observed, checkmate means never having to say you're sorry, then on the chessboard of life Tomas is the sort that rarely apologizes. Since immigrating to America, he'd begun an import-export business, taken up golf, and soon after taken up Lisa, a woman not much older than me, perhaps in her early forties. Nine months after their honeymoon in Monte Carlo, Lisa bore Monika a half-brother eighteen years her junior. Tomas, in deference to his commanding officer during his years in the Czech Army, named his son Stanislav. They all live together in what Monika has described as a modest home in Ossining, which I have yet to visit. The man maintains a blog, Drop and Give Me Venti, devoted in equal parts to exercise and coffee. He can pull off a wily game of chess, often beating me and even taking a rare game from Butch. (He stopped playing Monika sometime last summer, the summer of '09, when it became clear that her skills had outstripped his.) Just over six feet tall, with hair like copper wire, green eyes, and skin that ripples with underlying muscle, Tomas is an imposing fellow.

But if there was one thing that bothered me about this inescapable man with his imposing physical frame and his superhuman ability to conjure, on demand, success, money, and luck in equal measure, it was this: at not quite ten years older than myself, Tomas felt uncomfortably close to something like a father-in-law—and I was living in an apartment he was paying for.

Not that there was any need to feel awkward. I had been told in no uncertain terms there was no need to feel… *uncomfortable* is the word I believe Tomas had used that night at The Slipper & the Fez. But frankly, it was hard not to. For nearly fifteen years, ever since I had received my fellowship at NYU, I had not been—let's call things what they are, shall we?—a dependent. And what was I supposed to have done? Turned down Monika's—no, Tomas's—offer to live with her?

The water was hot, and I got in the shower.

♞ c2 ♞
AN UNEXPECTED GUEST. LABD. LOVE AMONG THE BOHEMIAN RICH.

The evening had started off in my old apartment—the one I was living in before I met Monika and whose $3,000-per-month rent I had been paying those past fifteen years. (A New Yorker could safely sneeze at the price tag; in April of '09, a slick, top-end suite at "The Stuy"—a dominoed arrangement of nearly one hundred brick-red high-rises squeezed up against the East River—was yours for a cool nine grand.)

At six o'clock and right on time, the small orange LED on my intercom panel flashed, indicating someone at the building's front security door—a recently added feature "For the SAFETY and CONVENIENCE of our VALUED TENNANTS." I pressed a button to activate the intercom, and Monika's voice came over the wire. "Hey, Martin! It's us. Ready?"

"You bet!" I said, but I couldn't suppress a sigh as I pressed the button to unlock the lobby door.

It wasn't that I was unexcited about our dinner plans with Tomas. The cordial air of spring had recently broken the winter that had clung to Manhattan like black slush to the side of an MTA bus. Monika and I had been dating for almost six months. Grownups once again occupied the White House. Life was a fine affair. Dinner with Monika and Tomas at a new restaurant Monika had mentioned to me—The Slipper & the Fez—was sure to be equally fine.

But something was up. *Something* was brewing between Monika and Tomas when they suggested this latest dinner out. While I waited for her to come up the elevator, I gave my neck a spritz of Obsession and laced up my black wing tips, sharp against my tan chinos. I had just finished knotting my tie when there came three light raps at my hallway door.

There was Monika. Boy, did she look like something that night, standing there in maybe a thousand bucks' worth of clothes. Even decided to wear her diamond choker. She stood needlessly on tiptoe to give me a kiss. With two long strides, someone followed her in, and for a wonder, it wasn't Tomas.

"My God, Butch!" I exclaimed, pleased and somewhat bewildered.

"Just Butch will suffice," he said, clapping a brown, weather-worn hand on my shoulder. "I am very excited about this dinner out with your woman and with Tomas." From the pocket of his hoodie, Butch produced a Swisher Sweets cigar and a lighter. He lit the cigar and tossed the lighter into the maw of his olive drab duffel, which he had flung onto my coffee table. He sat on my couch, rested his feet near his duffel, and with the two fingers that held his cigar, he pointed at Monika's necklace. "Marvelous on her, isn't it?" Without waiting for a response, he pulled a book from his bag, rummaged around in the bag until he found a highlighter, and sank into a space all his own.

Monika beamed. "I've finally gathered up the courage to wear it again, Martin." As she said this, I noticed her hand brushed lightly across her diamonds, as if unconsciously verifying their presence. I began to understand. The dinner was for the four of us, and it was to be yet another gesture of thanks from Tomas to myself and Butch for the rendering of certain services.

The previous fall, Monika's necklace had been stolen. The theft occurred at a chess tournament Monika was competing in. Butch and I had been observing the tournament, and the two of us became embroiled in the drama. Through the power of our chess skills, our logic, and no small amount of luck, we discovered the perpetrator: a dirty cop named Duski. But at the critical moment when Butch and I were to trap Duski during a game of chess at Washington Square, things went wrong. With miraculous timing, Tomas had come to our aid. Fisticuffs ensued, and the three of us (myself, Butch, and Tomas) subdued the perp, bringing the investigation to a satisfying close.

In the aftermath of the adventure, Monika and I began dating. Tomas had already thanked Butch and myself several times for retrieving the necklace, but from my perspective, the person I had to thank for my magnificent girlfriend was currently resting his ratty Converse All Stars on my coffee table and stinking up my apartment with his nasty cigar.

Monika went up on tiptoe again and kissed me, this time just a quick brush on the cheek. With her lips close to my ear she whispered, "Father is planning to give you a final thank you. I want you to just… go with it." She looked at me with a gleam in her eye as her hand lingered absently over her diamonds. It was a gesture that would fade as the months went on.

I didn't press Monika regarding her mysterious statement; if she'd wanted me to know more, she'd have said more. She called for a cab. Within a half hour, Butch, Monika, and I were eating dinner with Tomas at The Slipper & the Fez.

We sat cross-legged on embroidered pillows around a low, square table, eating Moroccan food with our hands. Monika was around the corner to my right, Butch to my left. Across from me was Tomas. He wore a salmon-pink polo shirt, mustard-colored linen slacks, and a pair of green suede bucks that looked brand spanking new. Within minutes of being seated, we found our table covered with meat-filled pastries, lamb couscous, glasses of hot mint tea, and a hand-painted ceramic plate of citrus, figs, and grapes. Steam laden with cumin and coriander rose from a low, wide tagine filled with a stew of fish and chickpeas. Two baskets of bread were kept overflowing by the many waiters who scurried about in their scarlet fezzes and matching slippers. Propelled by the heavy rhythms piped through hidden speakers, a belly dancer shimmied from table to table, all snake arms and fingers, with a sinuous spine and a sequined top that jiggled as her hips shot bullets and threw knives.

Tomas said, "Note with interest the slightly fat gentleman sitting by himself in that corner. He has his laptop out, and he types passionately. What do you make of him, Butch?"

"Ooo… are we doing LABD?" asked Monika with piqued interest. "Nice!"

"Looks like LABD," I said.

This was a game we had played—and enjoyed—before. Tomas, upon devising the game some time ago, had instantly become set on naming it. Always eager to expand his English and having at some point picked up a certain outmoded vernacular for *detective*, he had wanted to call it Let's All Be Dicks. An almost-chortling Monika, explaining the modern usage of that term, was ultimately able to dissuade him, although her father's acquiescence had been grudging. I suggested a more modest name, such as Guessing Gumshoes, but this he shot down immediately, and as a compromise we all settled on calling the game LABD.

Butch, attending now to Tomas's question, stroked a non-existent beard and raised one eyebrow, which, in sharp contrast to the rest of him, was impeccably groomed. This idiosyncrasy of Butch's hygiene is a testament to his firm belief that he can use his eyebrows to mesmerize his chess opponents, after the manner of his favorite world champion, Mikhail Tal.

After brief consideration he said, "When the subject arrived, I noticed him point out to the maître d' one of the few places that has a raised table and chairs, with seating for only one or two. I would say that our man desires seclusion within a public place."

While Butch spoke, Tomas arranged grapes from the platter into rows and columns. As we made our observations, he would scoop up portions of the rows and eat the grapes. The more important Tomas considered an observation to be, the more grapes would disappear. This was an element of the game I hadn't seen before, and I wondered whimsically to myself if Tomas would find the technique compatible with foods other than grapes.

Monika piped in. "He may have just needed a comfortable place to use a laptop. Or we could both be correct! Perhaps he is writing his paramour a love note, even while he waits for her. How romantic!"

Tomas ate two or three grapes. "M-clip," he said, using his pet name for Monika. (It's short for "money clip." The sobriquet is due to my lady's tendency to carry large amount of cash. I don't see how she tolerates it.) "I'm afraid I must disagree with you. The subject's face lacks the look of one desiring company. Note the concern buried deep in the furrow of his brows. See the way his eyes shift about the restaurant! They do not stray to the entrance, as would those of a lover in waiting." He scooped up an entire row of five or six grapes and started eating them.

"But what of the small Moleskine diary that he consults as he types?" said Butch. "It looks the sort of thing a person might keep intimate thoughts in."

Monika shot Butch a grateful look. Tomas ate a few more grapes, chased them down with a great gulp of mint tea, and said, "The diary is the perfect vehicle for recording sudden thoughts at times when it is not expedient to use an electronic device. Such might be the activities of a critic, who keeps notes as he eats and does not wish to grimy his keyboard.

I suggest this man is working within his professional capacity. His intense, deliberate writing is that of a restaurant critic!" Two entire rows of grapes went down.

"If so," broke in Butch, "then he is neither a very successful nor competent critic. For as I walked past him a few minutes ago on my way to the restroom, I detected on his body the distinct aroma of a cologne that I happen to know is sold at Duane Reade for $9.95. And notice how he does not order a full meal, but contents himself with hot tea and baklava. Who critiques a restaurant on the basis of tea and baklava?"

Tomas grunted at this contradiction and popped a single grape in his mouth.

Butch waggled a finger. "No, Tomas. Our subject is of limited means and savors being absorbed in thought, indifferent to his surroundings. Observe his age. Young twenties? I would say he has not experienced enough cycles of culinary fashion to be a published critic. This young man, he studies intently, and he craves the clamor of crowds and the comfort of cheap calories. Although I cannot make a claim with the certainty of a deduction, I tentatively infer that our subject is a student."

Monika said, "What do you think, Martin?"

I considered our man. Desirous of seclusion, yet in a place that was crowded. A note-taker. Far from being indifferent to his surroundings, as Butch suggested, he scanned a scene that fairly burst with sensory input. He would often bury his face in his hands, shaking his head in self-doubt, this gesture of uncertainty frequently followed by repeatedly hitting a key located on the top right of his keyboard. *The backspace key.*

"He's writing a novel."

Monika and Butch laughed in affirmation. Tomas said to me, "My God, M-doc," (his pet name for me—a reference to my doctoral degree, which he holds in an absurd and oversized regard) "I do believe you have the winning move. A writer! Well done." This verdict pronounced, Tomas polished off what few grapes remained, reclined on his cushion, and munched on a fistful of stew-laden bread. After a few minutes of serious eating, Tomas cleared his throat, grabbed his tea, and raised it. The three of us duplicated his gesture.

"Martin and Butch," Tomas said, looking at each of us in turn. (I noted the use of my full first name.) "Over these last months you have proved loyal and good friends beyond the mere retrieval of my daughter's necklace—a piece whose material value, while considerable, is nothing compared to the value your friendship holds in my heart." Here he touched his chest; out of the corner of my eye I saw Monika unconsciously reach for her diamonds. "And I know it occupies the same place in the heart of my dear Money Clip. Thank you, Butch; thank you, Martin."

We all clinked glasses and took swigs of mint tea.

But Tomas wasn't finished. He leaned in over the table, and for the first time that evening he stopped eating. "When I first came to America ten years ago as an ambassador from the Czech Republic, it was a job. Just a job. I had no intention of leaving Prague. But then, two years later, after the attacks on New York, I thought, maybe, a show of solidarity…"

Monika intervened. "There was also that business contract with the exporter."

Tomas nodded toward his daughter. *Yes, that too*, the nod said. "As I say, with a show of solidarity and a good business contract, I made my winning move. I immigrated here, with Monika at my side." Now he looked fully at Monika and beamed.

I thought he was done, and I began to sit back.

"And whenever I remember myself making that move," he continued, whereupon I resumed my former position of attentiveness, "I like to imagine myself making it with the gritty ruse of a chess player who has just added a new opening system to his repertoire." A sweep of his hand took in all three of us. *You woodpushers know how it is*, the hand said.

I glanced at Butch for a clue. Where was this going?

"For years," Tomas continued, "you begin all your important games the same way. For sake of discussion, let's say you like to push your king's pawn forward two squares, and you're happy with that. You're getting the game you want. The occasional loss doesn't bother you. It's merely proof that your opposition is real! Your games are challenges met on the battlefield of the mind—stretching your abilities, putting to the test your courage and your will."

I looked again at Butch. He was nodding his head. It was all making perfect sense to him. Or maybe he just didn't care. A quick glance at Monika revealed eyes that drifted thoughtfully across the table. *She* knew the plot of this one-man play. But was she concerned that Father might be going a touch off-script?

Tomas went on. "Then one day you become *un*satisfied. Maybe you get bored, or you start to lose too many games. Maybe you just lose your way. So you do something. You make a *new move*." He was looking firmly at me as he said these last two words. "You switch to the queen's pawn. You—"

But I never got to hear what else a person might do. A new voice, high-pitched and wheezy, with a dash of Italian, thrust itself into the monologue.

"Mr. Tomas! Is everything perfect for you and your guests?"

Immediately, Tomas sprang up and took the newcomer's extended hand into both of his, pumping it vigorously. "Chef Tonio!" he cried.

Chef Tonio had on a white double-breasted chef's jacket that covered a respectable paunch. The sleeves were rolled up to reveal hairless forearms and hands. In place of the traditional chef's hat, an oversized royal-blue fez came down to just above his eyebrows. I instinctively looked at the man's feet and saw what I expected: a pair of matching royal-blue slippers. The Slipper & the Fez—here before me was the restaurant incarnate. The name, though. Tonio? It didn't sound particularly Moroccan.

The man gestured expansively with his arm. "I trust that everything is to your satisfaction." Though he gazed solely at Tomas while he said this, we all took the liberty of offering various affirmatives.

Chef Tonio turned his attention to the rest of us, and his chestnut eyes grew wide as he looked down to where we still sat on our pillows. He pointed to the table. "The food?"

I had imagined the food to be previously included in "everything," but we all nodded and repeated our compliments.

"The decor?" He spread his hairless arms and raised his smooth hands, and his eyes scanned the entirety of the high-ceilinged hall that was his fiefdom.

Again, we offered our congratulations.

"The music? Does it not transport you to another place, free from the concerns of the world?"

I stole a quick glance at Monika. A shadow of a grin tweaked her cheeks, and she slid her hand into mine under the table, giving it a pleasant squeeze.

"Very exotic," said Butch. "I believe the primary instruments are—"

He was cut off. "The menu, it is rich and varied? The carpet, soft beneath your feet?"

We nodded our assent.

"The fish tank?" Tonio pointed across the room to where a colossal aquarium, looking entirely out of place, took up most of a wall. "Does it not mesmerize you with its colored fish all swimming about?"

We agreed that it did.

"And Shara?" With an air of finality, the chef thrust a finger and a most unsubtle glance toward the belly dancer. She was working a table with some Japanese businessmen, arms undulating, hips rattling. "Truly, she is the delight of this world?"

Tomas took Chef Tonio's hand once more and shook it. "My friend, your entire restaurant is the very definition of delight."

The man was finally satisfied. "And to think," he said, "none of this would be here without Tomas." When no one said anything, he looked at Tomas and said, pertly, "You haven't told them?"

"You tell them," said Tomas, sitting back down and starting in on some pastries.

From seemingly nowhere the chef produced a white linen towel and began rubbing his already-clean hands with it, one finger at a time. "I wanted it to be a Moroccan place. My relatives thought I was crazy, wanted me to do pizza, maybe some nice spaghetti. Never let it be said there's anything wrong with pizza. But I wanted my restaurant to be the kind of place where things happen, and pizza won't do."

I looked at Monika. We shared a quiet chuckle at the chef's haphazard thoughts. As for Butch, the look on his face suggested that everything the chef said was being bookmarked and stored away.

"The best pizza in New York is in New Jersey," Tomas offered.

"But then I think to myself," Chef Tonio went on, "I want it to be a fish kind of place. I don't mean seafood, I mean like the ocean. I can't make up my mind. So I set it up Moroccan. Opening day, nobody comes. Then right around one o'clock, this man—this good man, Tomas—shows up. I tell him my problems: Moroccan? Or ocean? He tells me that whenever he can't decide between things, he does both! So I keep Shara, I set up the fish tank, and my place goes blockbusters!"

I regarded anew the man who sat across the table from me, dressed all in pink and yellow and green like he sent the Easter Bunny to proxy-shop at Tommy Bahama. Yes, I decided, Tonio's story rang true.

As amused as I was by the story, I saw that Monika's hand was beginning to twitch. I looked at her; she was definitely anxious. I remembered the one-man play whose script had long since been abandoned. What could Monika be wanting to happen? Where was the plot supposed to have gone? I looked at Tomas. As far as he was concerned, everything was under control, so I returned my attention to the chattering chef.

"This is why every time Tomas comes to my restaurant, his check is on the house!"

Tomas lifted a finger and swallowed his food. "You know, Tonio," he said, abandoning the honorific title, "I bet my guests would love to see your kitchen. Would you mind?"

"What chef in this world would say he did? Come, my friends!"

We all started to get up, but Tomas looked across the table at me. "Stay here, please," he said.

At these words, Monika gave my hand two quick squeezes and my heart a smile. Her anxiety had disappeared. Which was very interesting, since mine had just shot way up.

Tomas and I watched Chef Tonio lead Butch and Monika through a pair of swinging doors into the kitchen. When the doors swung shut behind them, Tomas leaned forward, rested his elbows companionably on the table, and grinned at me. "What do you make of him?"

I glanced back toward the double doors. Through the round portholes I could see a splotch of royal blue bobbing up and down. Tonio was speaking. A waiter carrying a tray of dinnerware swept through the doors and had to swerve to avoid a collision, as the chef's white-clad arm swept a wide arc. I imagined Butch throwing a salvo of technical questions at the chef. Tonio would be in his glory answering them.

"He's fun," I said.

"Bit of a character, if you ask me," said Tomas. He tugged at a piece of bread. "But he's good."

"Makes a terrific b'stilla," I offered.

"None better." Tomas went to reach for a loaf of the sugar-dusted pastry, then paused and retracted his hand a bit. "He's right, you know, about restaurants. We mark the milestones of our lives in food. Weddings, business deals, funerals…" He changed his mind and tore off a chunk of pastry after all. "Oh, yes," he said, "things happen in restaurants." He popped the piece of b'stilla into his mouth, the muscles of his jaws rippling the taut skin of his face as he chewed. "Why do you suppose that is?"

Taking the question as rhetorical, I said, "Who knows?"

Tomas reclined, keeping his eyes fixed on me and crossing a green shoe over a mustard-colored thigh. "You can do better than that."

The one-man play was in its second act, and it had become a chess game of sorts. Should I play the board or the man? Butch is always a proponent of playing the man.

I reflected on him. Here was that rare type who does exactly as he feels without the slightest need for approbation and yet manages somehow to avoid being a complete ass. Thinking next of his question, I recalled Abraham Maslow, the twentieth-century psychologist who coined a theory he called the pyramid of needs. It went something like this: Most people spend the bulk of their time and energy satisfying the most basic of their needs (food, shelter, safety), leaving ever-decreasing resources at their disposal as they climb the pyramid toward life's more sophisticated desires (relationships, self-esteem, creativity). Only at the top, after all foundational requirements have been satisfied, is a person free to finally exercise their most meaningful inner potential.

I suspected that Tomas had never heard of Maslow, and I never much credited his theory, myself. But I was also fairly confident that, were such a pyramid to leave the abstract and take on stone and mortar, Tomas would be living at the very top of it, in a penthouse suite, where he would serve an endless buffet, free to any tenants of the baser needs who popped up for a meal. Whether Maslow was full of shit or not, his theory felt to me the perfect approach (the winning move, as Tomas himself would put it) to the question at hand.

I ventured my answer. "In restaurants, folks enjoy a sense of security. There's lots of people around, safety in numbers, everyone sharing in a mutually understood business, fulfilling a common need." I paused for a moment, then added, "Which is to eat."

"Good," said Tomas, waiting for more.

"The atmosphere will be pleasant, since the management wants people to be comfortable."

"Point being?"

"People feel welcome."

"The same could be said of a retail store."

"Yes," I agreed, "but, once seated, nobody window-shops a restaurant. Everybody eats. And because everybody is eating, waiters attend to everyone's needs equally, without prejudice."

"In theory," remarked Tomas.

"In theory."

"Making the patrons feel…?"

"Self-esteem in the presence of a common yet plentiful prosperity, as food arrives that none of the patrons had to shop for, prepare, or clean up after."

"All of which adds up to…?"

"Restaurants free people to focus their energies on their true, unencumbered selves."

"Excellent! You're a smart guy, M-doc, and I'll tell you what else: you don't bore Monika. You don't talk—" He leaned in conspiratorially and his face became sour. "You don't talk *cars*."

(*cars?*)

"Cars, jobs, *mutual funds*, for fuck's sake! She can't stand it. You take these other guys Monika has dated—"

(*other guys?*)

"—some guy who lives out of the city a bit, out in Ossining, where I live, or Yonkers, some bedroom community—and that's what all these guys obsess over. Anyone her age bores her to death. It's all 401(k) contributions and career planning!"

I started to object. "Tomas, *I* have a job—"

With a wave of his hand, Tomas brushed this non sequitur away. "Aw, c'mon, M-doc, that doesn't count. You're *established*. When's the last time you met Monika for dinner after one of your lectures and talked her ear off about what Boss-man Number One told Boss-man Number Two that afternoon at the big meeting? Or bored her with where you plan to *be* in five years, for god's sakes?" Tomas gulped some tea, then resumed his speech. "You see, M-doc, you're mature. That's what makes the difference. Fuck, you're not much younger than me! What are you, forty?"

"Exactly."

"Forty-nine," Tomas said, lifting a self-identifying finger and setting it back down near some grapes. I feared he was going to start lining them up again, but he plowed straight ahead. "Look. Monika has spent most of her life in close connection with me. She's bored fuckless by her peers. You're stable, you interest her, she thinks you're cute. You make *her* happy, that makes *me* happy, and *that's* the winning move in *every* game. So I've got another winning move for you." Now he *did* pop a grape in his mouth, but he kept it to just one. "I'd like you to move in with Monika, whaddaya say?"

For quite some time I didn't say anything. I mean, what *does* a man say to a father who propositions him on behalf of his daughter and asks him to move in with her? Wasn't this a little… backward? If only my undergrad education had included some coursework on life and love among the bohemian rich, instead of all those classes in medieval literature and etymology. Formal education, I thought to myself—and not for the first time—sometimes doesn't prepare people for life very well.

Monika's apartment was a luxury two-bedroom on the upper west side. Over the last several months I had been there frequently. It was where Monika and I first made love. It was where she introduced me (over a delicious Central European meal of goulash and kielbasa, with apple strudel for dessert) to the American side of her family: Lisa, her stepmother; Stanislav, her half-brother. It must be a very expensive apartment. Of course, Tomas was paying the rent—every dollar. Monika was a debutante of sorts. A career didn't seem to be part of her life's plans. Hall & Oates had all but written a song for her.

And is it really all that wrong, to take what is given you?

Maybe my face was transparent, or maybe my thoughts were simply those of any self-respecting person, for Tomas cut in, and he got straight to the point.

"I understand that you're a self-sufficient man, Martin, and that I am asking you to live under a roof that I provide. But really, there's no need to feel uncomfortable."

Let's see, now. Live with my girlfriend, save three grand a month on rent... and was it *really* all that wrong to take what was given you?

So it was said, so it was done, amen.

About a half hour later, as the four of us prepared to leave The Slipper & the Fez, Butch pulled me over to the side.

"Did you say yes?"

I looked at him, confused.

He elaborated. "Did you agree to move in with Monika?"

Nonplussed at first, I guessed that Monika had clued Butch in while they were touring the kitchen. But when I suggested this, Butch denied it.

"Then how did you know?" I asked.

Butch's heavy hand fell on my shoulder. "Come, now, Martin. It was my easiest inference of the entire evening. The wistful looks Monika gave to your apartment as if glancing around a place for the last time. The whisper in your ear about a proper thanks from her father. The moneyed control that Tomas exerts over his daughter. The obvious dismissal of the dinner party so that he could speak with you alone. The vacillating looks of anxiety and relief on Monika's face throughout the meal. The—"

I got the point. "You really don't miss much, Butch."

"Martin, I miss nothing."

Within the week, I was all settled in with Monika. And if Tomas began to feel one-third father and one-third father-in-law, at least there was that last third that felt like a friend. In the past ten months since I moved in with Monika, he had been true to his word and never given me outward reason to feel uncomfortable.

♞ d2 ♞
THE QUEEN NOTEBOOK

"Martin, you've got to see this!"

Our kitchen was cozy with the aromas of coffee, toast, eggs, and bacon. I walked in, raking my hand through hair still damp from the shower. The 1 percent, even in Manhattan's upper west side, comfy and plush,

Chapter 2

pack themselves in pretty tight. A small, white Formica table—pushed up against the galley kitchen's one free wall and warmly lit from above by a Tiffany chandelier—displayed the tail end of breakfast for two. Tomas was at the stove; Monika sat at the table's near side, her china cup still holding a sip or two of black tea. Across from her, half-full of coffee, a custom-printed mug displayed a picture of Tomas, Lisa, Stanislav, and Mickey Mouse. The picture had been taken a few years ago, when Lisa was experimenting with being a blonde and Stan was five, in what Tomas called his "Norman Chaney days," after the pudgy child actor from *The Little Rascals*. (The Czech Army, it seems, or at any rate Tomas's commanding officer, offered a quirky lineup of entertainment for the troops.) Since then, Stan had doubled his baby fat, added a pair of Coke-bottle glasses, and took it into his head that a buzz cut would make him an astronaut.

In the table's center, a pile of freshly peeled orange rinds covered a paper towel. A black chess king stood on one corner of the towel; I recognized it as the piece Butch had clutched in his hand.

"You've got to see this!" Monika repeated. It was well before 9:00 a.m. and already she was nicely made up and wearing a teal cashmere sweater loosely cinched with a thin leather belt over a pair of skintight blue jeans. I took what she was holding out to me: a spiral-bound chess notebook with a queen sketched in black Sharpie on its cover.

"What's this?" I asked, taking a seat.

Monika was about to answer when Tomas plopped a heavy bowl in front of me filled with four or five scrambled eggs slathered in melted cheese and dusted with dried tarragon. Then came a mug of coffee, a handful of bacon (tossed directly into the bowl of eggs), a plate of pancakes ("we saved the last three for you, M-doc!"), an orange ("put the rinds on the pile; I'll work them into tonight's dinner"), a knife and a fork, and finally, a rapid fire of fixings: butter, syrup, a carton of half-and-half.

My breakfast delivered, Tomas sat down. He wore a pair of blue-and-white pinstriped seersucker pants and a button-up short-sleeved shirt with a tropical print. His top three shirt buttons were open, revealing a wiry carpet of red chest hair. Had he been vacationing in the French Riviera in July, the look would have probably worked.

"Notebook," he announced, answering my question while at the same time helping himself to a slice of bacon from my bowl. The Lord giveth, and the Lord taketh away.

Monika said, "It's one of the notebooks Butch wrote about in the journal I was reading while we were at the ER. Apparently, there are five!"

"You found one already?"

Tomas interrupted. "Stan had it. When Monika called me this morning and told me what Butch described in his writings, I remembered he had lent something like that to Stanislav at his most recent lesson. I brought it right over."

I flipped it open. The first page was a poem. It was the Queen verse from Butch's assortment of haikus.

Queen

Queen! You are my heart,
Cut from my chest—powerful.
Go fight. I'll stay here.

As I skimmed the rest of the pages, I became increasingly amazed. Over the past year, Butch had expressed a growing interest in fiction and creative writing, but I had no idea he had pursued this passion to such an extent. On page after page, Butch described life in the park through his interactions with his opponents. A few of the entries bordered on poetry. Hell, one of the entries *was* poetry.

Nestled among his writings were ten swindle puzzles of the type Butch presented in his journal. In each, Butch is saddled with a losing position.

Chapter 2

Rather than playing the objectively best move, plodding along toward certain defeat, he attempts to trick his opponent by offering a piece that, if taken, would allow Butch to salvage a draw.

"Go on and work them out," Tomas said. "The two of us have already had a crack at them. I think you'll get a kick out of it."

"But shouldn't we be discussing observations?" I objected. "Clues? Theories? There are things Butch wrote that might lead us to his attacker. And the contents of his bag! Shouldn't we be mulling—"

"Monika and I have already talked matters out as far as we could get without you. When you read through the notebook and then report to me your version of events, we'll all be on the same page."

"Except for the contents of the bag," Monika added. "We haven't looked at any of that. We left it all until you were up. Once you've read this notebook, then we'll discuss everything. Sound good?"

It sounded good. I sat back in my chair and chipped away at my breakfast while I did the same with Butch's puzzles. Over and over, I turned the black king in my hands as I read.

Swindle #1—A sleight of mind

White: Bouncer
Black: Me
Date: February 9, 2010

Master Lin teaches that the student of the martial arts must learn to direct his adversary's own energy against himself. So it was in the game illustrated below. From the moment that he sat across from me, my opponent—burly, bald, and bold—exuded an intimidating air, with his uncouth speech and his outstretched arms, knuckles cracking in my face. Perhaps I had allowed myself to be intimidated and calculated poorly, thus accounting for the ruination of my king's safety, as you can plainly see. Even if it meant accepting a draw, I wanted out of this game.

I am by profession a player of games—a trickster, a hustler, a confidence man. Sleight of mind driving sleight of hand, I moved my queen in a way that made it appear as if I had accidentally overshot the square I'd been aiming for. I hit my clock and then cried out in feigned anguish. My opponent bit.

Black to move

Where did Butch place his queen?

[NB: Butch did not provide solutions to the puzzles in any of the notebooks we were eventually to find. I later consulted him and transcribed the solutions he gave into a section in the back of this book called "Back of the Notebook."]

Chapter 2

Swindle #2—Offsides

White: Me
Black: Number-One Fan
Date: December 19, 2009

This season is turning out to be a fantastic one for my New York Jets. Looks like we're heading to the playoffs again! The city brings in a lot of outsiders when our team does this well. Nobody had to wonder why this particular opponent was in town: Jets jacket, Jets pin, Jets hat. Green-and-white makeup on his face, a regular A-number-one fan. Top of the heap and all that jazz.

Maybe it was the makeup that threw me off. What happened to my kingside attack? One minute I was making my way down the field; the next thing I knew, I'd fumbled the ball.

I had to find a way to salvage a draw. Nothing like a queen sac to throw an opponent off his game.

White to move

How did Butch sacrifice his queen in order to save himself from a humiliating loss at the hands of his green-and-white adversary?

Swindle #3—A game between rivals

White (large): "The Bish"
Black (small): Me
Date: January 8, 2010

Butch was beginning to get very tired of sitting by himself in the park and having no chess to play; once or twice he pushed some pieces around on his board, but there was no opponent and no money on the table, *and what is the use of chess*, thought Butch, *without opponents or money?*[10] So after what seemed an awfully long time looking around the park for a victim, and not seeing so much as a single tourist or businessman, Butch decided it shouldn't be *very* odd if he were to play chess with one of his colleagues instead.

Presently, Butch stood up and walked down the path, along the wooden benches where his friends sat behind marble chess tables. He thought it was indeed a sad party of chess players who were gathered there, some of them sleeping, and not *one* of them playing any chess! *For if there is no one in the park to play chess with me*, Butch reasoned to himself, *then it must also be the case that there is no one in the park to play with anyone else! Oh, dear, what a sad state of affairs this is!* And even though he had only just gotten up a minute ago, all this lack of playing had made Butch quite sulky, and he was looking for a place to sit down again when a cross voice came from behind him.

"Now whatever could be the matter with *you?*"

Butch turned around to see a tall black man sitting behind a chess table. Butch sat down opposite from him. A long and braided beard smelling of peaches and patchouli swung from the man's chin, and his eyes were covered by a pair of sunglasses that had *very* thick, dark lenses. In each of his hands, the man was twirling a bishop; one of the bishops was normal-sized, while the other was quite large. If all of this wasn't odd enough, a white, mitered hat sat precariously on top of the man's head, making him look like a Byzantine priest. Butch was about to laugh when it occurred to him that doing so might be rude; then he thought it might be rude *not* to

---

10 A parody of the opening line of *Alice's Adventures in Wonderland*. All those irresistible references to chess in Lewis Carroll must have sparked a creative streak in Butch.

Chapter 2

laugh, and that it all depended on the man's attitude toward Byzantine priests. Since Butch hadn't any knowledge of this subject, in the end he pretended not to have noticed anything at all.

"Now whatever could be the matter with *you*?" the man repeated, even more crossly than before.

Somewhat foolishly, Butch blurted out, "It's not me! It's my mind!"

"What kind of talk is *that*?" said the man.

"My mind doesn't seem to be working *properly* these days," Butch said, correcting himself and wondering what the man had to be quite so cross about.

The man sat back on his bench and began stroking his long, smelly beard. After what seemed a terribly long time, he finally spoke. "Recite *The Tragedy of Ebert*."[11]

This didn't seem to Butch to be very fair, requiring him to recite such a ridiculous and extraneous poem! Nonetheless, he cleared his throat and tried his best:

> Upon a checkered field of squares
> The King lined up his men;
> All white were they, and doughty, too—
> They numbered six and ten.
> "Prepare!" cried he, "for fratch and fray!"
> But would not say just when.
>
> He called up his enlisted troops
> To march off first to war:
> "Albert! Bebert! Colbert! Dilbert!"
> He named his left-hand four;
> "Ebert! Filbert! Gilbert! Hebert!"—
> These others made four more.
>
> Yet still the King would not consent
> The battle to begin,
> But called upon his nearest page,

---

[11] A poem! Any pastiche of Lewis Carroll wouldn't be complete without one.

A beefy boy, though thin—
"Ebert," thought he (his *nom de guerre*),
"What trouble am I in?"

"Take heart, my son," the King beseeched,
His voice quite soft yet gruff;
"To win the day we must be made
Of hard and sordid stuff."
"Mefears," the boy kept to himself,
"That shan't be quite enough!"

The King knelt down upon the ground
(The boy was short, you see)
And with his sword he pointed toward
His constant enemy.
"Behold, across the grid from us,
His blackened effigy!"

Then looked the boy across the way
To see some awful sight;
But what he saw were sixteen men
Who'd look like him, if white.
"Can someone say," he asked the King,
"The purpose of this fight?"

His words were lost to time and space,
The King was there no more;
He'd risen up, he'd sallied forth,
He wallowed in the war.
"Just pawns," sighed Ebert, "in a game."
(Forgive the metaphor.)

Then wood on wood and click on clack!
The carnage did commence;
The dueling kings barked their commands,
Not one sat on the fence;

Chapter 2

And one by one the men went down,
Each to his lord's defense.

As Ebert, too, was carried off,
His eyes staring at death;
He looked behind, to bless his Sire:
Some muttered shibboleth;
But what he saw did stop his heart,
And steal his final breath.

The King stood o'er his vanquished foe,
Who lay there in defeat.
"That trick you played three moves ago—
It nearly had me beat!"
Then with a wink he lent a hand,
And helped him to his feet.

The black King rose and, dusting off,
Said with a haughty air:
"Next time the castles shall be switched!
Next time I shall not err!"
Then with a nod he sauntered off,
Back to his starting square.

Upon a checkered field of squares
The King lines up his men;
All white are they, and doughty, too—
They number six and ten.
"Prepare!" cries he, "for fratch and fray!"
And on it goes again.

"Your mind is working fine," the man in the hat said in his dour voice, still twirling his bishops. "Do please get to the heart of the matter."

"I'm not playing chess at all like myself these days!" exclaimed Butch.

"Who, then, are you playing chess like?"

Butch gave an exasperated click of his tongue. "You know what I mean."

"I'm afraid," said the man, "that I do not."

"What I mean to say is that I am making lots of draws."

"Then why didn't you say that, if that is what you meant?"

"Because," said Butch, thinking himself rather clever, "my mind isn't working right."

The man considered this, and Butch waited for him to make an equally clever retort; but after a minute he simply said, "Go on."

"I am making lots of draws," Butch repeated, not knowing what else to go on about and thinking this man really wasn't very much help.

"And what, pray tell, is the matter with draws?"

Growing irritated by the man's lack of sense, Butch said, "Well, how am I supposed to make my five dollars if I keep drawing?"

"I see your point. I'll tell you what you should do. Play me a game of chess. If you win, I'll tell you what's wrong with you."

"And if I lose?" asked Butch, with some concern in his voice.

"Then you pay me five dollars, of course," said the man, quite shortly, as if this were the most obvious fact in the world. Then he put his hands behind his back and presently brought them out again, closed into fists. "Pick," he said.

Butch pointed to the man's right hand. The man opened it, and it held the small bishop.

"Oh, good," said the man. "You're going to play with the small pieces, and I'll play with the large. Large goes first." Then he got out a green drawstring bag and dumped thirty-two chessmen onto the board, all black.

"But—all the pieces are black!" said Butch in his most scandalized voice.

"What does that matter?" said the man. "Your pieces are small, and my pieces are large. Anyone can see the difference. Now, are you going to sit there all day, or are you going to move? I've already pushed my King's pawn. As I told you, Large goes first."

It was quite difficult on Butch, all the pieces being the same color. *And what good fortune it is for me*, he thought to himself, *that the board is connected to the table, for wouldn't it just take the cake if the man had brought his own board, and all the squares were black as well?*

What with the hardship of studying the board, Butch ended up in the unfortunate position below. Happily, he was able to swindle a draw. And

Chapter 2

so, in the end, Butch neither paid his exasperating opponent five dollars nor received from him any insight into the compromised functioning of his own mind.

Black (small) to move

Can you spot a way for Butch to swindle his galling opponent?

Swindle #4—Take my queen, please

White: Me
Black: Ink 'n' Pink
Date: November 30, 2009

When I was a youngster, white women came in blonde and brunette and maybe the exotic redhead. Today, it's a Crayola factory. And tats are not just for truck drivers anymore. This young lady was ink and pink all over. But if the outside of her head resembled cotton candy, the inside was pure grey matter.

I was down the exchange and a pawn and feeling bad. I thought I could draw a bead on her king, but my own monarch didn't have much cover himself. Then I saw it. If luck were with me and the girl in pink overreached, I would yet come out of this alive.

White to move

How did Butch tempt the colorful young lady into a misstep?

CHAPTER 2

Swindle #5—Right of second refusal

White: Baggins
Black: Me
Date: February 5, 2010

I was down two pieces, and my short, curly-haired opponent had me teetering on the edge of the crack of doom. A swindle (or two) was all I had left to my game.

If only there were some way to deflect his protection of the squares around his king. I made an offer that he could refuse—and then I made a similar offer.

Black to move

Can you find Butch's swindle "or two?"

Swindle #6—Live bait

White: Smalltalk
Black: Me
Date: January 16, 2010

Many people do not realize that chess is a social game—a contest of ideas and perception, qualities of the human spirit. A chess professional must take full advantage of these psychological aspects, and it is for this reason that I prefer chess in the park to chess in a tournament hall, where speaking is forbidden.

The park player knows how to use words as suits his need. Is the opponent ready to quit? Not sure enough of himself to sit down? Assure your cash source that he is worthy of the game. Is she feeling outclassed? Might she soon get up, take her money, and walk? Admire her talent and pay her homage. Is he getting the best of you? Distract him with remarks spun of the finest fool's gold. Entice his intellect to follow the flashy spangles.

Sometimes the chess professional will face an opponent adept at the sparring of words. But *this*? This man with his never-ending drivel about the weather and where he spent his every summer?

I could take no more of it. I didn't know if I was losing or winning, and I didn't care. I just needed it to stop. I offered bait, my opponent bit, and I was never happier for the half point.

Black to move

Can you find how Butch coaxed his motor-mouthed opposition into an early draw?

CHAPTER 2

Swindle #7—A quiet sacrifice

White: It's Been Real
Black: Me
Date: January 30, 2010

I have written elsewhere of my duel with the Energizer bunny of intolerable prattle. In the present game I faced his opposite. The thin lad sat down wordlessly, set up his pieces, and proceeded to play eight games without a single utterance coming from his side of the board. The first seven games I won, but in this last, I was relieved to come away with the draw.

I think that as soon as the silent sentinel took my queen, he knew he had thrown away a likely win. A few more moves and the game was over. He stood up, fished thirty-five dollars out of his jeans pocket, and handed it to me.

"It's been real," he said, and he walked away.

Black to move

Butch wasn't doing very well this game, as Black. He was down two pawns, and his kingside was drafty. Can you find a way for him to swindle his way out of a loss?

Swindle #8—Old dogs, dirty tricks

White: Me
Black: Melvin
Date: February 2, 2010

I had not seen my old student for quite some time. Melvin! A treat, to be sure.

Over a thermos of hot soup, he told me how he had been devoting himself these days more fully to his career in hotel and restaurant management. As he recounted to me his most current developments, I gazed across the park toward the King's Corner—the place of Melvin's employ. Two autumns previous, my ever-faithful servant, Martin, and I had headquartered ourselves in that very hotel. We had been making our investigations into a situation of the most fascinating variety, involving chess, women, and crime.

The catching-up with Melvin completed, we began our game. As we played, I was pleased to see that, rather than growing rusty, my erstwhile student had honed the abilities I had so diligently labored to cultivate in him.

Black to move

White is about to promote on c8. Can Butch allow this and yet manage a draw?

Chapter 2

Swindle #9—Trash talkin'

White: The Grandmaster of Disaster
Black: Me
Date: February 7, 2010

Already he was sitting at my table.

W: Chess?

B: Of course.

W: What do you play for?

B: Five dollars.

W: Five dollars to me if I win?

B: If you win? Of course five dollars to you.

W: If I win.

B: If you win. If I win, it's five dollars for me.

W: Draw?

B: Draw? What draw? Who plays for a draw?

W: No, I'm just saying.

B: If we draw, then we just play again, right?

W: Yah, sure.

B: You're good with the clock? Five minutes?

W: Sure. What's this, black? I'm playing Black?

B: You want the white pieces? You can have the white pieces. I'm easy. There's no trouble here. The man wants the white pieces, he can have the white pieces. Ooo! Just like *that* he goes! Okay, okay. Let's see what you've got.

W: This is just a regular move.

B: A regular move, he says?

W: A regular move.

B: You look like you're trying to hurt me now.

W: No, never. I'm not trying to hurt nobody. I'm just playing some pieces.

B: Well, now, that's looking aggressive to me. That's looking aggressive.

W: Where's that bishop? That bishop on this square, or over here?

B: The bishop's right here. It ain't going nowhere.

W: Oh, you do like that, now. It's like that, now, is it?

B: Yah, I like that. I'm liking that okay.

W: Let the record show he likes it.

B: What? Hup! Here he comes, now. Here he comes. I best get out of the way.

W: There's nothing to fear here.

B: No, I think I better get out the way.

W: There's nothing to be—Ho! Are you letting me have that? Can I have that?

B: Sure, you can have that. I'm not causing any trouble. You can have anything you want.

W: Uh-oh. Here he comes. But what if I do *this*?

B: Is that for real?

W: I don't know what you're talking about.

B: I think you're a master.

Chapter 2

W: I ain't no master.

B: A master! The grandmaster! I'm playing the grandmaster of disaster over here!

W: Aw, now you're just saying anything. What? Is that a queen sitting behind that pawn? You didn't think I was going in front of that, did you? Tell me you didn't think that. Tell me you weren't thinking anything like that!

B: I was thinking nothing of the kind.

W: What happens, I go here?

B: I dunno. What happens, you go there? It's a question.

W: It's a good question. You're gonna find out.

B: I'll find out. It's no problem.

W: My move, right?

B: I think so.

W: I think I need to cover that up. You don't mind if I cover that square?

B: You do what you need to.

W: What I need is to get this piece out of my face.

B: What, you didn't like that piece? What did that piece do to you?

W: Get it out.

B: Oh, now we're getting serious.

W: Out!

B: We're getting serious now. Where you from?

W: Who, me? I'm from around.

B: Okay, I heard of that. That's okay. I heard of around.

W: Uh-oh. What are we playing for again? One million dollars?

B: One million dollars, yah, that's right. This is looking good for you.

W: But I gotta see it through now.

B: Absolutely.

W: No point in getting this far if I can't see it through.

B: Absolutely not.

W: Let's get rid of that pawn.

B: It's yours.

W: Another one? You're giving me another one?

B: Absolutely.

W: And now it's check— No! Sonofabitch!

B: Good game. Want another? I think we should play another.

Black to move

White is about to promote on c8 and finish Butch off—to say nothing of his hanging queen. Can you find Butch's swindle against the grandmaster of disaster?

BLACK TO MOVE AND DRAW

Chapter 2

Swindle #10—A sinister plan

White: Two Left Hands
Black: Me
Date: January 11, 2010

Ask most people what separates man from animal, and you will likely hear an appeal to the brain—or possibly to speech. I respectfully disagree. For what would profit a man if he gained the capacity of a computer, but lost his hands? If a snake or dolphin were to come into possession of the knowledge of the universe, how would such intellect be exerted? Observe how the root word *man-* denotes "hand."

My opponent in the game below seemed to have two left hands. He was constantly dropping pieces and knocking them over. I thought it fitting, then, that I should swindle him twice—and with a single move. One piece of bait would lead to checkmate. I knew better than to hope for that. But the other offering, leading to a draw, was much more subtle. Much more sinister.

Black to move

How did Butch lay two traps at once?

♞ e2 ♝
OF M&M's AND KINGS

As the walrus once said, the time had come to speak of many things.

I lay the queen notebook down on the table. Next to it, I placed the black king—the one Butch had clutched in his bloody hand. Monika had left the kitchen, but Tomas was still here, futzing about. The dishes were all cleaned and put away; the paper towel, previously loaded with orange rinds, now boasted a pile of finely chopped zest, ready to add a zing to whatever recipe Tomas had in mind to cook later that day. On the stovetop, steam curled from under the cocked lid of a small, copper pot. To judge from the tang in the air, Tomas was reducing a barbeque sauce. Above the pot, the clock on the microwave said 10:35. I had spent almost two hours absorbed in Butch's chess puzzles and his life in the park. I told Tomas I was done.

"M-clip!" he called into the living room. "We're ready to get rolling, here!"

Monika came in, and we resumed our positions around the table.

I was bursting to get to several points. "The way I see it, we could talk about this queen notebook a little, but—"

"Wasn't it amazing?" said Monika. "Did you have any *idea*? Take that poem, for example—"

"Lewis Carroll," I cut in. "A brilliant tribute to a brilliant poet. Clearly, Butch has been immersing himself in literature and creative writing with the same rigor he applies to all of his passions—"

"Nothing is worth doing that isn't worth overdoing," stated Tomas.

"Now, look. We could discuss this," I said, patting the sketch of the queen in front of me, "but mostly what we need to do is go over some things Butch said in his journal. Especially his note to me. There's stuff in there that could give us an idea what happened to him. Also, we've got to see if anything can be inferred from the contents of his bag."

"All of that," Tomas agreed. "But first, in order to get us on the same page, I want to hear your recollection of last night, M-doc." He sat forward and planted his elbows on the table.

I consented to this. As if to include Butch in the conversation, I picked up the black king. I found myself shifting it from hand to hand as I related

Chapter 2

to Tomas everything I could remember, beginning with my stuffing a copy of *Atlas Shrugged* into a doorjamb and ending with our trip to the ER.

While I spoke, Tomas opened the cupboard above the refrigerator and pulled out a pink plastic bowl filled with M&M's. He grabbed a handful, spilled them onto the table, and returned the bowl to its spot. Then he began sorting the candies into monochromatic columns according to their number. At least a dozen greens formed the longest column, all the way to the left. Three browns went on the right, with the rest of the colors lined up between in descending order, forming a triangle. Every time I came to a point that particularly interested Tomas, he'd eat a few of the candies, taking from whatever column was longest, thus maintaining the shape's proportionality. Damn if it wasn't the grapes from The Slipper & the Fez all over again. Give Poirot his little grey cells and let Sherlock Holmes smoke his pipe—Tomas has his geometrical food arrangements. Short of clues, what else does a detective need?

Tomas listened patiently to my account, stopping me only twice. The first interruption came as I narrated my description of the chess area in Washington Square. He made me go over that twice. Then:

"You say the park was deserted, save for two people at a single table?"

"Yes."

"Given the hour, the cold, and the dark, I'm not surprised it was so empty. But this one table, where people were playing chess—you said something about the squares and the snow?"

I told him again about how the snow was falling so hard, even on the board, that, at least from the distance I stood, it made the squares and the pieces all look smushed together.

Tomas downed an M&M or two. He squeezed his eyes shut as he visualized the terrain. "And the bag. It wasn't just sitting on the bench, in which case whoever attacked Butch could have just walked off with it. You found it among some grasses in the gardens between the benches and the street?"

"That's right."

Monika spoke up. "Butch fled and wanted to get out of the park as quickly as possible. He wouldn't have taken the winding, deserted path through the length of the park."

"At which point he dropped the bag under duress, walking through deeper, untrod snow. That sounds right." Tomas ate a few more M&M's.

"But why wouldn't his attacker have pursued him?" asked Monika. "Finished him, grabbed the bag?"

"Unless the attacker was driven off by someone," I suggested.

Tomas polished off half the remaining chocolates.

I shifted the king to my other hand. It occurred to me that I kept moving it around because it felt odd somehow. It was too large—at least two inches taller than the usual design.

The second interruption came as I was narrating my return to the Ninth: how Monika had opened the door to let me in the Bobst, and I saw the EMTs carrying Butch up the stairs on a gurney.

"M-clip," said Tomas, "you told me this morning that the paramedics had showed up with the police in tow, right?"

"Just one cop, yes."

He picked up an M&M and examined it carefully. After a time, as if speaking to himself, he said, "There was activity in Union Square around that same time last night. Lots of chess going on down there, at Union Square…"

Union Square. I *did* recall hearing something about that, somewhere.

"Wait a minute," Monika said, "are you suggesting the attack on Butch had something specifically to do with chess?"

The M&M stopped halfway to Tomas's mouth. "Maybe. I'm beginning to get a bead on it. Don't rush me." A pause. "Do you recall who the officer was?"

"His name?" Monika asked, incredulously. She thought for a second. "No."

"It was a man, then?"

"Yes."

"Hmph." Evidently, this wasn't the desired answer, for the delayed M&M was returned to the table, and Tomas tried again. "You're sure not a woman?"

"Father! Honestly—"

"Okay, okay, not a woman. Did the officer take your information?"

"Yes."

"Can I assume he inquired how a stabbed man," Tomas jabbed at the table with his index finger, "came to be in your particular location?"

Monika nodded. "Yes, something along those lines. I explained that Butch was friends with Martin, and that he just showed up at the door, bleeding."

Tomas looked at me. "There will be initial police involvement. After all, you called 911. You should expect a call from the police, probably today. But beyond an initial report, and with no additional cause or threat, they probably won't follow up about a person they perceive to be homeless. When it comes to the police, all crimes matter—just… some more than others. Let me handle that end of things. I know some folks down at HQ. If this case is going the direction I'm starting to think it is, I have a guess at the officer they'll put on it. Now, if you please, M-doc, let's finish your story."

I told the rest without further interruption. When Tomas was satisfied that he had assimilated everything, he swept up the remaining candies (exactly one M&M of each color remained) and chased the lot down with a gulp of coffee. Then he said, "There's missing pieces, but I have a hunch what lies behind this attack."

Monika leaned forward. "And?"

Tomas lifted an admonitory finger. "M-doc," he said, "let's go over those items from Butch's journal that have been gnawing at you."

While Monika went into the living room to fetch the journal, I examined the black king some more. Its interior weight was bulging against the green felt circle on the bottom. It seemed to me that this would cause the piece to sit on the board tilted. Highly annoying. I pushed against the weight with my thumbs, trying to get it aligned.

Monika returned with the journal. I set the king down and took the small book, flipping through the pages, reminding myself of the points I wanted to make. I cleared my throat and began my literary analysis.

"From the opening passages, the reader plainly sees that Butch struggles as he writes. Psychologically, I mean." I paused, waiting for peer review. Monika's face was thoughtful and slightly downcast, feeling her friend's pain; Tomas sat forward, eager—a spider waiting in a dark corner of his web for a clue, like prey, to come across his path. I continued. "The frequent allusions to deception, darkness, and infirmity are suggestive of internal conflict. The writer 'takes bait,' and ominously refers to 'last days.' His diction is unequivocally tenebrous—" I stopped. Tomas and Monika were sharing confused looks, bordering on pained. I was losing them. I took a deep breath and plowed on. "He writes: 'Yin and yang,' 'light and darkness,' 'the black king and the white knight—'"

"That's it!" burst in Tomas, bringing my speech to an end.

"What do you mean?"

"Black king and white knight! The black king is, of course, a self-reference.

But this White Knight—have you heard of it?" Monika and I looked at each other and shook our heads. Tomas continued. "New drug out of China. Meth derivative. Supposedly laced with Adderall. Or maybe it's Adderall laced with meth—"

"Adderall?" I recalled the comments I had made to Postdoc last night about cognitive-enhancing drugs. "That's a prescription drug for people with ADHD. It's popular on campus with students pulling all-nighters and cramming for exams."

Tomas guffawed. "Take your Adderall and infuse it with crystal meth. From what I've read, the effect is like inserting a quantum computer in your brain. It's a product specially designed for enhanced pattern recognition, cognitive recall, and focus. In a word, it's a chess player's ambrosia."

"Hence the name!" exclaimed Monika. "White Knight!" She raised an eyebrow, and the gesture reminded me of Butch. "What exactly are you suggesting?"

Mindlessly I picked the black king up off the table and for the next ten minutes futzed with it while Tomas talked about popular street drugs and how Prague had spilled over with them when he lived there. He spoke of how the NYPD was cultivating suspicions regarding a new drug trade that was taking root in Washington and Union Squares. He went on to heroin and opioid addiction, cocaine and prescription drug abuse.

Unbidden, a thought entered my mind: *As your physician, I strongly disapprove of your habit!*

He spoke of his belief that many chess hustlers were addicted to these things; he spoke of White Knight and how it had been first targeted at academics, of its side effects: paranoia, cognitive distortion, and long-term deterioration of the grey matter.

A bloody hand gripping a black king.

He spoke of the way it stimulates short-term concentration and the attraction it would have for someone like Butch, whose very livelihood—

This... damn... felt circle... isn't properly affixed to the base of the king.

—hangs on seconds.

I was listening, trying to find some winning move, trying to fix the green felt circle on the bottom of the king. Frustrated, I tore it off. A rolled-up plastic bag of white crystals fell from the bottom of the king.

Chapter 2

♞ f2 ♘
SIXTY-FOUR CIRCLES. MARTIN TAKES A CALL. MONIKA MAKES A SUGGESTION.

All families argue.

We sat around the coffee table in the living room. Outside the balcony door, thick February clouds roiled the sky, pulling a veil over the city, threatening fresh snow. Wind pressed against the glass, and though the hour was shy of noon, the failing light was muddling the air into twilit hues. Monika's face, too, had darkened, her eyes like cut emeralds, fixed on the small baggie of white crystals that now sat on the low table before us.

Monika started to pace the room, turning on lamps.

It was an unfortunate comment from Tomas that had ushered in her discontent. Moments after the drugs had hit the kitchen table, Tomas had pulled the baggie toward himself. He'd opened it and with a moistened finger lifted one of the white shards to his tongue.

"Yup," he said, his eyes rolling back in his head as if checking the taste against a mental catalog of drugs, "it's White Knight." Then: "I can see the appeal this particular drug would have for Butch. The cog—"

Monika's interjection was immediate and furious. "Father!" She stood up, one hand a fist planted on her hip, the other pointing a finger at Tomas, her nail a scarlet dagger. "If you think Butch would be taking these drugs, then you don't know him!"

Tomas was unfazed. Whether he accepted his daughter's categorical denial or merely put a pin in the idea, I couldn't tell. He simply shrugged his shoulders and said, "M-doc, I believe now is the correct time to inspect the contents of our friend's duffel." Then he'd taken the drugs and the oversized king, and we'd headed to the living room.

While Monika walked around turning on lamps, Tomas rummaged through the objects I had left out the previous night. Some of Butch's items he investigated carefully—a matchbook, a take-out menu, a highlighter—while others he dismissed with hardly a look. As he finished with each, he added them to a growing heap on the coffee table. Occasionally he would ask me a question: where had Butch purchased a book, how much cash did Butch usually carry with him, what were his favorite restaurants. I knew the answers to some, but mostly his questions appeared pointless. My chief desire was to discuss the letter Butch had left for me on the back page of his journal. In my estimation, that desperate epistle was where we needed to start.

Tomas finished inspecting the last of Butch's belongings and was about to put everything back into the duffel when something inside caught his attention. He reached in and pulled out a handful of green circles.

"What's all this?" Like a kid discovering sand at the beach, Tomas let the green pieces of felt sift through his fingers back into the duffel, then grabbed them up again into his fists.

"They're the bottoms of Butch's chess pieces. They must have fallen off over the years. I didn't bother taking them out last night."

Tomas said nothing.

"Are they important?" I asked.

"Well *that* remains to be seen, doesn't it?" He walked over to the coffee table, gently pushed aside the drugs, the king, and the green zippered bag containing Butch's chessmen, and instructed me to return everything else to the duffel—but not before fishing out every last green circle. While I did this, Tomas cleared a spot in the middle of the table onto which he spread all the little felt circles that I handed him. Then he dumped out the chessmen.

He counted the circles. "Sixty-three? You're shitting me, M-doc; sixty-*three?*"

"That's all there were."

"Nonsense." In rapid succession, he looked at the bottoms of all the chessmen. Sure enough, one pawn still retained its felt padding. Working deftly around its circumference, Tomas peeled the circle off the base of the pawn and placed it with the rest. Then he sat on the couch and stared at the pile.

I stood by the balcony door, the winter-seized city darkening early behind me, watching as Tomas studied the sixty-four circles arrayed in front of him. Out on the patio, the wind got caught in some piece of furniture. Like a chess clock, it began marking time, punctuating the silence with a wooden, metronomic clicking.

Taking a position on the loveseat, Monika watched from the corners of her eyes, a deflated but still palpable indignation lingering in her crimsoned cheeks. Myself, I hadn't thought to react in anger to her father's suggestion that Butch could be using drugs. But although his hypothesis probably merited consideration, I found myself agreeing with Monika: using drugs didn't fit with Butch's psychology. It wouldn't be logical.

Tomas began grouping the chessmen according to size. Butch's king claimed a spot all its own to the right of the drugs. Then he did the same with the green felt circles. Alas, some technical difficulty ensued, and after a few failed attempts he changed course and turned his attention back to the baggie. This he rolled up tight and slid into the large black king from which it came. It fit, of course. He then made the same attempt with Butch's regular chessmen. The baggie fit into none of these.

Monika rolled her eyes. "I told you, Butch wouldn't take drugs. That big ol' king you've got there probably belonged to some other chess player."

Tomas ignored this. "M-clip, may I borrow a dollar?"

"What for?"

"Now, now." Words spoken by a man playing whatever move the game called for. "You know I never carry cash with me."

With another eyeroll, Monika reached into her front pocket and produced a one-hundred-dollar bill. "Here," she said, handing it to him. She glanced my way as if to say, *What's all this?* I shrugged my shoulders. But maybe I was getting an idea.

Tomas's fingers splayed and flexed as he rolled the C-note into a tight, thin tube. *Great Scott*, I thought, *is the man going to snort up?* No, he was trying to slide the bill into the bottoms of the chessmen. Like a magician, he demonstrated to both of us that it fit into none of Butch's pieces. Then he tried the big king. The bill slid in—just clearing the base.

Monika sighed. "The point of this is what? I'm telling you, Butch would not spend money on drugs. He would calculate that they aren't good for his—"

She paused. Had she been about to suggest that the reason Butch wouldn't take drugs is that it would harm his chess? Had Monika considered that this drug was explicitly designed to *improve* one's chess? Was she thinking of the financial windfall that their friendship had meant to him? Is *this* where all those L-notes and C-notes that she had so generously been giving him were going? Into a drug dealer's pocket? I began to see Monika's consternation from a new angle.

She shook her head. "Anyway, the money didn't fit into *Butch's* pieces." She aimed a finger at the baggie. "Neither does that meth you've got there."

"White Knight," corrected her father. "But that's hardly—"

He cut himself off. Time passed to the sound of the metronomic clicking from the balcony. Then, all at once, Tomas found his winning move, and it was back to work on those circles.

He gathered the felt circles into piles and from there into a series of columns. These he ordered from left to right by decreasing diameter. Monika leaned forward, resting her chin in her hands. I stepped closer to get a better look. *Jove's right ball*, I thought to myself when I saw the geometrical arrangement, *if it isn't the bloody M&M's and grapes all over again!*

This time the columns formed *two* triangles. Each was very acute and comprised six columns: sixteen pawn-sized circles, four each for the rooks, knights, and bishops, two for the queens, and two for the kings.

Tomas explained. "There are six types of chess pieces: pawn, knight, bishop, rook, queen, king. Each piece has a slightly different-size circle at its bottom. But look. I have two sets of felt circles. On the left, you can clearly see that all six pieces are represented. These circles match the bottoms of Butch's chess pieces." Gleefully, Tomas crowned the top circle of each column in this first triangle with one of Butch's pieces. Each one exactly covered its corresponding circle.

I caught Monika's eye. She saw what was coming next, and the darkness began to lift from her face. She was facing a purely intellectual pursuit.

Tomas continued. "Now consider the circles comprising the triangle on my right. They match none of Butch's pieces—only the black king that contained the drugs. And here was the difficulty that obscured the solution to this puzzle: I had neither six nor twelve uniquely sized circles. Can either of you guess why?"

Monika spoke up. "Some larger piece from the smaller set happened to have a footprint that matched one of the smaller pieces from the larger set."

"Precisely!" said Tomas, beaming at his daughter. "But once I *assumed* that there were two different sets, I easily found a way to partition the circles that would account for all sixty-four pieces, thirty-two pieces from each set."

"You are saying that there are two sets," I ventured, "of different sizes?"

"Correct. And where did this larger set of pieces come from that Butch obviously has some connection to?" He turned to Monika. "Would you play chess with pieces of this size?"

"Hell, no," she said. "They're not tournament standard. How could one *think*? But if you like, let's agree that Butch in fact dealt with these pieces. In what capacity? We all know that one of Butch's favorite passions is crime. Not the committing, but the investigating."

Tomas smiled. "Without question, my dear. This, then, is the solution to the puzzle. The drug dealers come to Washington Square with a set of extra-large chess pieces. Inside each piece is a baggie of White Knight. Their clients, previously equipped by the dealers with a matching set of pieces, have already put money inside of their pieces. The two parties play chess, they capture one another's pieces, and voilà, the deal is made."

"All under the nose of anyone who happens to be watching," I whispered. "Brilliant."

"Quite clever," Monika agreed.

Behind us, snow began to fall on the city in great, white clumps. The wind must have died down, however, for the clicking on the patio had stopped.

The phone rang. Tomas strode ahead of me into the kitchen, anticipation writ on the angles of his face. "Maybe it'll be the police!" he said, picking up the receiver and positioning himself in the doorway so that we could see him, one elbow propped against a wall. "Hallo, speaking?"

A voice came through the phone, but I couldn't make out words. Tomas twitched with excitement as he spoke. "Of course, Anne, hello, it's Tomas. This is the residence of Martin Malloy—"

I yanked the receiver from Tomas. "Hello," I said, "this is Dr. Martin Malloy."

"Mr. Malloy." The voice, androgynous as roadkill and twice as flat, cut a thick slice of Brooklyn. I decided it was female (I suppose I had gotten a clue with "Anne"), but it was low and rather raspy.

"This is Officer Schnapp of the NYPD. You have an office, number L-918, situated at the Elmer Bobst Library, New York University."

I paused a moment before realizing that a response was expected. "Uh, yes?"

"You have an office mate: one Patrick MacGroddy."

"Yes?"

Chapter 2

"Mr. McGroddy spoke with the on-the-scene officer at the aforementioned premises on or around 10:45 p.m. of the previous evening, February 14, regarding an African-American male who had collapsed to your floor due to an abdominal wound, and for whom you placed a 911 call."

"Yes?"

A flipping of papers, one at a time, as if through a notepad. "According to this officer's report, your officemate claims to have placed the call himself."

"Oh, yes, of course. Pat called, I'm sorry—"

"Mr. MacGroddy placed the 911 call."

"Yes. I'm sorry, I was confused—"

"You were confused last night, when Mr. MacGroddy placed the call."

Officer Schnapp's tendency to frame questions in statement form was beginning to grate. "No, I was confused now, when I said that I placed the call. I'm sorry, I thought you meant in general about the call, that it was placed from my office—"

"You are amending your statement to claim that Mr. MacGroddy placed the call to 911."

"Yes."

The soft scratching of a pencil on the other end of the phone. "The officer also took a statement from a Caucasian female, one Monika Pervilieva."

"Per*fi*lieva. With an *f*."

More pencil scratchings. "Ms. Perfliefa shares your office."

"No, Ms. Perf—*Monika*—is my girlfriend."

"And you can tell me what you know regarding how the injured man came to be on said premises."

"The injured man—Butch—is my friend. He comes to my office sometimes."

"Butch." The word was spoken perfunctorily. For a fleeting moment I imagined Butch was being addressed directly, as if he were standing there alongside the officer, providing his recommendations to the NYPD for how to proceed with their investigations. "You could provide the victim's last name."

It was awkward, not knowing the last name of a man I had considered a friend for over a decade. I winced as I said, "Not exactly."

"And you can describe to me the nature of your relationship to the victim."

"I know the victim from chess. He plays in the park. Washington Square, I mean. Butch plays chess."

"You have played chess in Washington Square often, with the victim."

"Yes?"

"You were not present at your office the night previous, when the officer entered the premises, in attendance with the medical personnel."

"Yes—I mean, no."

"No, you were not in your office at that time."

"That is correct."

"And your location, at the time the victim entered your office."

"In my office. I mean, then."

Officer Schnapp paused. "You were not present at the time that the medical personnel arrived."

If this kept up, I would soon be discussing designer drugs and little green felt circles. "I was... outside."

"You were standing outside of your office."

"No, I was outside of the library."

Pencil scratchings. "You fled the premises upon the arrival of your injured friend."

"I... Wait, what? No, I didn't flee. It was crowded, and I needed to get some air—"

"There is more you could tell me regarding the incidents of the previous night insofar as they may be helpful to my understanding of the circumstances regarding the victim's injury."

I looked to Tomas and Monika for moral support. Tomas was sitting on the couch. He had pulled his button-up shirt out of his pants so that it hung loose over his lap, his legs were crossed at the ankles, and he was munching from the bowl of M&M's. I was a movie to him. Monika sat next to him. I couldn't read her face. I told the officer I had no more information.

Officer Schnapp thanked me for my time and gave me a phone number for reporting any recalled facts. I was told to have a nice day. I hung up.

Tomas stood up and slapped my shoulder. "You did great, M-doc!"

"Father," Monika said, "I have an idea. You have a lot of connections at the NYPD, right? Why don't you go down there and find out what you can. Make sure they stay on task. Meanwhile, Martin and I will start pursuing some of these leads."

"That's a *terrific* idea," he said, and tucking his French Riviera–style shirt back into his seersucker pants, he exited in a swirl of Coppertone—for even in February, Tomas smells like summer.

Monika looked at me and raised a canny eyebrow. I sat down on the couch next to her. "That was a pretty slick move, getting rid of your father like that."

"Oh, it wasn't just for that. He'll find things out. He really does have his connections, you know." She smiled and gave me a kiss, a quick smack on the lips. "I just thought it was time you and I got talking about whatever it is that's on your mind. You mentioned the letter that Butch left for you in his journal. You've been wanting to get to this part ever since breakfast. I can tell these things."

I retrieved the journal from the correspondence desk and opened it to the back page. Monika read the letter out loud. As she spoke, the words of my friend seemed to me like annotations that a grandmaster left behind for his apprentices to study, while he himself strove against an unknown opponent in a real-life *kriegspiel* in which the pieces were invisible and each move cryptic and inscrutable.

> Martin—
>
> I would liked to have explained everything in person but I hid it from them and now if you're reading this then things went wrong and I was right to have taken measures. Begin at the home of the black king, then pace off the keys. The key you need from each notebook is the one I give back to you. New York City is my chessboard, Check the legend.
>
> Have fun,
> Butch
>
> P.S. The poems I composed on the next page will help you on your quest.

P.P.S. Where the queen lays down her crown, seek the King in Yellow.

P.P.P.S. STAY OUT OF THE SQUARE AT NIGHT!

Monika read the letter for a second time and then once more, this time with many pauses and breaks. Before we could make our move, we would need to first consider all the pieces on the board. So I made a pot of coffee, Monika grabbed a Guinness from the fridge, and for the next hour and a half we discussed the case.

♞ g2 ♞
HEADING OUT. GOING UP. THINKING BACK.

The first actionable item we could identify from Butch's letter was to find my copy of Robert Chambers's *The King in Yellow*. The small hardback's vivid yellow and red jacket made it easy to find in its usual place on a bookshelf in our second bedroom. The book showed no sign of having been disturbed. I suggested that Butch's second postscript might refer to something other than this particular piece of literature. Monika noted, however, that Butch might have his own copy, and anyway, neither of us could make out what was meant by "where the Queen lays down her crown." We earmarked the issue for later investigation.

We then turned to Butch's first postscript, which alluded to the poems he had written. Monika read each of the poems out loud:

> At the end of the day
> Should you come to a wall,
> Order these numbers
> And order them all:
> 18, 13, 3, 24,
> 7, 9, 16, 1 and no more.
>
> Little Jack Horner
> The King's in his Corner,

Chapter 2

> Eating his curds and whey.
> If you want to play with him
> He'll charge you by the day.
>
> Some students are new,
> Some students are old;
> A hat's as good as a hanky,
> As long as it pays in gold.
> What would you say to a brother-in-law
> Who is five plus four all told?
>
> The King was in his Master's hall,
> The Queen was yet a pawn;
> In Honor's case does fortune rest
> For all to look upon.
>
> Nestled in the twists and turns
> Of proud Vienna,
> You'll find this game close to home.

"The first one sounds like we might need to find a combination lock," I said. But I had never seen a combination lock with eight numbers, and without knowing where to look for it, there was nothing more to do with the first poem.

Monika pointed to the second poem. "I suppose 'the King' is a self-reference, like Father said. But Butch doesn't charge by the day to play chess."

The third poem was easy. "Stan is nine years old, right? I guess he's my brother-in-law. I mean, not officially, of course—"

Monika cut me off. "Anyway, we have that one."

We moved on to the fourth poem, but neither of us knew what "Honor's case" meant, although I suggested that if "the King" were Butch, then the "Master" might refer to Master Lin, his kung fu sensei.

"'Close to home,'" said Monika, looking at the last poem. "Whose home do you think he means?"

We weren't sure, but we decided that one obvious line of attack would be to visit Butch's apartment, hoping to find anything that would help.

"We can get the key to his place when we visit him," Monika mused. "I hope it'll be in the pocket of his pants. I don't remember any key coming from the duffel."

"There wasn't one," I said. "As for his pants, the key probably *is* there, but I doubt that the *pants* will be with Butch."

"What do you mean?" asked Monika.

"Cops will have taken them. Evidence. Don't worry," I continued, seeing the look on her face. "I know where he keeps a spare."

This time, a simple "Butch Doe" got us past the nurse at the triage desk. A wrinkled doctor in hectic green scrubs led us through a maze of corridors, keeping about twenty feet ahead. After a final turn, and with a jab of his finger off to our left, he disappeared around a bend.

The ward was a hallway of semi-private rooms. Curtains, pulled around beds, hung from an overhead track, fabric walls carving private spaces out of the larger antiseptic white. Butch's bed was a manifold of plastic tubes, glass monitors, metallic instruments, and beeping things. Monika broke into a trot and was soon at his side, pulling up a chair, cooing to him as her hand stroked his arm.

His eyes were closed. An accordion tube coming from his neck provided his air. I noted the gentle rise and fall of his chest and laid a hand on Monika's shoulder.

"What do you think?" she said, looking up at me. "Is he in a coma? What... What does it mean?"

"We could get a doctor," I said, "or ask one of the nurses walking around."

Monika is not one to conflate a wish for a fact. "And you know what they're going to say, right?"

"Yes," I said and sighed. "That they can't release medical information to us, as we're not his relations."

I looked down at Butch. Poor bloke. I pulled the curtain around on its tracks to give us some privacy, then I hunted for a key I knew wouldn't be there.

Finding nothing, I pulled up a chair next to Monika and took a few minutes to simply be with Butch before we left for his apartment. Where the spiritual might pray, I, an agnostic, took inventory of my thoughts, feelings, and remembrances toward the beloved and resolved, in the company of whatever there was of his presence, to do right by him. To judge from her face, Monika, an atheist, was doing whatever atheists do, which I presume to be very much the same thing, and such is the religious difference between us.

Before Monika came along, the subway got me everywhere. Now it's all taxis, all the time. After a twenty-minute ride uptown, I told our cabbie to pull over. Monika paid the fare, and I stepped out onto the curb.

The mid-afternoon sky was the color of ash, and though the snow had stopped, the wind was back and the cold bit hard. I pulled my coat tight and scanned the street. The apartment buildings in Butch's section of Harlem make a six-story wall of grey brick, with storefronts along street level. Metallic fire stairs spell out a string of black Zs, connecting ranks and files of windows down to the second story, where fire ladders can be extended to reach the ground. Iron bars cover the windows of the shops. Some of the businesses at the time were shuttered, and half the awnings were missing. On Butch's building, a sign advertised Zhang's Dry Cleaners: "ALL GARMENTS 99¢! (AND UP) DROP-OFF SERVICE."

I attempted a spot of humor. "Monica, did you forget to bring the laundry?" She gave me a deserved jab on the arm and rolled her eyes. I rolled my own as well—up to a pair of windows on the fourth floor: Butch's place.

Before entering the apartment building proper, however, I had a quick job to do. "Stay here," I said, "I'll be just a second."

Monika glanced up and down the street and said, "I'm coming with you."

She followed me into Zhang's. I went straight to the back of the joint, where a pair of grimy doors advertise an M and a W. "I can do this part by myself, though, huh?" I teased. She rolled her eyes at me. I went in, did what I needed to do, and came out.

"You couldn't have waited to get to Butch's for that?" she asked.

For answer, I held out a keyring. Unlike Butch's regular set, this one *didn't* have a miniature Rubik's cube dangling from it. The key did, however, have a friend I'd never seen before: a tiny thing, with a thin silver stem and an *X* on the handle that wasn't exactly an *X*.

"Butch keeps a key to his apartment in a public men's room?" Monika said, scandalized.

"Trust me, you wouldn't find it, even knowing it's in there," I replied. "Anyway, it's smarter than what a lot of people in this country do."

"Oh? What's that?"

"Put it under their door mat."

"That's stupid," she declared.

I took the silver key off the ring and showed it to Monika. She knew nothing about it, of course, but she took it anyway and put it in her purse. I put Butch's apartment key deep in the pocket of my coat, where I had already stowed the queen notebook and the journal.

"Here we go," I said.

To the left of Zhang's stands an unpainted wooden door with a solitary diamond-shaped window at eye level. No key is required to open this door. Beyond it, a narrow corridor leads to the base of a staircase. As we climbed, I recalled our previous visit to Butch.

He had declined our offer to stay with us over Christmas Eve, and so we decided to bring some holiday cheer to him. Monika had purchased a woolen sweater and matching hat at Macy's, each Kelly green and thick, to keep him warm while he played chess. She had it all wrapped up in a great big gold box with a red bow. I was excited to give him the second volume of *Petersen's Anthology of Great Literature*, thrilled that my erstwhile fiction-averse friend had recently discovered the joys of reading for pleasure.

That night, as we made our way up these very stairs—a sparkly gift bag swinging from Monika's hand (having been unable to decide between a gift bag and a gift box, she had naturally chosen both), me thumbing through the copy of *Petersen's*—the whole building seemed to be in the holiday mood. From the first floor, Bing Crosby crooned about a long-ago Christmas in Killarney; from somewhere above, a hip-hop artist was making the yuletide gay with a throbbing bass beat and a steady drone of indistinct words. A string of blinking lights wrapped around the second- and

Chapter 2

third-floor banisters had crazed the walls with red, green, pink, and gold. The air was thick with the smell of roasting meat.

Even Butch's place had gotten in on the act, in its own sort of way. He greeted us at the door and showed us in. The place was a mess, as always. Under the best of conditions, chaos rules his apartment, with the flotsam of his daily life splayed everywhere. The only sanctuary from the tempest is his beloved bookshelves, on which he meticulously orders his books, newsmagazines, newspapers, and other fact-bearing material.

That night, however, even these had been deconstructed. Piles of books lay everywhere—in corners, on furniture; even the bathroom floor wasn't exempt. Large swaths of shelves were left empty. On one cleared-out shelf, a small ceramic Christmas tree, dotted with multi-colored plastic nibs that glowed by means of a white bulb hidden inside, seemed to possess a sense of calm.

Our Christmas Eve with Butch had been nice, but the evening left me wondering what was going on with my friend. I knew he often reorganized his books, and maybe that was it. But where Butch would normally have discussed the ingenuity of his new categorization scheme or perhaps the most recent findings of the CERN Large Hadron Collider, that night the man had uttered hardly a word. He appeared happy but distracted, answering questions only on a superficial level. When we left that night, Monika and I agreed that something besides mistletoe and the music of Johnny Mathis was hanging in the air.

Now, as we climbed the stairs, getting close to the fourth floor, Christmas seemed a distant spirit. The string of lights was still here, wrapped around the banister, unplugged and dead. The smell of roasting meat had been replaced with a twang of Pine-Sol and the hint of tired wood. The only sound, besides the tapping of our shoes on the steps, was an occasional muted honk from the street.

Outside Butch's door, I got out his keys, handed them to Monika, and bent to re-tie loose laces on one of my shoes. I heard a sharp intake of breath from Monika as she opened the door. I looked up to see her standing stock still, rosebud lips parted, green eyes wide. I thought maybe the place had been ransacked. I barely had time to wonder how I would be able to tell before I stood up and took in my own gasp of air.

The room was immaculate. No. More than that. It was *decorated*.

Centered on the wooden parquet floor (which, in the absence of strewn-about clothes, I could actually see) lay an oval Persian rug. This served as a focal point for the furniture, which displayed a serene minimalism. An embroidered quilt hid the couch's fabric, which I knew to be stained and stubbly. The coffee table was adorned with a bonsai tree in its exact center. The table itself, now revealed as a pane of glass set in a brown rattan frame, reflected a pool of light that streamed in from the window—a window that now had curtains. Only the aroma of nag champa, together with the extensive shelving (once again filled with books), assured me we were not in the wrong place.

We stood there, absorbing it all. I took off my coat and was laying it on the coffee table when all at once my heart skipped a beat. The smell of nag champa was coming from a bamboo incense burner on a small side table. The burner was still lit, releasing a trail of blue-white smoke. I looked at Monika to see if she had noticed. I could tell by her gaze—calculating, but hardly alarmed—that she hadn't. I laid a hand gently on her arm and pointed to the wisps of smoke curling up from the incense burner. Smoke that could only mean one thing.

♘ h2 ♞
QUEEN ACTIVATION

Someone was here. But who? I'd never heard of a burglar who cleans up when he's done, decorates the place, and leaves behind burning incense. What kind of calling card is that? Maybe Butch had a relative? A mother he never told me about? The door to Butch's bedroom was closed. We had been fairly quiet so far; whoever was in there probably hadn't heard us come in.

Monika and I exchanged a conversation that began with our eyes, moved the plot along by means of a few hand gestures, and wrapped up with a shoulder shrug.

Are you going to go in there?
I'm not going to go in there. Do you want me *to go in there?*
No. What, knock?
Not a good idea.

Chapter 2

Well, what then?
What? How am I supposed to know?
I dunno.

I was done with the Charlie Chaplin act. I aimed myself at the closed bedroom door, hitched up my pants, and with somewhat less force than I intended called out, "Hello?"

From behind the door came a dull thud. Then a second's pause, a few hurried footsteps, and the sound of something scraping heavily against wood. A grunt.

Whoever was in there wasn't coming out to greet their adoring public. They were heading out the window to the fire escape.

Was it a drug addict? A junkie who had searched the place by putting everything neatly away as he was done with it? Did he have a knife? Maybe one that had recently been used on my friend?

I strode to the bedroom door and threw it open. Across the room I could see the silhouette of a person straddling the windowsill, half in and half out of the window. The figure turned its head and paused. In the half-light of the afternoon, I could make out a pair of eyes. Those eyes started wide, then narrowed into slits.

The figure reversed course, back into the room. Too late, I realized my peril. Behind me, I heard Monika coming to the doorway. In front of me, the figure reached for a chair, picked it up, and lifted it over its head as it ran toward me.

"Martin!" cried Monika.

The eyes, belonging to what I could now see was a young woman, shot wide. As if... she recognized me? I ducked to the left and saw her try to check her overhead swing.

"Martin?" she said. Her voice sounded incredulous as the chair came down.

			T				
H				E	R		
	O						
		O					
	K				I		
		E					

Chapter 3
THE ROOKIE

♞ a3 ♞

"WHAT ELSE DO YOU KNOW?" TWO DOWN. THIRD WHEEL.

A GIRL SLAMS ME over the head with a chair, and right off the bat I'm suspicious—even if it did go wide at the last second, just as Monika yelled out my name. Suspicious, and maybe a little brash. "Who are you?" I said.

The girl took a step back, farther into Butch's bedroom. Eyeing me up, not bothering with Monika at all. "I could ask the same of you. You're in my apartment." Petulant and defensive, like she was the injured party.

I started in on her. "I think you already know—"

From the doorway behind me, Monika cut me off. "This isn't your apartment."

"That's right," I said. "And anyway, I think you already know who I am. How?" Getting right back to it.

While the kid paused to get her story straight, I gave her the once-over. She was Asian. Her clothes looked like they had surrendered at Yorktown: tan leather boots, hardened and riddled with cracks; grey woolen pants with threadbare patches on the thighs and a rip at the knee; a blouse the color of clotted cream that actually had a nice sheen to it, tucked neatly into the pants, fastened all the way to her slender neck with small, square, black buttons—but the sleeves were fraying at the cuffs, and the collar drooped. Then I noticed the earrings. Large gold discs, plopping a big ol' Asian calligraphy-inspired plus sign onto each lobe. The plating of each disc was flaking away, revealing the base metal in a few spots. A secret admirer could have given them to her in the seventh grade. In fact, I could have mistaken the petite, lithe woman standing in front of me for a teen playing dress-up, had I not looked into her dark eyes, penetrating and nervous. This was no kid.

"You're Martin," she finally said. "Butch's friend."

"And who are you?" Monika said.

She looked only at me. "I'm Shannon. I'm with Butch."

I gave a short bark of a laugh, maybe out of surprise. In the thirteen years I had known Butch, I had never heard him speak of a lady friend.

By this point, Monika had come all the way into the room. Shannon backed up to the bed and sat down. She was trembling. "Where is he? Where is Butch?"

Monika held out a hand to her, and for a moment this mysterious woman resembled a scared dog, beaten by some previous master, contemplating a morsel offered by a stranger. "Butch has been injured," Monika said. "He's in the hospital." Her hand found Shannon's.

Shannon began to look up at Monika, but as she spoke, her gaze strayed off to the left. "What happened?"

"Butch was stabbed—"

Shannon gasped.

"He's okay! I mean… he's alive. He's—"

"Where?" Now she was looking off to the right.

"Butch is in a coma at NYU," I said. "Langone. He'll—"

"He's in good hands," Monika said.

Shannon spoke then to both of us, and the beaten pup became a Rottweiler. "What else do you know?"

A strange question. Not *Tell me everything!* That would be the query of one who wished to know about Butch. This person wanted to know about *us*. What we were up to.

"First tell me how you know me," I said.

"I want to see Butch." She stood.

"Of course you do—" Monika began, but I cut her off.

"How do you know who I am?"

Shannon went for the door. "Follow me," she said. "I have something to show you." The instant we got out to the living room, she shot back into the bedroom. I went after her, not wanting her to get a leg up on us or escape out the window again.

Instead, she grabbed something off Butch's desk and rounded on me. "I told you to stay out!" she said, somewhat inaccurately. Then her arm went out straight as a pike, palm forward, into my chest just below the sternum, and she just… walked. I was driven back into the living room by a force I could hardly believe.

Shannon had retrieved a notebook and was holding it out at me, pointing at it. "Is this you?"

The notebook was identical to the one Tomas had brought us, only with a hand-sketched drawing of a rook on the cover instead of a queen.

"Is this you?" she repeated. She had flipped the cover open and was pointing at a note inside, scrawled in a hasty pencil.

> Martin—
> Find the others and put it all together.
> Be careful. They're looking too.
> Butch

"Are you the Martin in this note?"

"Yes. Butch obviously left that notebook here for me. I would like to have it." I extended a hand.

Shannon slid one hand through her hair, a steel blade slicing through black silk. Then she gripped the notebook in both hands. She wasn't going to give it up. She said, "Do you know who *they* are? And do you know what it is they're looking for?"

"No," said Monika.

I said, "If we did, do you think we'd tell you?"

Shannon sighed. Her eyes drifted off like she was calculating something. "Look," she said, "before Butch left here last night, he gave this to me. He told me you might be coming by. I think…" Now her eyes were shifting all over the place. I wasn't believing a word this woman was saying. She was showing more concern for that notebook than for Butch. "I think Butch wanted us to work together. This thing is full of chess puzzles. From what Butch wrote in this message, I think he made several of these notebooks." She was up close now, smelling ancient and exotic, the way old moth balls smell ancient and exotic. "If you have some of them, I'll help you. I play chess. If you have them, we can pool our resources—"

"Monika here is a chess grandmaster. We don't need—"

Monika *tsk*ed, affronted. "I am not a grandmaster!"

"Whatever. Master, then. The point is—"

"I'm not a master either, Martin. I'm 2178. Twenty-two more points to go."

"Whatever! Mate me! The point is, we don't need her help."

Monika threw Shannon a look: *Men!*

"Shannon," she said, "could you excuse us, please?" Then she grabbed my arm and pulled me into Butch's kitchen. I had never seen the square little room so clean.

"What do you think you're doing?" she managed to hiss, even in the absence of sibilants. "That poor girl just found out her boyfriend was stabbed!"

"I understand that, but I don't—" I dropped my voice to a whisper. "I don't trust her."

"Martin, this is Butch's *girlfriend!*"

"Her eyes shift."

"What?"

"Her eyes. They go to the right. That's when you jog your memory. That part's okay. But then they go to the left, and that's when you're accessing the right hemisphere of your brain. The *creative* half."

"What are you going on about?"

"Oh, come on, everybody knows this. If your eyes go to the left, you're making stuff up."

She planted her hands on her hips. "Where did you get this?"

"I don't know," I sort of lied. "Everybody knows it."

Monika said nothing and did it with feeling. It's a technique she inherited from her father and subsequently perfected.

"Okay, maybe I got it from a Stephen King book. What's the *difference*? Do *you* trust her?"

This time *her* eyes shifted right, left, all over the place. After a while she said, "I don't know, Martin. But has it occurred to you that she might have more notebooks than just the one she showed us? Or that Butch may have shared vital information with her? Might she have a clue who these other people are or what we're all supposedly looking for? Or that—"

"Okay, okay. Jesus. I get the picture."

"Good," she said with a kiss. She does that—gives me a kiss when I do something right. "Now. Shannon naturally wants to see Butch. We can use this. I suggest that I go with her to Langone while you stay here and search the apartment. Don't make a mess—this woman is down-market Martha Stewart. She'll know if anything's been moved. Can I presume you've read *Misery*?"

For answer, I planted my fists on my hips and tried the say-nothing trick myself. It didn't work.

She said, "It's by Stephen King—"

"Of course I know it's by Stephen King!"

"Right, then. Move nothing. We let her see ours, and in exchange, she lets us see hers. Check?"

The diplomat's daughter and I went back to the living room. Earlier, when we entered the apartment, we had tossed our coats onto the coffee table. Now they hung from a coat rack I had never seen before, and Shannon sat on the couch reading the queen notebook that I had buried deep in my coat pocket along with Butch's journal, which also was sitting beside Shannon on the couch.

I guess we were sharing.

Shannon looked up. I braced myself for the lip I was about to get for holding out on her. Instead I got, "These are fascinating positions!" And her head went right back down into the notebook. The woman had just been told her boyfriend had been stabbed, perhaps mortally, and she's doing what? She's working chess puzzles.

I suppose I had no room to judge. Chess is a drug. Don't let anybody tell you otherwise.

"Shannon?" Monika sat down next to her on the couch and nudged her arm. "Shannon?"

Shannon looked up, slightly vexed, probably for the broken concentration.

"Martin and I would like to apologize for barging into your place—it's lovely by the way—and we agree with you that we should pool our resources. Because you're right: Butch is definitely in trouble."

Shannon's eyes grew wide. I couldn't tell if she was going to cry or kill Monika. Then her eyes softened a bit, going from steel to mere iron, and she said, "So you have a notebook. Do you... did he give you anything else?"

Monika said, "More notebooks? No, we just have the one, plus his journal."

"No, I mean anything else."

"Such as?"

Shannon clammed up. Monika and I traded a glance. What was *that* all about?

Monika shifted gears. "How about we go to the hospital? This way you can see him. Then we can discuss these notebooks. There's a lot we all need to talk about."

Shannon put down the queen notebook and picked up Butch's journal. "This one is critical," she said. "I want to hear everything you know about it."

"Of course. We can talk in the cab on the way over to Langone. Maybe get some food. Will that work for you?"

As the ladies put on their coats at the hall door, Shannon looked back to where I was sitting on the couch. "What about him?"

"Martin really wants to study that rook notebook of yours," said Monika. "He's going to stay here, if that's okay with—"

"Like fuck he is," was Shannon's immediate reply.

"What's that supposed to mean?" I said.

"You're not staying in my apartment."

"This isn't your apartment!"

Monika tried to get a word in. "I think what she means is—"

I trampled right over her. "Do you know how many times I've been here? Made myself at home? Even slept on this couch? You flounce into Butch's sights, what—a month ago? two?—hang a few curtains, and suddenly you think this is your..."

Oh, dear. Already I had said too much. Somewhere in that speech (was it the curtains?) I had tripped a switch. Shannon's face was a furnace. Her hand, shooting to her hip, made an instinctive flexing motion as if clutching at

(a knife)

something that would normally hang at her hip.

The border between bravery and folly is often porous. I thought Shannon really was about to kill me when Monika walked up to her side and placed a gentle hand on her shoulder. Looking at me, Monika said brightly, "Think about it from her point of view."

"Yyyyeah." I took a step back. "Well." It seemed that I was going to survive. "How about you two go see Butch, and I... I'll just hang out at Zhang's with this notebook."

♘ b3 ♘
THE ROOK NOTEBOOK

I dined that afternoon from a laundromat vending machine. Laundromats are great places to get work done. Everyone assumes you're waiting for your clothes, and they leave you alone. If your laundromat is particularly high-end, there might even be a pot of coffee. Zhang's coffee tasted like it had been ground only just that morning.

Ground. As in, dirt.

I got down to work.

Like the queen notebook, the rook notebook began with its associated haiku and a hand-drawn sketch:

Rook

From the King's fortress
He peers into enemy camp:
Success is likely.

There followed ten swindle puzzles of the type I had grown accustomed to. They were every bit as intriguing as the others, and I once again found myself immersed in Butch's world.

CHAPTER 3

Swindle #11—A meager offering

White: Waif-er Thin
Black: Me
Date: December 21, 2009

My opponent looked as thin and waif-like as some of my less successful colleagues here in the park. I felt bad taking his money. Still, the dignity of the profession must be maintained.

After winning several games, I suggested to my opponent that he try his luck against a lesser foe. Rochambeau, for example, off to my right a couple of tables, was currently napping at his bench and would gladly be woken for chess. Across the path and down a few benches, Cue Ball was unoccupied and calling out for a taker. But, no, my gangly combatant insisted on one more game.

It turned out to be his best. Somehow, a miscalculation put me on the defensive. From across the table I could feel my opponent's anticipation. I needed to use his emotional energy to my advantage. I offered a piece of bait that he did not have the discipline to refuse, and I secured the draw. He didn't recover any of his money that game, but at least he put a stop to his losses.

I passed him on to Cue Ball.

Black to move

How did Butch keep money from flowing back to his poorly nourished prey?

Swindle #12—A loss of the right rook

White: Me
Black: Bazooka Joe
Date: January 31, 2010

Was it a kind of psychological ploy? Over his right eye, the boy wore a patch held in place by a thin black strap that pressed tightly into his pimply skin. I was reminded of world champion Mikhail Tal and his alleged ability to hypnotize his opponent with his evil gaze. Maybe something like this was the young lad's *modus operandi*?

In the following position, I had two rooks for the queen. But I wasn't fooling anyone; I was busted. Maybe if I got rid of one of the rooks?

White to move

Which rook did Butch offer as bait, and how did he achieve the draw?

CHAPTER 3

Swindle #13—Law and order

White: Penelope Plainclothes
Black: Me
Date: February 9, 2010

The overworked informality, the buried air of authority, and above all, a sense of invincibility that can never truly be left at the precinct: I can always tell an undercover cop. Could this officer's recent surge in interest in me, and indeed in the whole chess scene here at the park, possibly reflect a newfound admiration for the world's greatest game? Perhaps. But I would be foolish to misunderstand her increasingly frequent visits to my table as anything other than police interest in the larger game that has been playing out around these parts over the past several months.

Her queen had just captured on e8; my recapture would lead only to her rebirth and a slow and grinding death for myself. I found a way to distract the constable from the situation. I only hoped she didn't see the winning rejoinder to my trick.

Black to move

How did Butch outsmart the law?

Swindle #14—Hanging the rook out to dry

White: Me
Black: Sneezy
Date: February 5, 2010

Maybe one day I'll remember to carry wet wipes in my duffel, as Martin's sweetheart once suggested. "When you're playing chess with the public, you're bound to court germs," she had told me in that sweet voice of hers.

Martin, my friend, you are a lucky man.

My opponent's habit of sneezing into his hand and then immediately making some wet move proved Monika's point. My reticence to touch the pieces may have contributed somewhat to my downfall in this game. Happily, my opponent didn't see the trick I had in store for him, and I was able to move him on to Mongoose without owing him any money.

Poor Mongoose came down with a cold the next day.

White to move

How did Butch trick Sneezy?

Chapter 3

Swindle #15—In a "tale-spin"

White: The Author
Black: Me
Date: January 4, 2010

Spinners of fantastical tales charge their worlds with the uncanny, the elaborate, and the infernal. To them belong the eldritch[12] night, while their protagonists hunt vampires beneath a moonless New England sky and ogres covet the flesh of toothsome maidens from the gloom of hidden dens. Theirs are the unbranded gods whose stirrings drive worshippers to mad acts and whose extraterrestrial callers advance alien designs against the backdrop of an earthly frailty. Through appeal to the merely unordinary do such tale-spinners enchant their readers with a manufactured interest.

But the true patron of the extraordinary, whose concern inclines toward the ultimate, observing with gray forbearance the beat and stride of the bestseller parade, must demand the celestial and the baroque to yield to that most luminous product of the utterly prosaic and the purely organic: the human mind itself.

Taken blind on a watery bed by the groping elements, conceived through a primordial age when all took place in the dark (for there were none to see), life began. On soggy parchments of tidal mud were we drafted; between the firm covers of land and sea were we bound, publishing under the categorically non-fantastical genres of biologic descent and statistical determinism our billion-year tale of emergence from grimy element to ineffable self.

And yet: Inquiry. Astonishment. Love.[13]

To one who would spin a tale bereft of the pulp-mill horrors, favoring instead the extraordinary ordinary of human thought, what advice could I offer? From the available stockpile of human psyche a writer so inclined must select for his muse the richest of all subjects—a mentality in which the conflicting dualities of self-confidence and self-flagellation,

---

12 Like Lovecraft, Butch certainly views the world from a unique perch.
13 My goodness. Butch gets a girl, and suddenly we are writing haiku, searching our emotions, and channeling literary talent! My friend is full of surprises these days.

circumspection and bold trial, foresight and rash instinct compete to form the ultimate in cognitive turbulence. I must, in other words, recommend the urban chess player.[14]

Up from the fabled roots of its forgotten Oriental heritage and across the desert countries of an Islamic sultanate, the game of chess swept into a medieval Europe. Across the plague-ridden lands it found its definitive form among the knights and castles, the clerics and the royalty of a feudal economy. Consider the minds that steered the world from across an ocean. Napoleon Bonaparte! Marcel Duchamp! Ludwig Wittgenstein! These had no truck with the lesser avocations: from their left hemispheres, chess demanded calculation; from their right, creative force. To those who would synergize the cerebral parts into a cognitive whole, the game of kings presents itself a Truth Divine; to those who are by temperament dour and by disposition theocratic, a devil's snare.

Then, America. Quickened by the pulse of a newer world, the industrialists grew wealth for themselves through their specialized labor and sprawling railroads, condensing the hours in a day and contracting the distances between points. As the tempo of life increased, so did the modes of its expression. The constancy of Bach and Mozart gave way to the riffs of Coltrane and Monk, and in the speakeasies of American cities, jazz nightly created the world *ex nihilo* and *ad lib*.

Nor was chess immune to the hastening beats of change. Here, as in music, speed and self-invention succeeded precision and orthodoxy—and among none more than those who make the public places their home and who fight for survival (for the depth of the industrialist's weal was surely not mirrored in the breadth of its reach): the chess players of Washington Square Park!

It was one such investigator who, exploring the plight of the common man, gathering what thoughts and inspiration he might find, wandered into my corner of the park one late morning. It so happened that he was a very fine chess player, and over the course of several games (a fair amount of cash traveling both directions of the board), we had each landed the other in a

---

14 Butch has declared himself the ultimate writer's muse.

fair share of horrors. Below is the position that sticks most in my memory from that encounter.

Black to move

Butch, playing the black pieces, made a move that allowed him to follow up the careless capture of his rook with a draw. Can you find the move?

Swindle #16—A matter of relocation

White: Mr. Arms
Black: Me
Date: January 26, 2010

His arms reached my bench—slabs of beef swinging from meat hooks, each terminating in a stocky hand that gripped an invisible suitcase, accounting for the empty space that flanked either side of the white A-shirt that clung to his torso like a crust. As he sat, he tried to move the marble table, unaware that it was bolted to the ground.

"You pay me if I win?" was all he wanted to know. I informed him that five dollars went to the winner, to be financed by the loser. A grunt signified assent to terms. We played. He didn't move the pieces; he relocated them against their will.

In the position below, I was Black. As the result of an oversight, my queen had become one of those pieces moved against its will. Or rather, against *my* will. To come eventually to the point, it had been relocated off the board.

Happily, I found a drawing resource contingent upon my densely packed opponent's acceptance of my piece offering.

Black to move

What piece did Butch offer, and how did he swing the draw?

CHAPTER 3

Swindle #17—Under construction

White: Hard Hat Matt
Black: Me
Date: December 30, 2009

The man with the round head and rounder body didn't need to be wearing a hard hat for me to infer his occupation as belonging to the building trades. When you're around jackhammers and pneumatic tools all day, I guess you get used to shouting at your co-workers. Lots of construction these days, downtown.

I was playing the white pieces and was none too happy. A piece sac on a7 against his castled king hadn't gone quite according to plan. Then I spotted the potential draw. A draw isn't much to shout about, but in this case I was happy to get it.

White to move

Butch is playing White and he is down a piece. Are there any drawing tricks you can find to help avoid an embarrassing loss to his hard-hatted opposition?

Swindle #18—Hanging by a thread

White: Buzzy
Black: Me
Date: January 9, 2010

A mosquito buzzes past a spider in search of blood...

There are three essential modes by which chess in the park is monetized. In the first, the player collects pay upon a win but pays out nothing on a less fortunate result. I surprised Martin once by informing him that many visitors to our great city prefer this scheme to a straight wager, believing that a less-hostile web belongs to a less-formidable spider.

The second mode of money-making requires that the quarry pay to play. This is employment suitable for those less skilled with the pieces but possessing a profound knowledge of human nature and the weaving of webs.

The third and most honorable way is the straight wager. Each combatant lays his five dollars on the table, the sum going to the winner. Under this praxis, it is purely one's skill with the pieces that is put to the test.

... Where the mosquito seeks blood, the spider weaves his web.

The man who kept circling my table before finally sitting down and getting caught in my web knew how to handle a tough spider. In the position below, White is about to promote on g8. I made it out only by the thinnest of threads.

Black to move

What snare did Butch set for his opponent in hope of avoiding a loss?

Chapter 3

Swindle #19—Searching for Bobby Fischer

White: Me
Black: Prospect
Date: February 10, 2010

"Hey there, young man! Game of chess before school?" I tapped my skull. "Get that brain working?"

"Can I, Dad?" the boy asked. The father paused, then shook his head and continued apace.

Sometimes I employ shame. "Where's your courage?"

It worked.

Looking at the board from behind his black-framed glasses, the boy played as if he were immortal. Our game went wild, with both kings exposed and hardly anything coming off the board. Suddenly my rook and bishop were forked. I concluded that I could swindle a draw only if the kid took my rook. So I covered my bishop and hoped for the best.

The father stood tableside, arms folded over his chest. I needed a distraction. "You remind me of a game I played with Bobby Fischer, young man! Do you know who Bobby Fischer was?"

The boy gave his head only the slightest shake as he scanned the board. But the comment wasn't meant for him.

"You played Fischer?" The father stepped closer. A cold cloud of breath spilled over his chin. Naturally, he accepted a comparison between his child and the greatest chess player our species has ever produced.

"I did indeed, sir! The year was 1965. I was about your boy's age—seven, might I guess?—when Bobby Fischer gave a simultaneous exhibition right here in the park." The child's potential having been made clear, it was now necessary to take fate's brush in hand and, with heavy strokes, draw the connection between history and the gravity of the moment. "It was a most fateful day in my life. Very formative." The father continued to nod as I spoke. "Yes, sir, very influential. Fateful day for a young chess player, that day in the park." More nodding from the father. "A very powerful force in my chess development, being in the presence of a master like that." No further response.

I needed to press further. I turned my attention back to the boy. He still hadn't lifted his eyes from our cloth battlefield, and I could see his mind working, mentally replaying our game. He was hating the fact of our imminent draw. Very like Fischer indeed, this boy. A wonderful student he would be.

"You play very energetically, young man. May I make a suggestion for your improvement?" This offer was rewarded with a split-second glance from my prospect before his eyes returned to the plastic war spread out before him. With precise provocations, I practiced my professional pontifications. "Don't overextend your reach! Reserve your energies until your house is built! Then your attack will have more power."

"Did you hear what the chess master said?" the father asked. (Ah, this was going very well now.)

The boy looked directly at his father. "I want another game."

This time, I made sure the boy went down. Fast.

The father's defenses were broken. "Do you give private lessons?"

White to move

The young prospect almost did Butch in. How did Butch salvage the draw?

CHAPTER 3

Swindle #20—Dogfight in the park

White: Dog's Best Friend
Black: Me
Date: February 8, 2010

One of our city's dog walkers, finding a way to pass time while on the clock, helped all eight of her canine charges find a comfy spot on the ground around my bench, slapped a five on my table, and sat down to business. Three bull terriers, two Pekingese, two bichons, and a rescue napped on the ground while the two of us duked it out over the board.

I had a pawn on the seventh with no way to turn it into a queen—at least not and have it live. She had an extra bishop. A draw was the best I could hope for. I needed a place for my rook, and I found it.

Now I just needed her to take it.

Black to move

The dog lady *did* take it, and Butch secured the draw. How?

I finished the puzzles. I wasn't sure about a few of my answers, but I felt satisfied with my work. The light outside was now completely spent, and so was I. I put the notebook down next to an empty bottle of laundry detergent, folded my hands over its open pages, lay my head down on my hands, and took a nap.

♘ c3 ♘
I SAID I DIDN'T. BUDDHA, MANGA, CERTS. EIGHT BY EIGHT.

I woke up to Monika shaking my right shoulder. "We're heading upstairs. See you up there." She left me to regain my consciousness.

I sat up and looked at the notebook. On the final puzzle, a drop of drool had dried up on the a6 square, puckering the paper. I dragged myself up the four flights of stairs to Butch's place. I went inside and sat down heavily on the couch. In the kitchen, Monika was pouring St-Rémy into a paper cup. Melted snow was dripping off her coat and onto the parquet floor. I could hear Shannon moving about in the bedroom.

I attempted speech. "Hesemzbuffore?"

"Try that again?" Monika's eyes sparkled over the cup as she drank. Shannon came out of the bedroom with a red-and-white checkered towel to dry the floor, and she took Monika's coat.

My left shoulder was aching. I groaned a little and massaged it, wondering dourly if I would be able to distinguish the wood grain of the chair in the bruise, then cleared my throat. "Butch?" I said. "He was the same as before?"

Monika tossed her cup into the trash. "Yeah," she said, joining me in the living room.

Shannon went into the bathroom and returned with a bottle of Advil. She sat down next to me and held it out. "I'm sorry for hitting you before," she said.

I went for the Advil, but she pulled back a little and nodded at the notebook on my lap. "Were you able to solve any of those?"

I *tsk*ed and grabbed the bottle from Shannon's hand. "Yes. I think." I dry-swallowed one of the blue caplets. "Monika is going to be better at these puzzles than either of us. Monika?"

"Shannon and I saw Butch at the hospital, then got some lunch. I showed her his journal and we discussed a few points. Most importantly, we agreed that we're all in this hunt together."

I looked at Shannon. She nodded her assent, but not before grabbing the bottle of Advil out of my hand and returning it to the bathroom. By God, this woman was prickly.

"Okay, then," I said. "Where do we start?"

Monika laid Butch's journal on the coffee table so we could all see.

"Butch says, 'New York City is my chessboard. Check the legend.' Shannon and I were thinking that atlases have legends."

"I considered that as well," I said.

Looking around, Monika said, "There's got to be an atlas *somewhere* on one of these shelves."

"What else?" I said.

"Butch mentions keys," said Shannon. "'The key you need from each notebook is the one I give back to you.' In a chess puzzle, the key is the first move of the solution. Do you have any idea what he might mean by *give back to you?*"

I said I didn't, and that was the truth. Well, maybe I had a *little* idea. But that could wait, so instead I decided to just sum up. "The keys from each of his five notebooks are meant to be gathered and, I assume, somehow assembled. We're supposed to start at 'the home of the black king'—"

"Meaning here," Monika interjected.

"Yes, that at least is clear. But only one key from each notebook is meant to be identified."

"Hmm," said Monika. I saw it in her eyes; she knew I was holding back. It didn't matter. Whatever was discussed now between the three of us, she and I were going to have our own private analysis later. She said, "Then there's this business with *The King in Yellow*."

"I believe this could be a reference to a short story by Robert Chambers," I said to Shannon. "Do you know if Butch has a copy?"

Shannon shrugged her shoulders, splaying out her hands helplessly as if to indicate the vastness of Butch's book collection… and there went those drifting eyes again. How was I ever going to get anywhere when this woman kept lying to me?

I resumed. "Butch gives us five poems, each one obviously intended to point us toward a different notebook. I figure we already have the one whose poem talks about new and old students. That's this queen notebook. And now we have the rook notebook. I wonder which poem *that* one related to." I looked at Shannon. "How did you say you got it, again?"

She hesitated a little, then repeated her earlier assertion that Butch had left it for her. I let it go for the time being.

"How about some of these others, Shannon?" asked Monika. "Can you make any sense of them?"

We studied the poems, but nobody knew of lockers that Butch used that might utilize combination locks. We didn't know anyone named Jack. Monika observed that you call a judge "Your Honor," and suggested that Butch may have been interested in a court case. But none of us could think of one in particular. And taking a trip to Vienna was decidedly off the mark!

We were at an impasse, but I had a plan. I needed to snoop.

"Hey, Shannon," I said, rubbing my shoulder, "could you get me another Advil?"

When she walked off to the bathroom, I mouthed a message to Monika, accompanied by some hand gestures: *YOU take HER and search HERE*. Monika raised an eyebrow in confusion, and Shannon returned with a single blue capsule. No bottle this time. I sent it chasing after the first.

"Look," I announced, "I like what we said earlier about a legend and an atlas. Butch will definitely have an atlas. Wouldn't you agree, Monika?"

Semi-understanding lit her face. "Absolutely!" she said. "Knowing Butch, he'll have more than one."

"Let's start searching," I said. "Everything on his shelves will be organized according to some scheme. You two take this room. I'll get the bedroom." Shannon started to object, as I thought she might, but I just kept on. "Be thorough. Many of his books will be double-shelved."

"Come on, Shannon," said Monika, "you take this bookcase above the couch; I'll start by the kitchen."

I looked at Shannon to gauge her reaction. If she objected to something as ostensibly innocent as looking through shelves of books—books that weren't even hers—she would make herself look like she had something to hide. On the other hand, if she acquiesced, she could use this opportunity to build trust.

She paused a little, then said, "Sure."

Just as I thought. Two attackers, one defender. And that, chess fans, is how you grab the square you need.

At first, the bedroom was all shadows and dim shapes. Outside, across the street, splotches of amber were the windows of apartment buildings;

Chapter 3

a blob up against a wall was the chair that Shannon had swung at me. I felt on the wall for the switch. A lamp turned on across the room: a jade Buddha—fat, grinning, and green—squatted on the nightstand, holding a lampshade over his head.

I went to pull the door shut behind me, then realized I would only be stoking Shannon's suspicions, and I left the door how it was. I began with the books above the dresser. These were battered volumes of the *Encyclopedia Britannica*. The bookcase to the dresser's right held autobiographies alphabetized by author. Tucked behind them were tomes on military history. I proceeded to an array of milk crates stacked in files and ranks near the bed.

It was Butch's chess library. In one cube were classics: Reuben Fine, *The Ideas behind the Chess Openings*; Bobby Fischer, *My 60 Memorable Games*; Aron Nimzowitsch, *My System*. Another cube held the latest Sahovski *Informant*s; a third was devoted to endgame manuals. A light blue crate contained game anthologies. Here, too, was the most recent edition of *Modern Chess Openings*.

But hadn't I seen Butch's MCO in his duffel? I took the book out of the cube. It was a paperbound edition, and it looked and felt nearly mint. Riffling through the pages, I discovered a rectangular cavity cut into the middle of the book. The hole that Butch had gutted out (it must have killed him to do so) was the exact size of one of his notebooks. When I saw the name of the opening on the first page where the hole had been cut, I had all the proof I needed that Shannon was lying. I added this point to a list of points that I planned to discuss with Monika over dinner that evening.

Resisting the temptation to peruse the rest of Butch's chess library, I proceeded to the long shelf over his closet. This corner of the room was secluded by a tri-fold silk screen depicting geishas who played flutes and comforted their reclining clients with hand fans. Not for the first time, I noted Butch's indiscriminate attitude toward adopting both Chinese and Japanese influences.

I grabbed the chair Shannon hit me with and stood on it to inspect the shelf. Various holy books of the world's religions were here. No atlases. Just outside the door, I could hear somebody shuffling through some books. Maybe the ladies were having better luck?

Looking down the other side of the tri-fold screen, I spotted a small round table cluttered with objects. This bore further investigation. One end of the screen was flush against a wall. At the end nearer to the bedroom door, a narrow gap led to the sequestered space. I sucked in my gut, my back to the wall, gauging dimensions. I started to squeeze through and was almost in when my leg pushed against the screen, causing it to squeak at the hinges. Outside the door, the sound of shuffling books stopped. I heard a couple of footsteps. Monika called out, "Shannon, could you give me a hand with these?" The footsteps moved off, and I squeezed the rest of the way in.

I had just enough room to crouch in front of the low table. Here, Tupperware containers overflowed with batteries, a flashlight, a screwdriver and other hand tools, books of matches, packs of Swisher Sweets, an opened roll of Certs. This was Butch's personal corner—an allowed space within his own apartment. A concession. *Butch must really love this woman,* I thought to myself.

A glint of metal among the chattels caught my eye: Butch's apartment key. Shannon must have taken it from my coat pocket along with the notebooks when I was talking with Monika in the kitchen. I reclaimed the spare key for myself and didn't feel bad about it, either. Shannon would have her own.

I decided to check the closet itself. I slid open the door, quietly uncovering a collection of manga that ran from wall to wall above the hanging clothes. Then I saw it, and I was lucky to have done so: a strip of beige in a chaos of color. I took it off the shelf. It was a hardcover copy of *The King in Yellow* from which the cover had been ripped. I flipped through the book once quickly and then a second time page by page.

Not a thing from Butch.

No notes, no message, no clue.

Not even haiku.

"Got it!" cried Monika from the other room. For a foolish moment I believed she had found another copy of *The King in Yellow*, the one that Butch wanted me to find and that would solve the whole mystery. I returned the denuded book to its place, shot out from behind the screen (almost knocking it over), and went into the living room to see what she had found.

It was an atlas. Multiple atlases, actually. Just like she had said.

"There's the lot," Monika said, plunking down a pile of large books on the coffee table. Merriam-Webster, National Geographic, Rand McNally—all the big-name publishers were represented. "Everybody grab one and look up New York City."

For the next several minutes it was all ruffling pages and the nostalgic scent of old print from the secondhand volumes. Then—

"Look!" said Shannon. Opened before her was Oxford's *Atlas of the World*. Her finger pressed down on a map of New York. Drawn over top of a large chunk of Manhattan was a rectangle that had been divided into an eight-by-eight grid. The letters *a* through *h* along the width and the numerals 1 through 8 along the length gave it away for what it was: Butch had quite literally made New York City his chessboard (elongated somewhat in order to take into account Manhattan's rectangular shape). Hand-printed in a corner of the page were the words *X marks the spot*.

I looked up at Monika. "Butch really has hidden something in this city."

"And somehow," Monika said, "this map is going to help us find it."

"We must find the notebooks," said Shannon. "All of them. When we put all the clues together, Butch will lead us to it."

"But… to what?" asked Monika.

♘ d3 ♘
THIRTY MINUTES TO PEKING. REFLECTIONS ON A LECTURE. WE ARE ROOKED.

Monika and I were at The Great Wall of China, Butch's favorite restaurant. Earlier, Shannon had overheard us talking of going and had suggested the chocolate lychees for dessert. She claimed that Butch loved them. The concept seemed strange to me, and that was putting things nicely.

The air was funky with fish, soy, and garlic. I grabbed us a spot, one of those half-booths with the chair on one side of the table and the bench on the other, its stuffing pushing out in white tufts from behind patches of silver duct tape that held together its torn, yellow vinyl. I let Monika have the chair.

Over the ten minutes since we'd left Butch's apartment, I had been doing all the talking.

"—and why would she be running for the fire stairs and *then* turn around and attack me? Like she was afraid I was somebody else and then realized she could take me out? And she took our notebooks. Right out of my coat pocket! Butch's keys, too. We're lucky I got them back! Do you suppose—"

A waitress whose nametag said TAI asked us if we knew what we wanted. Monika ordered a Tsingtao and said she needed some time to look at the menu; I ordered tea. Tai left. I kept talking.

"Do you suppose Butch has been teaching Shannon kung fu? I mean, anyone can sling a chair. You should have felt how she pushed me out of that room. Just... *push*! Walked on through like I wasn't there. That's how it is with kung fu, you know. Concentrated power in small packages. Bruce Lee—"

"Martin?"

"Yes?"

"We're in a restaurant. Nobody here is going to kill you."

"Have you never read *The Godfather*? There's a scene in *The God*—"

"Martin?"

"All right." I sighed, looked around. In a far corner, a family of five—grandmother, mom and dad, twin girls six or seven years of age—was passing dishes around a circular table. Very cute. Opposite, near the door to the street, a fellow sat working a pair of chopsticks, slurping up noodles. Thirtyish, Chinese at a guess, with a stubby pipe on his table, unlit. I tried to recall whether I'd ever seen a Chinese person smoking a pipe, and I came up empty. Over at the waitress station, Tai tapped away at a cash register. Behind her, a pulled-back curtain embroidered with a golden dragon led to the kitchen, where a jumble of woks covered a wide stovetop. A silver pot breathed out a silent cloud of steam. The prime dinner hours were over; the place was shifting into low gear.

I turned back to Monika. "I bet this place has duck. You like duck?"

"It'll probably take a while," said Monika, "but yes, duck is wonderful. Are you feeling better now?"

"I'm in the mood for duck."

Tai came by with Monika's beer and a pot of tea and poured for both of us into a pair of white ceramic cups.

"You got Peking duck?" I asked.

"Half an hour." She glanced toward the kitchen then back to us. "You still have time."

"We'll take a duck," I said.

We sipped our beverages for a while, then Monika said, "Do you want to discuss the case? I mean for real this time. No kung fu bullshit."

I smiled. The tea had helped. "I do have a couple observations that I think you will find both rational and interesting."

"Would one of them have to do with Butch's comment about giving something back to you?"

"Yes, Sherlock, it would," I teased. "What makes you say this?"

"When Shannon mentioned it, you said you didn't know what Butch meant. Your eyes went up and to the left. I heard somewhere that that means you're making shit up."

"Nicely played. So, here's my thought. I'm sure you noticed in the queen notebook an entry that had a certain *Alice in Wonderland* whimsy to it?"

"Of course! I loved it."

"Yes, the poem was quite good. Then, in this most recent notebook we got from Shannon, Butch does *another* pastiche, this time in the fashion of H.P. Lovecraft." When we left Butch's, I had taken the two notebooks, and Monika had put Butch's journal in her purse. I now took the notebooks out of my coat pocket and handed the one with the rook on the cover to Monika. "See for yourself."

She paged through it to Swindle 15. She read carefully, whispering an occasional word or phrase out loud. *Eldritch. Plague-ridden lands.* She set it down. "Okay, so what's it all about?"

"Around a year ago, Butch started showing an interest in fiction. I wanted to encourage this, so I gave him an anthology of literature. You remember. The book we brought him last Christmas? *Peterson's Anthology of Great Literature*? It's an eclectic mix. Lewis Carroll is in it. Lovecraft, too."

"You're suggesting that by writing these pieces, Butch is 'giving back' to you what you gave him? Pieces of literature?"

"In so many words, yes," I said.

"In so many words? Cute."

"And here's another thing. *The King in Yellow* is *not* in the anthology. I think Butch wants us to find an *actual copy* of that book."

"We already checked your copy at our place," said Monika. "You didn't find anything."

"Correct. But while I was hunting in Butch's bedroom, I found *his* copy. And get this—the cover was ripped off."

Monika furrowed her eyebrows. "What? I can't imagine Butch doing that to a book."

"Right?! But there was nothing in the book. So here's what I want to do. I want to go back to Butch's tonight and snoop some more. Butch is very careful with how he arranges his books. I found the copy I'm telling you about in with a bunch of manga. I think that Butch has *another* copy of *The King in Yellow* that he wrote something in and that he placed among similar titles. He couldn't bring himself to part with the one he tore the cover off of, so he put that one someplace where he wouldn't be reminded of it."

"But that doesn't explain why he would rip the cover off in the first place."

"Well, I don't know. But after we're finished our duck, we need to go back and hunt for it—and for the anthology as well."

"And if Shannon is there?"

"Then you take her out for a coffee. Finally, there's this: Shannon is definitely lying to us."

"Come on, Martin. You're being overly suspicious of her."

"No, wait. We went through all those poems together with Shannon—the ones in Butch's journal that are hints to where the notebooks are hidden, right?"

"Right."

"And none of us, including Shannon, said we had a clue, right?"

"So far."

"But when I was in Butch's bedroom, I found a copy of the MCO. I thought this was strange, because he has one in his duffel. So I opened the book and guess what: he cut a rectangular cavity out of the middle of the pages, *in exactly the size and shape as one of his notebooks*. Would you care to guess which chess opening was on the first page where he cut the hole?" Not bothering to give her a chance, I said, "The Vienna Game."

Monika gave me a wondering look, and she pulled Butch's journal out of her purse. She found the page and read out loud, "Nestled in the twists and turns of proud Vienna…"

A blast of cold air came in from the street; the family of five was leaving. At his table by the door, the man with the noodles and the pipe was putting out some cash. Tai hollered some benediction (in Mandarin, I supposed) to the departing family, and then came over to us.

"Your duck is almost ready," she said. "Is there anything I can get you?"

I looked at Monika. "What was that dish Shannon suggested?"

"Lychee nuts with chocolate syrup."

Tai laughed. "Lychees with chocolate! You are maybe friends of Butch?"

"Yes," I said, "how did you—"

"That's his dish." Then she leaned over, put her mouth next to my ear, and whispered, "Lots of people know Butch." As she walked away, she called back over her shoulder, "After the duck, lychees with chocolate!" Almost into the kitchen, she glanced back at me once more, and she was no longer laughing.

Monika and I looked at each other. Neither of us had any idea what *that* was about.

While we waited for our duck, I asked Monika to work the puzzles in the rook notebook. I wanted to see if she'd arrive at the same answers I had come up with earlier that day. While she studied them, I reviewed the puzzles from the queen notebook. Our dinner came, and we spent the next hour or so in a companionable silence, rolling duck and scallions and hoisin sauce up into little round pancakes, thinking about chess, sipping tea, drinking beer, and burying ourselves in Butch's world.

The duck was gone and the puzzles solved. Lychees with chocolate turned out to be not so strange a dish as I had imagined. The bittersweet dark chocolate proved a welcome counterpoint to the fruity pulp of the nuts. I asked for the tab and checked my phone for the time: just after ten o'clock. The restaurant was empty now, save for us and the man who still sat at his table by the door. He had finished his noodles a long time ago. What was he still doing there?

As if in response to my notice of him, the man stood up and walked toward the men's. Monika excused herself to wash up. I looked for our waitress. The curtain to the kitchen was pulled shut, as if the restaurant wished to shroud from its patrons the sacred rites of closing—a quiet clamor of pots and pans being put away, fraternal commands shouted between workers, the smell of detergent on hot steel.

The man emerged from the bathroom. He walked toward me. He was short, I noticed, and his hands were behind his back. A few feet from my table, he stopped. Acting on its own, my hand covered the notebooks. Then I turned to watch him go past me toward the door and out onto the street. As the door shut, a crash came from the kitchen. I leaped to my feet. A voice behind me said, "Whoops!" I spun around to see a grinning Monika. "I think someone misplaced a wok," she said.

"Yah, I guess so. Let's clear our check and get out of here."

Outside, heavy clots of snow splattered the sidewalk and the streets. Orange light from overhead lamps caught the knobbles of the road, turning the asphalt into a wet, reptilian skin. Ahead of us, two women embraced; across the street, boys called out to each other and disappeared into a pizza shop.

On our way back to Butch's apartment, we walked hand in hand alongside a wrought-iron fence that separated us from a strip of brownstone stoops and half-lit alleyways. Then we crossed over the street, still backtracking the way we had come a few hours earlier. Off to our left and down the street about a block, I saw a dark shadow slip inside a door. The shape seemed familiar and feminine, and after catching the glint of an earring, I wondered if Shannon was tailing us. I ran off to discover which store she had entered and called to Monika to follow me.

I came to a large storefront window. Shannon, if that was who I'd seen, had disappeared somewhere around here. Pressing my hands and face against the cold glass, I peered inside, into the black. My eyes adjusted to the darkness beyond as the elements of a large room revealed themselves: a floor of wide, wooden planks; grey walls unadorned by mark or hanging; a solitary figure sitting in lotus position in the center of this stern space. A candle flickered next to him from inside a pale blue jar, mingling its light with what little the chamber had to offer and granting to the large space a sense of comfort. The man's silhouette seemed a living (but thinner) imitation of the jade Buddha that sat on Butch's nightstand.

I stepped back from the glass. Monika's stacked heels made light, staccato taps on the sidewalk as she approached. She read aloud the words

Chapter 3

that were painted in gold across the top of the window in a fake Chinese calligraphy. "Master Lin's Kung Fu Studio," she said, placing a hand on my shoulder. "Do you suppose Butch still practices here?"

I had been here once before, I remembered, and Butch had been quoting the wisdom of Master Lin to me ever since our first encounter nearly thirteen years ago.

I had just delivered my first public lecture at NYU as a new member of faculty. I was in the campus bookstore, ensuring that enough copies of my class textbook were available to my students, when I rounded a corner and slammed directly into a floating pile of books.

The books crashed to the floor, revealing the man who'd been carrying them. "Great Scott," I exclaimed. "Pardon me!"

"Dr. Malloy," the man said, the reek of tobacco coming from his mouth, "this is a most serendipitous convergence." Rather than stop to pick up the books that lay strewn about us, he launched into a question. "I was at your lecture today, 'From the Red Chamber to the Lighthouse: Reflections on a Trans-civilizational Approach to Philosophy as Autobiographical Literature'" (to this day it remains a matter of debate in my mind which amazed me more: that Butch *could* recite the title of my lecture verbatim or that he thought it *necessary* to) "and I am seeking your input regarding Schopenhauer's admonition against 'for ever reading, never to be read' in juxtaposition to the saying of Master Lin, that learning without reading is dangerous. Could you offer any?" As he concluded his query, his carefully trimmed eyebrows rose upward in parallel with the modulation of his voice.

"I'm sorry," I said, disoriented, "Master... ?"

"Master Lin," the somewhat alarming man explained, "my kung fu sensei." He then proceeded to clarify the subtle differences distinguishing the philosophy of his teacher from that of Confucius before offering some further thoughts on Schopenhauer in a return to his original question.

I must here confess to having registered very little of his oration. My only defense is my preoccupation with the various contradictory aspects of his character and countenance: the manicured eyebrows at odds with the stale stink coming from a mouth missing several teeth; the shabby clothes versus the man's intent to purchase a stack of books surely totaling hundreds of dollars; the rich, deep-black hair, oiled and tightly curled in an afro, looking downright youthful against his weathered and worn face; and, finally, his mental alacrity and perceptive recall (he recited passages from my lecture word for word) juxtaposed with a complete deafness to the annoyed comments coming from those who were forced to pick their way around us and over the books that still lay on the floor.

This last paradox reminded me of the singular attention that I often observe in chess players, whose vision and focus encompasses just the eight-by-eight board in front of them—and nothing beyond it. And so I wasn't surprised when, toward the end of his monologue, Butch mentioned playing chess in Washington Square. I was about to interject that I too played chess when I found myself invited to visit his kung fu studio that following Saturday. Master Lin's Kung Fu Studio was in Harlem, and he, Butch, would be testing for his black sash, third degree.

I was assured that my presence would be considered an honor.

Monika recalled me from my reminiscences with a question.

"Do you suppose Butch still practices here?" she repeated.

As I went to answer her, I looked up toward the window—and directly into a pair of eyes. I took a step backward from the man who was simply *there*, on the other side of the glass. He was elderly, with long white hair and beard, standing as motionless before me as he had sat next to the candle—for surely it was the same man. He held me in his gaze. Somewhere a door banged shut.

Although it felt a long time that I stood there, transfixed by that ancient face, it was probably not more than ten seconds before the spell was broken by a passing kid bumping into me.

"Martin?"

I turned to Monika. Her face was worried. Together we turned back to a window that was nothing more than an empty black square.

The rest of our walk to Butch's apartment was dominated by an awkward silence that I broke only when I put my hand into my coat pocket and discovered that our notebooks were gone.

CHAPTER 3

♞ e3 ♙
MARTIN TEACHES A TROPE. COLD DECEMBER LOVE.

The stairs squeaked as we climbed to Butch's apartment.

"Why do you keep looking behind us?" Monika whispered. The theft of our notebooks had shaken her.

"Because we don't know where Shannon is. I mean, she didn't necessarily go straight back to her apartment after rooking us, did she?" I was a little shook up myself. Until now, I don't think it had occurred to either of us that whatever trouble had found Butch would find us too.

"You really think it was Shannon who bumped you? I thought you said it was a kid." The trepidation had left Monika's voice, exorcised by the cleansing spirit of catching me out on an inconsistency.

"Maybe it didn't happen while I was being bumped," I equivocated. "Who else would it be?"

"What about that guy in the restaurant? The noodle slurper? You were looking at him quite a bit while we ate. He was short."

"Red herring."

"Meaning what?"

"A red herring is a literary device. A trope. Mystery writers use it when they want to send their readers down the garden path. I mean, come on. What are the odds some random guy we came across in a restaurant would want anything to do with chess puzzles? Now, Shannon, on the other hand—she's been acting suspiciously this whole time. Who besides her even knows about the notebooks?"

Monika had been trailing directly behind me. Now she pushed past and turned to face me; a hand on my arm. "So run this by me, Martin, because I'm not seeing it. Shannon stole our notebooks, right? Maybe she stabbed Butch, too?"

"Could be."

"Because that makes *so* much sense? Shannon starts sleeping with Butch, waits for just the right moment to stab him, and makes off with his estate of Japanese manga! Maybe she purloins the bonsai tree in the mix? What kind of fish does your mystery writer call *that*? Meanwhile, Butch is on to her. Our protagonist sets up an elaborate scavenger hunt, leading the investigators to a spot where he hid some of his more expensive John Coltrane albums and a roll of Certs—"

"Okay, I don't know, all right? I have no idea what is going on. Is that what you wanted to hear?"

Monika smiled and leaned in, and as she placed her cheek next to mine, the height from the extra step pushed the roundness of her bosom into my chest. "That, my dear," she breathed into my ear, "is *exactly* what I wanted to hear." Her warm lips brushed my neck. "Because I love you best when you have no idea what the fuck is coming next." She straightened up. "Now," she said, "what is it again that we are attempting to retrieve during this latest foray into our friend's lair?"

My thoughts seemed to have gone missing, so I paused a moment to find them before answering. "We're looking for an anthology of literature that I once gave Butch as a present. Also, for his copy of *The King in Yellow*, which I have reason to suspect will be filed among similar books."

"And if Shannon is there?" She nodded up the stairs.

I looked into Monika's emerald-greens. "Then, my dear, I'm going to ask for my half of Butch's manga. And visiting rights for the bonsai tree."

My girlfriend grinned, grabbed my hand, and led me the rest of the way up to Butch's apartment like we were two college kids escaping a frat party.

Shannon wasn't there, but the books were. The anthology we found easily. Monika kept lookout at the door while I went into the bedroom, where I noticed an obscure shelf I had previously overlooked near the dresser. The shelf held a stack of what I call coffee-table books. With no small pleasure I noted that the literature anthology was clearly the most beloved of them all. The jacket was scuffed, and the book opened easily to a few favorite selections. Flipping to the table of contents, I saw that five authors' names, including Lewis Carroll and H.P. Lovecraft, had been highlighted. When I read the names of the other three authors, my desire to hunt down the missing notebooks grew stronger than ever.

I brought the anthology to Monika to show her the highlighted entries.

"Well," she said, "you must be feeling good about yourself. Your theory was right. Now if Butch can just survive long enough to let us know what it's all about…"

I hunted for Butch's second copy of *The King in Yellow* and found it among the relatively modest fiction stacks in the living room. It was lumped not with horror volumes but amidst a collection of Gothic romances. This categorization scheme became even more interesting when I found the following inscription on the title page:

> Between the covers,
> we turn each page together—
> cold December love.
> —B

"Oh!" cooed Monika, who had strayed in from her post at the door, "he really *is* in love! Isn't it sweet, Martin? Can't you picture them? Butch and Shannon, lying in bed under the covers, 'reading' together? Cold December love!" She planted a kiss on my cheek.

I suppose I could have tried picturing that, but honestly, I didn't want to.

Nothing was coming together. Why had Butch torn a cover off a book? Had he then bought a second copy of that book? More vexing, a thorough scan of this second copy revealed nothing: no notes, no highlights, no marginalia. No information. I had no idea why Butch was telling me to read this book. It was enough to drive a person mad.

A thumping noise announced someone coming up the steps.

With an expression of alarm on her face, Monika said, "She's coming!"

♞ f3 ♞
THE WOMAN IN THE WINDOW

I grabbed Monika's hand and pulled her through the bedroom to the window over the fire escape.

Monika whispered, "Is this really necessary?"

"Shh!" I put a finger to my lips.

She tried again. "Can't we just talk—"

"Shh!" This time I put a finger to *her* lips. That worked.

Shannon had, possibly, stabbed Butch. She had, quite definitely, taken a swing at my head with furniture. We were leaving.

I opened the window, motioned to Monika to get our coats and turn off the lights.

We made it out onto the fire stairs in time, and I shut the window behind us.

I shall remember the moments spent outside of Butch's bedroom window thusly, as if from a dream:

I am standing to the side of the window, my back against cold brick. Harlem lights cast a harsh glow, throwing my shadow large onto the building. A wind rises, transporting on its frigid swell the street smells of frying chicken, collard greens, garbage. A shout from the street. I feel suddenly exposed, four stories into the night.

I look down through the black metal grating between my feet. Monika is descending the stairs, quiet as the breeze. She stops to look up at me, her face wondering. Why do I not follow? *It is because of the window*, I think. I need to look back. Know what is happening. Around the edge of the curtain, I can just see into the bedroom.

The light turns on and Shannon is there. She scowls. An angry bruise darkens her right eye. She reaches into her coat and pulls out two notebooks. She tosses them onto the bed. The coat comes off. Then she begins pushing the square, black buttons of her blouse through their holes, one by one, slipping the slick, antique white material from her skin. She is not wearing a bra; her arms make an X across her breasts, hands climbing shoulders, rubbing for warmth. She looks at the window, and the scowl on her face turns to astonishment. She feels the tell-tale pool of winter that hangs in the air, snuck in while the window was open, left behind by our anxious escape.

Her eyes find the gap between curtain and frame. I flinch back. Too late? *She knows we are here*, I think. She reaches for the blouse she has carefully laid on the bed. Starts to put it back on. Then she pauses. She is considering a different course. On the stairs below me, Monika is mouthing words. I shake my head, refusing communication, torn: Flee? Or get those notebooks? The notebooks are so close.

I look once more into the bedroom. Shannon stands in the center of the floor. In front of her bare feet lies the curved, silver blade of a Japanese katana—a steel serpent, waiting, holding back.

Chapter 3

Shannon's hands are at her waist now; she unzips her pants and strips them down her legs. I release a puff of steam from my mouth.

Monika whispers with the force of a shout: "What is going on up there?"

"Nothing!" I mouth back.

But for a pair of white cotton panties, Shannon is fully nude. Moonlight glints off hardened silver as she grips the banded hilt of the katana.

Slice! Her blade cuts an arc as she engages the space around her in a dance. Kicks describe precise distances between herself and some hidden foe; legs stab in and out, punctuating the rhythm of attack. A roundhouse kick lifts her thigh, swinging her foot into the jaw of an unknown assailant; a wide stance balances her onto the back of an invisible mount—

"Well, well!" Monika whispers in my ear. She points at Shannon. The gesture is unnecessary.

I look at Monika. She is amused. "Yes," I say.

Shannon stands once more in the center of the room. Her enemy is vanquished. Bowing low, but with eyes fixed in front of her, she lays the katana back on the floor. Then she retrieves her blouse and pants from the bed and hangs them primly in the closet. She folds her coat over her arm and exits to the living room.

Monika turns to me, indicating the street below with a tilt of her head.

"Not quite," I say. Opening the window, I crawl inside, grab the notebooks, and climb back out to the fire escape. "Okay. Let's go."

"Aren't you going to close the window?"

"No," I say, and we descend together toward the street.

Like most fire escapes, the stairs on the outside of Butch's building come down to the level of the storefront awnings. There, stairs from several apartments meet on a wide landing, where a heavy, iron ladder rests against the railing. This is connected by a pair of hooks to a cable that is counterweighted in order to allow the controlled descent of the ladder to the street.

Together, Monika and I hoisted the ladder over the side and let go. But the hooks were rusted through, and the ladder instantly snapped off the cable. With a metallic *boing*, the ladder hit the sidewalk, made a lucky bounce away from the plate glass storefront of Zhang's Laundry, and careened into the street, where it narrowly missed a passing car.

We looked at each other. "I guess we're dropping off," I said.

Monika looked over the railing. The distance to the sidewalk was about twelve feet. She grinned. "Age before chess rating!"

I climbed over the railing, crouched down, gripped the landing, and lowered myself nearly my full height. The drop wasn't so bad. I landed on the balls of my feet and hurt my left knee a bit. Monika tried the same maneuver, but her hand slipped as she was trying to lower herself. I caught her, mostly. Which is to say that my right shoulder got between her and the ground. She came out fine.

"Ooo, Martin," she said, seeing me rub my shoulder, "I'm sorry. Does it hurt much?"

"About the same as the other one," I said, recalling Shannon's chair attack.

"Well, they match, then. I'll pull the ladder off the street. Hail us a cab?"

We pulled away a few minutes later. I peered back through the rear window of the cab. Four flights up, looking like a scene from the cover of a Margaret Erskine paperback (except everything was backward; this time it was the guy running from the house, and the woman staying behind), Shannon stood outside on the fire escape under moon-raked clouds, her black profile silent against a lone, amber-lit window. The wind ripped through her hair, and although it was hard to tell, I believe she was still naked from the waist up.

♘ g3 ♞
SECOND IMPRESSIONS. MONIKA TAKES A STUDENT. THE ROOKIE.

Monika and I arrived at our apartment to find Tomas playing chess with a woman. The game was blitz—five minutes on the clock per side. Tomas was moving his pieces according to the *je ne sais quoi* that so singularly defines him, bulleting out a seemingly random move immediately upon his turn only to retract it, consider the position for a heartbeat, and then half the time make some completely different move.

By contrast, his opponent was a picture of circumspection, each move consuming at least five seconds, the chosen piece sliding on its cloth base to its destined square. The combatants' strategies mirrored their mechanics: Tomas's pieces went anywhere that promised excitement; his opponent's army held formation—the battle would come to them. No reason to get excited, nothing to see here, move along, move along.

Tomas spoke to us while on move, introductions coming in fragments.

"Hey, you two—" His bishop went to c4… no, it returned to e2, then forward again, striking a pawn off b5 with a wooden click. His opponent removed the intruder noiselessly with a pawn from a6.

"—I want you to meet—" He grabbed his queen's rook, tapped it on the board a few times, then slammed it into its counterpart on a8. His rook disappeared when his opponent's queen slid onto that square.

"—Anne—"

With crushing authority, he slammed a knight down onto c7, forking the enemy king and queen.

"—Schnapp."

The name was familiar. Keeping her eyes fixed on the board, the woman lifted her head slightly to address us. "Officer Schnapp or Detective Schnapp is preferred." Her correction delivered, she returned her full attention to the board. Nothing to see here. Move along.

Of course! The low pitch, the matter-of-fact tone, the thick Brooklyn accent—I had spoken with her on the phone that morning. But this person looked nothing like I had pictured. I had imagined a middle-aged woman whose shrewd, almost sardonic speech had developed over years of experience on the force. I saw now that what I had taken for a certain cynicism had to be something else.

I watched her closely as she played. She was young—younger even than Monika's twenty-six. She was plain in appearance, undecorated, neither beautiful nor unsightly. Innocence, not naiveté—determination, not cynicism—characterized her demeanor; this *ingénue* with the searching face looked perpetually moments away from some discovery that would put it all together and crack the case.

Her blonde hair was straight, hanging loosely to gently sloped shoulders. Her button-up shirt, checkered red and white like an Italian tablecloth, was open, her sleeves rolled into cuffs above the elbows. Under this she wore a beige thermal undershirt. The intentional rips in her jeans offered a down-market fashion. She sat on the edge of her chair, and when she leaned forward, cupping her forehead in her hands for concentration, she would cross her feet behind her. She had removed her tennis shoes, and her toes disappeared into the thick, white nap of the carpet.

Given the street clothes, Officer Schnapp was off duty. But what was she *doing* here? I looked to Monika for ideas, but she had left, probably to the bedroom.

After each game that Tomas won, which was all of them, he would offer Schnapp advice:

"Watch for the bishops on the fianchetto squares. They're snipers!"

"After I play Bxb2, you need to give back some material. I think maybe the pawn to d5. Try that."

"When I come at you on the flank, you should play into the center."

Schnapp scribbled notes with a mechanical pencil onto a small flip pad.

Tomas also provided in-game comments, usually accompanied with hand gestures. These were help of a lesser nature:

"Ho! You sure about dat?"

"Hup! I don't think your queen likes *dat* square!"

"Ooo, how am I going to get myself out of *dis* mess?"

I knew what Tomas was trying to do: sound like a hustler from Washington Square. But it was wrong, like a high school teacher trying to talk to their students about the latest boy bands. Or a foreigner trying to speak slang. Which, given that Tomas was Czech, went a fair way toward summing up the situation.

After one particularly brutal rout—the games seemed to be getting shorter and shorter, and although I kept waiting for Schnapp to exhibit some sign of impatience, she never did—Tomas looked up at me.

"How about it, M-doc?" he said. "Maybe you have some advice for the good constable?" (Here, in reaction to the informal address, came the only trace of irritation, however faint, that I would see on Schnapp's face that night.)

Myself, I was nonplussed. "I'm not the best chess player…" I looked to the closed bedroom door.

Tomas read my mind. "Yeah, maybe we should get Monika over here." He turned in his chair, craning his ropy neck. "M-clip! We could use some chess-master advice out here!"

Monika came out of the bedroom in a bathrobe-and-slipper set the same fire-orange as her hair. After watching a few games, she crouched down beside Schnapp and spoke sisterly to her.

"Your disposition is perfect. You remain cool in the face of aggression. But you move much too slowly." Monika looked up at her father. "I assume we're getting prepped for Washington Square?"

"That is the general idea," said Tomas.

Monika looked again at Officer Schnapp and raised an eyebrow. "A little undercover work?"

Schnapp hesitated, then said, echoing Tomas, "That is the general idea." She paused again and added, "I've been at it a while, but I lose most of my games."

Monika put a hand on Schnapp's shoulder: *don't worry, big sister will help.*

"The clock is a piece," said Monika. "You can be up a rook but down a clock, understand? In the end, it's the clock that'll kill you." Schnapp reached for her flip pad and mechanical pencil, but Monika placed her hand on Schapp's, arresting its progress.

"If you want to go up against the park," Monika said, "you need to put down the pencil and stop looking for the truth. The right move is the one that gets the job done and that comes off your hand as fast as possible."

Tomas stood up and indicated the vacated chair. "M-clip, how about you have a seat and give Officer Schnapp some games? I'm done for the night."

Monika sat. In an instant her side of the board was fully set up and she was adjusting the clock. She said to Schnapp, "I'm giving myself one minute. You still have five. Ready?"

And so it began. After two games, both of which Monika won with mere seconds remaining on her clock, Tomas slapped me on the shoulder. (I winced in pain, not that he noticed.) "Listen, M-doc, if you're hungry I've got some roast mutton in the broiler and gravy set to low on the stove. Help yourself. I'm going home."

I made a mental note to turn off the oven and stove. "Good night, Tomas."

He went to the door, then turned around and winked. "Oh, and by the way, feel free to make yourself at home. Good night!"

Chapter 3

It seemed like an odd comment until I realized I was still wearing my coat. I had been so surprised to discover Tomas playing chess with a stranger that I had never taken it off.

From one of the pockets, I pulled out the notebooks we had gone through such trouble to reclaim and set them on the kitchen table. The coat itself I folded over the back of a chair. Then I shut off the appliances, scooped the mutton and gravy into a Tupperware container, and made some space in the fridge. Finally, I retrieved my meerschaum pipe from its display cabinet in the living room and pulled up a chair to where Monika and Officer Schnapp were playing chess.

I indicated my pipe to our guest. "May I?"

She assented—the briefest of nods—and I smoked my pipe while I watched the chess.

After each game, Monika would replay all the moves, giving instruction. Sometimes these tips were quite specific:

"In the Sicilian, Black wants to break with d5. Try to prevent that."

In her dry Brooklyn drawl, Schnapp would re-state these lessons with the same probing tone and robotic diction that I remembered from our phone interview. "When I'm playing against the Sicilian Defense, I need to watch for any opportunity Black has to play his pawn to d5 and prevent that move."

At other times, Monika's admonitions were more general:

"When you're in a rook and pawn endgame, play very actively with your rook, and you will be rewarded."

Schnapp recited: "When all that remains is the rook, the rook is to be used in a very active manner."

Most of the time, however, Monika's message boiled down to *move faster*. I watched the chess until the tobacco in my pipe was consumed, and I retired to bed.

As I lay in bed, listening to the verbal exchanges going on outside between Monika and her new student, I realized that what I had taken for experience in Anne Schnapp was in fact almost the opposite. Here was the receptiveness of a child; the imperturbability of a robot; and an intense, blue wonder that was taking it all in, storing everything away.

A chess rookie she might be. But in my heart, I believed that if the NYPD wanted to plant someone among the hustlers who would quickly learn the ropes of park-style chess, they couldn't have picked a better officer. She was intelligent, a diligent learner, a sponge. Best of all, she was understated. Inconspicuous. Nobody would suspect a thing.

As I closed my eyes, my mind drifted into Anne Schnapp's future, and I foresaw a slightly older woman saying, "Lieutenant Schnapp or Detective Schnapp would be preferred."

So. The NYPD was going after the White Knight drug trade in Washington Square Park. What did they know? What *was* there to know? And how much of it was my friend caught up in?

♝ h3 ♞
MEDITATIONS ON A SLICE OF FRENCH TOAST.
TWO IS COMPANY, THREE ACROSS.

Right away I knew I had slept late. It was a good feeling. My only Tuesday class was Seminar in Literary Analysis, and it wouldn't start until 3:25. I'd need to stop by the Ninth first to gather a few lecture notes, but that could wait. It could all wait. My bedside clock said 9:18. It said I had tons of time. It reminded me that Tuesdays were easy.

I rolled over toward Monika's side of the bed, hoping to find her just waking. That happened a lot—her waking up just when I did. So often, in fact, that I think sometimes she faked it just to make me happy. Her hair would fan out against the white linen of the pillows and her irises would sparkle like emeralds from behind delicate, half-opened eyelids.

But she was already up. So I took a shower, got dressed, and poked my head into the living room. Tomas wasn't there. Neither was the NYPD. The apartment was, to borrow from the Irish, *sinn féin*. Ourselves alone. Everything from last night had been put away; the dryer rumbled softly in the utility closet. Outside, low clouds roiled above a grey and sleepy midtown. The Empire State Building was a distant pillar of lead, holding up the sky. Like I said, Tuesdays were easy.

I crossed the living room. Monika, in the kitchen, appeared and disappeared from view as she made breakfast. She was humming quietly to herself, occasionally singing out phrases from "Girl, You'll Be a Woman Soon." It had been a favorite tune of hers ever since last year's department

Christmas party. She and I, Postdoc, Sandeep Patel, and Rachel Lebowski had been standing around a bowl of eggnog listening to Burl Ives, when somehow Postdoc discovered that Monika had never seen *Pulp Fiction*. He made us all come to his basement apartment in Queens, right then, and watch it with him. By the time we got to the scene where Uma Thurman invites John Travolta back to her house and snorts herself half to death on what she thought was coke, but actually was heroin, Monika was convinced that Mia Wallace was the greatest thing to happen to the American movie screen since Jessica Rabbit informed Eddie Valiant that she wasn't bad, she was just drawn that way.

Monika won't be winning any *American Idol* contests, and her chances on *Iron Chef* are no better. But anything that comes off a griddle is well within her capabilities, and when it absolutely comes down to her making a meal, she can produce a reasonably tasty burger or, for a real treat, a Czech fried cheese. But her specialty is French toast.

"Smells good," I said, taking a seat.

Monika turned around. "What's the difference between sexy and kinky?"

"Well," I started to explain, "kinky possesses a certain connotation that—"

"No, no! It's a joke. What's the difference between sexy and kinky? You have to guess before I give you breakfast." She stood there, a flirty waitress, a plate in each hand and a grin sneaking across her face. A white puff of confectioner's sugar made a sweet handprint on her ass against the navy blue of her slacks, and there was another splotch of dusty white that I wished had been made by me on her fuzzy strawberry sweater.

God, it all just gave me *so* many ideas. "Sexy is in the bedroom, kinky is in the kitchen?"

She raised an eyebrow. "Not bad! Sexy is French lingerie.Ized Kinky," she leaned over and gave me a quick kiss on the lips, "is French toast." She set down the plates, each piled with thick, golden, white-dusted squares.

"All right," I said, eyeing the toast, "what exactly do you have in mind?" *My* mind had reached past Monika's plate, heading for strawberry fields, and my hand wasn't far behind.

"Tut, tut!" She gave my hand a light slap. "First things first. Breakfast, then the paper. Then," she poured me a cup of coffee, "we'll see."

Me, pointing to the French toast on my plate: "Should I be saving some of this for later?"

"Only if it's too soggy." She poured herself a Guinness and dug into her food.

We did the Sunday *New York Times* while we ate. (It had been overlooked the last couple of days.) Monika worked the crossword puzzle; I read the Book Review. Beyond a rhythmic rolling thunder outside, answered by the clothes dryer inside, our companionable silence was broken only by Monika occasionally asking for help with a clue.

"What's *Howard's friend?*" she said. "Six letters."

"Does it have a question mark?"

"Yes."

"Those are tricky. Any letters?"

"Not yet."

I went to the pantry to grab an orange. Butch's duffel was inside, pushed toward the back. Beside it was an open, blood-red Salvatore Ferragamo shoebox, inside of which were the queen and rook notebooks, the journal, the oversized black king, and the bag of White Knight: all the clues we had collected so far.

"What's this doing in here?" I held up Butch's bag.

"Father put it there last night. To keep from prying eyes, you know? I added the shoebox, with the notebooks and stuff."

Prying eyes. "Officer Schnapp, you mean." I returned to the table with my orange. "Did you find out anything more from her last night? Is she really doing undercover work in Washington Square?"

"*M.*"

"Huh?"

"First letter. Three across. *Howard's friend.*"

"Nothing comes to mind." I tried to get back to Schnapp. "Is she really going undercover?"

Monika continued working the crossword while we spoke. "She's a nice girl, Martin. Twenty-three, single, and laser focused. Two years out of the academy. She's got youthful looks, I'm sure you noticed, so they put her undercover at a high school. Eleanor Roosevelt, she said. She busted drug deals there. Did such a good job that when they got wind of this White Knight thing, they put her right on it."

"So this really *is* about White Knight? It's real?"

Monika set down the paper. "Of course it is. Father already told you. You've seen the stuff yourself."

"Well, yes, of course, but—" I was about to say, *But I don't automatically adopt your father's interpretation of everything*. I decided against. "But what did you think of Schnapp's chess skills? Is she going to be able to pull this off?"

Monika winked and pulled off a half-decent Brooklyn accent. "That would be Officer Schnapp or Detective Schnapp to you, pal."

We chuckled a little, and Monika went back to her crossword. "*N*," she said after a deep think.

"Which letter?"

"The last one. *Howard's friend*—starts with *M*, six letters, ends with *N*." She looked up at me. "You don't have a friend named Howard, do you?"

I smiled, but I still had no ideas.

Eventually, Monika got back to Schnapp. "She's a fast learner. Not hard to see why the department adores her. She's perceptive, takes direction, doesn't waste a word. If she ever learns to trust her instincts, she'll be a dynamo." Monika looked up and stared at the pantry door, as if being able to see through it with X-ray eyes to Butch's bag. After a moment she said, "I suppose they'll groom her for sergeant someday." She turned to me. "What was she like on the phone yesterday?"

"Mechanical," I said, thinking of her pencil.

"You asked how her chess was? Well, there you go." And with that, Monika sank down into another think. After filling in a few answers that had no connection to the dreaded Three Across, she put a grey look on her face that drew in the murkiness from outdoors. "We got our notebooks back from Shannon. What do you make of that?"

"I can't shake the idea she wanted us to take them."

Monika nodded as if she had been thinking the same. "But why?"

"I'm certain she knew we were on that fire escape."

Monika laughed. "Do you mean before or after we dropped the ladder into the street, and she stood outside, tits to the wind, watching us speed off in a getaway cab?"

I suddenly felt warm. Probably blushed. "She saw me through a slit in the curtain. I'm sure of that. Then what does she do? She performs a nearly naked martial arts routine right in front of me, and the whole time I'm standing there thinking… well… I dunno what I'm thinking—"

"Uh huh."

"—but she finishes her sword dance and just leaves the notebooks on the bed. What *is* that? Come on. She meant for us to take them."

Monika raised an eyebrow. "So, she stole the notebooks from us in order to give them back? But first, for our viewing pleasure, a nice little striptease? And the katana, just to let us know that if you can keep your hands off her tits, you can keep your hands?"

I sighed. "It makes no sense. I know that."

"Right," Monika said. "So we're nowhere on that. *I*."

"Yes?"

"*I*. Three across. Fifth letter. You *sure* you don't know a Howard?"

"None who are likely to be in a crossword puzzle."

Monika harrumphed. "So what do we do now?"

"Get more letters."

"No, I mean about Butch. What's our next move?"

"We find the rest of the notebooks," I said. "We've got the queen and the rook. Somewhere out there are the pawn, bishop, and knight."

"*L!*" cried Monika. "Third letter."

I recited the letters so far. "M blank L blank I N." A light came on. "I got it! *Melvin*."

"Why would Melvin be Howard's friend?"

"It's a movie," I said. "*Melvin and Howard*. True story about a guy named Melvin who befriended the eccentric billionaire Howard Hughes unawares and ended up in Hughes's will. Inherited millions of dollars." Something tugged at me. "Hmm. Interesting."

"What's that?"

I looked at her sideways. "You remember the King's Corner Hotel?"

"Of course. We were in the pub. You noticed me and then spent the next five minutes pretending to read a menu."

"Exactly." I blushed a little. "Well, there was a fellow who worked there by name of Melvin. Some kind of assistant manager. And if I'm correct, he was also one of Butch's first students."

Monika considered this. "Do you suppose Melvin might still be at the King's Corner?"

"Unless he got fired in the last couple weeks, he definitely is. Here, look at this." I went to the red shoebox in the pantry and retrieved the queen notebook. Returning to the kitchen table, I opened it to Swindle 8. "See? Butch wrote about Melvin just this month, and... blimey!"

"What?"

"Melvin is going to have our next notebook! He's the king in the corner!" I went to the pantry once more and this time brought out the journal. Turning it to the correct page, I pointed to:

Little Jack Horner
The King's in his Corner,
Eating his curds and whey.
If you want to play with him
He'll charge you by the day.

"See? You get charged by the day to stay at a hotel!"

"The nice ones," said Monika. "Let's just say that sexy is a hotel that charges by the day," she winked, "and kinky is—"

I cut her off. "I have to go to NYU this afternoon to teach my class. I'm going to stop by afterward."

"Sounds like a plan," said Monika.

Another wave of thunder rolled over New York, capped off by a splintering crash. The lights dimmed, then came back.

Monika's phone bleeped. She picked it up from where it had been sitting on the counter. "Text message from Shannon," she said.

"You have Shannon's phone number?"

"We traded numbers yesterday when we were at the hospital.... Oh, no. Shannon says to come to Langone right now." Monika looked at me with widening eyes. "Something is happening with Butch!"

```
T . . . . H E .
. B . . I S H O
P . O . . . . .
. F . F O . . .
. . . . . . . .
. . U . . . . .
R T . . . H S T
R . E E . . T .
```

Chapter 4
THE BISHOP OF FOURTH STREET

♝ a4 ♞
GONE, BOY

Can you come *to Langone? Something's up.* That's what Shannon's first text had said. By the time our doorman had hailed us a cab, there was a second: *They won't let me see Butch!*

We were nearly across Central Park, close to the zoo—a flock of blackbirds chose this moment to take flight over the iron fencing—when a third text came: *They just wheeled a body out of the room!*

Finally: *Nobody will tell me anything!*

This last text arrived while we were stuck on Park Avenue near Grand Central Station, Monika telling the cabbie he should have taken the FDR; the cabbie thickly mumbling something about construction; me asking if, really, it wouldn't have been quicker to have just taken the subway; and that was when the cabbie—very animated now at this comment of mine, the back of his checkered and denying turban bouncing from side to side as he shook his head—softly succumbed to the diplomatic magic of Monika, bringing it all to an end. "It is what it is," she said. I'll swear it on a stack of Strunk & Whites, that's what she said. "It is what it is." As if it meant something.

Our cab pushed through the gridlock, and soon we were trotting into the hospital waiting room. We found Shannon near a water fountain, pacing back and forth, wearing those same worn, woolen pants from yesterday and a button-up blouse just like before, but in a drabber tint of beige. Her face was drawn, as if she hadn't slept. When she saw us, she dropped the silent but heated argument she had been having with herself and said, "Butch is gone."

My hand found the back of a chair, and I lowered myself into it. I sat on a magazine. It was a copy of *Boys' Life*. I set it on a side table, along with *Vanity Fair*, *Esquire*, and *The New Yorker*. Good publications, all. I arranged the magazines in a tight pile, but it wasn't right, so I fanned them out. That looked better. That would do.

I looked up from the magazines and across the room to watch Monika and Shannon in conversation with Helga. The elderly triage nurse was sitting behind the window that shielded her from those who sought her help, wire-rimmed cheaters dangling from a chain of amber beads to graze her ample and grandmotherly bosom. She was pointing through the sliding glass doors to the street beyond. My gaze followed her finger to an empty drive. If I went back to Butch's bed, would I find it already empty? Had my last glimpse of my friend been yesterday, as he lay smothered in tubes and surrounded by monitors?

A man in a business suit appeared. He pulled Monika and Shannon to the side. As he spoke, Monika crossed her arms and narrowed her eyes. Shannon waved her hands about as she replied. This was beginning to look... legal. Like the hospital was denying culpability in something. But what?

A nurse in green scrubs joined them, conferring quietly with the man in the suit before turning to Monika and Shannon. Had there been "complications?" Was it the hospital's fault Butch had died? Did this nurse know why my friend was dead?

I was out of my chair and storming toward them when Monika broke away and intercepted me.

"What's going on?" I said, looking past her to the man in the suit. "What are they saying?"

Monika's face displayed a mixture of concern and frank incredulity. "Butch wasn't released. He just... drove off with someone. The hospital has no idea who, or maybe they aren't at liberty to say. I don't know. It doesn't matter. They are very upset. Making matters worse—"

"Wait. What?" I said, grasping blindly behind me for the arm of a chair but not finding one. "Butch is… alive?"

Her eyes grew wide. "Martin, you poor thing! Did you think Butch was gone?"

"That's what Shannon said. Gone."

Monika rested a hand on my arm. "Not that kind of gone."

I spent a moment taking this in. Butch was alive. Okay. But… not here. Okay… but then… "What's making matters worse?" I asked.

The expression of concern returned to her face. "Shannon heard someone say Butch was out of the coma. But then he disappeared, and apparently he hadn't been released, and nobody knows what happened."

"Typical!" I barked. Sure, Butch had been stabbed. Sure, Butch had been in a coma. Naturally, then, Butch had decided his own medical expertise was superior to the doctor's. "How just like Butch," I said, "to decide on his own—"

"No, you don't understand. Shannon doesn't think Butch *decided* anything. He had indeed come out of his coma, already been de-tubed and stuff, waiting for a doctor, and then he was just… gone. A nurse on a smoking break saw a man being driven off in a van. She thinks it was Butch."

I stared at Monika, blinking rapidly. "You are trying to tell me that—"

"Shannon thinks Butch has been kidnapped."

♟ b4 ♟
FATE OF THE CHICKEN-BUTCHER. A NEW HOPE.

"What do you think of this one?"

A late autumn sky breaks wide above a golden meadow. Beyond a distant tree line, the setting sun scratches the thin, low clouds, burning them with red streaks. Birds fly into view. Taking the fluid shape of a V, they flee the coming winter's wrath. A single bird, a black check against the silken white, drops out of formation. The bird circles lazily toward the ground to land on the exact place where, once, when the ground was less foul and the air more cruel, they'd buried the chicken-butcher.

I interrupted. "The *chicken-butcher?*"

"I know, I know," chuckled Postdoc. "Don't interrupt." He cleared his throat, leaned back in his chair to prop his feet up on his desk, and resumed.

In life, the chicken-butcher had often envisioned hell. Hell was him crawling on black, gooey asphalt, never finding the sacred herbs that had fallen ages ago among the deep cracks that spewed yellow steam, singeing his blood-caked fingers. Hell was him wringing the neck of a chicken as a torrent of puke-colored shit blows out of its asshole, burying the table on which he butchers his meat, burying him, sliding down his throat as he tries to scream. Hell was him cursing the goddamn kids who, in life, would stand in his shop, never buying fuck and playing their goddamn American "music" louder and louder and louder until his ears bled. The song never changed.

Hell would be all of this.

Then one day, five years before the killing fields, two hours after morning ablutions, and right before soup, the chicken-butcher died. And the people of his Kampuchean village carted his vulgar body to this remote meadow. They buried him and they went home, and not one of the chicken-butcher's fears of hell came to pass.

And now, if he listens, he can just make out the quiet scratching of a bird as it busily pecks above, pulling a worm from the dank and fetid earth, and then… utter silence, as the bird, sensing the presence of the damned, flees into a far and unknowable sky.

"Jesus," I said. "Remind me to be cremated."

"Yah, right?" My officemate closed the blue composition book he had been reading from and tossed it on his desk next to a pile of twenty or thirty others. "So what did you think?"

"I rather liked it!" I said.

"That's your professional analysis?"

I had been standing in the doorway while Postdoc read, having just returned from my afternoon lecture. Buying time to reflect, I took off my coat, hung it on the coat rack (globs of melting snow hit the floor), sat at my desk, and turned my chair toward Postdoc. I pointed to the pile of blue composition books on his desk. "What are those, anyway?"

"That there would be my dramatic monologue exercise," he answered, enunciating the last three words deliberately. "For my Cinema as Literature class. Three hundred words or less, stream of consciousness, third-person account. So, what did you think?"

I steepled my fingers together, reclined in my chair, and studied the drop ceiling. Nine stories above us, snow fell on the city. "Rich imagery. Clever transition from the above to the below."

"And back again," agreed Postdoc.

"Hmm. I think I would like to have known what it smells like in the chicken-butcher's coffin."

"If there even *was* a coffin," said Postdoc, "did you think of *that*? Maybe, too, the smell of his shop? All that glorious puke-colored shit."

I scratched my head. "I don't know. The shit implies the smell. But how did the chicken-butcher know what happened to the bird? It feels a little third-person omniscient to me."

"You mean, like, how did he know that it flew into the sky? That didn't bother me. Birds fly, right?"

"I suppose." I was about to ask whether birds migrated south for winter in Cambodia when I recalled the flock of blackbirds taking flight over the Central Park Zoo. Then I started wondering what even *defined* what the man could or couldn't have perceived after he had died.

My face must have turned sour.

"Hey, whoa whoa whoa, Marty. What's up?" Postdoc rolled his chair across the three feet of linoleum that separated his side of the room from mine. "You're all of a sudden looking marginally discomfited over here." He looked around as if he had never been to this side of the room before.

I said, "Remember Butch?"

"Could you be speaking of the guy who showed up a couple days ago half dead?"

I ignored the sarcasm. "Well, there's been a development."

Postdoc narrowed his eyes and said, "Uh-oh." If Postdoc came home and found his girl in bed with the plumber, the department chair, and his twin sister, he would narrow his eyes and say "Uh-oh."

"Do you mean… ?"

Chapter 4

"No," I said, "he's not dead. Listen, do you have about half an hour?"

"Yup."

It was closer to an hour before I had finished my tale, bringing Postdoc up to speed on everything. Well, almost everything. I omitted one naked martial arts routine from my account. It was entirely possible that, in the course of events, certain people might meet certain people. I didn't want Postdoc narrowing his eyes at Shannon and saying "Uh-oh." One nearly dead friend at a time, that was my new motto. Type it on a slip of paper and slide it into a fortune cookie.

"*Kidnapped?*" said Postdoc, genuinely stunned, when I got to that part of the story. Apparently, I had found something that transcended *uh-oh*. "And this White Knight stuff? Wow! It sounds like Adderall on steroids!" He furrowed his brows a little, imagining. "Let's hope *that* doesn't start making the dormitory rounds. Just think of what would happen to their essays." He cast a foreboding eye toward the pile of blue books on his desk. Then he leaned forward conspiratorially and said, "What's your next move?"

"Monika and Shannon went to Butch's apartment to see if he had simply gone home. I already got a text from Monika saying no dice. The last I heard, the ladies were on their way to my apartment. Monika thinks Shannon should be fully acquainted with everything we've got, so she's going to give her a shot at Butch's bag, see if she can spot anything we missed."

"And yourself?"

"I think we've got a strong lead to the next notebook. I'm heading over to the King's Corner Hotel. It's on Waverly." I gave my officemate a sidelong glance. "Got another hour? I'd love the company."

Postdoc shot from his seat and grabbed his coat from where it was draped over the chessboard atop our filing cabinet. A few pieces went clattering to the floor, where snow had melted into small, dirty ovals.

"Dramatic monologue!" he exclaimed. "Three hundred words or less, third-person account, *total rip-off* of a popular franchise. I'll start!"

I watched, mesmerized, as Postdoc seemed to gaze at some large, invisible object that had suddenly materialized in space in front of and above him, causing him to cock his head back at an angle. In a deep, melodramatic voice that just avoided outright corniness, he began.

"It is a period of unrest. Exotic drug manufacturers, distributing from a secret base, have infiltrated the pastoral chess scene in Washington Square Park.—"

I saw what this was. Postdoc was in a movie theater in his head. "*Star Wars* crawler text!" I said.

"Yes, Marty. Now shut it; I'm on a roll." He resumed:

"During a violent game, a rebel manages to steal a sample of the cartel's wares, WHITE KNIGHT," (Postdoc's eyes bulged, capitalizing the words) "a designer drug with enough cognitive-enhancing power to turn a rotting carp into a temporary chess grandmaster.

"Pursued by the cartel's sinister agents, Dr. Martin Malloy and his hottie Czech girlfriend race about lower Manhattan, custodians of a handful of quixotic notebooks that can save chess and restore tranquility to New York..."

His head resumed its normal angle, and he let out a breath. Very pleased with himself, was one Patrick "Postdoc" MacGroddy. "What do you think?" he asked.

I leaned back in my chair and steepled my fingers in mock thought. "I dunno. I would like to have been told what the park smells like."

Postdoc punched me on the shoulder. "Screw you, Marty."

"Hey!" I said, "I told you about the shoulder. Watch it."

"Sorry."

♘ c4 ♞

MAKEOVER. THE SILVER BALLS OF MELVIN T. DICKLEBERRY. MEAL VOUCHER.

Snow fell in clods as Postdoc and I walked to the King's Corner Hotel. We maneuvered around the Square, avoiding walkways hardpacked with the accumulation of several storms. A cut across the courtyard, a left on 3rd Street, a right on Waverly—our route was short enough that I barely had time to answer Postdoc's questions regarding Melvin before we were standing at the twin orbs that elegantly light the hotel's front entrance.

I described Melvin's physical characteristics—his thick glasses, his doughy skin that would appear stuffed into a liveried shirt, the thick hair in

Chapter 4

short, brown curls. I also mentioned his habit of continually reading from a stack of worn paperbacks that would sit at his side, while he maintained a work ethic barely sufficient to keep atop whatever light responsibilities defined the role of assistant guest services manager.

What I skipped was a certain wager Melvin had made with Butch two years ago, around the time I first met Monika. Their bet had staked a month's worth of free chess lessons in the Square against a peek at the hotel's guest manifest. I omitted this detail because one could never know what talking point Postdoc might suddenly decide was just the thing to break the ice in an awkward situation. Say, for example, if we were among people, and nobody had spoken for more than five seconds.

As we opened the hotel's frosted glass door, I anticipated the aroma of the Irish stew the establishment serves in its cozy taproom, Molly's Pub. Some say that, of all the senses, smell possesses the greatest power to evoke the past. The converse of this axiom is equally valid. For although I saw all that I had expected when we walked in—the art deco motif, the porcelain-tiled maze-work flooring, the tin ceiling, the oval portraits of starlets and fabled writers—it was the absence of the aromas of roasting beef and tangy sauces that first signaled to me something was wrong.

"Hoo-*wee*! Colder'n a witch's tit out there, wouldn't you say, sweetheart?" That was how Postdoc said hi to the young lady at the front desk.

Embarrassed, I glanced at the woman, expecting a look that was going to hurl my office mate right back out the door and bury him in the snow. Instead, she giggled coquettishly, the dimples on her cheeks lending her face a look of demure puckishness. "I suppose so!" she replied.

I approached the desk. "Hello. I'm looking for someone who might work here. A man named Melvin?" As I spoke, I read the woman's nameplate: CHELSEA—ASSISTANT GUEST SERVICES MANAGER.

Chelsea's blue eyes got big. "Oh! You must mean Mr. Dickleberry! He's not in his office now. I'll text him for you!"

Dickleberry? I thought. *Somebody named their kid Melvin Dickleberry?* I shot an amused look at Postdoc, who was occupied trying to grab Chelsea's attention. While I waited, I glanced down the corridor toward the pub. It was no longer named Molly's. Instead, a set of block letters above the entrance simply said PUB.

Presently, a dapper fellow arrived. His white tuxedo shirt was so crisp you could snap a piece off and have it with cheese, and his shiny black pants were held in place by a pair of leather suspenders. He wore a nice bowtie. His sandy-blonde hair and his five-o'clock shadow combined into one of those scruffy looks that can only be made right with time, gel, and celebrity.

"Melvin T. Dickleberry," he said, "Guest Services Manager." The white of his grin as he somehow managed to audibly capitalize each word of his title contrasted smartly with his unseasonably bronzed face. "How may I help you?"

"I'm sorry," I began, "I think you're not—"

"Hey…" The lesser twin of Brad Pitt wagged a finger at me. "I remember you." Maybe he winked.

"Really? I don't think—"

"Sure," he said. "You're Butch's friend. I don't forget people who land me in trouble." He glanced over to the front desk, where Chelsea and Postdoc were engaged in conversation. "You might recall a certain incident with a certain guest register?"

If this man was the Melvin I knew—and given what he said, he clearly was—then somewhere, a personal trainer, a dietician, and a makeover artist were being fast-tracked to sainthood.

"Now, look. I don't want any trouble," I said. "Whatever happened a couple years ago, your career seems to be going fine now."

As if reminded suddenly of his station, Melvin held up a calming hand and ditched the corny grin. "As I see it, yes. Now, how may I help you?"

Taken aback at the abrupt change of mien, I regained myself and asked what I had come here to ask. "When was the last time you saw Butch?"

He paused, calculating. Then: "Come with me to my office." He walked behind the front desk. (Chelsea and Postdoc were now giggling.) A crack appeared in the wooden paneling of the wall, then widened into a doorway. "Cee Cee." He snapped his fingers and pointed to Chelsea. "Back to work." Halfway through the door, he looked back over his shoulder. "Oh, and Cee Cee? Tell George to bring two chairs to my office."

"Yes, Mr. Dickleberry. Oh! Mr. Dickleberry?"

"Yes?"

"Do you think I could work an extra shift tomorrow night? You might be needing me. You know, the Atlantic Club meeting? In the ballroom?"

Chapter 4

"Don't count on it."

I followed Melvin through the hidden door.

Consider a room! Windowless, it could be anywhere. Nearly featureless, with off-white walls and Berber carpeting, it is disorienting in its very vacancy. A diffuse, natural-looking light comes from twin translucent panels in the drop ceiling, giving the illusion of skylights. Two empty, unpainted bookcases and a desk, its side pushed flush against one wall, are the only furniture. Extending from the far wall, a taut, black cord disappears behind the desk, where it presumably enters one of the drawers. The cord cuts the room neatly in half, causing one to wonder why the desk isn't simply pushed up against the far wall, so that in order to get behind it, it is not necessary to step awkwardly over the cord, lifting one leg at a time, placing it on the floor while straddling the cord, then up and over with the other leg.

Which is precisely what I watched Melvin do as he entered the behind-the-desk sanctum of his office. The desktop was empty save for a Magic 8-Ball and a Newton's cradle: five silver balls, all in a row, each suspended between two threads, precisely arranged to just touch each other.

A ringing came from inside the drawer. Melvin opened it, pulled out a phone, and set it on the desk. "Yes, Cee Cee. Have him bring them in." He hung up the phone and returned it to its drawer.

The office door opened. Outside, I could hear Chelsea giggling. A man in blue overalls entered with a folding chair under each arm. His complexion was of mashed potatoes; wisps of pale hair went in all directions.

"Just set the one up over there, George," said Melvin, pointing to the floor on my side of the desk. "I'll take the other."

The man unfolded one chair and set it on the floor, then handed the other to Melvin.

"Nice job, George. A real bang-up job."

"I do my best, Mr. Dickleberry."

"It is decidedly so."

George left.

Melvin indicated the chair, and I sat. He unfolded his own chair, set it down at his desk, and as much as one can in a chair of that sort, he reclined, tucking his hands behind his head. "You know, I never caught your name."

"Martin."

"Nice to meet you properly, Martin. Without a doubt."

I looked around. The whole thing felt wrong. Melvin was always reading. Now he sat vacantly in a vacant office with an executive plaything and a kid's toy on his desk and a phone stashed in a drawer. Where were his books?

"What happened to you?" I said.

As if he got this question all the time, Melvin appeared pleased and began answering in bullet points that sounded rehearsed. "One, I trimmed down. Low carbohydrates, a little exercise in the morning. Walk around the park, maybe take in a movie afterward. Two, I dyed my hair—"

I waved my hand at the emptiness of the room. "No, no. I mean *this*."

"Oh, the *job!*" He shrugged. "Well, Mrs. Abernathy wanted to take the hotel in a fresh direction. Minimalism, she said. All the rage, you know. Kumar was having none of it, so he left. That bumped Angie up to general and left guest services to me." He slid the Newton's cradle toward himself, pulled the right-most silver ball back a few inches, and let it go.

Click, clack, click, clack, click.

"And the stuff?"

Melvin looked around as if just now noticing the desolation of his surroundings. "Angie took it all upstairs to her new office."

"She took your *books*?"

"Hey, at least she left me her Magic 8-Ball. Terrific management tool. You might think about getting one yourself. Say, what do you do, Martin?"

"I grade a lot of papers," I said, adding "I suppose it could come in handy" under my breath. "Now, look, Melvin," I said, "when was the last time you saw Butch?"

"Butch? I see him all the time. He comes here to use the bathroom when he's working the park." Melvin grabbed the 8-ball and shook it, then peered at the answer. "Concentrate and ask again," he said. "What is it you really wish to know?"

Click, clack, click, clack, click went the Newton's cradle.

"Did Butch ever give you a notebook?"

"Describe it."

"Chess puzzles. Probably a haiku dedicated to a chess piece—"

"Yes," said Melvin, "I know the item."

Chapter 4

"You have it?"

Click, clack, click, clack, click.

"Consider the balls," said Melvin, rather unexpectedly. ("Yeah, Marty," I could hear Postdoc say in my head, "give your friend's balls some consideration, will ya?")

Melvin indicated the Newton's cradle on his desk. "What we have here, Martin, is a study in the conservation of energy. Something is given some initial momentum, a push. The object then lends that momentum to another. The pulse of energy continues through many points until it comes to a terminus, and suddenly, there is motion where none previously existed. The motion is returned, the pulse reverses itself, and where does it end? It's like contemplating the last digit of *pi*—"

("There isn't any," offered the Postdoc in my head.)

Click, clack, click, clack, click.

"—or wondering which ball will be the last to move when all the energy has been lost to noise and the system is left exhausted, cold, and inert. Jobs move on, governments are redressed, faiths re-interpreted. The pendulum of time swings..." ("Wow-*wee*, this guy's gonna make some fuckin' awesome upper-management material someday, Marty!" I imagined Postdoc saying. "He's talking about everything and saying nothing!")

"So you no longer have the notebook?" I said to Melvin. "It's moved on? Is that what you're saying?"

Melvin squirmed ever so slightly in his chair. "Yes."

"Can you at least tell me who you gave it to?"

Melvin picked up the Magic 8-Ball and gave it a shake. He held it up to his face and waited. Presently, he set it back down on his desk. "I cannot predict now," he said.

"Now look here," I said, "this has gone—"

Melvin held up a finger. "But I did finish Butch's puzzles. They were quite interesting." He paused for a moment, raising his index finger in an expression of thought. "Oh, yes, I remember now. I gave the notebook to someone I thought would enjoy it. A chess hustler, Bishop of 4th Street. If you play him, watch out. He really is a sly one."

I was done here.

Five minutes later, Postdoc and I sat in PUB together. Melvin had given us each a voucher for a free entrée.

Postdoc ordered Sandwich. I got Stew. Minimalism indeed.

"How is it?" Postdoc asked.

"Blech," I said. "Tofu."

♝ d4 ♝
OF MICE OR MEN. PEACHES 'N' PATCHOULI. GOOD FOR ONE FARE.

I walked out of the hotel's front door and down the steps. The weather was cold and grumbly, just like me. I let Postdoc go. Didn't need him for this part. I had the name of the guy I was after, and I knew where to find him. I headed to the chess circle.

Chess hustlers. They sit at their tables, playing or waiting to play. I rarely see them arrive, and I've never seen one leave. They're like the trees and the pigeons: fixtures, knowing neither heat nor cold. They play under the elms in New York, they play in the roundabouts in DC, they play on the beaches in Chicago. Somewhere in England, the land of Churchill's birth and mine, they play in the hills. If you come across one, don't expect to win, and don't expect to take money from him if you do. Some cat plays his sax on the street corner, and maybe you throw a buck in his case, maybe you don't. But you never take money out. Same goes for this lot. They're not in the chess business; they're in the cash business. Think of them as interactive street performers. It's best that way.

I reached the park. About half the players here I already knew: Cue Ball, Johnnycakes, Basic, Z, Rochambeau, the Argentinian. Their *noms de guerre*. Butch just went by Butch, and I liked that about him. No pretense. Unless, of course, Butch *wasn't* Butch. There was that possibility, and maybe it didn't matter.

Johnnycakes was closest, so I walked up to him. He used to be a full-time player "back in the day," by which he means the '70s. Then he got old and his brain gummed up and he had to get what he calls a "regular gig." For the last twenty years he's been driving limos for an airport hotel near JFK. My chess record against him is about even.

As soon as he saw me coming he perked up. "Hey, Martin," he wheezed, as he lit a fresh cigarette with the stub of the last one. "Your sweetheart not

Chapter 4

with you today?" Johnnycakes was one of Monika's first foils in her early years in America. Before she got good.

"No, sorry. Monika's got stuff going on today. Want some games?" As if I needed to ask.

"Let's do it." Within seconds, Johnnycakes had his f-pawn pushed forward two spaces, and my clock was ticking.

Like I said, I don't take money from these guys. But there still must be a point to winning, right? Here's the system I use with chess hustlers everywhere: I set a quarter on the side of the board, just beyond the first rank. When my opponent wins, I push the quarter up one rank. When I win, it goes the other direction. If I win past the edge, we forget that game and the quarter stays put. Eventually, I pay up: five bucks times whatever rank the quarter ended on. That's my system, and if you ever find yourself in the situation, feel free.

The quarter was on rank 3 when I started bringing the requisite trash talk around to the point.

"Any new players here these days?"

"You leaving me?" Johnnycakes wheezed. "Just when we gettin' started?"

"I'm not going anywhere till I get that quarter down a few ranks."

"You think you moving the quarter *that* way?" Air, forced through a broken-down calliope. "That's news."

By the time things finally started going where I was aiming, the quarter was on rank 5.

"You heard of Union Boss?" Johnnycakes said.

"Union Boss?"

"Yeah, he went by that up in Union Square." He kept playing while he talked. "You hear about the troubles?"

I did recall hearing something recently about Union Square. "Yeah. What was that all that about?"

"Drug bust. I don't go in for that funny stuff, Martin. Pall Malls is my thing. You smoke, Martin?"

"A pipe, maybe."

"Funny pipe?"

"Regular pipe."

"You a smart man, Martin, I don't care what the people say." He checkmated me.

I set up the pieces again. "You said something about Union Boss just now."

"That's what he went by." Pawn to d4. "*Boss*. Now he's down here at the Square, and all a sudden he's *Bishop*. Now I ask you," (*ask* came out *axe*, as is only proper in High Brooklynese) "can you make a doorstop outta that shit?"

"Bishop of 4th Street?" I asked.

"Ooh, you are a smart one. Whatchu askin' questions for, if you got all the answers already?"

"You know me, Johnnycakes. I'm just here to keep you on your feet."

"By my calc'lations, you're here to pay me thirty bucks."

I paid the man. Johnnycakes thumbed through the cash, adding it up. It disappeared into a pocket, and he pointed a gloved finger across the way. "You see that shiny black scalp over yonder?"

I looked. "Yeah."

"That's your man."

I rose and we shook hands. "Have a good one, Johnnycakes."

He smiled. "It's all chicken but the gravy!" As I walked off, I heard his high-pitched voice say to whoever was next, "Game of chess?"

Under the heatless gaze of a quickly dropping February sun, I imagined the Bishop observing me as I approached. Thick sunglasses, black as onyx; his black bomber jacket was of real leather, old enough to have been worn during WWII, with white, dirtied piping, deep scuffs on the lapels, and a grimy shearling collar. A long, braided beard began at his sideburns and disappeared below the level of the table. The beard glistened as if oiled, as did his scalp, which was the color of tar.

Like all chess hustlers, he had his pieces set up and ready to go. Unlike other hustlers, the Bishop of 4th Street had the black men in front of him, inviting his prey to play as White. His clock harkened to the days of my youth: analog, not digital, being of one substance with his board, by which all the pieces were made. This substance, a light-colored wood, was probably oak. The clock was tall, with large circular faces marking the time that remained to each player. The brass buttons that the players press to complete each move were spotted with wear and corruption. The wood

Chapter 4

under the button on his side of the clock had delaminated and was beginning to crack.

I sat down and pulled out my quarter, setting it just below the first rank. "Five dollars a game?"

His voice was double-aged bourbon. "Well, look at you, straight down to business. Tell me something." He pointed behind me. "How did you do with my boy Johnnycakes?"

I glanced back to where Johnnycakes sat playing chess. "About even, I would say." *Give or take half a dozen games.*

"Hmm! You must be good." He smiled. Two pearly white lines appeared between lips that resembled medium-well sirloin.

Please, I thought, *spare me the showmanship.*

He pointed to the quarter. "What's *this*?"

I began explaining my system with the quarter, but he interrupted me.

"But what happens if you win 'em all?" He picked up the quarter, flipped it between his fingers a few times, one to the next to the next, and set it down on the other side of the board. "The quarter goes over here?" He smiled again. "I guess I would owe you, then?"

"Oh—no," I started, "I'm not going to take any money—"

His tone went hot. "Mice, or men?"

"What?"

Hotter. "Mice. Or. Men."

I faltered. "I, um…" (*Squeak?*) "Men, of course."

His voice resumed its smoothness. "You have answered correctly. Now, I didn't catch your name."

"Martin."

He leaned back on his bench and stroked his oily beard. "And do you know my name?"

"Johnnycakes called you the Bishop."

He nodded encouragingly. "The Bishop of 4th Street, that's right! And if you were to lose a game of chess to the Bishop of 4th Street, what would you do?"

"Pay up."

"Correct again. You would pay what you owe, because unlike the pests and vermin that inhabit this city and sometime cross our paths, you are a man. And if I were to lose to you?"

He didn't exactly leave me any choice, did he? "You would pay me."

"Correct once more." He gave a single nod. "Now. Do we have the basis of an equitable agreement?"

In the past few hours, I had dealt with a hotel manager who supervised his staff by means of a Magic 8-Ball, a man dying of a chronic lung disease who pays money to make smoke that he then inhales, and now a chess hustler who makes his living by insisting he pay out to his opponents. "Yes," I said.

"Good," he smiled. Then he broke into a quick, scripted patter that reminded me of radio boilerplate for a prescription drug. "We play five dollars to the game. The game is clock move—your move is determined when you hit the clock, before which you can change your move. Five minutes, no increment, no delay. The little red flag on your clock drops, and I have anything on the board beyond my king, I win. You put your king in check, or don't get him out of check, I take your king, I win. You make an illegal move, I win."

This was all standard fare, and I nodded as he spoke. Then came the bomb.

"Black chooses what side of the board the clock is on, and I always play Black. Shall we begin?"

Wait. What? "What?" I said.

He repeated himself. I looked again at his clock and that worn spot on one side of it. His side. What did he say? He *always* played that side of the clock?

"Let me get this straight," I said. "You always play Black, and you always have the clock on the left side of the board?"

"That's right," he said, "I'm left-handed."

A fine story. "Left-handed you might be, but how do I know your clock isn't rigged?"

The Bishop rose. It was like watching the Christmas tree rise to splendor and glory out of the stage at a performance of *The Nutcracker* at Lincoln Center. His beard was revealed to end at crotch level, and as it swung, I inhaled the smell of his beard oils, like sweet, ripe fruit mixed with something ashen, sacrificed to a tribal god.

"What are you doing?" I was looking up at him, bracing for trouble. But his words contradicted his stance, and he played it nice and smooth.

Chapter 4

"You want to play my side of the clock? We've got no problem, Martin. We're all good, you and I. We just need to switch seats."

Taken unawares, I stood, and it wasn't until we were halfway to each other's side of the table that I realized the obvious. "This doesn't change a thing!" I said, as I sat on his bench. It was warm. He sat on my chair, and he switched the clock to his left side.

"How do you mean?"

"What do you mean, how do I mean? All we did was rotate 180 degrees! Our whole table-and-chair setup could be sitting on a merry-go-round, and you and I could take turns all day watching the sun set, and you would still have the clock on your left side, with that worn spot on the wood under your hand."

He looked at his clock as if seeing it for the first time. "I told you, Martin," he said, turning his innocent-looking face to me, "I'm left-handed."

"And that's another thing! It doesn't matter what *handed* you are. You're declaring which side of the board the clock goes on. *That's* the point."

"I'm playing the black pieces, Martin. Black chooses. That's how it works—"

"Yes, it is, and if you rigged the clock so my side goes faster—"

"Is that what this is all about, Martin? Are you saying I rigged this clock?"

"That's what I've been saying this whole time. How come one side of this clock is more worn than the other?"

"This side of the clock has always been my side. It's an old clock, Martin, and I'm an old man. Maybe you don't realize because of my healthful appearance, which comes from a vegetarian diet—"

"No, no, no. Both sides should be equally worn. Every time one side makes a move, the other side goes, right?"

The Bishop of 4th Street paused. After a while he said, "Well, if that's true, then how does that prove the clock is rigged?"

"I..."

"Wouldn't both sides still be equally worn?"

Uh-oh. I had made a tactical mistake, and he had me.

"Martin," he said. Reasonably, the height of civility. "We seem to have gotten off on the wrong foot. How about *you* play Black, and *I* play White, and then you can put the clock on whatever side of the board suits you. Would that make you happy?"

He was trying to shame me now. It was like when a student comes to my office with an essay that he got a lousy 62 on, but he has some trivial complaint about how I graded it, and I say, "You want a 63? Is that what you want, a 63? Would that make you happy?" And what kind of fool would I look, taking Black, when I could have had White every single game?

I sighed. "You're saying I can have White?"

"Yes."

"Every game?"

"That's right."

I folded my arms. "Why?"

"Because I like Black, Martin. It's my trademark."

I finally understood: this was about brand. In a city full of wood pushers, this guy had found a way to single himself out. Why, we may wonder, was his side of the clock so worn? To this day, I don't know. Maybe he hits the clock a little hard when he makes a move, maybe it's the oils that go from beard to hand to clock. I can only say that, over the coming weeks, during which I played him many times, I discerned no time discrepancy, and I blame none of my losses on a rigged clock. I was simply outplayed.

"Now," he said, "let's play."

And we played.

Strategy-wise, I divide chess hustlers into two camps: those who embrace mainline variations and those who, by means of dubious maneuverings, deviate from well-worn paths in order to avoid prepared lines of play from their opponents. The very best adopt a hybrid strategy, employing little-known lines that are yet perfectly respectable at master-level play. Butch is one of these.

During our first two games, the Bishop of 4th Street employed a strategy that fit neither description. His play was not eccentric or wild, but neither did his even-tempered moves possess any energy. He made few threats, and I went both games without ever having been in check. My pieces developed without serious resistance, and in each game I was able to find a winning plan that seemed to almost play itself, resulting in pretty checkmates.

"Well," said the Bishop in a mellow baritone that made Morgan Freeman sound like a dump truck driving down a gravel pit in the wrong gear, "it looks like the quarter is on your side of the board, and I owe you ten dollars. Will you have a little mercy on a fellow chess player and give me a chance to earn some of that money back?" He stroked his oily beard while the setting sun made a streak across his thick sunglasses, which I assume he wore to keep opponents from knowing where on the board he was looking. The gimmick is not without precedent. But the sunglasses never came off, even when it grew dark, and that amazed me.

Please don't think I didn't anticipate any of what was about to happen. It is well known that some hustlers will throw a game or two in order to lend a new customer a false sense of confidence. (Butch would rather die.) Suddenly, the fellow can't understand how it is he's only *almost* winning his games. How lucky the chess hustler has suddenly become! Of all the squares for that pawn to have been standing on! And how close he came to clocking out!

If the hustler is good, he will continue to instill in his client the belief that he, the client, is a superior player. If the hustler is particularly skilled, he will raise the stakes at the moment he begins to win.

I decided to preempt any such nonsense by initiating a stake-raising of my own. "You said you intend to pay up if I win, right? Mice and men, and all that?"

"Wait a minute. You leaving me, just as we gettin' started?" On some primitive level, chess hustlers are all the same.

"Not at all, my friend." Two can play at the schmooze act. "I was just thinking maybe we can, you know, change the stakes a bit."

My opponent's face belonged on a fox who just got an invitation from a particularly fat hen to the chicken coop for a bite to eat. "What exactly did you have in mind?" Then (the suddenness of the shift was almost comical), a look of astonishment, transmitting even through the sunglasses. "I hope you're not gonna raise these stakes too much, Martin. You're a terror!"

I gave this comment the attention it deserved and ignored it. "You know a chess player named Butch?"

The grin deflated a little and he crossed his arms. "New York's finest.

Everybody knows Butch." Then, redeploying his Visage of Alarm, "Martin! You're not tellin' me you can take *him*!" He sighed in resignation. "Oh, no, no, no! Maybe I should just pay up right now and send you on your way." The man reached into the pocket of his bomber jacket, as if searching for money. I had to hand it to him, this guy was good.

I said, "Butch had a student once by the name of Melvin."

"You're losing me now." His hand came out of his pocket.

"Well, Butch, you see, he made these notebooks. And Melvin had one of them. Now Melvin is telling me that, maybe, he happened to give his notebook to you."

The Bishop said nothing. It reminded me of Monika.

"After he was done with it, of course," I added.

"Done with it?"

The shift from silence to inquiry encouraged me. "You would have enjoyed this notebook. It's full of puzzles."

"Chess puzzles?"

It's always difficult to tell with a chess hustler, but I believed his interest to be authentic. "Oh, yeah. Chess puzzles. All made by Butch." I thought about the nature of those puzzles—based on swindles—and I took a trick out of the Bishop's own playbook. "I think you'd be very good at solving them."

A wry smile passed from his face as quickly as it had arrived. "You've seen these puzzles already, then?"

"Indeed. I'm collecting them."

The Bishop leaned back on the chair that was usually occupied by his customers, put his big oily hands behind his big oily head, and considered me for a big oily while. The longer he looked at me like that, the more certain I became: he had it. He had Melvin's notebook! He was just trying to figure out how to use this fact to his advantage. Which, if I ended up with it, was fine by me.

His hand dug into one of the deep outer pockets of his bomber jacket, and for a moment I believed he was going to produce the notebook right then and there. Instead he said, "And here you are, sittin' on my bench, sayin' you want to raise the stakes." He nodded slowly, as if debating himself. He stroked his beard. He twirled a bishop between his fingers. Finally, he took something out of his pocket. My first impression was of foreign coinage. The button-sized metal disc had a die-cut hole in its center shaped like a capital *Y*. Then I recognized it—it was an old New York City Transit Authority Metro token. GOOD FOR ONE FARE, the bronze coin said in all caps around its perimeter. Such coins were replaced by plastic cards quite some years ago.

The Bishop pointed to the quarter that currently sat on the left side of the board at rank 2. "*That* coin," he said, "is the Martin coin. Any time you want, you can cash out the Martin coin for one hundred dollars per rank. But *this* coin," he said putting the Metro token down on the right side of the board, just below the first rank, "this is the Bishop's coin. And I get twenty dollars for every rank it gets to on my side of the board. Now, you want that notebook? Here's what you gotta do." He pointed to the Martin coin. "You just get that quarter up to rank 3, and the notebook is yours."

I paused, considering the deal.

"That's instead of the money, you understand," he added.

I said, "All I have to do to get the notebook is win one more time?"

"Mm-hmm."

"And any time I want, I can quit and trade my quarter for two hundred dollars, less what I owe you on the other side?"

"Mm-hmm."

"And every time you win, I owe you twenty dollars?"

"Mm."

"I believe we have the basis of an equitable agreement," I said, whereupon I prepared myself to lose a whole lot of money. But dammit, I was going to get that notebook.

The slaughter was worse even than I had anticipated. Immediately, all semblance of passivity in the Bishop's play was replaced by moves of the most nefarious and beguiling nature. Every line he played was a gambit: usually he would give a pawn, but often it was a full piece. If ever his material sacrifice was recovered, it meant certain death. His endgame technique was flawless, and he never missed a tactic. But most of all, he was fast. Even if he couldn't recover his gambit, I was never given a chance to make good on it before my flag fell, and it was one more rank for the Bishop's coin.

Throughout this carnage, I was praised as a consummate player who was just getting (could you *believe* it?) the worst of all luck:

"That was some attack, Martin." Twenty dollars.

"You're a ferocious defender!" Forty dollars.

"I'm gonna have to watch out for those knights of yours." Sixty dollars.

"I'll admit to having gotten a *little* lucky on *that* one." Eighty dollars.

By the time my first session with the Bishop had concluded, I was firmly established as one of the best players to have ever played in Washington Square Park.

I paid up. One hundred and sixty bucks.

♘ e4 ♞
STREET CHESS

From 4th Street I took the B train to Columbus Circle and then the 1 Uptown Local to 72nd. From there it's a two-block walk to our place. Our apartment building is a gay, grey affair, with turrets, bay windows that corrugate the exterior walls, and flags that ripple in the wind. I can see why Tomas chose it for his daughter—with its mansard roof and dormer windows, it feels very Continental.

I had thought about getting off at Columbus Circle and walking the remaining dozen blocks, skirting the inside of Central Park's west edge, slowly letting the blare and boom of all the people yield to the serene haven of Strawberry Fields. In this way I often shrug off work and mentally shift to whatever caprice Monika has planned for us.

Halfway through my disastrous games with the Bishop, however, I had received a text from Monika that made me want to move along: *when ur finished hurry home*

Followed immediately by a second text: *shannon found something*

Then, a couple minutes later: *dont eat, going out*

I had texted her back: *Any word on Butch? Perhaps from the NYPD or your dad?*

Her response: *no. hope ur in the mood for chinese again!*

So I saved the fifteen minutes and stayed on the subway, expecting to find Monika ready to go when I arrived. I was rather surprised, then, when I walked through the front door to the sweet, smoky tang of paprika hanging in the air. The kitchen was a mess. Monika and Shannon sat at the table, picking over the remains of what had clearly been dinner. Monika

Chapter 4

beamed; Shannon eyed the cooking utensils like they were about to leap up and gore her through the throat.

"Goulash?" I said to Monika, holding my briefcase while searching for a corner of the table that wasn't covered in plates and bowls and glasses.

"Mm-hmm!" Monika replied. Pleased with herself, she was.

I greeted Shannon. She smiled back with the lost face of someone who had just eaten her last meal on death row and found it tasty. Life, it turned out, had been good all along.

I felt terrible for her, of course, with the ambiguity around Butch. But as she continued eyeing the appliances, I felt again my earlier suspicion that she was hiding something. I recalled that half-naked dance with the sword. Mental. I returned my attention to Monika.

"Hey, you. I thought you said we were going out for dinner. What's all this?"

Monika turned the palms of her hands upward in explanation. "By the time Shannon found the clue, I had already started dinner."

"Clue?" I asked.

"Shannon has been going through Butch's duffel." Monika addressed our discomposed guest. "Would you like to show Martin what you found?"

Shannon got up, walked to the counter, and returned with Butch's journal. She opened it to a spot bookmarked by a rumpled takeout Chinese menu and sat back down. Clipped, sullen, and borderline hostile, her tone somehow also managed to convey sheepishness.

"I was looking at this poem," she said.

> At the end of the day
> Should you come to a wall,
> Order these numbers
> And order them all:
> 18, 13, 3, 24,
> 7, 9, 16, 1 and no more.

She leaned back hard against the chair, her arms crossed over her chest. Monika said, "Remember, Martin? We thought maybe the notebooks were going to lead us to a wall of combination lockers."

"Sure," I said. "Did you find something like that, Shannon?"

She gave her head a single adamant shake. "No, it's not that at all. It's this." She handed me the takeout menu. It was from the Great Wall, and I recognized it as being from Butch's duffel.

I glanced at Monika. "Is this why you mentioned going out for Chinese?"

"Just read it," she said.

I looked at the top of the menu: Great Wall of China Restaurant. NO MSG. OPEN CHRISTMAS.

"It's from the restaurant we just ate at. So what?"

Shannon was now definitely scolding. "Look at the numbers."

I unfolded the menu. As I recalled seeing, several of the numbered menu items were circled. *Order these numbers...* Understanding dawned. "Are you telling me—"

"Yes!" cut in Monika. "The numbers that Butch circled on that menu match exactly the numbers he listed in his journal."

"When you come to a wall," I recited. "The wall is a reference to this restaurant. And when Butch says 'order these numbers'—"

"He means to order those items!" finished Monika.

Shannon spoke. "We go to the Great Wall. We order those items. All of them. Nothing else. If they don't give us a notebook, then..." She crossed her arms as she trailed off and completed her speech with an apprehensive glance at a spatula that was balanced on a saucepan.

I checked the clock on the microwave—7:35. "Well, if we're going to go out—and I suppose I'll be the only one eating—I'd at least like to dress." I went into the bedroom to fetch a tie and a change of socks and trade my Adidas for a pair of suede bucks. Out in the living room, Monika said, "Make yourself at home, Shannon. I'll be right out, and then we'll go."

Monika swept into the bedroom, closing the door behind her, and into the bathroom, where she turned on the shower.

I called into the bathroom, "Is it entirely necessary to sho—?"

"Shh!" She appeared in the bathroom doorway with a finger on her lips, and under the steady hiss of the running shower she whispered, "I don't want Shannon to hear."

Shannon! The crazy bird was out there with all of Butch's belongings, unattended. I went over and put my ear to the door. Outside was a busy clanking of metal and china. What was she doing?

I pointed to the door. "Do you think it's okay to leave her out there by herself?"

Monika rolled her eyes. "Oh, for heaven's sake, Martin. She'll be fine."

"It's not her I'm worried about."

In that special way she has that says everything, Monika said nothing.

"Oh!" I exclaimed. "So it's perfectly fine that *I* get the bum's rush out of my friend's apartment, but please, by all means, let's give *Shannon* free run of *our place?*"

Monika continued saying nothing.

"All right," I said, resigned. "You've obviously got something to tell me, so tell." I sat on the foot of the bed, taking off my socks.

She grinned. "You're going to be so proud of me! I did some sleuthing today. Real Nancy Duke stuff!"

"Nancy Drew," I corrected. "What did you do?"

"Well, after you left the hospital for work, Shannon suggested maybe we had everything wrong about Butch and that white van. She said maybe he just got a lift home. Then she said it again—she said she needed to go *home*. There was something about the way she said *home* that didn't sound like she meant Butch's apartment. So I played along and offered to go with her. She refused. You know how she does, very insistently?"

"There! Now doesn't that seem suspicious to you?" Scoring a point, or so I thought.

"Well of course it does. There's no doubt she's hiding something, Martin. I never said she wasn't. Now let me finish, will you? So I said to her, at least let me walk you to 3rd and 33rd. From there you can catch the 6 Uptown Local to 125th."

Monika paused. She was looking at me that way she does when she's telling me about some chess game she just played, and she needs me to know the position of every piece on the board at the climactic moment of the game, and I'm not allowed to hear how it all ended until I make at least some attempt to guess her move.

But I had no idea where this was going. "So what did you do then?" I started lacing up my bucks.

"I gave her a big hug and let her go on her way. Then—you'll be so proud of me, Martin!—I saw the M102, just about to pull away. On a lark, I hopped on. A bus! I got on a *bus!* I figured I could get off at 42nd, run to Grand Central in about two minutes, and with a little luck catch the 4 Express up to 125th. With all the stops that Shannon's local was going to make, I calculated I could get to Harlem two minutes ahead of her. And then—spy!"

My shoes were on and I was working the tie. "Kudos for riding a bus. Very proletarian of you, sweetheart. How do you know the schedules, by the way?"

"Father used to put me on them when I was a kid." She meant about five years ago.

"You got lucky, you know. Those schedules change. But I'm still not getting it. You outmaneuvered her. What did you hope for? If Shannon was going someplace other than Butch's, she might have been going anywhere."

Monika held up a concessionary finger. "True. But if she didn't get off there, it meant for sure—well, almost for sure—that she was going someplace other than where she said. And anyway," she placed her hands on her hips, "she *did* get off at 125th, and guess what?"

"Go on."

She sat down on the bed next to me in her fuzzy strawberry sweater and skintight navies, and her face was positively alight. "So there I am, my back up against a brick wall, watching the subway exit from around the corner of a building. Sure enough, about two minutes along—out pops Shannon. But instead of going west past Marcus Garvey toward Butch's, she heads *north*. I give her maybe half a block, and I follow her. Take a guess where she ends up."

It was like certain chess puzzles. You're given a position, and they *tell* you there's one and only one winning move, and then you *know* what it is, because what else *could* it be? The fact of the question implies the existence of the answer. "She went to Master Lin's Kung Fu studio," I said.

Monika rewarded me with a kiss. I love when my hottie Czech girlfriend gives me puzzles.

I thought I was ready, but Monika corrected my misapprehension. "Oh, dear, that is not the right tie for that shirt." So the tie came off, and after retrieving several of them from my side of the closet and holding them up to me, she picked out just the right one. I put it on. It looked almost the same to me as the one she had discarded.

Chapter 4

"Real Nancy Duke stuff!"

Finally, we walked out of the bedroom. Our kitchen was spotless—and empty. Shannon had cleaned up the predatory pots and pans, loaded the dreaded dishwasher, wiped down the terrible table, and fled.

Monika scanned the room. "I guess it'll be just the two of us for Chinese." The tri-fold takeout menu sat in the middle of the table. She took another look at it before putting it in her purse. "This is going to be a lot of food, you know. Maybe I should call Father to join us?"

"No, thank you," I said.

♝ f4 ♞
ANOTHER TRIP TO THE WALL. PASSAGES. LIKE CHOCOLATE FOR CHESS.

Our table at the Great Wall was red Formica with a burn mark in the shape of a tilde and ribbed metal around the perimeter like you sometimes see in fifties-style diners. The metal didn't quite make it all the way, and there were four sharp corners at the gap where the edging started and stopped. I took that side.

Our waitress, Angel, had gold-dyed hair plaited into twin braids that came over each shoulder, ending in red ribbons. Swiss Miss, Latina edition, set down a bamboo bowl of fried wonton strips and two menus, then left for another table.

Monika took out Butch's tri-fold menu with the circled numbers and set it in the middle, right on top of the burn mark, where we could reference it.

"What do we do with that?" she asked. She was talking about the bowl of wonton strips.

"I dip them in mustard," I said.

"No, I mean, do we send them back? Shannon said not to eat anything but the numbered items."

"Actually, she said not to *order* anything but the numbered items. Otherwise, we couldn't even get a glass of water."

"Oh, good." She sounded relieved. "I hope we don't have to *eat* everything."

"I don't know. And who is it that needs to *see* us ordering these numbers?"

"The waitress, maybe? The cook?"

Suddenly, this whole idea with the menu and the notebook seemed unlikely.

Monika said, "Maybe we could ask to see the manager—"

"All right, you two. Know what you want?" Angel had a pad of paper and a pen, ready to take our order. Her jaw worked a bit, cracking gum.

"Yes," I said. "We'll have number 1, number 3, number 9—"

"No!" interrupted Monika. Then, to me, "I'm sorry, I just thought maybe we're supposed to go in the order Butch specified."

Oh, hell, she was probably right. I had been ordering the items as they appeared on the menu. But in his journal, Butch had given the numbers in a very specific order. Yes. Of course he had.

I took the journal out of my coat pocket and flipped through the pages, trying not to look at the waitress. She must have taken me for something out of Bedlam.

"Okay," I said to her, "could you, um... we're just starting over now, okay?"

Poor, confused Angel. "Go ahead, sugar bunny," she said.

"We want number 18. Number 13. Number 3. Number 24. Number 7. Number 9. Number 16. And Number 1."

She ticked the items off with her pen. "Okay, I've got a Happy Family, a combination chow mein, mu shu pork, barbeque ribs, egg drop soup, Szechuan string beans, egg rolls, and beef with broccoli."

"That's great," I said, "but, you've got the numbers, right? All of the numbers?"

"I got your order, sugar." It was like the first day of kindergarten, and Angel was that kindly cafeteria aide with patience for small children. But only so much.

I said, "You got the numbers?"

Angel looked to Monika for help, but in vain. "Yes, sugar baby. Now do you want steamed rice or fried?"

"Is there a number for rice?"

"No number. The rice comes with the meal."

"We'll take steamed, I guess."

"Tea? There's no number."

I shrugged.

"Yes," said Monika, giving our waitress an empathetic look, "tea would be lovely."

Angel made a final tick mark on her pad and walked off rather more quickly than necessary.

We sat for a minute without speaking. Monika asked me what I was thinking.

"I don't know. About my grandfather, I guess." I smiled. "I got a letter from him a few days ago."

"This is the grandfather on your father's side?" Monika asked. "The one with the cottage in the country?"

"Margaret-on-the-Sea," I said. "Yes. You can smell the sea in every room. It isn't a big place. Here in the States they'd call it a Cape Cod. Little white matchbox, set back from a gravel road behind a row of green hedges. A flower box under each of the four windows at ground level. My parents would send me every summer to visit. They'd put me on the train at King's Cross. I was young the first time I went by myself. Nine. Would you say that was a little scandalous?"

Monika smiled.

"Gramps would meet me at the tiny country station. They sell caramel apples there. He would buy me one for the trip back. The whole ride, I'd try to spot glimmers of the ocean, like a ribbon that wound up and down, hiding just beyond the hills. I'd stay with him for a month. The entire upstairs is his library. I'd spend hours up there."

"It sounds wonderful." The tea came. Monika poured out for each of us. "The letter that you mentioned. Gramps is… okay?"

"He's not ill or anything. But Sophie left. She's the young lady who was doing for him."

Monika raised an eyebrow. "Doing for?…"

I smiled. "An old-fashioned expression, sorry. She was, you know, kind of a live-in helper. Cook, clean, provide companionship. He knew she would leave eventually, of course. But now he's quite by himself.

"And, yes," I continued, steering back to happier topics, "the place *is* wonderful. The upstairs library I just mentioned? Gramps did that by himself. Converted the attic. Cut a dormer window right into the roof. This was that very first summer I went up there. Margaret-on-the-Sea is far north, and the sky is clear. No light pollution, like they have in the city.

Chapter 4

At night the stars are so real, I felt like I was reading by their light. You get into the library through a trap door in the floor, and the bookcases go all the way around, floor to ceiling. The top shelves had to be angled, to fit the roof."

"Gramps built the bookcases, too?"

"That's right."

"And you would read up there?"

"Uh-huh. And play games. Gramps taught me chess, you know. He had lots of other games as well: backgammon, mahjong, xiangqi, which is Chinese chess. Cards. But mostly I'd read. I'd sit on the floor, or maybe lie down. Gramps had his green leather chair. But I wouldn't sit on it. Even when he wasn't there. That chair was his."

"Wait," she interrupted. "The green leather chair you brought from your old place? The one that's sitting in the spare room? That's—"

"That's Gramps's old chair, yes. When I moved to America, he insisted I take it. I think he wanted to make sure I never forgot him." I took a sip of tea. "As if."

"I had no idea." Monika's eyes twinkled.

"Well, one day, Gramps notices I'm reading the same books over and over. You know, *Frankenstein*, anything by Robert Louis Stevenson, *The Hobbit*. He gets a look on his face and he says, 'You know, Martin, books can take you to secret places. You just need to find the right ones.'" I paused to down my tea. "Now, you have to remember, I was nine."

Monika poured me another. "Go on."

"So I take it into my head that there's a secret passage behind one of the bookcases, and all I have to do is find some kind of trigger. Maybe put the right books in the right order, you know?"

"Like Nancy Duke!" she teased.

"Yes, like Nancy Duke. Gramps has hundreds of books, thousands probably, and I don't think there's a single paperback among them. Many are first editions."

"Sounds like a small fortune," said Monika.

"I'm sure it's quite valuable. That summer, I picked up every book he had, read a bunch of them, and ended up finding 'secret passages' to all over. Abbeys and monasteries, villages that sprang up along ancient riverbeds in South America, a Civil War battlefield—" I realized I was rambling.

"Anyway, the past week has been much the same, hasn't it? A notebook with its own secret passages has led us to all sorts of adventure. It's rather more literal than literary, but here we are now at the Great Wall."

"Martin?" said Monika.

"Yes?"

"Promise me you'll always be a romantic."

I promised.

A waitstaff parade came with the food. There was Angel; Tai, whom I recognized from yesterday; and a waiter I hadn't seen before, Xi. They set out bowls for the egg drop soup and a plate of pancakes for the mu shu pork. They put down plastic dinner plates and paper-wrapped chopsticks, and while Xi refilled our water glasses, Tai tried to find room for the Happy Family between the barbeque ribs and the Szechuan green beans. Angel resigned herself to setting the egg rolls on top of the Happy Family. Just when I thought the last item had found a spot on the table, the beef with broccoli came.

Patrons gawked.

"Gee, I wish I hadn't eaten already," Monika said. Xi, who was pouring out, almost lost hold of the pot and splattered a bit of tea onto the steaming heap of rice.

Angel was still trying to fit the beef with broccoli when I suggested she could box it up for take-home. Maybe the look she shot me was annoyance, maybe it was relief. Whatever it was, it wasn't amusement.

"We're sorry if we're making things difficult," Monika said.

Angel sighed. "How much you wanna box up?"

Fifteen minutes later, Monika and I were surrounded by brown paper bags loaded with take-out boxes, fortune cookies, and an absurd number of soy sauce and mustard packets. Our answer had been "All of it."

"Don't throw out the mustard when we get home," said Monika. "Father likes it on sausage."

"Sure." (An entire shelf in our refrigerator is devoted to condiments, and now you know why.)

"What do we do now?" she asked.

"Beats me." I searched each bag, hoping to find a notebook, stuffing everything back in as best I could when they all turned up naught.

Chapter 4

Monika pulled a C-note out of her front pocket and put it under the teapot. "We can at least give her a good tip."

"That should probably keep us from getting kicked out the next time we show up. Which I doubt will be any time soon."

Angel appeared. The sardonic note in her voice could not be masked. "Care for dessert?"

"No, thank you." Monika said.

Bloody hell... I slapped my forehead. "Yes!"

Angel shot me a look that tried to part my hair.

I didn't care. "Does dessert come with numbers?"

"We got ice cream," she said. "It's not on the menu. There's no numbers."

"Maybe you have a special dessert?" I was thinking of those chocolate covered lychees.

The muted aspect of her tone disappeared. "Sugar bunny, we got ice cream."

I sighed. They were out of the lychees. For a second, there, I thought I had something. "I guess we'll just take the check, then."

Angel rang up while we donned coats and grabbed bags. I explained to Monika my idea about the lychees. That maybe they were somehow the key. She said the idea had been a good one.

As we left, I looked back at our table. Angel was picking up her tip. Suddenly, something crossed her face, as if she remembered. "Sugar baby, don't go anywhere!" She disappeared into the kitchen.

In the time it took us to share a victory hug, Angel was back with a white, rectangular box. She dropped it into one of Monika's bags, thanked us for the tip, and wished us good night.

Out on the street, Monika hailed a cab. I grabbed the box. A cab must have been very close, because Monika was already opening the door when I handed the box to her. Inside was a slip of paper with a hand-written note:

Come again! —XI

Under it were six chocolate-covered lychee nuts. No notebook.

♘ g4 ♘
ENTER THE DRAGON. SAY HIS NAME. CITY STARLIGHT.

I stood at our pantry door. Ridiculously, I was hungry. Neither of us had touched our Chinese food, and Monika had eaten all the chocolate lychees on the way home. But I wasn't here for food. Into the blood-red Salvatore Ferragamo shoe box I returned Butch's journal. I added the slip of paper from Xi, as well as the tri-fold menu with the circled numbers. A dozen times or more I had cross-referenced the menu with the journal. But numbers, like words, can only be checked so many times before they lose all meaning.

Monika noted my mood and tried her best. "It didn't work out, sugar daddy, that's all," she chirped. Ever since the restaurant, she had been assigning me *sugar* names. In the cab, I was *sugar cube*, *sugar bear*, and, most alarmingly, *sugar lick*. In front of the concierge, I was *sugar king*. That one wasn't so bad. Then, in the elevator, she uncorked *sugar boo-boo*. The shtick was getting old. Fast.

"It's the end of the day, Martin. We'll go to bed, and we'll start again tomorrow. I always find sleep helps me work things out."

Work what *things out, sugar mama? You've got no job. You've got a sugar daddy, and it's not me. You spend your days shopping and playing chess. Your father's life makes your life possible.*

No, I didn't say any of that. One more time, I reminded myself that Monika, as Shakespeare might have put things, was from the womb of high school untimely ripped. Tomas had brought his then-seventeen-year-old daughter with him to a foreign country and never bothered to re-enroll her in school or encourage her to get so much as a GED, let alone a college degree. For all of that, Monika is well read, highly intelligent, and, perhaps most of all, resourceful. But Tomas simply must be of the belief that life is forever, and Monika thinks no differently. It's the only explanation I've ever been able to come up with for their shared position that things will always work out to their advantage.

So, no. I didn't say any of that. But I thought it, and something of it must have shown on my face, and that was enough.

"Well o*kay*, then," said Monika. "I'm going to take a shower now. You come to bed when you're ready." And she disappeared into the bedroom suite, and the water turned on, and the Steve Miller Band played "Wild Mountain Honey," and I sat in the kitchen thinking about Tomas, and Margaret-on-the-Sea, and starlight, and lychee nuts.

The light from under the bedroom door went dark. I went to the pantry, and from the Ferragamo-Butch shrine I retrieved the journal, the menu, and Xi's note. I read again the pertinent passages:

Come again! – XI

XI was in all-caps and heavily underscored with four pen strokes.

At the end of the day, if you come to a wall, order these numbers…

What had Monika said just now? "It's the end of the day, Martin." I looked at the clock on the microwave. It said 10:38. I had an inspiration. I grabbed the menu and found what I needed.

OPEN 365 DAYS! DAILY HOUR: 11 AM TO 11 PM!

I stood up, nearly knocking over my chair. XI wasn't just a name. It was Roman numerals. Eleven. The end of the day came to the Great Wall of China restaurant at eleven o'clock—and we had been there in the middle of it. I had 22 minutes to visit it one more time.

I rang the concierge and ordered a taxi. I grabbed my coat. To save time having to pay the cabbie with a credit card, I scooped a fistful of bills from the cash jar. I was at our front door when I realized that I couldn't just walk out. I crossed the living room and quietly opened the bedroom door. Monika was in bed. As I bent over her, she lay on her side, facing the middle of the bed, her hands placed palms together in the ancient, child-like gesture of prayer and tucked neatly under her head, her legs slightly bent, contouring her body into a gentle *S*. She smiled ever so slightly.

"Monika," I said. "I got it. I'm supposed to—"

Soft, like a breeze through summer lilacs: "You do what you need to, sugar love, and tell me all about it in the morning." A flash of emerald from under an eyelid, and her smile faded into the unmeasured, wayward passage of sleep.

I got to the Great Wall of China at one minute past eleven. The fare was $38.60. The smallest bill from the jar was a fifty. I gave the L-note to the cabbie and stepped into the icy night. The cab sped off.

"Hey!" I banged on the glass door of the restaurant. "I want to see Xi!"

The dining room was empty. I banged again. "I want Xi!"

A person appeared from behind the dragon on the kitchen curtain. One of the dishwashers, maybe. The person shook their head: no. "Closed," they mouthed. "Clooooosed."

"Xi!" I yelled.

A motion like an umpire calling safe at home plate. "Cloooosed!"

I held up the menu. "I want number 18! Number 13! Number 3!"

A woman emerged. It was the waitress, Tai. The other person looked up at her. *Good luck dealing with the likes of him*, that face said.

Tai walked across and stood at the door. "What do you want?"

"I want number 24. I want number 7. Number 9. Number—"

I stopped. Tai had taken a notepad and pen out from her apron and was jotting down my order. Was she getting me more food?

"I want Number 16," I continued. "And I want number 1!"

She stood there, chewing the end of her pen, reviewing the numbers she had written.

"Is Xi here?" I shouted through the door. "I think I should see Xi!"

She opened the door and put a hand on a hip. "I was the one who wrote that note. Did you enjoy your lychees?"

I started to answer, but she was already walking. She held aside the dragon curtain, and I followed her in.

The kitchen was narrow and the ceiling low. Dishwashers shrugged when they saw me, then went back to work. We squeezed past rows of gas burners and rickety metal shelves that held containers labeled in unreadable Chinese characters. The shelving leaned in like the kitchen was collapsing.

Coming to a closed office door, Tai paused, listening, then walked on past. We came to a place so narrow there was no room for anything. Here,

Chapter 4

steep concrete steps led down to a door with a breaker bar. An EXIT sign dumped red into the flaccid brown air.

Twisting myself sideways, I clambered down the stairs. Tai pushed through the door, and the cold hit our faces. We were at the bottom of a tight stairwell. I followed her up to an alleyway where walls blocked out the city and a blanket of atmosphere, heavy with unfallen snow and ruddied by the light of hidden towers, obscured the stars.

Tai rounded on me, holding me against the wall. Above us, a yellow bulb flickered inside its metal cage; Tai's sleeveless arm winked in and out of existence. A silver ventilation shaft blew hot exhaust around our bodies, rippling Tai's skin with goose bumps.

She put her face inches from mine. Her eyes were white holes in the night. "Say his name."

"Butch," I said.

Her contorted face and lips came to my ear. "Is he dead?"

"No." I paused. "I don't think so." How many lovers had Butch kept over the years that I knew him?

"Do you know where he is?"

"No."

She pressed something into my hand and fled back down the stairs. I watched her produce a key from her apron, re-enter through the door, and pull it shut. I wasn't getting back that way.

I looked at what she gave me. It was a notebook with a bishop sketched on the cover in black marker. On the back were the numbers Tai had written down. She had taken my order on the thing.

The alley rounded a corner and continued out onto a street. Presently, a cabbie was asking me where to. I started to give my address, then changed my mind. "Just drive."

"What?" said the cabbie.

"Drive. Anywhere. I'll tell you when I want to go home."

The cabbie looked at me funny. I waved a fistful of cash in the air.

"We drive," he agreed.

For two and a half hours I studied Butch's notebook. The night was gorgeous. Points of light from buildings and streetlamps pierced the window of my taxi like stars, and by these, together with the light from my phone, I read until there was no more left to read.

♝ h4 ♝
THE BISHOP NOTEBOOK

Bishop

Clear lines rake the field;
Bishop sees rocks of one hue,
Turns into big pawn.

CHAPTER 4

Swindle #21—A weighty decision

White: Beer Belly
Black: Me
Date: January 26, 2010

"The body is the kwoon of the mind." Such is the teaching of Master Lin, as is that of some of the world's better religions. What, then, of the abuse of the kwoon? How, then, this crisis of obesity in America? And yet I could not deny that this bulging belly of a man had put me in a bind.

In the position below I was playing the black pieces. My earlier exchange sacrifice had not panned out. I had an opportunity to win back the exchange on a1, but in so doing, I felt my position would still be worse. So I found other employment for my bishop.

Black to move

Butch seems to have a trick in mind for one of his bishops. Can you find it?

Swindle #22—Working it out

White: Twenty-Six Point Two
Black: Me
Date: January 30, 2010

In contrast to my obese opposition of a few days previous, the woman facing me today was fit in both mind and body. Indeed, I was surprised to see her suspend her jog through the park in response to my verbal challenge. She certainly gave me a run for my money. By the time this exercise was over, I was happy not to owe *her*.

In the position below, I was down two pawns. Only by working out the cheapest of shots did I trick the well-conditioned player of the white pieces into a draw.

Black to move

Can you find Butch's swindle?

CHAPTER 4

Swindle #23—A holiday hoodwink

White: Cookie McJingles
Black: Me
Date: December 23, 2009

Ah, December in New York. The streets a-twinkle, the smell of roasting nuts, the frosty air that bites the nose. The tourists' cash, awash through year-end goodwill. 'Tis the season! And lookie, lookie, Christmas cookie! Here's a whole family, taking in the Big City. Ma in her kerchief, Dad in his cap, Son looking like the boy from the Jean Shepherd movie, Baby Sister wrapped up snug and warm. Adorable! And Ma won't mind (will she?) if Dad, in his favorite Christmas sweater ("Ho! Ho! Ho! Merry F#@king Christmas!" in green letters appliqued to red polyester) engages with the local color?

    I was growing warm in my affections for the family man who sat across from me, his cheer paying out in five-dollar increments. If it weren't for Ma—red woolen mittens on hips, black-booted feet a-tapping, quite at the end of her merry measure—we might have played until the hour when all good boys and girls need to be tucked in bed, with visions of back-rank checkmates dancing in their heads.

    Perhaps a victim of the seasonal spirit myself, I put forth an lavish adventure. It failed, and I was left with the following position, from which I needed to bail. Happily, I spotted a swindle, good ol' Dad took the bait, and the family moved on.

Black to move

Can you find Butch's swindle?

Swindle #24—Posing a threat

White: Me
Black: The Photographer
Date: January 21, 2010

With some fancy-looking camera gear in tow, the affable fellow in the blue and gray knit cap smiled kindly, introduced himself as Brandon, and asked if he could take a few photos of me. Some of my colleagues can get a little touchy about strangers taking pictures, but I've got no problem with it. I am an apt and fitting resident of this, my world. (Frankly, any portrayal of the park without me would be the less for it.) After Brandon worked his photographic magic, I invited him to play some chess. If his photography turns out to be half as good as his chess, he will have quite a nice album.

In the position below I am playing White. Brandon had stopped my pawns cold, and I was getting concerned about his two connected passers. I figured I'd gift him a bishop and send him on his way with a draw. He snapped at the bait.

White to move

How did an offer of a bishop get Butch out of trouble with his photographer friend?

CHAPTER 4

Swindle #25—Nothing changes on New Year's Day

White: Me
Black: El Che
Date: January 1, 2010

The communist says it is the game that is important, and that each individual piece means nothing. I offered a piece to the man who sat opposite me in a ratty Che Guevara T-shirt. He took it, and I saved my game.

White to move

Can you discover how Butch swindled his radical opponent?

Swindle #26—Subtle is the game

White: Einstein
Black: Me
Date: February 5, 2010

I have no idea if the elderly man with the white, spindrift hair had a passion for physics, but as he sat down to play I believed I saw in his face the same starspun wonder that set Albert Einstein chasing the rhythms to which our universe dances. Myself, I have never been able to master the mathematics necessary to a full grasp of his theories. Mine, therefore, is but a diluted apprehension of the physical world—a way of thinking that those who know me, but not well, often call spiritual.

Among the secrets of the cosmos was how on Earth I had gotten myself into the pickle pictured below. Alas, my poor king was isolated in a cold, miserable corner, far flung from the scattered particles of his fragmented forces. It was then that I realized how one of my pieces could tempt my opponent into a fiendish draw.

Subtle was my move. Malicious? Yes, it was that, too.

Black to move

How did Butch tempt his highly esteemed opponent into a draw?

CHAPTER 4

Swindle #27—Divertissement

White: Me
Black: Sugar & Spice (and everything nice)
Date: January 5, 2010

Whatever snips and tails little boys are made of, I don't see what any of it's got over sugar and spice. And yet, the facts. Move for move, females play chess at a lesser caliber than the male of the species.[15] Could it be the physiology of the brain? Parental expectation? Nature? Nurture? Chess isn't a nice game, and maybe it's that simple. Ah, but the cruel games a woman can play.

I digress. The girl of perhaps nine was dancing about the park in her pink tutu when she spotted me. "Oh, Daddy, look, look! Chess! Just like we have at home! Can I play the black man, can I?" Whereupon she plopped herself down at my table and within minutes had quite swept me off my feet. Halfway through our game I became lost in my own analysis. I simply stopped playing and began revealing all my thoughts.

In the position below, I am far from any moves the girl made. I was illustrating for the little lady the motifs of clearance and pins, you see. I was about to forgo the present line of inquiry (Black is clearly better), when I found an amusing swindle.

White to move

Butch is playing as White. Can you find the swindle that caught his attention?

---

15 Butch has never been one to sidestep a landmine.

Swindle #28—Rodeo ruse

White: Ersatz Cowboy
Black: Me
Date: January 14, 2010

He thought he was a cowboy, a hard-riding pretender to the rodeo—fancy brown boots with pointed toes, ten-gallon hat pulled down over the darkened leather of his face. But somehow the fancy foot- and headwear didn't pair very well with the gray sweatpants tucked into boots or the golden paisley four-button that grazed the top of his sweats.

Like his ensemble, our game, too, seemed an odd pairing of ideas. Every time I thought I was on the verge of busting this bogus bronco, my plans hit the dirt. In the position below, I was white-knuckled in the face of numerous pawns driving down my range. I had but one remaining piece of rope. I needed to lasso him with it right then, or this ride would be over.

Black to play

Can you uncover how Butch swindled the roughrider?

Chapter 4

Swindle #29—A game between friends

White: Monika
Black: Me
Date: January 26, 2009

"The reader who wins through to the end of Popanov's tome," concludes IM Kim Kitsch in her book review for the January 2010 edition of *Chess Life*, "Barking Dogma: Reflections on *The Thoughts & Games of Philip Merano*" (New in Chess, 2009), "will at once be satisfied with the exhaustive handling of this famously quixotic GM's observations on the nature of the game, while at the same time being quite certain that they have had enough of GM Popanov himself."[16]

Whatever might be said in terms of IM Kitsch's *writing* (I particularly enjoyed some of her literary juxtapositions; I would never have thought to pair Popanov's treatments of Merano's "elements of pre-middlegame strategy" with various torture implements of the Spanish Inquisition; my friend, meanwhile, found unlooked-for mirth in the counterintuitive, if not wholly unreadable, use of adjectives in Kitsch's assessment of Chapter 3—Merano, Overprotection, and the Nimzowitschian Central Outpost—in which she describes Popanov's analysis as "square, nippy, and somewhat greenish"), we both agreed that the first aspect of Kitsch's conclusion (we leave to others to determine the desirability of any future work from Mr. Popanov) was diametrically opposed to our own experience of the book.

To be sure, *Thoughts & Games* does apply a certain unnecessary stiffness to the presentation of Merano's philosophies. But enough of form. The chief argument we must make against any claim to "exhaustive handling" of Merano's ideas can clearly (the adverb is pompous) be seen in a list that Popanov claims to have found among Merano's diaries, prayers, novel fragments, and cookbooks (most—but not all—of which appear to have recommended a thoroughgoing vegan diet combining strictures from the Qur'an, the Upanishads, and the fourth chapter of 2 Kings), cataloguing "The Different Possible Types of Chess Games."

According to Merano, these are as follows:

---

16 By god, if this isn't a pastiche of Jorge Luis Borges, I'll play the Babylonian Lottery while wallowing in the sacred muds!

1. games in which the kings have castled on opposite sides of the board
2. games in which one side has started with a material or temporal handicap
3. games in which one player is not really trying
4. games in which *both* players are not really trying
5. games that have ended prematurely
6. games that have been already played
7. games that have been played with non-regulation equipment
8. games whose results have been incorrectly recorded

It is wasteful to expound the obvious, namely, that apart from a simple case of mutual exclusion between categories three and four, the rest of Merano's groupings could all simultaneously serve to describe *a single game of chess*. What is needed, and what was missing from GM Popanov's otherwise comprehensive analysis of Merano's scheme, is a sufficiently liberal, if not Humean and skeptical, understanding of *identity*. We refer, of course, to Merano's notorious category six. To play a game of chess that has "been already played" presumes an agreed-upon understanding of what constitutes *a game*, such that the *same* game could be repeated.

Whether it was by philosophy or chance that a concrete formalization of this understanding was omitted from *Thoughts & Games*, that its absence casts a pall on the entire classification scheme cannot be doubted. The deficiency is clarified by two illustrations. The first is an account culled from the collected works of that blind and Argentinian poet—and, the two should not be confused, writer—Jorge Luis Borges. In it, Borges tells of another writer—this one of a semi-apocryphal historicity—who, in the twentieth century, invoking the *nom de plume* Pierre Menard, attempted to pen the authoritative *Don Quixote*. Borges treats his reader to the astounding if somewhat predictable conclusion that Pierre Menard's *Don Quixote*, having been authored under more refined and less accidental circumstances than the primitive sixteenth century of Miguel Cervantes, is of a vastly different (Borges goes on to suggest *superior*) quality than its eponymous progenitor.

The application to chess of Borges's insight—that Menard's work, being at once a definitive and original edition of *Don Quixote* while at the

Chapter 4

same time superior to Cervantes's work, proves the possibility of an object's (the word is used strictly in its philosophical sense) being logically differenced from that which it is nominally equivalent to—readily suggests itself in our second illustration. We refer to a pair of chess games that, from start to finish, employed an identical sequence of moves, but which should not, by any sober means of evaluation, be considered identical.

The first game—Nikolashvili v. Basilia, Georgian Championship 2002—had reached the following position.

Nikolashvili — Basilia

Georgian Championship, 2002

Also:

Jones — Struthers

Wilkes Barre Club Quads, 1974

It was the final round of the Georgian Championship, and Vakhushti Nikolashvili, playing White, needed the full point to secure the championship of his country. With a full hour remaining on his clock, Nikolashvili erred inexplicably with **42 Qb6?! b2! 43 Qxb2?? Nc4+**. He resigned eighteen moves later, when he became convinced that his opponent knew the proper knight-and-bishop checkmating technique.

But could any meaningful comparison be made between this game and Jones v. Struthers, Wilkes Barre Club Quads 1974? By an identical sequence of moves, the players reached the same position as in Nikolashvili. Unlike Nikolashvili, however, both players were down to almost no time on their clocks, which were operating on a five-second delay. Needing only a draw to clinch first prize (a charter bus trip into Philadelphia, Pennsylvania, to watch the Phillies play the Cincinnati Reds; the Phillies ended up losing, their lone score a home run by Mike Schmidt in the fifth inning), and keenly aware of Black's passed pawn and his dangerous knight but most importantly with the foreknowledge that Struthers had no understanding that he would need to force Jones's king into a dark-squared corner in order to checkmate him, Jones pounded out **42 Qb6! b2 43 Qxb2!! Nc4+**. Eighteen moves later, with both of Jones's remaining pawns captured, the game was drawn when Struthers's clock flagged.

Such was the topic of the conversation I was having with my friend over a delicious cup of hot chocolate she had so kindly brought to me. When we decided to finally delve into a nice, friendly game of chess, it was perhaps not completely improbable that we would walk right into a game that, as we played it, I remembered having seen before.

In the position below, I am playing White. I had only just at this point remembered that White didn't win this game. The good news is, I remembered the swindle that the former world champion played at this point to save himself from a loss.

Of course, this assumes that his opponent didn't find the winning move. Kasparov's opponent missed it, and so, too, did Monika.

White to move

Can you find the swindle that Kasparov and Butch both played in this position?

CHAPTER 4

Swindle #30—Playing up

White: VIP
Black: Me
Date: February 8, 2010

Occasionally, a VIP will slip unannounced into our midst, and then it's we hustlers who get the business handed to us. In the game pictured below, my position had begun crumbling from around the tenth move. That's when I figured I was up against someone big.

Obviously, my feeble attack on White's castled king had not won the day. However, I spotted one last attempt at preserving my five dollars. If my elite opposition found the right move, it would be lights out for me. But the necessary response to avoid my swindle was pretty hard to spot. In fact, it turned out to be a move even a grandmaster could miss.

Black to move

How did Butch swindle the visiting GM?

						P	
				A		W	N
	P		R				
O							
	M				O	T	
				I		O	N

Chapter 5
PAWN PROMOTION

♞ a5 ♞
STOREHOUSE OF WORLDS

NIGHT, AND THE sea is a distant murmur.

Summer rain taps on a window. Through the glass, white edges of distant ocean waves reach and recede, caressing the black and somnolent deep. The foamy surf crashes softly onto itself, yearning for hidden shores.

Untethered from its terrestrial moorings, Margaret-on-the-Sea floats.

These images, even in the gloom: green leather, churchwarden pipe, a billow of grey hair and smoke, watery eyes behind steel bifocals, basket of red apples.

These words, even in the silence: ink, pulp, story, passages, lives, places.

This single entity: storehouse of worlds on a pinewood floor.

The worlds are books and the shelves are their storehouse: shelves upon shelves, they extend upward beyond the feeble reach of light; left and right, they wrap around this attic room, hyphenated by the square-paned window that looks out to sea. Ladders slide on rails, run up and down the shelves, providing access.

From the chair, a directive: take the books. Skip the ladder, just float. Rules here are fluid things. Someone, after all, has opened the window, inviting in the tender stench of salt and living funk. Remove the books, the shelves slide away: a secret passage.

Straight back, farther into the books, away from where a white Isle of

Chapter 5

Lewis chess king sits on his floating green leather chair, smoking a pipe. Outside the window, the foamy white looms larger. The sea has made its move and has surrounded the world; this is what happens to cottages built on the edge of the water.

Deeper, farther in. The white king is a smudge now, hanging in the air over the roiling brine that spills into the room with each swell of the sea.

Even here, this far in, the water comes. Look: it laps at my feet. And where are you, my love?

At the end of the passage, an alcove. Here you are. In bed. Asleep, next to me all along, red hair spilling over naked shoulders. I slip a hand under your pillow, my other finds you. I caress your secret passages. You mount me, and I enter. The ocean comes in.

Crashing onto ourselves, we find the hidden shores.

I open my eyes.

"Good morning," you say.

We do it again.

♘ b5 ♞
SHANNONUS INTERRUPTUS. MU SHU BREAKFAST. I MAKE A SUGGESTION.

I came.

Monika came.

And someone, God bless them, came—knocking at our front door at around 8:30 that morning.

"I'll get it," said Monika. She got up, lifted her thick orange terrycloth robe off the dresser, and wrapped it around her naked body, which faintly shone with a layer of sweet sweat.

Coming back in from the living room, she said, "It's Shannon. She's still out in the hall."

"Somebody needs to fire Bryan."

"You leave the concierge desk out of this," she said. "And put on some pants."

I got half dressed. Boxer briefs from off the floor, a pair of 501s from my half of the bottom dresser drawer, and the first thing my hand found in the top drawer, which was a Levi Strauss T-shirt.

"What about you?" I asked.

"I'm good."

I looked at her and agreed. We went into the living room. I raked a hand through my hair and motioned to the door. "Go ahead."

In swept Shannon.

"Thank you for cleaning up last night, Shannon," said Monika. "That was nice of you."

Our guest cocked her head to one side and planted a hand on a hip. "So, did you get it? Where is it?"

Monika looked at me expectantly. I realized I hadn't told her about the notebook. I just assumed she knew, but at what point in the middle of sex would I have explained? Chess has its limits.

I went to the pantry to retrieve the latest addition to the Ferragamo shoebox. When I returned with the bishop notebook, I expected Shannon to pounce. Instead, she looked at Monika and said, "You take a look first."

"We'll look at it together," said Monika. Then, to me, "Were you able to solve the puzzles?"

"I think I got them. But you two go ahead and take a shot. I'm going to shower."

Fifteen minutes later I entered the kitchen clean, fully dressed, a spritz of English Leather, a little dab of Brylcreem. Much better.

Monika and Shannon were several puzzles into the notebook, pleasantly debating various chess moves. Shannon mostly ignored a mug of coffee, while Monika was about halfway through her first morning Guinness. I poured a cup of Kenya's finest for myself and sat down with the *Times*. I kept half an ear on their conversation, waiting from them to get to the Jorge Luis Borges pastiche in Swindle 28.

"Oh, look!" Monika said. "I remember playing this game with Butch."

Shannon gave the open page a flick with her finger. "What is all this? I can barely follow it, the writing is so dense. And where the heck is Wilkes Barre, Pennsylvania?"

After another half hour, Monika shut the notebook and addressed me. "I suppose this time the literary cue was that Georgie Porgie swindle?"

"Jorge Borges," I said with a sigh. "Yes. In the first notebook, Butch

Chapter 5

parodied Lewis Carroll. Then in the second one it was H.P. Lovecraft. In this latest pastiche, Butch channels the Argentinian master of the short story, Borges, even to the point of self-parody. If you ever get a chance to read 'Pierre Menard, Author of *the Quixote*,' I think you will appreciate Butch's sense of humor."

Monika rested her head in her hands and gazed up at the Tiffany chandelier. "Butch is so amazing, isn't he? So multi-talented. And all of that is self-taught, too." She sighed. "He was really developing a love of literature, Martin. I'm sure that was all thanks to your influence."

From Shannon, a caught breath and a stifled cry. She buried her face in her hands.

Monika looked horrified, and I understood: she had spoken of Butch in the past tense.

"Shannon," I said, "have you gone to the police to report the kidnapping? I'm sure—"

"Sure?" Shannon mocked. "You know nothing." She stared off into space a little. Then, deciding something right then and there, "No. No police. Butch has given this chase to you, Martin. We must follow where it leads. We must do right by Butch."

Monika exhaled. "Look, we've only got one more poem to figure out. We need ideas." She went to the pantry, retrieved Butch's journal, and handed it to me. "Read it out loud for us," she said.

I slid the journal closer to me, cleared my throat, and read:

> The King was in his Master's hall,
> the Queen was yet a pawn;
> In Honor's case does fortune rest,
> for all to look upon.

I sat back and sipped at my coffee. "Hmm. I don't know if I like that."
"Why?" asked Monika, hopeful. "What do you see?"
"*A pawn* and *upon*? It's not really a proper rhyme, you know. Or at any rate not a perfect one. You need a different consonant—"
Cutting me off with a sigh, she said, "The king could be a self-reference."
"But when does a king have a master?"
"A chess master, perhaps? Does Butch have a mentor?"

"Not that he ever told me. And what about the queen? What's that supposed to—?"

Monika gave my leg a bump under the table. I looked up to see her casting a sideways glance toward Shannon, who had resumed staring into space.

I said, "Maybe the king and queen are Butch's parents, and the pawn is a reference to his mother as a child?"

"A foray into his distant past might prove difficult," Monika said.

I moved on to the next line. "Case. Honor. Perhaps a reference to a judge?"

"Some criminal case that Butch took an interest in?"

We had been over this ground before and hadn't gotten anywhere. I considered the words *for all to look upon*. "Are court proceedings public?"

Shannon came back from whatever region of outer space she had been visiting. "All right, you two, enough. You know Butch, and you therefore must have heard all about Master Lin's Kung Fu Studio."

Monika and I shared a glance. I spoke first. "What do *you* know about that place?"

"Excuse me?" said Shannon. As if I were the exasperating one.

"We saw you go in there the other day," Monika said, somewhat inaccurately. Half co-operation, half manipulation—that's her game.

Maybe Shannon's game, too. She said, "I had already thought about this poem, and I think it has to do with Master Lin's studio. I went there to see what I could find."

Monika leaned forward. "And?"

"I left right away. I wasn't... I didn't see anything," she ended, lamely.

"Well, so much for that." Once again I was questioning the veracity of our strange co-conspirator.

Shannon stood up, pushing back her chair. "No! It's there. The next notebook. It's in Master Lin's Kung Fu Studio." She paused. "Trust me."

Monika, doing what she does best: "Listen, are you hungry at all? Let's have some breakfast." She opened the fridge. The shelves inside were stuffed with takeout boxes all labeled in large, black numbers scrawled in felt-tip pen. Several of the boxes were dripping grease onto the vegetable crisper and the deli tray.

Shannon grabbed the box labeled #8 out of the fridge, asked Monika

Chapter 5

where the chopsticks were, pulled a pair out of the indicated drawer, and dug in. After several minutes of uninterrupted dining, she spoke.

"It's like you said. The king is a self-reference. Master Lin's studio is where Butch took kung fu lessons for many years. Master Lin is the master; the studio is the master's hall."

I pressed. "And the queen?"

"I have no idea." Again, with the glance off in space. "It's probably just there to complete the meter of the line. You know, iambic pentameter and all that. I thought Monika said you were a literature professor, Martin. You should know this."

Ridiculous. There had been no pentameter, iambic or otherwise, in that poem. I let it slide. Well, almost. "I have not known Butch to be a man who wastes words."

"Easy now," said Monika, "let's not get at one another's necks."

"Shannon," I said, "what do you think Butch meant by *honor's case?*"

"That's how I know it's the studio. Martial arts studios are filled with trophy cases to show off the accomplishments of their teams and star individuals. Mark my words. Butch hid this notebook in plain sight, behind a pane of sliding glass."

"Okay, let's say you're right. You didn't find anything when you walked in there. Or so you said." A kick under the table from Monika. "So what's our next move?"

Shannon washed #8 down with a coffee that Monika had poured for her, then dragged a napkin across her lips. "We're going to infiltrate the studio. One of you two is going to sign up for classes. You don't need a black sash or anything. You're just going long enough to earn a white sash graduation. The ceremony is lengthy and very noisy. Plenty of opportunity for the other to break away from the crowd and snoop." She stretched out her arms in front of her, popping all her knuckles. Honest people, it seemed to me, do not eye others with looks of such nefarious amusement. "Now. Which of you wants to learn kung fu?"

"Hold on," I said. "I've got an idea of someone who'd be much better suited for this than either Monika or myself."

I sold them my idea.

My last lecture that day ended at 5:40—plenty of time to get to Grand Central Station before 8:00, when Monika, Shannon, and I planned to meet. I headed to Washington Square to try to win myself a notebook in the meantime.

The snow of three nights previous had turned the park's walkways into white hardpan. Across what had been the grassy areas, an enamel of ice reflected dusk's steel blue. Orange haloes crowned overhead lanterns. Pigeons pecked around benches and under the stalwart trunks of denuded elms. Beneath the trees, a dozen or more chess games were in progress, evidenced by a wide ring of bulky rayon coats and woolen scarves, knit hats fluffed with pompons, and puffs of white smoke hanging over the tables.

I hunted for the Bishop of 4th Street amid the murmur of trash talk coming from the tables and the clattering of actual trash on the street. I found him already engaged in a game. Not wishing to appear desperate, I left my nemesis for the time being and visited some of the other boards.

At the first table I came to, a Latvian Gambit was raining chaos on the board, queens ricocheting, kings wildly misplaced. Players at the next table scrabbled over a rook-and-pawn endgame. "Same hand! Same hand!" the man yelled at his opponent, who kept moving his pieces with his right hand and banging the clock with his left. Further around the circle, a fellow sat across from an empty seat. "C'mon!" he called when he saw me, "C'mon! I need a player here!" I moved along. "Aw, c'mon," he hurled at my back, "we got chess!"

I was halfway around the circle. Two men sat calmly at their game. Their stoic nature as they quietly sipped from large Starbucks hot cups was mimicked by their chess. I would likely have passed them over had I not spotted the oversized chessmen that barely fit inside the marble squares of their tabletop board. Not wishing to draw attention to myself, I retreated a step and watched from a distance. If Tomas's hypothesis was correct, crystals of White Knight were right now being traded for hundreds of dollars—drugs and cash alike stuffed into pieces that, in the larger company of wild gambits and unsound skirmishes, were quietly acting out an unassuming, almost conciliatory Italian Variation of a Four Knights Game.

The fellow playing the black pieces, confident of his game, leaned back in his seat—then looked up. As our eyes met, I recognized him as the man from the Great Wall restaurant, the slurper of noodles. The short guy with the stubby pipe. For an instant, he made a sudden movement as if to leave his seat. Then, as quickly as the recognition had dawned on his face, he disengaged from our eye lock and returned his attention to his game. It all happened so quickly that I wondered if I had imagined it.

I decided to return to the Bishop's table. I was just in time to watch my nemesis perfectly execute a complex knight and pawn endgame. With ten seconds remaining on his clock, he promoted his last pawn. Seven seconds later, he delivered checkmate.

The Bishop of 4th Street collected his money and looked at me. "Martin," he spake, in his most deific and treacherous baritone. We played eight games that evening. Every one of them was more atrocious than the last.

At first, our games resembled the style we had adopted previously: me, trying to stick to main lines; the Bishop, throwing me off with moves that seemed suspect, but against which I couldn't find concrete refutations. I'd feel I was getting a good game, when suddenly a passed pawn that my knight just couldn't catch would appear on the edge of the board. Or a mating attack would result in his king taking shelter behind one of my own pawns. Often, I would simply clock out.

All of this, while painful, was at least respectable. It was our fifth game when things took a turn for the downright insulting. His first move was a pawn to a6. Already this tested the boundaries of his customary eccentricity, but when he followed up with 2… b6 and 3… c6, I knew I was being toyed with. Five more moves, and all his pawns stood on the sixth rank. Eight minutes later, when my clock flagged, I could detect no demonstrable advantage to my position. And that was game five.

Six was worse. After moving his c-pawn forward one square on move one, he tucked his queen's knight into c7 via a6. This maneuver he repeated with his other knight, bringing it to f7. None of my pieces that game had anything to say to those knights.

At the outset of our seventh game, the Bishop seemed to return to some level of normalcy, developing his knights to their accustomed posts on f6 and c6. Then he returned them to their starting squares. I resigned that game when one of those knights nose-dived onto f3, forking my queen on d4 with my king, who had just captured a sacrificed bishop on h2.

Our final game of the evening scraped bottom. Mumbling something about "the Fred," the Bishop spent his first few moves running his king into the middle of the board. Then he started playing for real. I left that session feeling poor, and it had nothing to do with the $160 I gave him.

It was 7:30. I texted Monika to say I was on my way and walked briskly to Grand Central Station. Arriving a few minutes before 8:00, I found her in a coffee shop, seated at a crowded table. She glowed a little. Her eyeshadow was the color of her orchid slacks, and her glossy lips matched the tomato red of her blouse. It was a color scheme very few women could wield. Including, possibly, Monika.

Under the table, corralled by her legs, were two winter coats piled onto three overnight bags. The coats were Monika's and Shannon's. One of the bags was my black leather duffel, which I had packed that morning before I left for work. The others belonged to Monika, who had lent one to Shannon for our trip, presumably along with overnight toiletries and some clothes. But where was Shannon?

"Hey, Martin!" Monika said.

"Hey," I said. "Are we still good? 8:37 Metro-North Railroad to Ossining?"

"We're all good," she said. "Track 6, on time."

"And what about Shannon? Where is she?" I recalled how she had disappeared last night, just as we were getting ready to go out on our Great Wall caper. "Don't tell me the crazy bird has left us in the lurch again!"

"We've been to the department stores and the salon." Monika looked across to one of the women sharing the table, then back at me. "Well?"

I considered again the person sitting opposite Monika, my eyes alighting first on those adolescent-y earrings—huge, round, and ridiculous, featuring an Asian-style plus sign with a line underneath. How had I missed them? Shannon's long hair had been aggressively cut and styled into a shiny black bob. In place of her gauzy blouse, a frizzy apricot sweater hugged her form. A modest application of foundation mollified the lines of her face, and her brown eyes considered me from beneath mascara-enhanced eyelashes. Reluctantly, and only at the affable force of Monika's command, Shannon stood up and turned a full circle. Gone were the ripped, moth-eaten woolen pants—replaced by skinny jeans identical in brand and style to Monika's favorite. Impulsively, I peeked at her feet, perhaps expecting to see her in stilettos. Instead, she wore a pair of white Nikes. In the footwear department, if nowhere else, Shannon is a sensible woman.

I said, "You look nice, Shannon."

She said, "This boy, Stanislav. Is he *really* going to take kung fu?"

♝ c5 ♝
CHATEAU PERFILIEV. PRAY TO THE HAND. SHANNON GIVES A DEMONSTRATION.

When I had suggested that morning that it should be Stanislav, and not Monika or myself, to dive headlong into kung fu, I had imagined a persuasive phone call would suffice to set the kid to the task. Possibly the call could come from big sister, or maybe from good old "Uncle" Martin. (Butch, perhaps the only person who truly could have gotten the nine-year-old boy to come all the way to Harlem for kung fu lessons—or for that matter to play with LEGOs while sitting in the Cross Bronx Expressway—was presumably sitting in a kidnapper's lair somewhere, recovering from a recent coma.)

Monika, "improving on" my phone call idea, had suggested instead an in-person visit. She wished for all of us—Shannon included—to make the one-hour trip north to Ossining, where Tomas lived with his wife, Lisa, and Stanislav, their son. We were to stay overnight.

As usual, Monika had expertly sold her idea, and 8:42 that Wednesday evening saw the three of us pulling out of Grand Central Station on the Metro-North Railroad. Shannon and I sat across from each other in window seats. I watched the boxy buildings slowly give way to trees. Shannon's eyes reflected the moonlight as she silently studied the passing landscape. I wondered to myself what other things those eyes had seen over her thirty-some years of life. Next to Shannon, in an aisle seat, Monika sat, legs crossed, reading a paperback copy of *The Shining*. Our three coats and overnight bags took up the seat next to me.

As the city slipped away to the bedroom communities of Yonkers, Irvington, and Tarrytown, I began to feel the wisdom of Monika's choice. It was good to get out of the city, if even just for a night. More importantly, I knew very little of Monika's stateside relatives (barring the omnipresent

Tomas). Stanislav I had only seen in the context of his chess lessons with Butch in the park. I knew Lisa even less. These were the only relatives of Monika I was likely ever to meet. It would be nice to get to know them.

From the Ossining train station, a taxi took us to Tomas's home, a modest colonial with white picket fencing and clapboard siding on the corner of two residential streets. Shutters the color of Kraft Macaroni & Cheese framed the windows, while a lime green door seemed to exude its own light, even at 9:50 on a mid-February night. An elevated porch, also white, wrapped itself around the front of the house. I was surprised to see container flowers dangling above the railings. Even the plant beds surrounding the porch were in full bloom. More than the eruption of color, it was the species of flowers that dazzled me: petunias, dahlias, impatiens, celosias, and geraniums, all side by side and in no particular arrangement, and every single one of them out of season.

Monika saw my bewilderment and offered a single whispered word: "Plastics."

Monika, Shannon, and I climbed the half dozen steps to the front door, where we found a note taped beneath the doorbell: WE'RE OUT BACK. COMBO = M'S B-DAY.

We followed the porch around the house until we came to an area walled off from the yard by a tall fence of interlocking white wooden slats. A door in the fence was secured with a combination lock. Monika worked the lock, and soon we all stood in Tomas Perfiliev's outdoor sanctum, where night and day are one, summer is a substance that flows from Italian marble, and it's the rest of the world that lives in a dream.

"Uncle Martin! Uncle Martin!"

I heard Stanislav's voice and looked across an in-ground pool to a smaller pool: a rectangular hot tub, also in-ground, where Stanislav was waving his pudgy, pink arm above the surface of the water. Light from beneath the churning foam turned his Coke-bottle eyeglass lenses into twin blue circles on his smiling face.

"Uncle Martin! We got a hot tub! Come in the hot tub!" Then, "Hi, Monika!"

If Stanislav noticed Shannon, he gave no indication, as he briefly went under and came up again, spouting water from his mouth like a statue in a psychedelic Roman fountain.

"Slav!" scolded Lisa, who was submerged from the neck down next to him. "Do you think Martin and Shannon and your sister want to bathe in your spit?"

"Sorry, mum." Then, to the audience in general, "It's okay, everybody. Dad says the salt water's full of natural chlorine. Mum's just saying stuff. Come in! It's hot!"

On the other side of Stanislav from Lisa, Tomas was leaning back against the inside of the tub, hands cradled behind his head, elbows out wide, defining a large space around his person. Water glistened on the orange, wiry hair of his chest and under his arms. He called out, "M-clip! Did you bring the whole gang with you?"

"Yes," she said, "I suppose I did."

"C'mon, gang!" he said, a lean, muscled arm pumping out and back in again. Trying to scoop us into the tub. "Jump in! There's room and to spare. Grab a sausage. Have a beer. Get your swimsuits on first, if you insist!"

Shannon, now apparently my fellow gang member, looked around the place as if she had never seen anything like it. Then, too, maybe neither had I.

A kidney-shaped pool dominated the center of the sanctuary. Thin steam, illuminated from below, played across the water. The surface of the pool was rippled by water from a line of stone fountains, each in the shape of a different animal, that gurgled along the pool's outside curve. Hugged by the water, a large, tiled brazier opposite the fountains held glowing coals, keeping warm a lidded grill, where I guessed the sausages to be. On an adjoining table, bottles of beer, ale, and stout protruded from crushed ice inside a patinated basin. Here also were various eating utensils and a nearly empty bottle of absinthe.

Behind the brazier, a pair of tables held inlaid chess boards, reminiscent of those in Washington Square. In daylight, players would enjoy shade provided by two red and blue umbrellas advertising Cinzano in white all-caps. Off to the side of the tables, a shimmering waterfall cascaded from an overhead ledge. The sheet of water disappeared into a narrow drain, where it was doubtless recycled by some hidden pump.

From the marble paving tile, a narrow metal staircase painted the color of cantaloupe and festooned with plastic ivy and flowers spiraled up to a second-floor balcony that led to a sliding-glass door and what I assumed to be the master suite. To the right of the staircase, a row of copper shower heads allowed people to wash off before entering the house. To the left, a spotlight underlit a tall flagpole. An American flag hung listlessly above a second flag that I assumed to be that of the Czech Republic.

Crisscrossing the entire haven was a network of twine from which depended dozens of colored crepe paper lanterns. High above the twine, but not so far as to escape his influence, the heavens looked down upon Tomas, and the stars, too, belonged to him.

Monika said, "Shannon, would you like a soak in the hot tub?"

Shannon took one more glance around. "It's winter," she said.

"That's the best," Monika answered. "When you get out, you'll be coated with a layer of warm air that will last about thirty seconds. C'mon, let's get changed!"

"I didn't pack a swimsuit," I informed Monika.

"I got you covered," she said. "It's in your bag." Then, turning to Tomas, "Father, where do you want us sleeping tonight?"

Monika and I were directed to help ourselves to the guest room; Shannon had Stanislav's room.

"Don't worry 'bout me!" the kid said. "I get to sleep on the couch tonight!"

The indoor furnishings of Tomas's house seemed modest and predictable in comparison to their outdoor counterparts—aside from a universal gym set that occupied an entire alcove off the eat-in kitchen. Almost certainly designed for formal dining, the room was instead all black gym mats and mirrors. The latter constituted the room's three walls from floor to ceiling. Televisions are forbidden in Tomas's house.

The three of us went upstairs. Monika showed Shannon to her room, then took us to ours.

"Was this your room once?" I asked her, getting changed into my swim trunks.

"No," she said, "Father bought this place after he set me up in the apartment we're in now. Before that, we had a flat in SoHo. I guess he figured that once I was on my own and he had his business going, there wasn't a need for him to be in the city all the time."

"He wanted you to be more independent," I suggested.

"Sure," she said, checking the fit of her swimsuit in a wall mirror.

Chapter 5

It's not like he's never around, I thought to myself.

I got changed first. As I walked across the tiled ground to the tub, warmth soaked into my feet from electric heating circuits beneath the tiles. Then I settled into the hot tub, where blades of hot water operated on my aching shoulders. Shannon and Monika walked up: twenty toes wiggling twenty glossy nails, testing the waters. To my left, ten in midnight blue, to catch the enigma of her soul; to my right, ten in scarlet, to rival the fire in her hair. Two pairs of shiny legs slid into the water on either side of me, followed by matching tropical floral one-pieces, outlined in pink piping. The swimsuits had been purchased that afternoon, along with the pedicures and the hairdos and the makeovers. All of it now swallowed up by the foam, and we were so many floating heads.

The six of us sat in a rectangle. Across from me, Tomas nursed some dark, cloudy drink, alternating between that and a glass of water. "Feel that heat melt the cold in your bones, M-doc," he said. Without need for a response, he tilted his head back to consider the black sky.

While Tomas basked in the comfort he was providing for those in his fold, Stanislav, to his left, bobbed up and down in the water. He was putting on a show for Big Sister across from him, making faces and blowing wet raspberries into his arm. Monika shot a stream of water from her mouth, hitting Stanislav square in the face and causing him to erupt in laughter and me to be sure to ask Monika to give her teeth a thorough brushing before giving me any more kisses.

To Tomas's right sat Lisa. A woman of possibly my age, she'd laced the tie ends of her bikini top beneath prematurely greying hair pulled gently back into a ponytail to reveal an open and kindly face. She was speaking in soothing tones to Shannon—one hand compassionately extended, reluctantly accepted. I had just caught mention of Butch when I noticed the fourth member of the family. Splayed out low, jowls flopping onto the marble tile, a golden retriever shifted his eyes lazily between the conversations in the tub and a shallow dish being guarded by Lisa's free hand.

Lisa's ministrations to Shannon concluded with an awkward hug. Lisa stopped covering the dish with her hand, reached in, and withdrew a thin disk. Immediately, the dog sat up on its haunches. I couldn't see clearly what Lisa was holding, but the size and shape of it seemed familiar, taunting some long-buried memory. The dog's pink tongue lolled out of his mouth as he accepted the treat.

"So, M-doc, what do you think of my jjimjilbang?"

The sudden comment had come from Tomas. "Excuse me?" I said, turning to him.

"My jjimjilbang," he repeated, "what do you say?"

Shannon helped. "*Jjimjilbang*. It's a Korean bathhouse."

"Correct!" exclaimed Tomas, then turned back to me. "Fabulous waterworks, M-doc. They just built one down in Yonkers. Huge facility. Sixty thousand square feet easy, with pools, fountains, spas, massage rooms. Food and drink. Saunas. I could spend the whole day there, soaking up the steam. You can just curl up, take a nap." Landing on an idea, Tomas slapped the water. A fleck of foam alighted on his eyebrow. "You must come with me some time!"

"Careful, Martin," Shannon said.

Monika snickered.

"What?" I asked the both of them.

Monika leaned in. "Let's just say the Koreans don't have the same hang-ups about nakedness as Americans do."

Shannon was more direct. "Swimsuits are forbidden."

I shot a disbelieving look at Monika, who explained. "It's gender segregated."

"For the most part," added Shannon.

Tomas *tsk*ed. "*Nobody* has the same hang-ups about their bodies as Americans." His eyebrows shot up, as if he were remembering something. "Speaking of which!" He tapped Stanislav on the shoulder. "S-squire, we're about to run out of foam. Go give us another fifteen minutes, will you?" Turning back to me, he said, "I moved the controls over there. The jets shut themselves off, you see."

I didn't see, exactly, but Stanislav climbed out of the tub, disappeared into a small maintenance shed, and returned, splashing back into the water.

Roused, the dog sat up and whimpered.

"Sit back down, Skittles," cooed Lisa. "G'boy." She produced another thin, round cookie from the dish.

As she gave the treat to Skittles, placing it lightly on the dog's tongue, I finally recognized it. My family had never been particularly devout, and

Chapter 5

I had not been a practitioner in the C of E since the age of ten, when my mother discovered the bishop was sleeping with the organist and my father made the pronouncement that, anyway, there was nothing to the Christian religion that wasn't borrowed from druidic ritual. Still, some experiences never wholly abandon a person, and at that moment I could almost feel again in my mouth the gossamer texture of reconstituted paper and the taste of blanched flour.

"My God," I said, not quite realizing the irony as I pointed to the treat Lisa was feeding the dog, "is that a eucharist wafer?"

"Uh-huh!" With a look of gratitude toward her husband, Lisa said, "Tomas freed me from the shackles of religion."

Tomas tilted his head, indicating his wife. "Used to be an Episcopal priest." His arm disappeared under the water. Perhaps he goosed her, because Lisa gave a little yelp and shot a sly grin at her husband.

"I had been floundering in my faith for years," she said, "but could never quite muster the courage to split with the Church. Then Tomas came along and showed me how to be true to myself."

I looked at Monika. She was trading goofy faces with her kid brother, ignoring the conversation completely. Shannon's face, at least, registered a modicum of bewilderment.

"And the communion wafers?" I asked.

Lisa shrugged her shoulders. "I had some left over when I quit the ministry. One day I was out of Milk Bones, and I discovered Skittles here loves 'em. I kept my account open with Herod's, the ecclesiastical supply company. They ship direct."

"Don't even charge postage," added Tomas.

Suddenly concerned, Lisa looked at me with a hand over her mouth. Then at Shannon. "Oh, my. I hope I didn't offend? We're all happy atheists here, the three of us, but I understand if—"

Shannon cut in. "The first requisite for the happiness of the people is the abolition of religion."

"Ah, Marx!" said Tomas. He screwed up his mouth and scratched his head, as if trying to work out his exact attitude toward this unexpected comment. "Well. As a Czech, I can't say I particularly hold Soviet communism in high regard. But as theologians go, Marx sure did know a priest from a porcupine!" Tomas gave Shannon a collegial glance. "Opiate of the people and all that. Eh, Shannon?"

Shannon nodded her bland assent.

"And how about you, M-doc? It's been a while since we last discussed religion. Any particular views?"

"Still agnostic," I said.

"Ah, well." Tomas swirled his drink in consideration of this irresolute position. "You'll come around."

Monika said, "Perhaps another subject, Father?"

"Oh, I don't know." Pausing to reconsider the stars, Tomas proceeded in a measured, almost reserved, manner. "It seems to me that we all are here, in our own fashion, out of our individual and collective concern for Butch."

I felt the center of gravity in the group shift as he broached this subject seemingly without preamble. Shannon, especially, considered him with a focused gaze.

"I don't think it should be out of bounds," he went on, "to engage in frank conversation of a philosophical nature as we each undertake to do what we can in the present situation. It is only natural, in times of distress, to feel a desire to project, onto the face of the universe, however indifferent and ignorant we know its vacuous expanse to be, our deepest fears and wishes."

Lisa said, "Tomas?"

Tomas looked at his wife.

She fixed him with a stare, and with a single looping gesture from her finger, indicated the whole scene, as if hot tubs were no place for this kind of talk. "What are you talking about?"

Tomas pressed on. "It's like that woman from your parish." He snapped his fingers, trying to get her to read his mind. "You know."

Lisa said, "You'll have to give me a little more than that."

"The one who loved purple and wide-brimmed felt hats."

"Oh." The cheer went out of Lisa's smile. "We're discussing Mrs. Fields again."

"Yes! There's the calamity. *Mrs. Fields.*" Tomas pointed to the sky, as if holding the cosmos accountable for the mere existence of this person.

"What about Mrs. Fields?"

Chapter 5

Tomas rolled his eyes. "You know that ridiculous prayer diary she kept. How she'd get it out at meetings and check everything off according to how God answered: yes, no, or wait."

Shannon laughed. "That's nothing that a lucky horseshoe couldn't deliver. You may as well pray to my nose."

Tomas nearly stood up in his excitement, then sat down again. Quickly. "Precisely!" Then, aside to Stan: "S-squire, the foam. Go run and get the timer again, please?" Stan got out, and Tomas continued, glancing first at Shannon as he repeated, "Precisely!" and then again at the surface of the water. The roiling motion of the jets was beginning to calm. Suddenly, Tomas seemed unusually anxious.

I turned to Monika. "Is it me, or are you having difficulty following the present line of conversation?"

For answer, Monika stuck a hand right in my face and asked Shannon and myself to consider it. She explained how any deity could be replaced by a hand, and all prayers answered yes, no, or wait, without any observational difference in the result. Everything she was saying made perfect sense to me. Shannon and I were trying to share an agreeable nod behind Monika's hand when the jets came back on. Stan crashed back into the water, and Monika's hand returned to her side.

Lisa said to Tomas, "Are you saying that you wish you could pray?"

Tomas made a strangled noise, and Monika answered for him. "Well it is a little hard, isn't it, not being able to do anything? I mean, just at the moment? I think what Father means is that it would be nice if we all said something meaningful about Butch. Isn't that it, Father?"

Tomas, restored to his natural state of self-generated nirvana, smiled and nodded. "You got it perfect, M-clip." Then, turning to his wife, "L-word, how about you get us started?"

Lisa let out a breath. "You mean, you want me to say something—"

"Yeah," Tomas interrupted, "just, you know, say something. About Butch. Something positive, to let us get our focus on."

"Before, you wanted to pray; now you want a sermon?"

"No! Nothing like that. Just... say something nice. Then, we go around the circle. Everybody gets a word in."

"Okay." Lisa closed her eyes. She nodded gently as she took several deep breaths. She was taking her time, drawing on her years of experience as a shepherd of hurt souls, letting her mind come up with some homiletic turn of phrase to still the stormy waters.

She opened her eyes and looked at Tomas. "I really didn't know Butch."

"Gah! Just say something!"

"Okay." Lisa looked around at the group. "I just want to say that I feel very optimistic about the future of this man, Butch. I say this, not because of anything I know about him, but because of what I know about you. You, who are assembled here, in your devotion to him. When I see such manner of friends, lovers, and students, rushing to his aid—how can I not believe that all will turn out best for him?"

"Beautifully stated," said Tomas. "Now, who needs an absinthe?"

"But really," Lisa said, "I don't know him very well. I'm afraid that was all just old boilerplate. I think others should speak." She blushed and fed Skittles a communion wafer. It looked to me like she was embarrassed. Trying to shake the attention off. I suddenly felt awkward, whether for her or myself it was difficult to tell. I found myself struggling to put together something to say.

Monika spoke up. "It's like you said, Father. We're here because of Butch. I'm not just talking about our concern for him. I mean we're here *because* of him. His actions, his intent: they have led us to this point." Tomas nodded enthusiastically. Lisa, chin in hand, looked as though she might be taking in a sermon. Shannon held Monika in a cloudy and pensive gaze. Stanislav was attempting to hit his sister in the face with spurts of water that he was squeezing from his clasped hands.

I considered the white, foamy brine. "You mean to say Butch intended us to be here?"

"In this hot tub, right now?" Monika shrugged this off. "Nothing so fanciful. I'm just saying that Butch is a mastermind. I've spent many hours with him, learning chess. And not just chess. The way he thinks, the way he understands the world. Butch sees himself as a sort of chess-playing detective. Where Sherlock Holmes takes in the details of his immediate environment and makes deductions about the past, Butch looks *ahead*. Consider those notebooks. Think about what he's written in them, and how strategic and orchestrated it all is. It's like a well-played middle game in chess. Whatever it is that's going on behind the scenes, Butch likely knows everything about it."

Chapter 5

"Well, maybe that's what got him *kid*napped," I said. It came out peevish.

"If he even *got* kidnapped," Monika countered. "Maybe whatever happened to him is exactly what he intended."

"A strong point, M-clip," said Tomas, going for his glass of water.

Shannon spoke. "But we're not supposed to be doing this right now, are we? Solving this thing?" She looked at Lisa while she said this. "We're supposed to be saying good things about Butch. Something nice."

Lisa said, "I believe that was the idea."

"Look," Monika said, "I'm just saying Butch is an amazing individual. That's nice, right?"

Tomas, who had switched to his cloudy drink, held it up to me. "What do you have to say for him, M-doc?"

Maybe it was the setting. Maybe it was my imagination getting the better of me, conjuring up whatever hellhole Butch might have been sitting in at that moment. Maybe it was a lot of things, but something in me finally broke. What do I have to say for Butch? Is that the question someone was asking me? What did I have to say for *myself*: there was the bloody question of the bloody hour. I was sitting in a hot tub—a feckin', fuckin' hot tub—soaking my cares away, and beyond that, what? Solving chess puzzles? Shagging my girlfriend? Taking pleasure trips to the fine bedroom communities on the northern outskirts of New York? Coming here, to this house, to this place, where the Beach Boy from Prague had decided there was no point to looking for an endless summer when he could just make one of his own, and what else *was* there? What did I have to say for Butch? What did *any* of these people have to say for Butch? There. *There* was the fucking question. What were any of these ex-priest, narcissistic, jet-control-moving, exhibitionist, loony-bin—

I don't know what I said, or how much. What I knew was, someone was in my face. Monika. Then, briefly, Shannon. Then Monika again. It was she who got me to calm down. I don't know what I said. I don't know.

Monika took my hand, gently held it. I took a swallow from Tomas's offered water glass. Somehow, I managed to look around. The faces around me wore the patient humor of those who await the passing of a light sprinkle when it's time to take in the dishes from the picnic table and wrap up the leftovers. Stanislav broke the silence with a farting noise from his armpit. And somewhere, somewhere in the dank cellar of my brain, I felt love, and I told myself that I was one lucky bastard.

Tomas spoke. "I'd like someone to help me figure this out. Let's say I had some pixie dust."

Lisa eyed the drink in his hand suspiciously. Monika looked at him with all the shock of a waitress at IHOP taking an order of pancakes. Tomas said nothing more at first and sent Stanislav off once again to the equipment shed to restart the jets.

When Stanislav returned, Tomas continued. "Let's say you had some pixie dust that let you play a perfect game of chess." He twiddled his fingers at all of us, as if dispensing the stuff. "Can any of you tell me how many hits you would need in order to become the World Chess Champion?"

Lisa said, "May I ask what the point of this is?"

"No," said Tomas. "Think about this. Every two years, another world championship cycle starts, and every one of the millions of chess players on this planet has a shot at it." In response to a doubtful glance from Monika, he added, "I'm talking theoretically." He continued, "Now let's say that out of nowhere, some unheard-of nobody starts winning every game of chess that he or she sits down to play." He looked at each of us in turn. "How many hits of pixie dust would I need to give you? In order to become the world champion of chess, how many games would you need to win?"

"In order to face the reigning champion in a world title match, you'd need to first become the challenger," said Monika. "That means winning the fourteen-round Candidates Tournament. I should think ten games would likely do the trick."

Grateful for the tangent, I ventured to speak for the first time since my emotion explosion. "Plus the world title match itself. That's best of twelve. So, add seven more. That makes seventeen games."

"So far, so good," said Tomas. "And how does one make it to the Candidates?"

Monika screwed up her eyes and started calculating. "There are several entry points, but I think the most direct path would be the World Cup. That's a single-elimination, seven-round tournament, with each of the first six rounds consisting of a two-game match, and the last round is a four-game match. Six times two is twelve, plus four is sixteen."

"But the runner-up also goes to the Candidates," I reminded her. "So you could completely blow the last round."

"Okay," she agreed, "so scratch the last four games. Twelve, then."

"And you don't need to actually win both games of the two-game matches. A win and a draw would suffice to win each round."

"Do you honestly think you could pull off a draw against any of those players without the pixie dust?"

"Fair point," I said. "Twelve it is. Twelve plus seventeen, that's twenty-nine," I said, looking at Tomas for approval.

"Excellent," he said. "Now. The World Cup is a competition that pits 128 of the best players on the planet against each other. How do you plan to gain entry?"

"That one's easy," said Monika. "The top three or four contestants from each Zonal are invited to the World Cup. In this country, that means the US Chess Championship. Eleven rounds, a draw and a win amounting to the same thing, I'd say eight hits of pixie dust should guarantee a World Cup berth."

"I still don't see what any of this has to do with anything," said Lisa.

"How many games are we up to?" asked Tomas.

"Thirty-seven," I said.

Monika said, "And now you're going to ask how we gain entry into the US Chess Championships, of course."

"Exactly," said Tomas. "This is fun, right?"

"Yes," Monika said, "this is pretty neat. Because unless I'm mistaken, a totally random person could be guaranteed an invitation to the US Chess Championship by *winning the US Open*."

"Bingo!" exclaimed Tomas.

"Why the US Open?" I asked.

"Tradition," said Monika. "As the biggest single-section open tournament in America, in which anyone can play, winning first place has always been accompanied by an invitation to the following year's US Chess Championship." Looking at Tomas she said, "I think taking nine rounds should do the trick."

"All right," said Lisa, "I've been keeping count, and you're up to forty-six hits of pixie dust, given to some random guy on the street—"

"Or random woman," interjected Monika.

"Or woman," agreed Lisa, "who then becomes the chess world champion. May I now ask the point of this exercise?"

"Well, just think about it!" said Tomas, as if thinking were a mere formality. "Compared to chess, most sports are for wimps! What does a football team have to do to win the Super Bowl? Win, what, nine games during regular season? Then three more in postseason, and then the big game itself? What is that—thirteen games?"

Asked Lisa, "Point being?"

"Apropos the pixie dust? Nothing! But relative to *Butch*, think of it this way: Butch is a *self-taught man*, Lisa. Fighting every day in the toughest sport on the planet. He is way better off than you people are imagining him to be. Wherever he is, I'll bet he's got the whole situation totally under control." Tomas knocked back the rest of his drink. "I consider Butch my equal in every way. I'm not worried about him in the least."

"And Butch knows kung fu!" Stanislav said.

Addressing Stanislav, Shannon asked, "Would you like to learn kung fu? You could take lessons at the same kwoon where Butch earned his black sash a long time ago. Before you were born."

The boy spun about. I think he had been trying for a roundhouse kick when he lost his footing and succumbed to the water jets. He disappeared under the surface and came up dripping and panting. To his invisible choir of perpetual admirers he said, "Yay! Kung fu!" Then, to Shannon, "What's a kwoon?"

"It's a gym for martial artists. You could learn from a kung fu master."

"Let's not get ahead of ourselves on this, please," said Lisa.

Perhaps Shannon didn't hear. She said, "Get over here, kid."

I looked at Monika and subtly tipped my head toward Tomas and Lisa. It was time to explain our plans.

While the four of us spoke, Shannon was busy showing Stanislav some moves. She'd take up a stance or block with her arm, fending off a shadow opponent. Stanislav did his best to copy her. This went on for several minutes until Stanislav called out, "Yay! Demonstration, everybody! Shannon's gonna do a kung fu demonstration!"

Shannon was already out of the tub, extending a hand down. "All right, you," she said to me. "Let's go."

I gripped her hand, and she pulled. In an instant, I was standing next to her. She walked me over to the open ground beside the pool. Everyone else was out of the tub and watching from the chairs around the Cinzano tables. Everyone, that is, except Tomas, who was content to watch from the tub.

Shannon indicated that she wanted me to come at her with a strike to her face. She demonstrated the attack and then stood back, waiting.

"What are you going to do?" I asked.

"Just do it," she said.

I made the attack. With a sweeping motion of her arms and a pivot of a hip, she planted her fist in my gut, and I was introduced to the tiles on the ground. Clearly, she had pulled her punch and somehow softened my landing, because it didn't hurt. Too much.

I stood up, and she demonstrated another attack for me to try. This time, I was to push her into the pool with both arms.

She lowered her voice. "What was that, back there?"

I answered with a hushed question of my own. "What are you up to?"

Shannon whispered, "I'm not the bad guy, Martin. Now push me."

And so I pushed. Or at least, I tried. I ended up doubled over, my head in a vice grip.

Next attack, a hit to the chest. I prepared to attack, but first I said—

"What's your connection to Master Lin's studio?"

Stony silence.

"Do you live there?"

More silence. This time, it was I who had caught her off guard. From behind me, the family was cheering us both on.

"Answer me," I hissed, "or I won't hit you."

"Yes. I live there. Or I did, before I moved in with Butch."

I attacked. Before my fist could connect with her chest, she bent my wrist back, and I was helpless. She could have snapped my arm like a #2 pencil.

We were at it again for one final attack. This time, I was supposed to lunge for her with my whole body. I kind of knew how this was going to end, but I was on a roll. This was the most I had gotten out of Shannon since I'd met her. Plus, the pool would be a refreshing change from the hard ground.

"Is Butch alive?" I asked.

"Yes. I think so."

"Do you know where?"

She paused. "I have an idea."

"What are you doing about it?"

"Martin, don't press this. If you go after Butch directly, you will get us all killed. I need you—Butch needs you—to go after those notebooks. Just like he said. If you want to help Butch, that's his best chance."

"What are these notebooks all about?"

"I'm not going to answer that."

I lunged. I expected to be in the pool very soon. What I didn't expect was the passing view of the night sky and the stars that winked at me as I careened ("*Keee-ya!*" yelled Shannon) over her head. I went in.

As I floated on my back in the pool, Monika appeared, upside-down. She smiled at me.

I groaned. "Can we please go to bed now?"

The following morning, over breakfast, Lisa called Master Lin's Kung Fu Studio. The first available event for new applicants was an exhibition scheduled for noon of the following Saturday. Those who attended would get a 10 percent discount on a six-month membership. She signed Stanislav up.

♞ d5 ♞
IN THE HOUSE OF MASTERS LIN AND FENG

The day of the exhibition at Master Lin's arrived with no word from or news of Butch. Shannon invited Monika and me to Butch's apartment for lunch, where we were joined by Lisa and Stanislav. Tomas, who had business, had sent his wife with his apologies. Also deli sandwiches and potato chips, which made a welcome addition to the Dinty Moore beef stew Shannon provided.

The five of us ate and cleaned up. As we got ready to walk to the studio, Shannon said she would stay behind. This didn't surprise me. Whatever connection she had to that place, she clearly did not want to be seen there.

The weather had warmed, leaving mounds of grimy mush to melt in the crotches where buildings and sidewalks come together. Stanislav spoke excitedly while he walked, punching the air around him and telling incomprehensible tales about Power Rangers and mutated amphibians. Monika squeezed my hand and grinned. "Someday?" she said.

I gave her a dubious look that she coyly ignored. Perhaps she meant that, someday, Stanislav would earn a black sash from Master Lin. Or—alternative interpretation—that, someday, the kid would get himself lost on the New York City Subway. Yes, those were two possible interpretations. Either was fine.

Mirrors without smear or smudge covered the walls of the studio, floor to ceiling. Considering the recent lunar new year, I had expected perhaps a red-and-gold tissue paper dragon for decoration. Instead, a forgotten Christmas garland sagged in lazy Ws along the tops of the mirrored walls.

The floor was beautiful: wide, hardwood planks, highly polished. Pushed into a far corner of the room, a drooping potted plant begged for water. On top of a meticulously organized reception desk, a Keurig coffee machine collected dust; its clear plastic water reservoir revealed its empty condition. *Indications of neglect*, I thought to myself, *cohabiting with evidence of fastidious care*. Even the smell of the place—a mix of linseed oil, jasmine, and warm sweat—was a study in contrasts.

Monika, Lisa, and I took our seats. Rows of folding chairs faced a squat, temporary-looking stage. Between the front row and the stage, three instructors in grey frog-button tops and black canvas shoes were directing all aspiring students to sit on red mats. Most of these were kids ranging in age from seven to ten. I spotted Stanislav, his meaty face jiggling as he laughed, switching his attention between a few chattering prospective chums. At one corner of the matted area, a cluster of teenage boys sat down, trading glances. Two adults started to sit, then decided to go back to where they had been leaning against one of the mirrored walls.

As I was watching Stanislav talk to his new friends, the instructors leaped onto the stage. There were six. An additional three must have come from behind a golden curtain that covered the back wall. They formed a single line and faced the audience in regimented attention. In unison they shouted, "Ha!"

A quieting force descended on the room. Unless I was imagining it, the lights dimmed. The stage burst into action as each of the grey-uniformed instructors flew into wild acrobatics. Kicks, punches. Flexible and powerful, the combatants favored fluid, circular movements that swept them low to the ground or high in the air. Some made dramatic blocks; others hurled themselves backward, away from the incoming blows, landing on their feet, leaping forward again in counterattack.

Then the weapons came out. Swords cut wide arcs as the instructors ducked or leaped over them. To my surprise, one bloke took a pike thrust full in the stomach. Then, with a single backward step, he grabbed the pole and twisted, sending his assailant flying.

Another instructor cleared everyone off the stage with twin flails, one in each hand, making deadly circles of whirring steel, whipping the air. With a double *thwack*, he embedded the flail's spikes into the stage floor. Then he fended off bricks thrown at him by those he had driven off the stage, crushing each weighty projectile in midair. The broken chunks fell to the ground in a hail of ruddy stone. Then all six instructors were once again on stage, each holding a plank of wood. One by one they held the planks up, snapping them in half with a foot, a head, the tip of a finger.

Finally, the six once again faced the audience in their regimented line, and all was silent. A woman walked onto the stage. With small, efficient movements, as if attempting invisibility, she took away all the pieces of broken wood and brick and disappeared whence she had come. A stunned applause rippled through the room while she worked.

I leaned in toward Monika. "That was amazing!"

She whispered back in a tone that made me almost hear her eyes rolling, "You'd like Cirque du Soleil. I'll get us tickets some time."

Lisa, sitting on the other side of Monika from me, said, "Wasn't that amazing?"

Monika turned to her. "Oh, yes!" and in a tone of pure conviction, added, "Slav will love it!"

Whatever it was about the show that was putting Monika off, I was glad to see she at least remembered our mission.

The instructors filed off stage. One of them pried the twin flails out of the makeshift floor, while another grabbed the gold curtain that led backstage and pulled it halfway open. A man in a tangerine robe sat in lotus position on a small rug. His white beard was long and narrow, and it serpentined down his chest like a gossamer dragon. Here at last was Master

Lin himself, who had startled me two weeks ago when he'd appeared in the darkened frame of his storefront window.

He rose. In slow steps, each one clearly causing him pain, he walked to the front of the stage. Twelve years ago, this man had presented Butch with a black sash. Maybe the creases around Lin's eyes hadn't been so deep then, but now they intensified a gaze that missed its mark—or perhaps saw something just beyond vision. Silken hair grew out from his ears a bit too wildly in white, cottony tufts, and it clung like a silver shadow to a sunken and hollow face. His hands, calloused and large-knuckled, scrunched his robes as they clutched at his stomach. Here, I thought, was a withered man, an unkempt man—even, perhaps, a dying man. But unless I missed my guess, this was not a broken man. For proof of this, I would have to wait. But not for long.

Master Lin spoke. He kept his sentences short and ended each phrase with a labored intake of breath. It was impossible not to feel his agony.

"Welcome to my home. For fifty-three years, I am the master. I have trained many in the ways of kung fu. My grandchildren were first. You, too, can be trained. Feng will be your teacher. We live here, my grandchildren and I. One's home is where all true struggle takes place. But, as Lao Tzu said, the student is greater than the master—this must be, or the world cannot be." This last statement had come out in a single effort, and Master Lin took several rasping breaths as he recovered. The hand he pressed against his abdomen went white from the pressure. "And so, as long as any student of mine is here, this also is his home. Feng will show you now the nature of kung fu. This is all I have to say."

The audience did not have time to react to this before the curtain at the back of the stage was opened fully, revealing a man dressed in black who stood on his head. To my amazement, his arms were stock-still at his sides, exactly as they would be were he standing upright at military attention. The man was simply inverted. I did not notice that his eyes were closed until, suddenly, they opened, and I saw at once that he was a heterochrome: his eyes were two different colors—one blue, the other such a dark brown that it appeared obsidian. A greenish bruise spread from his lip onto his cheek.

The man, whom I took to be Feng, remained this way for a while, his eyes scanning the audience. To his right, Master Lin had resumed the lotus position on his small rug. Feng, too, had a rug. It was off to one side. Apparently, he needed nothing between his head and the stage. It was only later that evening, when Monika and I were discussing the day's events, that she brought up a third rug that I had not noticed, and which lay empty to Master Lin's right.

With a sharp *crack*, Feng landed on his feet on the stage, dead center. Over the following weeks, Tomas, Monika, and I put forth many theories on how this was done. None of us believe any of them.

The grey-clad warriors flew at Feng, the six against the one. In whirling circles high and low they attacked, some with weapons, others wielding only hands and feet. Feng dodged most of the attacks and absorbed a few blows. These he followed up with counterattacks that sent his assailants across the stage, sometimes onto the floor, where the mesmerized children gaped at each other in awe and delight.

Just like in the movies, though, they attacked only one at a time. In real life, I always figured people would just gang up. But who was here for real life? Best-case scenario, Stanislav would get some exercise, maybe shed a little stubborn baby fat, improve his gross motor coordination. Nobody used martial arts in real life. *Except Butch, that day in the King's Corner Hotel*, I reminded myself, *when he apprehended the jewelry thieves.* Okay, there was that.

The deadly flails were out again, mad as bees, creating a steel net as they slowly approached Feng. He stood there, one eye a piece of coal and the other a patch of sky, calculating the motion.

I was squeezing Monika's hand. "How's he going to get out of this one?" I whispered.

She leaned in. Her hair caressed my cheek, and the aroma of lilacs slipped through the ambient stench of sweat. She cupped her hands around my ear and with a mouth full of breath she said, "My toenails match the color of my panties."

She was simply telling me what she thought of the demonstration, of course, but to hell with her, the swinging flails were close now, about six feet from where Feng stood, watching and calculating. With a howl, Feng leapt in the air, landing on his attacker from above. It was as if a small slice of time and space between Feng and where he needed to be had simply ceased to exist. His assailant got up, took his flails, and walked away.

This time there was no hesitation. The audience clapped wildly as Feng stalked the stage with the casual prowl of a tiger pacing back and forth in his cage, eyeing the crowd on the other side of the metal bars. The difference in this case being that there were no bars.

In literature, villains come in types. You have, for example, your Architect, pulling invisible strings, staying one step ahead of the outmaneuvered hero. You've got the Disturbed One, marching to the beat of a different drummer, and wouldn't you know it, that drummer's always one mother of a bastard. Then there's the Fallen Angel. He was a good guy, once. He wants you to know that. That was Before, of course. Before his privileged position at some government agency was revoked. Before the thing that happened to his kid happened, and the True Nature of the World was revealed to him. And now, all those government secrets are sure coming in handy.

As I sat there squeezing Monika's hand and watching the man who eyed us from his stage, I decided that if Feng were a villain in some novel, he would be the type who gets his very own John Williams theme music.

Now an instructor was wheeling a table onto the stage. On the table was a section of a brick wall and a small black velvet pouch. Feng walked up to the table and assumed a stance that made him look like he was riding a horse. He curled his hands into fists and rested them on his hips. Then he extended his left arm until the fist, now turned knuckles-up, just touched the wall of bricks. His right hand cocked backward a few inches. I heard him draw his breath in through his nose and exhale from his mouth. He did this twice. Then a third intake, very sharp, a loud *kee-yah!*, and his right hand smashed into the bricks, sending a chunk out the back side.

That job finished, Feng turned and faced the opposite side of the stage. There, another instructor held a brick in each of his upturned palms. Feng took the velvet pouch from the table and removed something from it. He held it up to the audience. A shimmer of light reflected off something thin, about two inches long.

"Is that some kind of a needle?" I asked Monika.

"Yeah," she said, "I think so."

Feng placed the needle between two of his fingers and aimed cross-stage. He threw it. If it hit the brick, I couldn't tell: it had disappeared. Unfazed, he produced a second needle from the pouch and repeated his throw. This needle, too, disappeared.

PAWN PROMOTION

BLACK TO MOVE AND DRAW | 235

He smiled the kind of smile you never want to see on the face of an enemy.

A few seconds later, both bricks turned to dust and crumbled to the floor. Again the room clapped, while a woman, the same one as before, appeared with a broom and dustpan and silently cleaned up the mess.

With that same smile that was more peril than pearl, Feng turned to the audience. "Thank you for coming, everyone! Our demonstration is almost concluded. But first—"

He reached for the velvet pouch and pulled out three more needles. These he placed between the fingers of his left hand. Then he turned to face the back of the stage, where his grandfather sat, and—

Ha! Ha! Ha! He hurled the needles at Master Lin.

The old man raised a hand, palm forward. When Feng was finished, Lin stood up, pulled the needles from the palm of his hand, and calmly returned them to Feng. It was as if all the pain had left his body. Master Lin walked off stage, ceding the crowd to his grandson.

The studio erupted in cheers. I turned to Monika. "That was incredible!"

"Forget Cirque du Soleil," she said. "I'll get you a magician for your next birthday."

"Oh, come on—" I started, but just then Master Feng held up a silencing hand. The noise in the room died.

"Thank you, everyone," he said, "for attending our demonstration of the ancient art of kung fu. Did you like what you saw?"

More cheers from the crowd.

"As my grandfather, the illustrious Master Lin, said, you too can be trained. You can all get your black sashes. Who here would like to earn a black sash?"

A peal of delight from the kids sitting on the mats.

"It will mean hard work. Dedication. Sweat! Blood! Exertion! Perseverance!"

("Money!" Monika whispered in my ear.)

But if Feng was anticipating another gleeful reaction, it was a mistake. I was quite sure, to tweak a phrase, that the kids didn't know half of those words half as well as their parents should like, and that they liked less than half of them half as well as they deserved.

Feng tried again. "But if you come, and you try, you can learn."

Continued stubborn silence from the crowd.

"Then you can get your black sash!"

The audience once again erupted with shouts and claps. Everything was back on track.

Feng pointed toward the reception desk. "Please, parents. Check out the various membership packages we are offering. Thank you!"

Mission accomplished, Feng had started to climb down from the stage when one of the instructors approached him and whispered something in his ear.

He listened for a few seconds, then hopped back on stage. "I am reminded to tell you, please do not try these things at home." He appeared to be finished, then had an afterthought. "When you get your black sash, *then* you do these things. Now go get your memberships, and I will see you in class!" He walked off toward the front desk, where a group of parents was already forming.

"Well, that was something," I said to Monika.

This time, I saw her eyes roll. "Oh, yeah, it was something, all right."

I shot a glance across Monika to see if Lisa had caught any of these comments. But she had left, presumably for the front desk. Good.

Turning back to Monika, I said, "Now what are you coming off all negative for? What if Lisa heard you talking like that?"

"She didn't."

"Fine. But what's with the attitude?"

Monika hoisted an eyebrow. "Really?" I was reminded of Spock, the chief science officer aboard the USS *Enterprise* (except that Spock probably never once said, "Really?"). She folded her arms and repeated, "Really? Needles and exploding bricks?"

If Monika was Spock, then I guess that made me Dr. McCoy. The one always ready to toss logic to the cosmic winds in order to embrace the fullness of human experience. The romantic. "Well, I don't know," I said. "Why *not* needles and exploding bricks? Why should everything have to make sense for you to enjoy it?"

It was like she read my mind. "I did make you promise to always be a romantic, I suppose." She looked over to the front desk, where Lisa was filling out a form. "It looks like we got what we needed."

"But you don't believe any of this," I said. "You think kung fu is fake."

"Oh, I don't have a problem with kung fu. Look how Butch handled those jewelry thieves."

"Exactly!" I said. "Nice to see you haven't forgotten."

"No," she said, "I just don't think that throwing a bunch of needles at bricks—probably fake bricks, I might add—has anything to *do* with kung fu. And that Feng person? What a hack! He obviously wants to yank cash from gullible parents who all want to believe their kids are the next Bruce Lee."

Ouch. I thought about Butch and the chess lessons he gave in the park. The parents all thinking, with a bunch of twenties thrown his way, that he could turn their budding prodigies into the next Bobby Fischer. Was what he did for a living any different than what Monika was accusing Feng of?

I didn't know, and at the moment I didn't care. I wasn't going to get any further on this subject anyway. There was, however, one thing Monika had said earlier that needed clarification.

I lowered my voice. "And what's all this about your toenails and your…" I hushed my voice further. "Your panties?"

Monika grinned. Any imagined resemblance to Spock followed the discarded logic of the good McCoy out to the cosmic winds, where together they would sail the fathomless seas of the universe. "That," she said, "was a statement of plain, simple fact." She stood needlessly on her tiptoes and planted a kiss. "Now how about you and I make ourselves useful and go hunt for a notebook?"

We made a circuit of the main room of the studio and found a total of two plexiglass trophy cases. Each was filled with pictures, sashes, plaques, and, of course, trophies. No notebooks.

"I think if it were in one of these, Shannon would already have it," I said.

"True," said Monika. "And I suppose you're wondering if that would mean *we* have it? Anyway, Shannon said something about a back hall."

I scanned the room for points of egress and spotted two curtained passages. One was behind the front desk. The other was in a corner of the room opposite the stage, where, I noted with a modicum of concern, the kids were now largely ignoring the postscript advice of Master Feng and throwing punches intended to just miss each other.

The curtain *not* behind the front desk seemed a good place to start. After all, there had to be bathrooms. Maybe this would lead to them, and maybe there would be a trophy case along the way.

I was just pushing back the curtain when someone put their hand on my shoulder. I turned to face one of the grey-clad warriors.

"I think you're going to want to come with me," he said. Before I had a chance to wonder, he pointed across the room to a commotion. It was centered around a kid who was kneeling on the ground, cradling a hand. "That boy belongs to you?"

Oh, God save the queen, it was Stan.

We crossed the room, and I pushed through a circle of boys who had gathered around him. Stan was sitting on the floor, being tended to by one of the instructors. The instructor was kneeling on the ground with his back to me. He held one of Stan's hands sandwiched between his own. The gesture nagged at my memory until I recalled how, eleven nights previous, on the floor of my office, Monika had held Butch's hand, blood all over her Prada gloves while my friend passed into unconsciousness.

At least Stan wasn't bleeding. In fact, I realized, he wasn't even actively crying (despite the fresh tear tracks down his cheeks). Those high-pitched, involuntary squeals I was hearing were more like giggles. The instructor was massaging Stan's hand, pushing here and pressing there, asking questions and giving instruction: "Does this hurt? How about now? Wiggle your pinky."

Stan noticed me. "Hi, Uncle Martin! I went on the stage and hit the brick wall. It's really hard!" (Stanislav is now admitted to Harvard, where he will be studying pre-law.)

Apparently satisfied with his examination of Stan's hand, the instructor turned around. His eyes—one black, the other blue—focused on me. He rose, towering over me by a head, and extended a hand. "Master Feng at your service." I introduced myself in turn, and we shook. "This boy is yours?"

I said he was.

"Nice kid." Feng tousled Stan's hair. "No broken bones, no cuts." He looked down at Stanislav, who was beaming at him. "How you doing there, little warrior?"

Stan went to give a thumbs up with his right hand, winced, and used his left instead.

Feng returned his gaze to me. "Take him to the doctor for x-rays, to make sure. But he's fine. I can look forward to teaching him in class?"

Stan answered for me. "Yay! Kung fu!"

Chapter 5

♞ e5 ♞
SPRING TRAINING. $200-A-DAY HABIT. A LITTLE HELP FROM MY FRIENDS.

By tradition, winter begins with the solstice on December 21 and ends three months later with the vernal equinox in March. In New York, we have our own ways of marking the passage of the seasons.

Winter in New York is your booted foot in a puddle of icy street water as you navigate an uncleared sidewalk. It's a commuter from Jersey City Heights pepper-spraying (why?) a group of misplaced German tourists who weren't smart enough to leave with the rest when the red and green lights went dark and the storefront decorations were put away, formally marking the end of the previous season. (The name of this previous season is Christmas, and it has nothing to do with winter or Jesus. It's short for "The Christmas Shopping Season"; it begins somewhere in September, and it ends whenever Macy's and Lord & Taylor say it ends.) Winter, as I was saying, is bundled up bodies and downturned faces. It's a PATH train delay due to a frozen track switch. It's getting up and going to work in the dark and coming home and going to bed in the dark, and if it weren't for the pizza, you may as well be eating and working and sleeping and fucking in Norway.

Now, spring is different, and although lines of demarcation rarely come painted in bright pastels, there are telltale signs. David Letterman once said that you know it's spring in New York when a dog-shaped rat emerges from the subway and sees its shadow. So, there's that. There's also the tourists. They can come out, now, and they do—along with the bikers and the daffodils. At the first hint of thaw, the young, sensing liberation, go around with too few clothes, while the wise retain their coats. Eventually, even the garbage collectors go shirtless, as each day that passes brings an additional slice of sun. Instances of pepper spray (why??) come fewer and further between, and trucks that once held their ground selling hot, sugared nuts are replaced with trucks that drive around with ice cream, playing tinny renditions of "The Wheels on the Bus" and "Turkey in the Straw" and generally sounding like something out of an old creep flick.

As the mood of the town brightens, little by little you feel more like a person and less like a person-sized rat in a concrete maze. You breathe in the regenerate air, and you know that spring has come to the city.

It was the last Thursday in April, and Stanislav had been one busy boy. Over the space of two months, he had learned several sequences of kung fu moves that he called *taolu*, or forms. (Lisa referred to them as "Slav's dance moves.") Damage to household items had been acceptably minimal. Tomorrow, Master Feng would preside over a ceremony that included a test of these forms. If Stan passed, he would earn a white sash.

A bunch of kids had signed up at the same time as Stan, and they were all getting tested at once. Shannon informed Monika and me that the ceremony would take a long time. (Meant as a simple matter-of-fact statement, this declaration created in me an omen of dread akin to what I'd felt during a recent visit to the Met, when Monika and I sat through the full six hours of *Götterdämmerung*. For a month afterward, I owed Monika favors. Happily, many of these favors were satisfied in the bedroom.)

More importantly, Shannon was certain that the testing and fanfare of the ceremony would occupy the complete attention of the instructors. The idea was for me to slip through a curtained passage (she described the one I had found during the exhibition; it indeed led to the bathrooms, as I suspected), go to the end of that hall, and find a certain trophy case. From this, I would retrieve the notebook.

A simple plan, really.

Stanislav was not the only one who had been busy over the past two months. While spring was hard at work tossing winter out on its meddlesome ass, most days, I was able to get to Washington Square for a game or two (or nine or ten) of chess with the Bishop of 4th Street. I'd fit them in here and there: between lectures, on break from grading sessions with Postdoc, at the ends of the slowly lengthening days. I'd take my lunch in the park. Some days I'd even get up for a game or two (or three or four) before work. After all, a single win was all I wanted. All I needed was the notebook the Bishop had promised me. Just one more game, that was all I needed. Just one.

But the games were all a bust. In fact, it sometimes seemed I was getting less of a high out of each one. And if I was surprised to find the

Chapter 5

Bishop sitting there every time like a mahogany god awaiting my supplications, with his greasy black beard and dilapidating chess clock, his pieces all set up and ready to go, always taking Black, always with his thick sunglasses looking like polished stone—a little math cleared up the mystery. At twenty bucks a game, I was single-handedly putting the man in an entirely new pay grade.

Despite my continuous contributions to the Bishop's coffers, I never saw the bottom of the cash jar in our kitchen. It was the Parable of the Talents from the Bible, in which a master gives money to his slaves, hoping they will multiply that money to the best of their abilities, rewarding those who succeeded with even more, and punishing the one who failed by taking away even what little he had. Except that in this topsy-turvy, socialistic version of the fable, the worse I (the slave) did, the more money Tomas (the master) would throw into the hole, sending good money chasing after bad, and always blessing the ritual refilling of the cash jar with a benediction: "You'll get him one of these times, M-doc!" "Keep on keeping on, M-doc!" "He can't win 'em all, M-doc!"

Nor was Tomas my only very present help in time of need. Monika tried her best to train me in the ways of chess mastery. Given the garbage moves that the Bishop would troll out at the beginning of every game (warding off any opening preparation on my part), memorization was off the menu. No, this was a deeper battle between me and my nemesis. This was a matter of tactics, positional understanding, and, in a great many cases, endgame technique under severe clock duress. Because three pawns and a bishop facing two pawns and a knight might be a lovely situation to savor when your legs are crossed and you're sipping a coffee as a timer harmlessly marks off the better part of a sedentary hour. But when you're perched on the edge of your bench and the twenty seconds you've got is ten less than your opponent's thirty, you're simply up a pawn and down a clock, and every tick is the sound of inevitability.

Shannon, too, lent a hand. She showed up at our place nearly every evening, that strange woman, insisting that I play chess with her. She was very intense as we played, asking questions about what I thought the Bishop would do against this or that move, running her hands through her hair, reciting a record of past moves that I had said the Bishop favored. Every so often, however, she would forget about the Bishop and allow what I felt was her true playing style to come through. Then, she was a trench warfare artist, favoring closed formations, tirelessly maneuvering her pieces behind castle walls, only to explode the position with some sudden sacrifice. Of all the games I played during those months, these were my favorites.

Through all of this, I didn't complain. I was addicted to chess, and Shannon was an easy fix. And I never pestered her with questions, regardless of my worry about Butch.

"Martin, don't press this," she had said. "If you go after Butch directly, you will get us all killed."

Of course the three of us did plenty of worrying in Shannon's absence as we did our best for the one person whose chess help I could have used the most and whom we all missed dearly. Tomas was able to convince Shannon to let him pay rent on Butch's apartment. He also kept in contact with Officer Schnapp, mostly in connection with her ongoing investigation into the possible drug trade in Washington Square, being careful not to "go after Butch directly."

We all kept an ear to the news, and none more than Monika, who combed the paper daily for any mention of Butch. Frequently, she would wonder out loud what the kidnappers could possibly want with him, and what the odds were they would simply off the man. At these times, I would point out that Shannon seemed quite confident that, at least for now, Butch was alive. I would remind Monika that Shannon endorsed a plan that would require two months to come to fruition, and that this would probably not be the course of action undertaken by someone who thought Butch's death was imminent. Shannon knew more than she was allowing herself to say—a fact which, in this case, paradoxically provided me a certain amount of comfort.

Statistically speaking, it was only a matter of time before I would take a game from the Bishop of 4th Street. Then, finally, we would have all the pieces to this puzzle. I had no idea what Shannon was going to do then. Neither did I have any idea what more I could be doing to hasten the coming of that day. But with a little help from my friends, I was going to try.

♗ f5 ♘
TAKE BOOK. ENTER HOLE. LIGHT TORCH.

It was pouring the next day when we cabbed into Harlem for Stanislav's white sash test. The wipers slapped away buckets of grey water as we drove. Monika gave our cabbie an extra-nice tip as we pulled up to Master Lin's.

This time, the whole family was here. Tomas and Lisa had saved the two of us a pair of seats next to them. Back row, perfect for slipping off on adventures. Where the makeshift stage had been during the exhibition, about twenty students sat on a polished hardwood floor. Dressed in white uniforms, they were taking last-minute direction from a grey-clad instructor. I spotted Stan, his face rapt with delight. Was it my imagination, or did the kid resemble the Pillsbury Doughboy ever so slightly less than he had two months previous? If Monika and I didn't end up with a notebook today, at least somebody was benefitting from the effort.

I leaned in toward Monika. "I guess I'll wait for the ceremony to start before I go notebook hunting. Do you see Master Lin anywhere?"

"No," she said, "but Feng just showed up." She pointed ahead and to our right, toward where the front desk sat, just inside the street entrance. Feng had emerged from the curtained doorway behind the desk. His large frame bent slightly as he walked, as if pushing through a hole he had found in the space immediately in front of him.

I scanned the room. "I'm going to want to see a total of six grey friends before I start poking around in places I'm not supposed to be." I counted three instructors in front with the students. Behind us and to the left, another one stood near the curtain that opened into the hall to the bathrooms. That hall was my objective. A fifth instructor was mingling with some parents near the storage racks. "I count five," I said.

Monika nodded her head. "Over there. One just came out behind Feng."

I looked over to spot Feng walking briskly toward where the students awaited their examinations. Behind Feng, the sixth instructor (a little shorter than the rest, with mousy eyes and a pointy chin) was scuttling along in the wake of his master. I remembered him from the exhibition—he was the one who had grabbed my shoulder and alerted me to Stan's hand injury.

Checking around the place one more time, I said to Monika, "Looks like we've got everybody accounted for but Lin."

Feng reached the front of the room. He raised a hand and the place fell silent. After a short speech praising the efforts of the students, he gave a nod. The twenty-some students and the six instructors all stood. They bowed to each other, bowed to the audience, and bowed to Feng. Then one of the six yelled, "Ha!" and the entire group began jogging in a rectangle around the testing area. The sash ceremony was begun.

After a few minutes of exercises and stretches, I whispered to Monika, "Maybe Lin's not here today?"

"Let's wait for warmups to be over," she said.

But the warmups were done, and one by one, the students began performing their *taolu*. Still no Master Lin.

"I'm not waiting anymore," I said. "I'm going."

Poor Monika. Her eyes were already glossing over with boredom. She said, "Sure you don't want company?"

I grinned. "Bored already, huh? Let's not attract attention. I won't be long. Down the hall, past the bathrooms, through a curtain into another hall, and there it'll be. Shannon made it sound quite simple."

Monika gave my hand a squeeze. "If you get in trouble, just say you're lost."

"Right." I gave her hand a squeeze back, got up, and left.

I was through the curtain. A narrow hallway led off to my right. Framed pictures of kung fu masters hung on the walls. Halfway down the hall, on the right, a pair of doors were labeled *M* and *W*. I checked the men's, hesitated, then did the same with the women's. Both rooms were empty. The hall ended fifteen feet farther along at another curtain. This curtain was threadbare and looked very old, with large Chinese characters running its length. Above it, black-on-gold letter stickers spelled out EMP OYE S ON Y.

I thought, *If I get caught, maybe I'll pretend I wasn't able to read that.* I heard nothing on the other side of the ratty curtain. With a single glance behind me, I walked through.

I was in a wide hall brightly lit by overhead fluorescent bays. Worn carpeting indicated living quarters. The muffled *kee-yah*s of students performing their *taolu* came through the near wall to my right. On the wall

Chapter 5

opposite me were three doors. Door number one was across from me and a little to the left; door number two was about ten feet to its right. Both were shut. From behind number two, a cheesy male TV voice was saying, "Like sands through the hourglass, so are the days of our lives." Farther down the hall, the third door appeared to be open a crack. Beyond this, at the hall's far end, was a metal railing.

To my left, the hall terminated at a window, where rain beat against the glass. Between this window and door number one stood a trophy case. I approached it.

The objects on these shelves were not meant for public display. The glass cabinet, meant to show off the achievements of students, was instead being used for storage. Binders, reference manuals, and loose scraps of paper were piled together and bookended with shoeboxes. Jars of paper clips and rubber bands were scattered about, as was the occasional framed picture. It was a clutterfest, and I wasn't prepared for it. I tried to remember: had Shannon said anything specific regarding *where* in this trophy-case-cum-office-supply-center I was supposed to find our missing notebook?

I didn't think she had. I thought to myself, *Maybe she doesn't know. Maybe she's just guessing. For all we know, the notebook is hidden somewhere on Staten Island or in a janitor's closet on the thirty-fifth floor of the Empire State Building. Maybe Butch hid it behind a toilet paper dispenser in a Port Authority men's room.*

From down the hall came the faint clatter of applause. Someone had just earned a white sash. I took a deep breath and tried again. Where in this mess would Butch hide something that he wished to be found?

I glanced again at those framed pictures. Most were of old men in garb I took to be martial arts uniforms, but one stood out: it was a boy and girl in their pre-adolescence, the boy perhaps twelve, the girl ten. They were posed for a professional family shot, the kind where you kneel in front of a backdrop the creamy blue color of childhood, and they tell you to say cheese, and you do it, just to get it over with. The girl, in square, black-framed glasses, resembled a Chinese version of Velma from Scooby-Doo, Hanna-Barbera's answer to Hercule Poirot. But the boy? He was no Fred. Not unless Fred had a brown eye and a blue eye. It was Feng, of course, gritting his teeth like he was about to shit a chopstick, and the girl would be his sister. Only a brother and sister could look so awkward together, only a parent would keep such a picture, and only a grandparent would frame it for display. Beneath the pic lay a spiral-bound notebook with a sketch of a pawn on the cover. I slid open the door to grab it, and that's when I spared another glance at that girl.

I had come so close to not recognizing her, and it took me a few moments to understand why: the girl in this photo did not look like she was ready to kill *anybody*. She didn't appear likely to be the type who would stare at cooking gear as if it were about to jump her. And she didn't look so desperate to intimidate someone that she would expose herself in front of them and dance half-naked with a sword. This girl, in other words, was happy. *We're going to help you, Shannon*, I thought. *Somehow, we're going to rescue Butch.*

Even as I thought these thoughts, however, I felt their inadequacy. I slid the notebook into my back pocket and shut the trophy case door.

Now, the commonsense thing to do at this point would have been to return the way I had come. But in the books and in the movies—take my word on this—*nothing you want ever comes from people following good sense.* I know, I know. You malign the protagonist who pursues the vampire down, into the cellar, alone and with naught to defend herself beyond the odor of garlic that lingers on her breath from that evening's repast, and for offense a mere single vial of holy water, secreted away from the rickety chapel that stands on the hill outside, sad and ineffectual against the darkness. "Fool!" you mentally cry from the comfort of your oversized theater seat. Your arm is wrapped around your date, and with your free hand you indulge yourself in popcorn. "Fool! Adorn thyself," you implore the heroine, "in an entire *garland* of garlic! Get thee to a Wal-Mart and purchase for thyself a Super Soaker! Fill it with an entire *baptistry* of the liquid stuff and be done once and for all with these cartoon evils that rely on the incompetence bestowed upon thee by the sadism of the screenwriters!"

Against which indictment I shall merely repeat: nothing you *truly* want, in a movie or a novel, ever comes from people following good sense.

Plus, Shannon had told me explicitly to waste no time getting back once I had the notebook. She didn't want me snooping around. Given this, what choice did I really have?

So instead of going back through the threadbare curtain to the main room, I walked the short distance to where the rain was pelting at the window. Outside, across a narrow back alley, I could see a mossy and windowless brick building that bordered a penned-in parking lot.

It was at this point that my cellphone bleeped.

A voice came from behind door number one, followed by the sound of a hand on the knob. I'd never make it back to the curtain in time. Opposite the trophy case was an archway. I slipped through into a large, dimly lit room.

It was an eat-in kitchen. To my right was a round table set for two. Yellowing appliances and dingy cabinetry lined the walls along the length of the room. A window above the sink allowed a grimy light to sneak in through the bars.

The center of the room had what I needed: a long, butcher-block island, above which dangled cooking utensils, pots, and pans. I scooted around the island, squatted, and crawled back toward the front. The island's feet allowed enough clearance that, if I lowered my head to the ground, I could see underneath through to the archway.

I was just in time to see her arrive, quiet as a cat. I thought I had accounted for everyone, but I had forgotten the diminutive woman who, during the exhibition, had slipped almost invisibly onto the stage to clean up the bits of brick and pieces of broken pine board. She walked into the kitchen far enough that I could see only the bottom half of her. Her hands went to her hips, and I imagined her head turning left and right while she scratched at her temple, wondering where that bleeping sound had come from. All I needed for things to really turn south was another text.

I felt in my pocket for the silencing switch on the side of my phone and flicked it. Then I held my breath for what felt like ten minutes, but which was probably more like ten seconds, until Ninja Cat Lady turned and left.

Putting the damn phone on Do Not Disturb, I read the offending text. It was from Tomas: *Hey, M-doc! How's the mission?*

Impossible, I thought, and rolled my eyes before proceeding to examine the kitchen more closely.

On the wall opposite the archway, I spotted a possible exit. It was a six-panel wooden door, its antique white paint crackled and peeling. The door was latched with an old-fashioned black brass rim lock set with a white porcelain knob. Reminding myself that Ninja Cat Lady was still out there prowling the hallways, I went to the door and slowly opened it.

Closing it behind me, I found myself at the foot of a twin bed. The room was illuminated by a curtained window. To my left, a pair of sliding doors suggested a clothes closet. A system of cubbies and shelves honeycombed the righthand wall and the portion of the wall above the head of the bed. Most of these shelves held paperbacks, but centered on the largest shelf, right over the pillow, was an empty katana stand. I paused, recalling once more the long, curved blade Shannon had wielded the night that Monika and I had watched her, slack-jawed, from the fire stairs outside Butch's bedroom window. If Shannon had brought that vicious instrument from this room to Butch's apartment, I hoped she had at least wrapped the thing up in a blanket before walking the streets of Harlem with it.

But *had* she brought it from here? Shannon, I now knew, was a granddaughter of Master Lin. She lived, or had lived, somewhere in this place. She would have had her own room. Could this be it?

I pulled back the lacy curtains that concealed the window above the side of the bed. Like many first-floor windows in Harlem (although the grade of the underlying block elevated this room to almost second-floor level), it was barred. I looked out onto a side alley through the rain-streaked glass. At the base of the neighboring building, I could see a pair of metal cellar doors. Craning my neck to the left, I looked down the length of the alley to where moving cars indicated the street. To the right, another set of black metal bars, barely in view, hinted at a nearby window in that direction.

I was at the bookshelves, preparing to peruse the paperbacks, when I thought I heard a series of distant, rhythmic grunts. The muted noises seemed to be coming from the other side of the shelves. Before I could explore, I heard something much more alarming. Out in the kitchen, Ninja Cat Lady had apparently returned, and this time with help. A male voice and female voice were exchanging words in a language I presumed to be either Mandarin or Cantonese. The woman sounded earnest; the man, confident and self-assured. I didn't need to know Chinese to imagine the gist of their conversation:

But something *must have made the noise!*
You checked all the other rooms?
Yes. But I was scared to look too closely.
If there is something to find, I will find it. But you will see that there is nothing, silly woman.

Chapter 5

Or maybe they were discussing cheese. Either way, I was in trouble. Once again, I needed an exit, and once again, I was given only one option. I slid open the closet door, stepped inside (pushing aside some hanging pants and blouses), and slid the door shut—just in time to hear them enter. This time, the imagined conversation was blessedly short:

See? There is nothing here. You are a silly woman who hears things.
Fuck you and the horse you rode in on.

They left. I exhaled. At least I had learned something: this was definitely Shannon's room. The clothes here were thoroughly her—scratchy, ripped woolen pants and silky button-ups that had seen better days. The smell, too—mothballs and old jasmine—was undoubtedly *eau de Shannon*.

I gave it a few minutes and decided it was time to leave. As I shifted my weight to get purchase on the sliding door, I felt a floorboard wiggle. I knelt down and explored in the relative dark with my hands. Beneath a pile of shoes, I discovered a removable panel. I pulled it aside, uncovering an opening in the floor about two-foot square. Dank air wafted from the blackness below. I got out my cell phone and turned on the flashlight. (*Torch*, if you don't mind getting British about it.) The light revealed a drop of about eight feet to a cement floor.

Did I really want to do this? If I got caught, I was well past the point where I could blame it on getting lost on the way to the bathroom. But then, this was a basement—not a one-way entrance to some great underground empire. There would be a way out that avoided being eaten by a grue. I opened the compass app on my phone and pushed the phone into my pocket. Then, lowering myself into the opening and doing my best to maneuver the trap door panel over the open square that soon loomed above me, I let go and dropped the remaining two or three inches to the ground.

I was in a large basement, unlit and musty. A long plastic pole leaned against the north wall, looking deliberate and out of place. Above me, out of reach, was the half-covered square hole through which I had dropped. Using the pole, I jiggled the panel back in place until the upper world was gone. Then I returned the pole and had a look around.

My torch cast a pallid glow on the cinder-block walls. To the east, a boiler lay dormant in a corner. A mazework of dull copper pipes and valves connected the boiler to the rooms above. Running my torch along the wall to the south, I was startled by a pair of reflective white circles that resembled monstrous eyes. I soon descried the shape of a forklift hunkering behind and realized that I was seeing its headlights.

To the west, numerous plywood warehouse crates, all alike, occupied the bulk of the room. The labels were mostly in Chinese characters with a smattering of English letters and numbers and revealed nothing of the crates' contents. Wandering among the crates, I came upon one with its lid askew, a crowbar up against the side. A glance inside revealed thick plastic sheeting. Pulling this back, I discovered dozens of fabric bolts wrapped tightly into long cylinders.

Continuing in the same direction, I maneuvered around the crates until I arrived at the west wall. Here, a rickety workbench appeared to have recently been used for a craft project. A fine-pointed knife, a bottle of glue, and a small unlit desk lamp sat on the bench in front of a low-backed stool. The workbench abutted a pegboard wall, from which depended an assortment of hand tools. Curiously, a whiteboard displayed the names of various chess openings: *King's Gambit, Queen's Gambit, Center Game, Smith-Morra Gambit, Wing Gambit,* and *Coca-Cola Gambit* were written in a single column in red felt-tip pen. All the names except the bottom one, *Coca-Cola Gambit*, had been struck through. I searched the area for signs of a chess game but found nothing, and I resumed my exploration of the basement.

To the right of the workbench, a wide metal double door in the north wall looked foreboding and locked. On the opposite side, a narrow door in the south wall had slats for ventilation. Choosing the friendlier-looking option, I opened the south door. Behind it, cement steps led back up to an indoor light.

As if in reaction to this discovery, a thud came from the ceiling, sounding remarkably like someone landing on his ass in the studio above. I thought of Stanislav and wondered if he was performing his *taolu*.

I climbed the cement steps. At the top of the stairway I came to the metal railing I had seen earlier from the opposite end of the residential hall in which I now stood. I had returned to the hallway, but from the other side. At the hall's far end, I could see the window that faced the back alley. To my left and very close, a curtained entranceway stood half-open behind the front desk. It looked out toward the seated rows of parents and spectators. I couldn't risk walking past that opening. The way forward was barred.

I was preparing to return quietly back down the stairs when I happened to notice door number three—the one that, from the other end of the hall, I had been able to tell stood slightly ajar. I investigated. Behind the door was an office. Perched atop a metal filing cabinet, a black and white TV monitor displayed a rotating series of camera images being taken from around the premises. I watched in dread as various areas I had recently traversed flipped past one another on the screen: the main room (proud, clapping parents), the bathroom hall, the hall that I was currently standing in, the door between the kitchen and Shannon's room. Also, several perfectly black screens that I guessed covered the basement. If this was so, they would recently have shown me walking around, holding up my cell phone. Terrific. I could only hope that Ninja Cat Lady had given up the chase—and that no one would curl up with a bucket of popcorn later and decide to view the recorded security footage. But who watches security footage on days when, seemingly, nothing has happened? I decided there was little to be concerned about.

I retreated to the basement, and it was then, for the first time since snooping around, that I got a little scared. I wondered what had taken so long. Shannon clearly felt anxiety about this place, and here I was, hiding behind kitchen fixtures and jumping down dark holes in the floor. In desperate need of a way out, I crossed the room to the metal double doors, expecting to find the keyed silver knob unyielding. Instead, the door swung open to reveal a dark passageway.

I whispered an adage of my grandfather's—*in for a copper, in for a pound*—as I took a step into the passageway… and let the door click shut behind me. Not my best move of the day. Too late, I turned around. If the door had looked locked before, it now resembled something you'd find in a bank. Or maybe a prison.

Above the knob (now quite *definitely* locked, thank you *very* much, lords and ladies) was a bright, shiny numbered keypad. It was at this moment that I began serious consideration of that skittish little bitch demon named Panic. She had, until recently, been content to pace about the lower circles of my consciousness. But the dodgy imp had spotted me, and she was crawling up the ranks. Fast. Any second now I would taste her sulfurous breath as it coated the inside of my mouth and feel the shattered nails of her fingers grip cold and tight around my heart.

But not quite yet. There was still the passage ahead. If that ended in a brick wall or an uncrossable bottomless black chasm in the dirt floor, then—I told myself—*then* would be the perfect time for a rendezvous with Madame Bitch Demon.

I took another look at that dirt floor. In the amber circle of light cast from my torch, I could see where tire tracks had formed ruts running lengthwise along the passage. Doubling back the way I came, I saw that the tracks disappeared under the double doors. I recalled the forklift. Okay—the forklift took the crates of fabric down this passage into Master Lin's basement. But the meaning of it? I tried to picture Feng sewing homemade kung fu uniforms for his students. The imagery wasn't working.

I turned back to find the other end of the tunnel. If there were doors at the other end and they were similarly equipped with a numbered keypad, I would be trapped, and good.

But when I came to the end of the tunnel, I discovered that the doors there had no keypad on either side. Apparently, somebody wanted to restrict access *into* Lin's basement, with no precaution against leaving. I took a deep breath and felt the bitch demon heave a sigh of bitter disappointment.

So there I was in another basement. Equally unlit, equally musty. To my right, occupying the bulk of the floor, were dozens more warehouse crates, presumably loaded with linens. From beyond them I could hear a steady rumbling, as of rubber mallets drumming on metal. Ahead of me, a wooden staircase led up to a closed, white door.

At this point, having dodged panic and wandered so many forbidden paths that an inordinate sense of invincibility had deadened my normal misgivings around such basic misdemeanors as trespass, I yet exercised sufficient caution that, when I climbed the stairs and slowly cracked open the door, I can at least say that I did so as quietly as possible.

I found myself at one end of a small laundry room. Several washing machines and dryers were here, all of them running. Beyond them, I could peer through an open doorway into a much larger room, where several Asian women sat hunched over tables. Some were operating sewing machines; others sewed by hand. Apparently, the building across the alleyway from Master Lin's studio was a tailor shop, and the tunnel I had just walked through connected them.

I was considering what would happen if I simply excused my way across the store and out the door to the street when someone called out, "Xiang!"

Chapter 5

A woman whose back was to me looked in the direction of the summons. It was Shannon. Later, Monika and I would theorize about the significance of Shannon's working next door to the studio, in view of the connecting tunnel and the one-way lock that appeared to be newly installed. But honestly, my first thought at that moment was how strange it was that a seamstress should always be wearing such ratty pants.

I didn't want Shannon to know I had done anything beyond simply retrieve the notebook from the case, as instructed. So, it was back to the basement. I sought out the drumming noise I'd heard earlier. It came from a pair of nearly horizontal metal cellar doors that lay closed above a short set of concrete steps. The doors were secured by a wooden two-by-four that ran through both inside handles. Anticipating the deluge, I took Butch's pawn notebook from my back pocket and tucked it under my shirt. Then, with the full realization that there would be no way for me to cover my tracks, I slid the two-by-four out of the handles, set it on the floor, and opened the cellar doors to what little light remained of the day—and to the onslaught of the rain.

I exited the cellar. Immediately soaked, I nonetheless stood for a moment, studying the lay of the land. Directly in front of me and up almost a full story were two barred windows. Not much building existed to the left of these before the corner of the side and back alleys. I recalled looking out of the window in Shannon's room and seeing the cellar doors from which I had just emerged. There had also, I remembered, been a set of bars to my right, indicating a second window. Looking at them from the other side, then, the right-hand window belonged to Shannon's room. I was trying to work out where the left-hand window must lay relative to where I had been when someone appeared behind the murky glass. Mindful that Ninja Cat Lady might still be prowling about, seeking the source of the sound she'd heard, I shrouded my face with my hand and ran down the alley toward the street, around the corner, and in through Master Lin's front door, probably looking like a lunatic who had just crawled out of the East River.

At first, I foolishly imagined the applause that erupted upon my entrance was for me. But of course it was for some kid who had just completed his *taolu*. As discreetly as one can while dripping water with each step, I walked to the back row and sat down next to Monika. My butt made a squelching noise as it hit the black vinyl seat of the folding chair. I pulled the pawn notebook out from under my shirt.

"Hey," I whispered to Monika, "look what I—"

But there was no point in finishing. Monika was sitting with her head tilted ever so slightly back. Her eyes were lightly shut, and she was snoring.

I looked past her to Tomas. "How did Stanislav do? Did he go yet?"

"He did great," said Tomas. Then, noticing my notebook, he pointed to it. "Hey! Nice work." As if all of this were the most natural thing in the world, he reached across Monika and slapped me on my shoulder with a wet *thwock* that sent vagrant droplets of water onto her face. She was so out, she didn't budge, even when Lisa took out a handkerchief to wipe her off.

If I had been afraid of my excursion taking too long, I needn't have worried: the ceremony dragged on for another two hours. During this time, Monika slept while I once more immersed myself in the world of Butch's chess adventures and his encounters with the wide assortment of people who visit his table at Washington Square Park.

♘ g5 ♘
THE PAWN NOTEBOOK

Pawn

Outside passer, run.
Resurrection on the eighth:
Philidor's soul reborn.

Chapter 5

Swindle #31—Candidate moves

White: Me
Black: The Advocate
Date: February 9, 2010

My discourse with the towering man with the power tie and steel wool hair flowed naturally into such topics as chess in schools, affordable housing, and the prospect of raising the minimum wage to fifteen dollars an hour. It was clear that I was facing a deft politician. I approved of his views and guessed at an Italian heritage, which hypothesis was corroborated when he produced a slice of pizza from his lunch box but challenged when he began to eat it with a fork and knife.

In what was to be our last game—and yet at a time that I foresaw to be only the beginning of the man's presence in the public eye—I was losing badly. If only there were some way to snooker the man into something nefarious…

White to move

Can you find Butch's swindle?

Swindle #32—The scariest game

White: Skinhead
Black: Me
Date: January 13, 2010

I cannot be certain, but I believe several of the tattoos on the man's skin represented crimes against our species. Here in the park we serve all races, colors, creeds, and orientations. I do not fear those who would attempt to intimidate his fellow man. One must first be psychologically derailed before one can be physically dominated. And quite apart from my excellently honed kung fu skills, which would protect me in any event, I do not derail.

But this man? This man frightened me. Do not misunderstand: I did not fear for my life. From out of the bag pieces come and are developed. They play their role in the game; they are returned to the bag whence they came. Eternal recurrence.

I was not therefore scared for my life, but for the very course of life's game—beginning with the unsoundly developed piece who sat miserably at my table as the dying day cast a pall over his glistening scalp, his tattoos twitching with the movements of his bare arms. Perhaps accosted by the symbols of violence adorning my opponent's skin (that pore-ridden border between a man and his physical environment by which we deign speak of a "body"), I found myself in the jam you see below.

Black to move

Can you spot a ray of hope in Butch's desolate position?

Black to Move and Draw | 257

CHAPTER 5

Swindle #33—My craft and art

White: Mr. Negative
Black: Me
Date: February 1, 2010

Chess can be a sullen art.[17] By a long ago choice did I eschew the tournament halls' ivory stages in favor of the park, where my charms mingle among the strut and trade of the common man and my winter wages come oft in the still night, beneath the moon's silent rages. But the secret heart of the nightingale path is grieved by those towering proud who regret my wages and pay no heed to my craft.[18]

Such a one was my present client: a man of negative energy, whom I am not inclined to otherwise describe. I am afraid Master Lin would not be pleased with me—I had allowed my opponent's negative energy to diffuse my focus. All chances for a win were kaput. A perpetual check seemed my only hope of avoiding a loss. But then I saw another.

Black to move

Oh dear! Butch has been put into quite a temper. Can you discover the swindle by which he tried to stave off his demise and return to sunnier psychological climes?

---

17 Homage to Dylan Thomas, perhaps? I am intrigued.

18 Yes, definitely Dylan Thomas. I have often contemplated the hardship of Butch's chosen lifestyle. Hustling chess is not a profession for one who requires public praise or recognition. It seems that Butch has found in Thomas a poem that echoes some of his angst.

Swindle #34—The proper use of wealth

White: Rich Uncle Pennybags
Black: Me
Date: January 18, 2010

"I like a little competition," the portly man said in his portly-man voice. He stood very close, as one does who conspires, extending a black-gloved hand for me to shake, then sliding it under his double-breasted overcoat to produce a money clip: a thick, golden X that folded perhaps thousands of dollars into a tight, green wad. "Do you like competition, Mister…?"

I reclined against my bench, folding my hands behind my head. "They call me Butch, and I play for ten thousand dollars a game." I took a slow drag on my Swisher Sweet and let the blue smoke drizzle from my lips into the cold morning air.

The man, who had begun to sit, stopped halfway down, his richly trousered ass hovering inches above the wood. Unblinkingly he stared at me; the frosty puff of breath that covered the pink O of his mouth seemed frozen in time and space.

I shrugged my shoulders. "Or we could just play for five bucks."

My joke had run its course, and the invisible clock that marks the time remaining to the world resumed. With a barely audible thump, the man sat down. His blue eyes reflected a stray sunbeam, and we shared a warm laugh.

People will say that a rich man can't know who his friends are. They'll say his friends are leeches, that they're only around for the money. But if a witty man were to curtail his jest, or a friend with a mutual interest were to suddenly abandon that interest, what would anyone have to say to that? Make friends with dishonest wealth. I believe it was the Christ who said that.

The rich man and I played twenty games, after which one of those tightly clipped hundred-dollar bills slid across the table in my direction. I had to slide a fiver back for change, though, because our last game had ended in a draw. Indeed, I was lucky not to have lost it.

Chapter 5

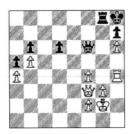

Black to move

Butch almost lost this game. How did he trick Rich Uncle Pennybags and escape with a draw?

Swindle #35—One for the birds

White: Tuppens
Black: Me
Date: February 4, 2010

Where Master Lin has taught me the art of war, it is Tuppens who shows me the art of peace. We were playing pensively, without a clock; me talking, her breaking off small pieces of Wonder bread, tossing them onto the frozen ground. Feeding the pigeons. Light from an overhead lamp cut through the mist, casting a gauzy veil around the place where we sat. Under it, her brown skin, creased and thin, appeared nearly translucent. Plastic, like old 35mm film.

"My child, you seem distressed."

I looked around. Off toward the fountain, a pair of cops kept each other company. At our feet, the pigeons feasted. We were alone. I told her what I was up to. For a while, she let me go on. Then, getting rid of the last of the bread along with the last of my threats to her kingside, she fianchettoed her king's bishop and looked at me through rheumy eyes that held light, but almost no color. "I think you might find, when all this is done, that maybe it's not."

"What do you mean?" I centralized my knight to d4.

A few minutes passed before she spoke again. As she often does when deep in thought, she softly half-sung, half-hummed a tune. Finally she chased my knight away with a cool pawn to c3. "I understand why this mess bothers you, Butch. You thinkin' it's the crime."

Scratch. A flame from my match lit my Swisher Sweet, briefly comforting my face against the pressing cold. "I do," I said, puffing my cigar to life. My matchbook was down to its last strike; I dropped it into my duffel. It was time to finish things. I slid a rook onto the open e-file, seeking to invade.

"Well, maybe it is." She went to move her king, thought again, and checked me with her queen instead. On her left ring finger was the flat band of silver that is her solitary adornment. Four decades ago, when she first taught me chess, that ring bore three words: INQUIRY—ASTONISHMENT—LOVE.

Time has dulled things. These days I give her rook odds, just to keep things interesting. The king move would have been better.

She continued. "But there's the journey, Butch, and there's the journey back." She pulled another loaf of Wonder Bread from the huge denim bag that she rolls everywhere on her squeaky Duane Reade grocery cart. "This time, you got yourself involved with the pieces. This time, you gonna have to think past the checkmate to the pieces that got took along the way."

Everything she's got in the world is in that bag. Yet somehow, the birds always get fed.

She got me into a fork with her bishop, and after a few moves my position sank into trouble. I went into a deep think. As has happened so many times over these past several weeks, I spotted a trick I could play that, if she succumbed to it, would pull off a dirty draw.

I think she saw it and just walked into it anyhow.

Master Lin would never have approved.

Black to move

Poor Butch! He seems distressed. Can you find a swindle that would at least get him out of his chess troubles?

Swindle #36—End-times prediction

White: Second Coming
Black: Me
Date: February 8, 2010

"Lord, save me from your followers." It was something my grandmother used to say.

Apparently, the world had once again been scheduled for immolation, and once again the Almighty had missed his deadline. Not to worry. While Rochambeau, Cue Ball, Mongoose, and the rest of us welcomed the raincheck and patiently awaited Armageddon's recalculation from the Scriptures, there were a few end-timers hanging around who had decided that New York was the room to be in when it happened. Some of them, it turned out, played chess.

By a kind of miracle gone wrong, I found myself on the losing end of the tribulation pictured below. As you see, I was down the exchange. Rather than do something about White's center pawns (and what, pray tell, was there to do?), I decided to make a feint, betting that my fanatical friend would misread the signs and capture something untoward.

Happily, this was one prediction that came true.

Black to move

How did Butch, playing Black, tempt his opponent beyond what he could bear?

CHAPTER 5

Swindle #37—Turning the tables

White: Me
Black: Wizard Beard
Date: December 15, 2009

Nothing undermines one's chess quite as insidiously as overconfidence. Consider the behavior of the man in the long, silvery beard. The wizened old man sat down opposite me and without any apparent concern for my own moves shot out... e6,... c6,... Qb6. By his third move I had him for one strange fish.

I went all out on the attack. But somehow, even though everything had felt right, I found myself with a compromised castled position. Worse, my own attack against the enemy king's fortress had petered out after a bad piece sac. I saw now that if I tried to recoup my piece with gxf3, it would be mate on g2.

My confidence was shattered. I stole a glance at my opponent. With a hand that was nothing but scabs and chipped fingernails, he was looping his beard up into his face, gently sucking on its silvery hairs. How was it that I was losing to this? I decided to turn the tables and encourage the wizard's own overconfidence. So I invited him farther into my king's house. As soon as he touched his queen, I knew I had saved my game.

White to move

Butch's king is in trouble. Yet, he saves his game by further compromising his safety. How?

Swindle #38—When the rook is on the seventh rank, and check aligns with pawns

White: Throwback
Black: Me
Date: January 20, 2010

The long-haired cliché in the Grateful Dead T-shirt and tie-dyed bandana had been throwing my pieces out of harmony the whole game. I saw one last chance to avoid a loss, but it would require my granola-oriented opponent to take the bait.

Black to move

Is Butch having visions, or can you find a way to trick White into aligning the pieces just right so that Black can salvage a draw?

CHAPTER 5

Swindle #39—These aren't the draws you're looking for

White: Jedi Knight?
Black: Me
Date: January 27, 2010

Every time I see this young man strolling the park he's wearing some different piece of *Star Wars* attire: a coat that's all white-and-blue panels, making him look like R2-D2; a woolen cap that pulls down over his head like a Stormtrooper helmet; even a pair of pants matted with thick, brown hair that turns the fellow into Chewbacca. Today, it was a black sweatshirt with buttons all over it like Darth Vader.

The Force must really have been with my opponent, because my game was in big trouble. Maybe I could pull off a little Jedi mind trick?

White to move

Butch needs help. Can you find a way to "force" the draw?

Swindle #40—An imperfect storm

White: The Greatest Generation
Black: Me
Date: February 9, 2010

"Mind if I have a seat?"

His clothing, like the grizzled old man who wore it, appeared battle worn and designed for rough service. Soon I had the old general pegged: he was a trench-warfare artist. A soldier who knew how to sit out a storm.

Indeed, my storm was all but spent. Had it not been for the general's too-rapid acceptance of one of my foot soldiers, I would've been a casualty.

Black to move

How did Butch, playing Black, swindle the old war dog into a draw?

CHAPTER 5

♞ h5 ♟
BLACK COFFEE

For Dr. Martin Malloy, professor of literature, the trip began like this.

I.
"Tell me more"—You regard me
with unhurried eyes, cast from time
to time over your shoulder, as you go about
my kitchen, serving me coffee, listening as I
tell you about the mission—how it went,
the parts I am willing you should hear.
For the first time, this is nice between us;
you don't want to be fighting with something
like this. It should be easy. I do not even mind
how you showed up on our doorstep, minutes
on our heels—damp ratty pants, one wet shoe
dumped over the other on our welcome mat;
me, wriggling into a dry sweater, a towel draped
over my shoulders; my girlfriend already in the shower,
singing about rain and the saccharine mysteries
of love. I do not mind as you poke among my pantry
shelves for the sugar, your back to me,
not that I wanted any of it:
the sugar, your back, your designs.

II.
"You must understand"—You speak to me

of your contempt for the city, and I remember
your room: how black were the iron bars
that lined up outside your one window, how black
the heavy ancient lock outside your door, the hole
in your floor—and I do not mind. Nor do you mind
as I reveal to you, unwittingly, unguardedly,
(it is taking hold now in my brain, I am slipping)
these recollections; my knowledge of your world.
You describe to me your perfect world, and it sounds
(*like Margaret-on-the-Sea*)
like the side of a box of tea from Celestial Seasonings.
You tell me all these things, and though the coffee
is somewhat bitter, still, none of these things do I mind.

III.
"How do you feel?"—You sit across from me
now, eyes searching, no longer patient.
It is happening: I sense, I recall, I infer;
I know that which cannot be easily known.
In my bathroom, the singing stops, and I smell
the conflicting fragrances; Monika has run out
of shampoo and has opened a bottle of a different
brand. In our bed tonight, her hair will be a craze.
From the whiteboard that hangs in your brother's lair,
I recall the name of every chess opening written there
in red—and I know now the code that will unlock
the keypad door. The dampness of your slacks?
It is not severe enough for you to have walked

all the way from the subway; no, you took a bus,
and as you emerged, you stepped off with your right
foot—for the one shoe is wetter than the other, and
when you walk you always begin with your left
(I have noticed this about you), and so it is
that the odd number of steps on that bus will have you
planting your right foot down into a puddle in the street.

IV.
"Are you ready to play the Bishop now?"—You ask me
so nicely. So sweetly. Without needing to, I go
to the pantry, to the shelf where you poked around
for the sugar I did not want. A scarlet box, open
as a raided tomb: the Salvatore Ferragamo shrine lies
adrift, and next to it the Black King, looming large
beside a baggie that moments ago held crystals
of White Knight, and that I already know
will be empty.

Yes. The answer to your question is

	W		H				
I	T			E			
K							
						N	I
						G	
		H					T

Chapter 6
WHITE KNIGHT

yes.

Yes, I am.

♝ a6 ♞
THE GLOWING EDGES

THE FOCUS WAS good and all, right away after three, maybe four sips of the bitter excuse of a coffee Shannon had given me, but it was on 5th Avenue, down four-sevenths of the way from 69th to 68th, which is to say approximately 514 feet down the block, stuck in gridlock, when the stuff really kicked into gear and all of a sudden I truly started to see the chess application—the whole point, you might say; it's all about seeing the variations, the possibilities inherent in the position—any situation, in fact—like the situation with the genius standing with the *Times* over his head, Arts section damp and dripping (the rain having slowed a bit from a rate of one, maybe one and a half inches per hour to at most one-sixteenth of an inch per hour; you could call it a drizzle and I wouldn't argue the point) but the genius had the Arts section over his head, and instead of holding it perpendicular to the direction of the precipitation, he had it angled obtusely away from his forehead, his worry lines creased up like a washboard so that I took him for a stockbroker, so that the thing (the paper, I mean, not the forehead) was basically useless, and *this* was the moment my cabbie chose to start getting downright hostile to my suggestions for speeding up the trip to Washington Square, as if shifting lanes a few more times was a (metaphorical) bridge too far for a Manhattan cabbie (since otherwise bridges are generally not an issue), and I had taken the time to look out the window and start in on the crossword puzzle (some of the clues were particularly knavish) when I got distracted by an article (I had to fill in some of the words) about the upcoming premiere of Rossini's *Armida* at the Met—which performance, I surmised, given history, I should *not* attend with Monika—and I had just started in on the next article on the back of the Financial section that he (the stockbroker, not Rossini) was holding upright in his right hand (they were predicting the Fed would hold the rates steady—an obviously myopic conclusion given what was happening in commodities futures the next column over), and it's *then* that the broker fellow sees me reading his paper, and like I should apologize, he shot me a dirty look. But the chess! How could I have been so careless? I saw everything, now—how, every time the Bishop played Owen's Defense, I'd been allowing a critical weakening of the h1-a8 diagonal; how every time I started in against his kingside castle position I let him trade off to a place where his knight could maneuver around my bishop, hemmed in on one color square or another; how I'd been too aggressive in the opening against Hedgehog structures and not aggressive enough when all I needed to do was create either a passer that would tie down his knight or a chain of levers that would allow an active king to infiltrate the center; and it was then that I realized I never even took cash out of the cash jar and how little that was going to matter, because everything there was to see, *I saw*. I saw it all, broken down in front of me: nature—no, *not* nature, but rather the contents of my own mind, usually inaccessible even to myself, now laid bare and pieced together like a jigsaw puzzle with all the matching edges glowing in color, describing to me the interconnectedness of all things. Not that this had stopped me from knocking over the hat stand on my way out the hall door, Shannon laughing, but honestly, gross motor skills were not in play at that particular juncture, and she bloody well knew it.

So, fuck her.

Now as I said, all of this heightened concentration was good and all, but the business with the edges and suddenly stressing over the hat stand, or me not knowing whether to hit Shannon or kiss her for lending my brain the extra CPU cycles, was only going to result in a bunch of constantly shifting gears in my brain when I played the Bishop, which, given the breaking of the gridlock and the number of traffic lights between my current position and the Square and given the statistical likelihood of hitting each one red or green, I calculated would be within eighteen to twenty-two minutes—and none of the aforementioned concentration was going to come to fruition if it (my mind, not the cab) operated according to a will of its own, focusing on whatever tidbit satisfied its caprice at any given moment. No. I had to be able to harness my mental kinetic energy on a single point—a singularity, if you will—so I shut my eyes, recalled the crossword in the stockbroker's newspaper, every last Across and Down, and finished the puzzle just as the cabbie pulled up to Washington Square, thereby *proving* that the outcome of the upcoming game was a matter of non-deterministic certitude, and that in fifteen minutes I would have the final missing notebook in my hands… and *there you were*, sitting in your forever place, not minding the drippings of the day, as if you, too, knew the hour of my coming, and that here, in the fullness of time, you and I would simply *play*; and if our

♘ b6 ♞
SWAN SONG

game felt a little like screwing with each other's heads, well, don't look at me through those thick black plastic lenses of yours as if you thought I didn't know that when two people do these things to each other over and over again so many times it almost becomes a theory unto itself, or why it was that I fought, or that home is anything other than where the struggle is. I began with e4, and

You answered with c5, and right away

the game was different. As you transposed

from a Najdorf to a Schveningen, I knew

two things: (1) that in order to know the rules,

it sometimes helps to first break them;

Chapter 6

and (2) that since when do *you* employ *theory*?
Since when do you so casually transpose
from one ECO code to the next? What gives
you the unexpected right?

To turn the tables, to move into murky waters—
this was my aim. A database in my head churned,
coming up with an alternative to throw you
from your charted course. On e4, I sacrificed
a pawn; on e6, a knight. These pieces I offered you,
initiating a countdown that would resolve when you
either: (1) decided to accept my final sacrifice—
my rook on f1 for your knight that, in six moves,
I foresaw would invade on g3; or (2) declined.

Move after move you surprised and delighted me.
We were two "boys in the engine room," pumping,
pumping (John Lilly, *The Center of the Cyclone:
An Autobiography of Inner Space*, Julian Press, 1972),
secreting calculation "like the liver secretes bile"
(Pierre Cabanis, unknown reference—a leftover
from high school biology, lodged in my brain
one thought to the right of pi and two to the left
of Jenny Clayton's phone number).

And when the time came, how then?
Did you accept my saucy sacrifice, plunging
us into variations beyond count? No—

you blinked, and we hurtled toward an insipid
denouement, an ending that would leave you
without resource on a formless and empty board.
For formality's sake, I checked: one minute
seven seconds left to me, forty seconds for you.
I was up two pawns and you were down a clock.

Calmly (for it could almost be said I was bored),
I swapped our queens, then the last pair of bishops.
Mechanically (for what was left but unthinking
technique?), I picked off the pawns left weakened
by your inaccurate defense. Small moves—these
were what had been lacking from my chess.
Prophylactic maneuverings. I could have been
asleep. The game was over; you just hadn't seen it.
Or maybe you did, for

    the Bishop of 4th Street looked up from his board, hands spread, and I knew it: something was wrong. And still for the time being I sat there, perceiving a future self lecturing my present self: *things could yet take a turn; you could let the game play itself out.* But the truth was it was with a loathsome sort of innocence that the Bishop shrugged and said in his baritone voice, insouciant and rich, I don't have it anymore. I really don't, Martin. I mean, I *had* it, I *did* have it, I won't lie, but I gave it to her, and by the time I had said, To whom? I was already standing, because all of this was happening fast, too fast, and I repeated—loudly now, my body taut, like a chain pulled by gears across the marble chess table, *Goddammit, to whom?* and then I was having a go at him, shaking him, once for his bad chess, twice for his pointless blather. (*Her?* He had given the notebook to *her?* Could he mean Shannon? So help me gods, what was that woman's game?)

    But the Bishop looked up, first at me, then behind me, pointing, and

Chapter 6

I saw that his thick black plastic lenses had shifted so that they were half on, half off his face, exposing a single eyeball (a sightless, hardboiled egg of an eye it was; the other one, still obscured by a lens, I assumed to be functional) and I followed the direction of his finger and, turning around, found myself being addressed by a large police officer.

Sir, I'm going to need you to step back and calm down. Then, to the Bishop:

Are you hurt, mister?

To which the Bishop responded, It's all cake but the frosting! And the cop to me:

Sir, can I please see some identification?

To which I said something amounting to no, and the cop said:

Can you state your full name, sir?

I am Dr. Martin Malloy, I said, and the cop replied, Dr. Malloy, could you please recite the alphabet backwards for me, starting with *z*? Take as much time as you need. And not requiring any time at all I did so, whereupon the cop asked me to list as many countries in Europe as I could in alphabetical order, and when I got to Azerbaijan he interrupted me and asked me if, starting with the fifteenth digit to the right of the decimal point and working backwards, I could recite the square root of two, and when I did that as well, he said:

Sir, please come with me to the squad car.

Was there a problem with my answer? I asked, and maybe he thought I was being a wise guy and maybe he didn't, but he said:

Sir, I will be giving you a summons today for reckless behavior. Please come with me to the squad car.

And not wanting any more trouble, I shut up.

So, I thought to myself as we walked, *Newton's cradle has been rocked; the notebook has been passed. In order to pursue it I will need once again to follow the click and clack of machinery that Butch, months ago, set into motion.*

Maybe it was the walk or the construction of a set of reasonable, connected thoughts. It felt as if the plug at the bottom of a filled washbasin had been pulled. The drug was wearing off, and my brain was slowing down.

My thoughts were once again my own.

WHITE KNIGHT

BLACK TO MOVE AND DRAW

Chapter 6

We came to the squad car. The squad car was there. Blue and red lights flashed. My custodian helped me into the back seat, behind where his partner was sitting shotgun. Even with her back to me, I could see her shoulder-length blonde hair and petite frame.

The cop who had been handling me said to her, "Looks like we might have a code C here."

♚ c6 ♚
COMING DOWN. REVERSE JEOPARDY IN THE BACK OF AN NYPD CRUISER. COMING UP.

The second cop spoke in a familiar Brooklyn drawl. But it was her perfunctory manner that gave away her identity, even as she was turning around to face me.

Officer Anne Schnapp said: "Martin," (she was fully turned around now, and I felt I was looking into the face of a robot that a programmer had tried, but failed, to imbue with human emotion), "you have been posing a threat to the public, but you won't be a problem for me this evening."

"Yes," I responded, recalling Schnapp's practice of phrasing her questions in the form of an answer.

"There is no need for me to cuff you, as you are not under arrest and will be sitting in the back of my cruiser without incident."

"Yes, officer."

"Nor will there be need for me to take you to the precinct in order to ask [axe!] you a few questions."

"Yes, officer."

Schnapp paused, then said, "By which you mean no." With her pale blue eyes, she contemplated me.

"No," I said. Presumably attempting to parse *this* response, Schnapp paused again, whereupon I said, "That is correct, officer." Another pause, and I said, striving to contain my exasperation, "Yes?"

Satisfied, she turned forward, leaving me to reflect on the difficulties inherent in natural language processing. Presently, I heard the rustling of papers coming from Schnapp. The steel mesh between us prevented me from seeing what she was doing, so I sat back and waited while the police radio squawked and the rain, picking up again, pelted the darkening windshield.

It really had been a tremendous game of chess. Now that my mind was back to its usual level of cognition, I amused myself trying to mentally replay some of the highlights. I was soon chuckling out loud as I recollected the ease with which I had invited complications. Knowing that my brain had access to a powerful calculating machine had transformed chess into almost a different game entirely. And was that machine still in there, somewhere? Lurking around my grey matter, bored and underemployed? Were we all of us so many PhDs, working as baristas at our local Starbucks? Should the whole world be taking White Knight with breakfast?

As I was thinking these things, I became aware of the various aromas that the NYPD cruiser had to offer its back-seat clientele. There was the homey scent of vinyl upholstery being warmed by the air that blew from the heater vents. (Even in mid-April, New York can get nippy when the sun goes down.) There were the salty, airborne remains of whatever grease bomb Schnapp and her stocky partner had recently called dinner (burgers and fries was my guess). And one of them (let's hang it on Schnapp and call it good) had spent some time in the perfume department before leaving home that morning. But from behind all this came the ghost of another smell, faint but unmistakable: the ugly, acidic penumbra of puke.

There are things that, once noticed, cannot be unnoticed. I tried to divert my attention from the puke smell by replaying my game with the Bishop move by move, coming up with different defenses for Black. But the effort was in vain; the computer in my head had locked me out. Worse, I could feel the temperature of my body beginning to fluctuate as the drug wore off, leaving behind a drained and exhausted mind. No, White Knight would not be showing up next to Vitamin A on an FDA Nutrition Facts label.

The puke smell that had previously lain dormant in the meat and bones of the car was growing now, perhaps encouraged by the warm air that blew from the vents. The stink was finding its way down my esophagus. Soon, it would be rapping on the door of my stomach, asking for a conjugal visit with whatever it found there.

Schnapp ceased her paper shuffling and turned back around to me.

Chapter 6

In a tone that you might hear being used by a bored grocery store checkout clerk inquiring about a customer's day, she asked, "You are feeling better now."

I stared at her, honestly confused. I felt like a cold pile of shit on a hot sidewalk.

She explained: "You are not fidgeting or talking. The drug is wearing off."

And what was I supposed to say to *that*? Something left the confines of my stomach and started crawling upward.

She went on. "You were, perhaps, offered a hot beverage today."

Recalling the drug-infused coffee Shannon had given me a few hours previous, I said, "I had coffee."

Schnapp and her partner shared a quick, knowing glance. She continued. "This coffee—you made it yourself, or it was offered to you."

"Sh—" I began, then stopped myself. I was about to say, "Shannon gave it to me," but simply said, "It was given to me." The use of the passive voice pushed bile halfway up my esophagus. The bile was gaining steam.

Schnapp's partner turned back around, folded his arms across the white-shirted barrel that was his chest, reclined, and shut his eyes. He may as well have said out loud, "I've heard all I need. My purty little blonde partner here with the silicon personality and Brooklyn charm will do the rest."

Schnapp handed me a sheet of printer paper. On it was a picture of a woman. The shot had been taken in Washington Square from a distance of about three chess tables. I imagined Schnapp in plainclothes, trying her best to play chess with some random hustler, covertly taking this shot with her phone while pretending to text. The subject was staring directly at the camera, and she was clearly Shannon.

"Yes?" I said, handing the paper back to Schnapp.

She asked, "This is the woman who gave you the coffee."

There was no getting around this one. "Yes," I said.

Don't press this... you will get us all killed... These remembered words from our lovely night in Ossining. The bile had almost reached my mouth.

I thought I knew what was coming next: Schnapp would ask me who this woman was. Instead, she turned back around, and I again heard the shuffling of papers. Maybe she already knew, or maybe she was working her way up to it. But when she turned back to me, she was holding out a chess notebook. On its cover was a sketch of a knight. Anne Schnapp said—and this was the only time I'd ever heard her use a question mark—"I have been trying to work these out, and I am stumped. Do you think you could get this notebook to Monika? I was going to swing by this evening to give it to her, but it would be quicker if you took it."

And so it transpired that all I had needed to do was wait. The Bishop hadn't given the notebook to Shannon; he had given it to Officer Schnapp. The last thing I remember before I covered the back seat of Anne Schnapp's car with vomit was telling myself that it really had been a tremendous game of ch—

♞ d6 ♝
TWILIGHT

"... Unit 14, reporting..."

"... around to the side..."

"... give me that number..."

"... done my shift. Going out tonight?..."

"I'M A-SWIMMIN' WITH THE FISHIES!"

Great green clouds of purple and red.

♞ e6 ♝
GENERAL PURPOSES. STRAY CHUNKS. THE KING IS COMING.

I came around to a gentle touch on my shoulder and a familiar voice:
"He's coming to."
I opened my eyes. Monika stood over me, smiling. I was in a chair, my left arm on a wide, padded armrest. An IV tube came out the back of my hand. To my right and left were similar oversized chairs with similarly tubed-up patients. I was in a hospital ward.
"Where am I?" I asked. "When is it?" I meant *What time is it.*

Chapter 6

Monika said, "You're in Bellevue Hospital. You're fine, Martin."

"It's a hospital for nut jobs!" said another voice, and a not-so-gentle hand came down on my other shoulder. I looked up at a grinning Tomas.

Monika *tsk*ed and rolled her eyes. "Father! They use it for general purposes now." Then, to me, "It's still Friday. Almost midnight. The police brought you here."

"Yeah," added Tomas, helpfully, "after you blew your cookies all over the back of Anne Schnapp's wagon and then passed out in the chunks! Well done, son."

Monika shot her father a quick-and-dirty, then returned her attention to me. "I was able to get most of it out," she said. With her hands, she started combing through my hair like a barber checking one last time to make sure the job is perfect.

"Bah! Never mind that, M-doc," said Tomas. "We love ya. You're a winner!" He pointed off to my right, where a chess notebook sat on a folding chair. It was the last of the five. We had them all.

I brooded again over the inconsequentiality of my campaign against the Bishop. I needn't have played a single game! But chess is a drug. I had gotten my hits for free (thanks to Tomas), and it had been one hell of a trip.

"It came from Schnapp," I said, meaning the notebook. "The Bishop gave it to her."

The two of them traded nods, like that settled that. Monika said, "We saw her hand it to the attending nurse."

"But why would he have done that?" I asked. "Why did the Bishop give it to her at all?"

Tomas said, "The heat was on. He'd moved his gig down here from Union Square, where the drug busts have been hot and heavy."

"The Bishop is the kingpin?" I said, looking up sharply. Monika pushed my head back down with a firm hand, continuing her search for stray vomit chunks.

"No," said Tomas, "if it was him, this would already be over. I'm just saying he didn't want any police entanglements. Probably figured anything you were willing to pay almost a thousand bucks for was maybe something he could hand over to the cops. You know, as a gesture of cooperation."

"Sorry about that," I said.

"Sorry about what?"

"The thousand clams."

He shrugged his shoulders. "The rivers are full of 'em."

Just then, the patient to my left—an old woman with slippers made to resemble a pair of dogs, whatever breed it might be that are fuzzy and pink and look like they stuck their tails into wall sockets—suddenly yelled out some nonsense. A nurse came on the quick and ministered to her.

"Okay," I said, returning my attention to Monika and Tomas, "but why would Schnapp hand over the notebook to me?"

"She would have no reason to think anything of it," said Monika. "As far as she's concerned, a chess hustler gave her a bunch of puzzles."

I looked up at my girlfriend. Satisfied with her work, she was standing in front of me now, arms folded across her chest.

"Schnapp wanted your help with it, you know," I said. "Said she was stumped."

"We got along very well, that evening at our place," Monika said. "I like her." Under her breath, she added, "Needs work on her square control, though."

"Anne Schnapp is a rising star in the force," said Tomas. "Mark my words, one of these days they're going to give her one mother of a case."

I remembered something. "The police are on to Shannon. Schnapp showed me a picture of her in the Square. Asked me if she had drugged me."

Monika looked at her father darkly. Tomas said, "All it means is she's a person of interest."

"She drugged me!" I repeated.

Monika placed a hand on Tomas's arm. "She dumped that whole baggie into Martin's coffee, Father. If he had drunk that whole cup, who knows? Maybe he could have been killed. Or worse, suffered permanent brain damage."

Tomas considered this. "She needed you to play the Bishop," he said to me. "She wouldn't have let you drink the whole thing."

From off to my left: "WHERE DID IT ALL COME FROM, AND WHY DOES IT TASTE LIKE CHICKEN?" It was the patient with the slippers. She was pointing up at the ceiling, demanding that it divulge to the world its hidden answers. I looked around for the nurse, but he had left.

I picked it back up with Tomas. "Then why dump the whole thing into my coffee?"

"Maybe she was getting rid of evidence," said Monika. "Killing two birds with one stone?"

"Cheep cheep," I said.

Giving up on the ceiling, Slipper Woman turned to us for the answers. "WHY DO BIRDS SUDDENLY DISAPPEAR?"

Ignoring this as best he could, Tomas said, "Did you give Schnapp Shannon's name?"

"She never asked. I threw up before she got the chance."

"Clever!" Another slap on my shoulder.

"What's our next move?" asked Monika.

"We do what we always do," I said. "We solve chess puzzles." I nodded toward the notebook on the chair. "I assume you've already looked at them?"

Monika perked up. "Yup! Got 'em all."

"YOU LIKE MY BABIES? THEY'RE ON MY FEET! YOU WANNA GIVE MY BABIES A PET? GIVE MY BABIES A PET!"

"Look, M-doc," said Tomas, "They want to keep you overnight for monitoring. One night in the nuthouse will be comfortable enough." While Monika shot her father an admonitory glance, he looked over at Slipper Woman, then back again. "Why don't you solve these puzzles, and we'll reconvene in the morning. Figure out where to go from there."

"We're getting close, Martin!" said Monika.

"And the police?" I asked.

"The summons is all taken care of," said Tomas.

And *is* it wrong to take what is given you?

They said their goodbyes and left, Monika turning around at the door to toss me a kiss.

The nurse came back—tall, dark, and harried. "Anything you need?"

"Yeah," I said, "I need my fix."

The nurse raised his eyebrows. I indicated the chess notebook.

"Oh!" he said and handed it to me. "Here you are, Dr. Malloy."

From off to my left came, "THE KING IS COMING! THE KING IS A-COMIN' AND I'M A-SWIMMIN' WITH THE FISHIES!"

♞ f6 ♞
THE KNIGHT NOTEBOOK

The following is a transcript of Butch's knight notebook, read during my overnight in Bellevue Hospital. The literary reference in Swindle 50 was obvious—a nod to the somewhat nauseating Sartre. After convincing myself of the solution to the final puzzle, I laid the notebook aside and shut my eyes. Slipper Lady had long ago fallen asleep. The ward was blessedly quiet.

We now had all five moves from the notebooks that Butch had hidden. Five moves that, starting from "the home of the black king" and using Butch's atlas, were meant to lead us to the location of our hidden quarry.

Meditating on this, I slipped into a dreamless sleep.

Knight

Ripples on square pond—
Eight-fold sphere of influence.
Watch out! You are forked.

Chapter 6

Swindle #41—Dark Knight: a self-reflection in black and white

White: The Batman
Black: Me
Date: January 29, 2010

"Batman your favorite superhero?" I asked the boy of about eleven to distract him from our chess game, which had somehow taken a bad turn. I figured the question wasn't too much of a leap, given the iconic black-on-gold symbol spanning the width of the kid's hoodie.

"You betcha, mister," came the boy's true-to-period response.

"How come you like Batman so much?"

"*The* Batman."

"What?"

"*The* Batman," the boy repeated, emphasizing the definite article while simultaneously playing a strong queen to d5. "Get it right."

"Well okay, then," I conceded. "How come you like *the* Batman so much?"

"No superpowers," the boy said, trading his QB for my knight on f6 and creating a permanent weakness in my kingside camp. "Just his mind and his strength."

"You don't like superpowers, huh?"

"Nope."

"How come?"

"Not real." The boy's knight came to h5, and if I didn't want to get mated in about two moves, it was going to cost me a pawn. At least.

"What makes Batman a superhero, then? What kind of superhero doesn't have any superpowers?" If I could distract the kid for even one move—just a breathing space, to consolidate my position...

"*The* Batman. C'mon. Get it right."

"Sorry. What makes *the* Batman a superhero?"

"He fights villains."

"Cops fight crime. Cops aren't superheroes."

"Cops fight *criminals*. The Batman fights *villains*."

"Villains, huh? You got this all worked out, dontcha." Oh, lordy. There was a bishop sac on f7. If the kid found it, it would be the end of me. I continued with the distraction. "What's a villain?"

"A villain is someone who makes the Batman outsmart him if he wants to win." Rather than hurling itself into my castle wall, the boy's bishop had retreated to b3. My position would survive. For a few more moves, anyhow.

"Example?"

"You know. The Joker. The Penguin. The Riddler. He's my favorite, the Riddler."

"The Riddler's your favorite, huh? Who's that?"

The boy looked up from the board with disbelief on his face. "You don't know the Riddler?"

"Yeah, I know the Riddler." Of course I knew the Riddler. Who doesn't know the Riddler.

"Right." The boy returned his attention to the desperate theater that was my kingside defense. Then, a queen trade! *Phew!* The ladies were off the board! Stemming the tide of the boy's attack, however, had cost me a second pawn.

"What do you like about the Riddler?" I asked.

"He makes puzzles. The Batman and the Boy Wonder have to solve the puzzles. Then they solve the crime."

"So you like it when the criminal is smart?"

"*Villain.* Get it right. No."

"What?"

"It's a *villain*, not a criminal. And I like it when the *good* guy is smart, not the bad guy. Look. If you have superpowers you don't *have* to be smart, get it?"

"And the Batman doesn't have any superpowers."

"Right."

We had reached the position pictured below. All that remained of my forces was a single, dark knight. If I was going to secure this draw, I was going to have to stop not one but *two* pawns from promoting. Using the full power of my words, I made my final push.

"So you're claiming that the defining essence of an object is often to be found in the absence, rather than in the possession, of certain characteristic attributes, as well as in attributes belonging to an object's environment, rather than to the object itself—to wit, the Batman's identity as a superhero due to (a) a lack of superhuman powers, and (b) the intellectual status of his opposition?"

Chapter 6

As I spoke, I moved my dark knight to a square where the boy could capture him.

He did so. In a matter of seconds, the poor kid realized his mistake, and our game ended in a draw. The boy stood up and started to walk away.

"Hey," I said, motioning him to my side of the table. "Guess what."

The boy stopped and turned around. "What?"

"The Batman was always my favorite, too." I reached into my pocket and pulled out a fiver. "Here, kid. This is for you."

"But I didn't win."

"This is truth. But sometimes what we are is defined by the attributes of our environment. Understand?"

"Not really," said the boy, but he took the five dollars anyway. As he walked off into the twilit park, I observed the surrounding Gotham. And what I saw was white and black, light and dark, good and evil, and everywhere, struggle.

And I? Was I the Batman, or was I the Riddler?

"I'm Batman," I whispered. Then I corrected myself. "*The* Batman."

Get it right.

Black to move

Can you find a way for Butch to offer his opponent a dark knight in the hopes of tricking him into a draw?

Swindle #42—A well-suited end

White: 007
Black: Me
Date: February 4, 2010

It is said that the clothes make the man. This is inaccurate. But something about this man with his pleated dress slacks and studded-up tuxedo shirt brought me to reconsider the idiom. He played with a formality whose stiffness was exceeded only by the crisp, cardboard-like ring that was his starched collar.

The man's demeanor was reflected in his game; I was slowly suffocating. If my king's breathing space continued to diminish, it would soon be checkmate. My choices were to capitulate to suffocation or try for a trick.

Black to move

How did Butch escape the snares of his rigidly dressed opponent?

Chapter 6

Swindle #43—Catch as catch can

White: Me
Black: Rain Man
Date: December 7, 2009

The fellow playing Black was apparently the sort who expects rain at any moment, with his long black umbrella and his Columbia rain jacket. While I generally appreciate the habit of prophylaxis, I thought he would have done better in something with a warmer lining.

Not that the weather provides any excuse for my sorry play these days. Study the position below. How could I have been so careless? I recall being shocked at discovering that somewhere along the way I had lost an exchange! Fortunately, I also discovered a most ingenious drawing mechanism. I needed only for my opponent to not anticipate the inclement weather I was sending his way, and I would be assured of a draw... in a particularly extraordinary manner.

Our games were over and it was time to pay up. I was displeased when the man turned his pockets out and claimed to have no cash. For payment, he offered a cheesy plastic figurine of a Mexican wearing a sombrero and taking a siesta with his head down on his knees and his arms wrapped around his legs.

Like I say, I was displeased. But what recourse did I have?

White to move

In what extraordinary manner can Butch save his game?

Swindle #44—Skating on thin ice

White: Me
Black: Girl on a Skateboard
Date: December 26, 2009

I sometimes do not process thoughts efficiently when around the female of the species. I have shared this fact about myself with Martin on more than one occasion, attempting to discern the variables determining how and when this is so. Apparently, this unease of mine is not palliated by a subject's tender age.

In the position below, my opponent was a girl of perhaps fifteen. She wore her New York Giants cap backward and kicked around on a neon green skateboard. (It was unscratched—a Christmas present, I presumed.) While we played our game, she rolled the skateboard back and forth under the table with her feet. I lost my concentration. Then I lost an exchange. Soon, her three outside passed pawns were barreling down my queenside. It was time for me to bail.

But how? It took me a full minute, what with the skateboard sending up a racket from under the table, but I found just the way to trick my young adversary.

White to move

What bait did Butch lay out for his teenage nemesis?

CHAPTER 6

Swindle #45—By dawn's early light

White: Me
Black: Captain America
Date: February 9, 2010

7:45 a.m.— My first client of the day was a young fellow in a leather jacket with an American flag embroidered on the back. The flag was so large that it spilled over onto both sleeves.

Unfortunately, everything I tried against my chess compatriot resulted in nothing but a missing piece from my army. I no longer liked where my game was going. Happily, I found a way to entice my fellow countryman to capture another piece and thereby avoided a loss.

White to move

How could losing another piece prevent Butch from losing his game?

Swindle #46—Shades of the past

White: The Professor
Black: Me
Date: February 8, 2010

The tightly pressed sardonic smile; the shifty eyes, calculating from behind a pair of perfectly round eyeglass lenses; the thin dome of oily black hair, scraped back over his considerable cranium—why, this man looked like none other than that great pioneer of hypermodern chess, Aron Nimzowitsch!

Alas, none of the threats I made against him came through in their execution. In the game pictured below, my prim and bespectacled opponent had developed a small but meaningful advantage over me. Rather than continue to lose slowly, I made a move that would have convinced even the most novice of onlookers that I had lost not only my game, but my mind.

I then stunned even myself by pulling off a difficult sequence, securing the draw.

Black to move

Butch is playing the black pieces. Can you find the bait and the entire sequence of moves after its capture that will result in a draw for him?

CHAPTER 6

Swindle #47—Agitated

White: Me
Black: Maryanne
Date: January 20, 2010

GM Yasser Seirewan once quipped, "I have made twenty exchange sacrifices in my life. Eighteen of them were unintentional." In the game pictured below, I had made many moves that resulted in unintentional consequences. My castle wall had been breached and my king's position compromised. I am becoming increasingly distracted these days. As much as I would like to blame these deficiencies on the charms of the lady who sat across from me, I'm afraid that the source of my agitation runs deeper.

White to move

How did Butch offer a piece, thereby provoking a draw from his opponent?

Swindle #48—Sonic warfare

White: Me
Black: American Idol
Date: January 2, 2010

Where silence in the tournament hall is golden, trash-talking is a quintessential element in the variety of chess we offer to those who visit the parks of America's best cities. Like city life itself, chess is a game of courage—a testing of body and mind. It is a war of psychology, played out in thought, word, and deed.

Singing, however, is beyond the pale. Ditto for humming, whistling, and making clucking noises with the tongue. The man who played opposite me was an adept in all these auditory vices. He had quite gotten under my skin. Perhaps this explains how I found myself in the present predicament. My only hope was to offer a swindle.

White to move

Butch, playing as White, is down substantial material. How did he lose even more and pull off the draw?

CHAPTER 6

Swindle #49—Bananarama

White: Monochrome
Black: Me
Date: January 21, 2010

From his knit beanie to his twill button-down, moleskin trousers, and canvas boat shoes, the man was dressed entirely in yellow. If Martin had been here, he'd surely have described him as a highlighter. Somehow, I was losing to him. So mentally distracted these days I am, even by the most transient of external stimuli.

I returned my concentration to the game. Things didn't look good. Soon, White (Yellow?) would dislodge my king from d6 and march his pawn to promotion. It was then that I realized how to offer my monochromatic friend some more material.

Black to move

Can you find a way for Butch to swindle the thing in yellow?

Swindle #50—Existence precedes essence

White: The Thin-Framed Man
Black: Me
Date: February 9, 2010

The others have left, and I see the man now: his thin frame tilts against the black iron fence that runs along 4th Avenue, the southern border of Washington Square Park. It's been dark for some time; I wonder to myself if the short, hooded silhouette is the person who was following me earlier. I was taking my noontime walk around the circular fountain that lies at the park's center. In the winter the fountain doesn't run; it's a hard, white eye gazing at the sky from among the barren trees. I think at first the man, not realizing my circular trajectory, believed himself to be following me toward some set-upon destination. Three-quarters of the way around the fountain he broke off pursuit and sat down on a bench, kicking away a small huddle of pigeons that pecked among some bags of fast food abandoned to the cruel and dirty ice. I imagine the hooded man must have felt somewhat foolish.

As I watch the leaning figure, my hand reaches for an empty soda can that stands to the right of my chessboard. I ought to know from the shallow dent in its side—the can is empty. Recently I've developed a habit of crushing cans. I crush them as I finish them. I don't notice the dent (perhaps I'm distracted by the leaning man), and I lift the can uselessly to my mouth. The dry metallic hole scrapes at my parted lips, reminding me that I'm probably hungry. It's just this pain that pulses, quite irritably now, along the ropes of my neck: it so often keeps other feelings at bay, away from my conscious self. I've been like that a lot today. I don't know myself. It sounds like it should not be a very probable thing, that a pain in my neck should mask a hunger in my stomach or a thirst on my lips, but I find myself believing it nonetheless.[19]

I do not fear the leaning man, but it concerns me that perhaps I should. Does it mean something to have fear, yet not feel it? Fear, like hunger, being masked by this pain in my neck? I know... it sounds unlikely. I don't notice the man has started toward me until he suddenly is near enough that

---

19 All that is missing is a reference to the Self-Taught Man.

Chapter 6

I can see his face. A slant to the eyes hints at a Chinaman; his cheeks, drawn in and narrow—dented, like my can—give the impression he sucks on sour candy. But with his hood down, none of this is clear. In fact, now that I see the totality, I realize I can't be sure of specifics. This is what it's like to believe things—you must pick. He offers me a cup of coffee that I probably shouldn't take, and it's warm.

Warmth, too, is a feeling[20], and feelings, like objects, stack. I lunched today at Antonio's, earlier than usual. I had woken with a taste on the roof of my mouth like an artificially sweetened sulfur. It was 7:30 when I exited my apartment building, and I realized the whole city was like that today. A taste of sulfur, or maybe a smell, I don't know—the senses at some point meld: the icy smell of the buildings that loomed beside me on my walk to the subway; the sepia-toned echo of the train; the coarse smoke that rose from my Swisher Sweets cigar to graze against my skin, failing to mask that sickening, saccharine sulfur. I had hoped Antonio's pizza would drive the taste of the city from my mouth.

Behind Antonio in his wide, greasy undershirt, a pile of pans sat in a strainer that drained gray, bubbling water into a metallic sink. Suddenly and for no reason, the entire stack fell with a crash. No one had touched it, but Antonio, incensed, yelled at his Mexican dishwasher. That bothers me. I think, "What has changed to cause something to happen?" Everything today seems to change at will, without need for external cause. Maybe it's the thought of the coffee that is causing the feelings piled up in me to come crashing down, like Antonio's pans. Or maybe the pile just fell on its own. I can't be sure.

I go for the coffee, and the cacophonous crash inside my brain leaves behind a solitary feeling, a loneliness that disgusts me. I thought I had taught myself to manage it. Like an isolated pawn on d4, to suppress, blockade, attack, and eventually eliminate it; like a criminal element in my mind, to keep under lock and key. This is what all of us self-taught men[21] in the park do to survive the hands that daily move our pieces—the smiling,

---

20 This is how it is with Sartre—you must just keep on going.
21 There it is.

rational others who sit across our boards and play us, while we sit alone in their midst.[22]

"I think you have something of mine," is all the hooded man has to say.

"I play for five dollars," is all I have to say back.

"Very well." The hooded man presses my clock and watches as I move my white knight to f3. "Have it your way."

This game was not one of my best. In the position below, I am playing as White. I had tried various tricks throughout the encounter, but the hooded man seemed to perceive all of them. I had one last attempt at a swindle. He fell for it, and we ended up owing each other nothing.

White to move

Can you find Butch's last stand?

---

22 Does Butch feel all this? How much of this is expository, and how much is fantasy? I am deeply worried for my friend.

♞ g6 ♘
HARD-BOILED. THE COMMUTATIVE PROPERTY OF ADDITION. X MARKS THE SPOT.

I got home from the hospital around eight that morning. The living room was empty; the sounds of a hair dryer came from the bedroom. I hadn't eaten, so I wandered into the kitchen. My place at the table was already set: a covered bowl, a fork, a small plate with two hard-boiled eggs on it. I lifted the cover off the bowl and found white rice, still steaming.

"Food for the infirm," chirped Monika. She walked in looking like food for the incredibly robust. Her orchid blouse practically jumped off her lime green pencil skirt. She gave me a peck on the cheek and asked how I was feeling.

"Ransacked," I said. Hospitals are no place for the sick. Slipper Lady had awoken early—very early. I sat down at the table and started cracking the shells of my hard-boileds. Maybe a little too aggressively.

Now that we had the last notebook, all we needed was to connect the dots. Which meant we needed the atlas. It was at Butch's place, so we texted Shannon and agreed to meet her there. I finished my eggs, showered, and got into a fresh set of clothes. Monika grabbed a taxi—my second one of the day, and it wasn't even nine. The morning sun drew the lines of our shadows onto the brick walls of Butch's building. We made the long climb up the five flights of stairs to his apartment. The door was cracked open, so we stepped inside.

"Oh, no!" said Monika. "What happened?"

"Ransacked," I said.

A line of demarcation ran down the middle of Butch's living room: everything to the right—mostly books—was trashed and lying wounded on the field. Everything to the left lay untouched. Shannon acknowledged us with a flash of fury from her eyes, then got back to the mess. Even in her anger, she handled the books carefully, referring to each book's front matter before placing it back on the shelves, clearly following some opaque categorization scheme. Monika bravely offered help and was shooed away.

"The atlas!" I said. "Did they get the atlas?"

"They wouldn't have known about that," said Shannon, not stopping her work. Her words were ice. "It's with the reference books, where it always is. Feel free."

"Did they take anything?" asked Monika.

That stopped her, and the look she gave us was something I never wanted to see again. She said, "They. Got. My. *Sword!*"

She swept away into the bedroom. The slamming door drowned out whatever it was she said next, which might have been "some bitch" or probably "son of a bitch."

Monika and I looked at one another and exhaled. After taking a moment to recoup from the force of Shannon's anger, I retrieved the atlas and set it on the coffee table, then found the entry on New York City, where an eight-by-eight array of what was intended to be the squares of a chess board had been superimposed over Manhattan. Monika opened her purse, took out the five notebooks (surely the intended target of the perps) and laid them next to the atlas. After a few minutes, Shannon emerged from the bedroom. This was the first she had gotten to see the knight notebook. We waited for her to peruse it (which, given her agitation, she did with amazing focus). Then together we reviewed the key moves, one from each of the five important puzzles.

From the notebook Butch had given to Stanislav, we all agreed that Swindle 3, with its whimsical nod to Lewis Carroll, was the puzzle of interest. In that position, White makes an offer of his queen, which Black does well to dodge, but which, if accepted, leads down a rabbit hole to perpetual check.

From the notebook hidden among the "twists and turns" of the Vienna Game as found in Butch's *Modern Chess Openings,* Swindle 15 captured the atmospheric density of Lovecraftian horror. White moves a rook deep into Black's camp, seemingly abandoning its twin to doom. If Black accepts, a knight appears, heralding a repetition of moves from which there can be no escape.

The complexity of Swindle 29, from the notebook given by Tai at the Great Wall of China restaurant, was matched only by that of its accompanying prose. In this puzzle, Butch takes the step of outright naming Jorge Luis Borges, perhaps in case his literary intentions had not previously been understood. It must have been a stroke of purest genius that led him to find

Chapter 6

a subtle spot for his bishop in that position. Unless Black picks the winning continuation from the garden of forking paths, he will be lured into a draw.

In the notebook found at Master Lin's studio, we gained poignant insight into Butch's life as a chess hustler. Although not written as a poem itself, Swindle 33 gives away Dylan Thomas's "In My Craft or Sullen Art" as the muse Butch must have leveraged to discuss the loneliness of his profession and his societal status. The austerity of the position mirrors the cold poverty that continually presents itself to me as a possible interpretation of his life—and could the slight move of a black pawn be perhaps symbolic of his self-perception? If captured, the pawn will lead White into a frozen stalemate.

A queen move, a rook move, a bishop move, and a pawn move: these, we already had. And although Monika and I agreed on the critical move from the knight notebook, we waited to hear Shannon's own conclusion.

She looked up from the final puzzle. Her eyes were damp, and a tear dripped from her chin onto the open page. "Take it," she said. "It's number fifty, of course. But I don't understand the position."

"It's Jean Paul Sartre," I began. "The existentialist musings, together with the general pathetic—"

"I don't care about the author. Just tell me the move."

Monika pointed to a square in the position in Swindle 50. "We think that if White moves his knight here—"

"Fine," said Shannon. "I believe you." She looked at me, and her eyes did not shift. "I believe both of you. Now, do we have all the moves?"

"Yes," I said.

"How do we order them?"

"I don't understand."

"The moves. We use the atlas and start here, at his home. Then we move about the map, using the answers from the puzzles. But how do we know which move to make first?"

Monika chimed in. "I had wondered that, too, especially since Butch says nothing about it in any of his notebooks. But then I played around with it one day on my board and realized that the order doesn't matter. Look. Let's say we start at e8, and we take a bishop three squares down and to the right to h5. Then we take a knight and hop down and to the left, onto g3. Okay so far?"

"Okay..." said Shannon.

"So now let's mix it up. We start at e8 again, but hop with the knight first, down and to the left..."

Shannon finished for her. "...you'd get to d6, and then the bishop would go down and to the right three squares to g3. Jesus, I'm an idiot."

"Not at all!" said Monika. "Look, we're chess players, right? Order matters all the time." She paused. "Come to think of it, I guess the order *does* matter a little. I mean... if you went off the board..."

"You'd be fine," said Shannon. "Just mentally extend the grid."

"That doesn't sound like an idiot to me," said Monika.

And to think I had been about to launch into a lecture on the Commutative Property of Addition.

On the map, Butch's apartment was in a square that covered a good part of central Harlem. Placing my finger on that square, and with Monika calling out the moves, I went back and forth over New York—but more north than south and veering somewhat more to the west than to the east.

After she called out the last move, my finger was pointing to Fort Tryon Park, above the Hudson River.

"That's a big square," said Monika. "It covers quite a lot of ground. I don't see how—"

Pointing to the corner of the page, I said, "You see here where Butch wrote *X marks the spot*?" Using one of the notebooks as a straight edge, I drew an X across the square and pointed to its center. "That's where we need to go."

"Nice!" said Monika. "Then what? I mean, after we get there?"

"I think I know," said Shannon. "And if I'm right, I'm going to need to get into the studio. Just for a second."

"Why? What's there?" asked Monika.

Shannon thought for a moment. "A key," she said.

And her eyes shifted to the left.

CHAPTER 6

♘ h6 ♞
FAMILY EMERGENCY. OPENING LINES. OPEN AND SHUT.

Shannon is a beautiful woman, if a bit beaten up around the edges. The bruises and cuts that had landed on her face the night our notebooks were stolen had mostly healed. But other markings on her body—her knuckle pads, various scars and gouges on her forearms, a dent on the skin of her forehead—I was afraid were permanent fixtures.

But the blonde wig she had just put on? Travesty. The thing looked like nesting material. It had been her idea; she claimed everyone at the studio would be busy teaching class, and that if she went in disguise, she might be able to slip into her room unnoticed. Frankly, I held an opposite opinion, but I choose my battles and hold my words, and sometimes that works out. I had doubted, for example, that there would be a wig shop in Harlem at all—a point on which I was immediately corrected. At least she had removed the big, Chinese-plus-minus-sign earrings. That was a help.

It was just past 9:30 a.m. when we left the shop. Shannon was a kind of wispy Chinese Tippi Hedren having a bad hair day. Given how close everything was, I said we should walk—the weather was that fine. But everyone wanted to hurry, so we got a taxi. In ten minutes we pulled up to the front of the kung fu studio and got our first surprise of the day.

"Closed," said Monika. She was looking at a sheet of paper taped to the inside of the glass door. SATURDAY CLASSES CLOSED, FAMILY EMERGENCEY, it said. Underneath this, *Practice at Home!* had been scrawled in red ink like an afterthought.

Monika asked, "Do we have a Plan B?"

"Actually," I said, "we do." I turned to Shannon, preparing to speak, and found her staring, ashen faced, at the note on the door.

"Shannon?" Monika said, placing a hand on her shoulder. "Are you okay?"

She said, "We need to get in there."

"We could go in through your shop," I offered.

That got her attention. "What do you mean?"

"You're a seamstress. You work right there." I pointed to the brick building across the alleyway.

"What do *you* know about anything?"

"You're not the only one who knows things they don't say."

She glared at me, and Monika stepped in. "Martin, do you have a way in?"

Shannon answered for me. "No, he doesn't."

"There's the tunnel," I said.

A pause, then, "What do you mean, *tunnel*? We're not going through any tunnel."

"You mean because of the keypad lock?"

Now she was really flustered. "Next you're going to tell us you deduced the combination?"

"No," I admitted, "I didn't deduce it." I waited for Shannon to exhale before adding, "I inferred it."

"What?"

"Deduction," I began, "is predicated upon *a priori* reasoning, whereas inference—"

"Lose the lecture notes, *M-doc*. I meant how did you know?"

The indiscriminate and indelicate use of my sobriquet stung. As if I were some kind of know-it-all! I said, "I figured it out whilst in a drug-induced state, thanks to *you* putting—"

"We needed that notebook!"

"Enough!" said Monika. "Martin, do you have a way in?"

"Yes."

"And Shannon," she said, "isn't that what you wanted? A way in?"

She nodded.

"Then let's go."

And that, for the time being, was that.

The three of us entered the tailor shop. The same ladies from yesterday were all there, sewing away as if they had worked through the night. One of them looked up, and Shannon invented some rationale for our being there. The seamstress nodded her head and got back to her stitching. Shannon tossed her Tippi Hedren wig onto a table, got those big ol' earrings out of her pocket, and put them back on.

We descended to the basement, and I soon found the double doors that opened to the tunnel. We entered, and I closed the doors behind us.

Monika had turned on her phone's flashlight. "You came this way yesterday?" The blackness ate her words. Tire tracks in the ground, doubtless made by the forklift, led into the dark beyond.

"It connects to the studio." My whisper, too, dissolved into a tight space that was just wide enough for the three of us to walk abreast.

We walked for a minute or two, Monika and I trading quiet encouragements to keep going. Presently, we came to a halt at the double doors that, just as before, were secured by an alphanumeric keypad lock.

"Okay," said Shannon, "you said you know the combination. What is it?" As if against her better judgment, she added, hesitantly, "And how *do* you know?"

"Your brother has a whiteboard above his workbench. It shows the names of several chess openings: the King's Gambit, the Queen's Gambit, the Center Game, the Smith-Morra Gambit, the Wing Gambit, and the Coca-Cola Gambit. All these opening have something in common."

They both thought for a moment, then Monika spoke up. "They're all defined by the first three piece movements of the game—two moves by White and one by Black."

"So far, so good," I said. "What else?"

This time it was Shannon. "All three moves are by pawns."

"Correct again. Therefore?"

Monika's green eyes lit up in the pallid light of her phone. "In algebraic notation, pawn moves are represented by exactly two characters—a letter and a number. All of those openings therefore yield a six-character alphanumeric sequence!"

Shannon asked, "But which opening do we use?"

"The one that wasn't crossed out: the Coca-Cola Gambit." Turning to the keypad, I pressed g-4-g-5-f-4. The door swung open with a sharp click.

"Opening lines," said Shannon, nodding her approval. "Very clever. All right, I'll admit it, you're good."

"Thanks for the drugs," I said companionably. "I couldn't have done it without you."

The three of us stole across the unlit basement, Shannon and I jockeying for position at the lead, heading for the stairs we both knew lay on the other side of the jumble of crates littering the floor.

Emerging from the stairs, we came to the hallway leading to what I had taken to be the bedrooms of Master Lin's family members. *Excepting*

Shannon, I reminded myself. She'd claimed a small room off the kitchen, with barred windows and a closet with a hole in the floor. I looked at Shannon, and for what turned out to be the last time, I wondered.

The hallway doors were all open. We could hear quiet voices speaking in Chinese. Monika shut off her flashlight. Shannon pulled us back a few stairs.

"Is that Mandarin?" I asked.

Shannon put a finger to her lips. She was listening to the hushed conversations above. Her face had gone ashen again. Finally, she said, "It's my grandfather. They're wondering if he is dying."

Before Monika could offer a word of consolation, Shannon took charge. "My room is straight down this hall and to the left, through the kitchen. Obviously, we can't take the short route. We're going to need to go back up these stairs, through a curtain on the left, and across the studio floor to the hall where the bathrooms are. At the end of that hall is another curtain. When we go through, we'll be exposed for a few seconds while we hook around to the left, and from there into the kitchen. Once we're there, we should be safe."

"Assuming no one is in the kitchen," I said.

Shannon did not respond to this. I looked at Monika, who shrugged her shoulders.

"We're good?" asked Shannon.

"For shaky definitions of the word," I said.

"Then everybody take off your shoes and follow my lead."

Shannon peered over the top of the stairwell for several minutes, waiting for a clear shot. Then she whispered, "Go."

Within seconds we were out on the floor. In full view of the street windows, we swept silently into the bathroom hall, shoes in hand.

The next stage of our operation took a little longer. While Shannon assessed the situation, peering out through a crack in the curtain, Monika and I stayed back a few feet. I had been in this exact position yesterday, and I knew what the problem was. Although the kitchen was directly opposite the wall that we were leaning against, the entrance was a good ten feet down the hall. Shannon was waiting for everyone to be well inside the rooms before we ran for it.

And how many people was that? I wondered. I listened as best I could to the conversations. There was one female voice. I thought of the Ninja Cat Lady. There were also two men, at the least. Master Feng seemed a likely candidate for one. The second could be anyone. Perhaps one of the instructors?

From time to time there were periods of silence. During these interludes, I imagined a frail and dying Master Lin speaking from his bed to his loving family. Surely, during one of those intervals…

"Go!" whispered Shannon.

We slipped through the curtain and raced down the hall in single file. Shannon led; I took the rear. She hooked left into the kitchen, followed by Monika. Still running, I took one look back. A large and familiar head was just ducking through the middle door and into the hall. The door was hinged on the side nearer to me, so that it came between me and the bulk of Feng's massive body. And then I was around the corner.

The kitchen was empty. Across the room was the door with the white ceramic knob and antique rim lock that led to Shannon's room. She opened it and with a silent wave of her arm beckoned us in. Hoping that Feng wasn't coming this way, I ran. I didn't breathe again until I heard the faint but solid click the door made when Shannon shut it behind us.

Monika sat on the bed while Shannon rummaged through a dresser drawer. Outside the window, a lone black bird perched on the iron bars. The room looked the same as it did yesterday. My gaze rested involuntarily on the closet door that hid Shannon's secret escape.

"What is it that you're looking for, again?" I asked.

"A key."

And how could it have been that either of us believed for a moment that Shannon, who tries to keep everything (and everyone) in order, would not have known *exactly* where this key was?

"Do you figure there's going to be some kind of lockbox when we get to Fort Tryon Park?" asked Monika.

Shannon paused. And how did I not see the treachery in her eyes? "I could use a little help here," she said. "Monika, can you look in the nightstand? No, not that one, the one on the far side of the bed. Thanks." Pointing to the shelves fastened to the wall above her bed, she said, "Martin, could you look up on top of those? Just go ahead and stand on the bed—yeah, that's right, don't worry about it, it's rubbish. That's good—right up there."

This is where we were—me standing on Shannon's bed (the hard mattress barely gave beneath my weight), staring at an empty katana stand; Monika kneeling in front of a nightstand that was nothing more than a couple of stacked cardboard boxes—when we heard Shannon say, "I'm sorry."

I heard it in the tone: the gig was up. I spun around, expecting a repeat of that first encounter with her, when she nearly crashed a chair over my head. But there was no attack. She stood in the open door, holding a key made of the same black metal as the rim lock.

"I'm going to Fort Tryon Park. Don't follow me." Then she pulled the door shut and locked us in.

Monika went to the door. Finding it immovable, she turned to me, and I saw something in her eyes that I had never seen there before. I started to think it was fear, but then she spoke.

"Martin." She sat down next to me on the bed. "I am so sorry. You were right about her. You were right all along. We should never have trusted her."

So *that* was it—she had been *wrong* (I hadn't realized just how seldom that happened), and she was *embarrassed*.

Life is full of new experiences.

I of course didn't say any of that. I put my arm around my girlfriend and told her the truth: I would be nowhere without her.

There was no reason to let her fester in the dumps any longer than necessary. Shannon had learned that I knew about the basement and the tunnel—but she had no reason to believe I knew about the trap door in the closet floor. Things had happened so fast that I'd never gotten a chance to tell Monika about it either. But that was one fact that I felt would surely lift her spirits.

I went to Shannon's closet and slid open the door. "Come over here," I said. I pushed aside some boxes that lay in the corner. (*Boxes?* asked an alarmed part of my brain that I wasn't listening to.)

"Yes?" said Monika.

I got down on my knees and tried to pry up the secret trap door—the one that I had put back in its place yesterday, *from below*. But nothing budged. There was no trap door—only a trap. The floorboards had been nailed down and boxes placed over what had been our only means of escape.

THE HOME OF THE BLACK KING

Chapter 7
THE HOME OF THE BLACK KING

♞ a7 ♞
THE KEY TO XIANG LIN

FIVE, MAYBE TEN minutes, I sat half in, half out of Shannon's closet, forearms slung over the points of my knees, trading stares with a blackbird that sat perched on the bars outside the window. Monika was calling out points from her text convo with Tomas: We were trapped in the kung fu studio. We knew where Butch had hidden IT. IT was in Fort Tryon Park. We had been on our way there when Shannon locked us in her room. Now she was on her way to Fort Tryon by herself.

Oh, and just to be crystal, we were trapped in the kung fu studio.

Tomas told us the cavalry was on its way.

"He means himself?"

"Yeah," she said. "He means himself."

"From *Ossining*?"

"Mm."

She was sitting with her back against the wall where a headboard should have been, feet crossed one over the other. She patted at a spot where her purse lay next to her on the bed. "C'mon."

I got up and sat next to her, shifting her purse onto the cardboard box nightstand. A muted conversation was seeping through the wall. Seemed to be English.

Monika pointed up to the shelves of books. "Could you—"

"Shh." I raised a finger. "You hear that?"

Chapter 7

"I tried. It's too muffled to make anything out."

I tried as well but couldn't make sense of the few words I could get—*Cunningham*, *drowned*, something that might have been *California*. I gave up. Monika had been pointing at the shelves; I asked her what she wanted.

"Let's distract ourselves while we wait. Prescribe a book for us, doctor?"

Really? I stood on the bed to search for a book. Where Butch would have sorted them by content, Shannon's books were arranged by height, in keeping with her more physical sense of order. I found a patch of modest-sized novels.

"Maugham?"

"Stuffy."

"Goethe?"

"Which?"

I looked. "*The Sorrows of Young Werther*."

"Sad."

"... Patterson?"

"Bland."

"Thank you. Daphne du Maurier?"

"Ooo! Is it *Rebecca*?" She cleared her throat, then, "Last night I dreamt I went to Manderley again." Her lilting voice attempted Joan Fontaine, and her green eyes shone. "Read it to me!"

"You want me to read you a four-hundred-page novel?"

She sighed and rolled her eyes. "No, I want you to go over to that door"—she pointed to the spot where Shannon had walked out on us and made us her prisoners—"pick the lock, get us out of here without anyone noticing, race up to Fort Tryon Park with me, arrive there ahead of Shannon, magically find—"

"All right." I sat down on the bed. "So. *Rebecca*?"

Monika took the book from me and riffled the pages. "It is rather long," she admitted. "Maybe a short story? Something we can finish before someone discovers us. Calls the police."

Or worse, doesn't call the police. But then, Tomas was on the way, right? Nothing to worry about. Out loud I said, "You want me to read you a short story?"

Monika cast her eyes upward toward the shelves, and what else was I to do? I stood on the bed, put Mrs. Danvers in her place, and searched for something to entertain Monika.

Nestled between the pomp of John Updike and the pith of Raymond Carver, I found what I needed. The flame orange and canary yellow spine made me wonder how I hadn't spotted it earlier: *The King in Yellow*. (Not Robert Chambers's best work, but as so often happens, his most well known.)

"Monika!" I pulled the book from its shelf and sat down next to her. "Look!"

"My god," she said. "*Another* copy of the *King in Yellow*? What did Butch say? 'Where the queen lays down her crown—'"

"'—seek the King in Yellow, '" I finished.

I turned the book over in my hands and saw at once that it wasn't a book at all, but a case made to look like a book. So this was the mystery of Butch's coverless *King in Yellow*. He had ripped off the cover and used it to fashion a case. Believing that our chase would lead us here, he had hidden it in plain sight, trusting I would spot the colorful spine. The case was oversized, creating a deep fore-edge beyond what would have been the book block. I gripped the covers and pulled. There was the ripping sound of separating Velcro, and the entire case came off, revealing a hidden book within.

I took the book from the case. It was a journal of some type, its pages locked shut by a silver hasp with a small keyhole. The cover was tan with an awfully familiar symbol in black on its center: the Chinese calligraphy plus-minus sign that Shannon wears on her earlobes. It gnawed at me that I had seen this symbol once, a long time ago, and it seemed that this feeling had been with me ever since I'd first laid eyes on those earrings. It also struck me that I had seen this design somewhere else, much more recently.

I had just worked out the more recent sighting when Monika's cell phone rang—and rang loudly. Startled, Monika silenced the ring in exactly the way I would have done in her position: she pushed buttons until it stopped. We looked at each other, horrified, and then turned our heads slowly to the door.

One second. Two. Three.

Then: "M-clip? You there? I was thinking of picking up sandwiches. You still like Rosato's? M-clip?"

Monika closed her eyes in resignation as I stared, aghast, at her phone.

♞ b7 ♞
THE BROTHER OF XIANG LIN

The door shot open and she stood there, hands pressed on her hips. Her Chinese left little to the imagination: *What in hell are* you *doing here?* Then, tossed over her shoulder, a word I understood:

"Feng!"

I traded a glance with Monika. She was standing there, holding Shannon's journal; the false *King in Yellow* lay on the bed like something naked and empty and ready to scream—and Feng was on his way.

Monika's purse gaped open on the nightstand. It gave me an idea.

I turned my back to Ninja Cat Lady and got between her and the bed. "Put it back," I said to Monika. I pointed to the shelves.

The tone of my own voice pained me, and the glance Monika shot me told me everything she wanted me to know about how she felt, forgetting to silence her phone. The hurt in her face shifted around a little, and she said, "Is it checkmate already? Martin, I'm sorry—"

"Hey," I said. "Checkmate means never having to say you're sorry. Now put it back." I risked a wink—and a slight nod to her purse.

And, by Jove, she got it.

She handed me the journal and folded the false cover into a hollow rectangle. She made a show of standing on the bed and reaching for the shelf. ("It came from up here, right?") While she did that, I dropped the journal into her purse.

I spun back around. Feng was already there. He leaned against the door jamb with a coiled grace. Ninja Cat Lady moved to the window; Monika still stood stupidly on the bed. Feng took in the scene. His blue eye was the one in charge; the other was just there to set the tone. The tiny room felt very full.

Eventually, Feng's gaze settled on me. "Now, either my sister had a much higher opinion of your ability to remain undetected than was warranted or she was perfectly fine with you being discovered. Which do you think it is?"

There wasn't any answer to that, so I took a pass. Feng shifted his eye to Monika, still standing on the bed. "Really," he said, "I'm not so dangerous as all that. Please." He indicated the floor and then extended a hand up.

The room was small enough, and he was big enough, that he didn't have to move to do it.

Monika took his hand ever so briefly and alighted next to me.

Feng observed us for a few seconds in silence, then spoke softly in Chinese to Mi Fan. She threw us a resentful glare and left the room.

"Look," I said, "we broke in. Guilty. If you're going to call the police—"

"Police?" Feng smiled. "Please."

Then he did something that almost made me laugh. In a show of indifference, he examined his fingernails. He blew on them a little, even buffed them on his shirt. This, of course, is essential Bond (James Bond) villain behavior, classically begun in 1959 by Auric Goldfingernail from the Ian Fleming novel of the same name; exhibited the following year by Wax Zorin in *A View to a Cutie-kill*; continued most convincingly by the archvillain Ernst Stavro Blofeld, alias Dr. Shatternail, in the short story *You Only Clip Twice*; and, I am led to understand, will find its most contemporary manifestation in the person of Nails Done in the upcoming film *Cosmetics Cart Blanche*. Yes, movie villains are always examining their nails. It's the universal signal they're about to get down to business.

"Given my sister's absence," said Feng, "and your unfortunate imprisonment in this room, I believe it's fair to say that Xiang—I understand she's been calling herself Shannon these days—wanted you... out of the way for a bit." He went back to his nails. "And if she would place you in my hands to achieve her goal," he continued, still glancing down at those hands, "she must have been in pursuit of something quite important." Now, finally, he looked up—and the threat in his eyes, both of them, was quite clear. "Would you care to say what that might be?"

Monika and I exchanged glances, but neither of us said a word. We knew a destination only, not what awaited us there.

Feng went back to looking eminently bored. "Either you know something of value to me and are therefore useful, or you know nothing and are of no value to me."

The sound of footsteps heralded the appearance of another gentleman. I recognized him from the kung fu demonstration. He stood just behind Feng's left side, he placed his feet a shoulder width apart, and, naturally, he crossed his arms over his chest. The threat was now complete.

Chapter 7

Feng said, "I encourage you to weigh your options carefully," and returned to his fingernail inspection.

I met Monika's eyes one more time, and one more time, I hoped she got it.

"The MacGuffin is in Fort Tryon Park," I said.

Feng forgot all about his nails. "The… McMuffin?"

I sighed. "The Mac*Guffin*. The trope. The thing that everyone is looking for."

Feng's henchman shifted his weight and uncrossed his arms. He was waiting for his cue to beat the living daylights out of me. "We don't know what it is!" I added, perhaps a little hastily. "But we know *where* it is."

Feng considered things for a moment, then nodded toward Monika. The henchman crossed in front of him and gripped Monika's arm.

"You will tell me now where it is," said Feng.

I looked at Monika. She was wearing the same expression on her face that she had during that first martial arts demo we'd attended with Stanislav: aggressively unimpressed ennui.

"We will show you where it is," I replied. "Monika and I, together. If we hurry, we just might all get there in time."

I thought the man towering in front of me had been standing upright, but now he straightened all the way up, adding another inch or so to his height. "Excellent," he said. "I will have the van brought around to the front immediately."

As I trailed Monika out of the room, I noticed that the conversation seeping through the wall behind Shannon's bed had stopped and been replaced with music. I caught a few snappy chords and a familiar melody and decided it was Captain & Tennille. I took a final glimpse outside the window. The blackbird was gone.

The van was a white Ford Econoline with a red and gold Chinese dragon slithering along beneath the passenger windows. Chinese-menu lettering spelled out MASTER LIN'S KUNG FU STUDIO. Underneath that was a phone number and a quote: "He will win who knows when to fight and when not to fight." I questioned the marketing value of that particular slogan.

Feng slid open the side door for us and climbed into the passenger's seat. I slid in next to Monika on the bench in back. Behind us was a large space half filled with gym equipment. Litter-free upholstery and a whiff of pine suggested the interior had been recently cleaned. Feng said something in Chinese to the driver. A face appeared in the rearview mirror, and a hand gripped the steering wheel. The driver started the engine, and we pulled away.

Feng turned around to address us in English. "We're going to take MLK over to Broadway, then up Riverside to Fort Tryon Park. You take it from there, Martin. Oh, and in case you get ideas." I looked at him. The evil in his face could no longer be hidden. He held out a white bucket. It was from KFC, and it still held a few crumbs of Extra Crispy at the bottom. "Your cell phones, please."

We dug them out and dumped them in.

We had been driving for some minutes when I became aware of Monika gently elbowing me.

"Martin," she whispered. "Help me out, here."

I didn't respond right away. Something was familiar about the face that too often showed in the rearview mirror, like he was making sure we were all still here. I looked to see what Monika was up to. She had gotten out Shannon's journal and was prying at the clasp with a nail file. The symbol on the cover reminded me of my earlier revelation. I just hoped Monika hadn't cleared out her purse in the last few months. "There's a better way to do that," I whispered.

A woman's purse is a magical thing. Things once lost are found; necessary objects materialize *ex nihilo*. I think P.L. Travers knew all about this when she had Mary Poppins pulling lampposts and umbrellas out of her carpet bag. I told Monika what I was looking for …

… and there it was. Delicately, for it was quite small, I took the key—the one I had found with Butch's spare, at Zhang's Laundry. I examined it. The first time I saw it, I had thought of the design on its head as being almost but not quite a capital *X*. Now, when I turned it on an angle, it was that same plus-minus symbol that showed up both on the journal and on Shannon's earrings. *And on something else, too.*

I inserted the key and twisted. The clasp silently unlocked.

"You," I whispered to my girlfriend, "are practically perfect in every way."

"I know." She smiled. "You're just lucky I am and that it's still there. I cleaned out my purse last week. Must have missed it."

"If we'd needed to, I think we could have just ripped the thing off with your nail file."

"Fair enough."

The driver's face appeared in the rearview mirror. Monika got to work filing a nail, perhaps with a little more vigor than necessary.

We had unlocked Shannon's secret journal, and we would now unlock the mystery of Xiang Lin.

♘ c7 ♘
THE MYSTERY OF XIANG LIN

This felt entirely different, entirely *worse*, than delving into Butch's journal and notebooks. Butch and I knew each other well, he respected my opinions and accepted my eccentricities, and he thrived on criticism. But this, what I was doing, was wrong. An invasion of privacy. What I held in my hands was not some chess journal, or even a diary, but a *writer's* journal. A diary would have been less bad.

The entries started off short and entirely in what I thought of then as kanji, but which I later learned to call hanzi—the Chinese word for the characters that compose both Chinese and Japanese written languages. I assumed that the language itself was Mandarin. (This was later confirmed.)

Eventually, the entries started to lengthen. Dates indicated that this lengthening generally coincided with Butch's increased interest in fictional literature, as I understood it.

Even better, English translations began appearing on the right-hand side of each page layout, opposite what I assumed were the original Mandarin sources on the left. I was particularly delighted to see the occasional marginalia written in Butch's compact script, suggesting various editorial modifications. It was as if Shannon, inspired by Butch and coached by him, was practicing her writing, and the smallest leap of imagination led me first to the delightful vision of him taking an interest in her prose, and then to thinking of him taking the treacherous step of stealing this, her beautiful, highly personal journal. What did I need to see that he couldn't have simply written in his own journals?

The entries lengthened and lengthened as Monika and I paged through the journal. Finally, we arrived at Shannon's most recent entry. It was clearly autobiographical in nature, with certain names being replaced, presumably (although I remain unclear regarding the efficacy of this) to hedge against possible use as evidence.

The writing was in a beautiful, flowing script:

They say the entire operation has been jeopardized. They tell me you are the cause of it. I fear for you. I fear for your life. Already, he has killed those who stand in his way.

And yet, I play their game. And I wait.

I cannot say how long my brother has been at it. I know only that my involvement began the day our grandfather announced the cancer in his stomach. Once proud and full of focused power, my grandfather was now old and haggard; my devotion to him allowed me no choice but to assist in Jian's operations. The money was more than could be made in a lifetime of tailoring clothes. Jian assured me of this. The money was meant to help our ailing grandfather. Jian assured me of that, as well.

I could have lived this way. I could have lived with all of it. But now it has spread beyond me, and you are involved.

A quarter century ago, my secret love took root. As a child I would watch from behind the curtains as you moved about the floor, the beautiful beads of perspiration, crystals on your mahogany skin, occasionally falling to the mat, marking a path in sweat as you performed whatever taolu grandfather demanded. When you passed by where I hid, the world would smell like spice.

You named yourself Beau and you were eighteen. For you, kung fu was never about fist and foot. I knew that about you, even then. It was a love affair with the Chinese path. You are a man of knowledge and many passions. But the passion that stood alongside kung fu and above all else was your delight in what you at first (out of respect?) called xiangqi, but by which I later learned you simply meant chess.

After lessons, when the other students shed their uniforms and bragged to each other about the movies they would watch and the girls they would watch

Chapter 7

them with, I would watch you. You would open your olive-green bag and bring out your chess set. Right there, on the kwoon floor, you would set up your men and challenge anyone. Grandfather sometimes played. His losses were met with grace. Once, Jian challenged you. Within moments, my brother was checkmated. He threw the king across the room and never challenged you again.

All of this I watched quietly from behind the red embroidered curtains.

My love grew with the years. You I could not have, but your passions I could share. Each night after evening meditations, I would get out my own chess set. It was a mere toy: thin, plastic men on a folding cardboard square; a gift from grandfather on a long-ago rainy day. While the family slept, I would read the works of Reuben Fine and Bobby Fischer and move the men from square to square, seeing in their motion the same rhythms that you and grandfather would make as you sparred along the floor.

Now grandfather is ill, and Jian is sicker yet, in a way that medicine cannot reach. This newest drug from China is targeted toward chess players—and my brother remembers my abilities.

Go to the park, he says, the one where the derelicts play chess for money. Slip some of the white crystals into a cup of coffee. Offer it to them. They will accept, for they are poor, he says, and it is their nature to take whatever is given them. Then, he tells me, I am to play them a game. I am to fight hard, while yet being sure to lose. And I am to ask: did my opponent like what they just had? When they agree, I am to supply them with an over-sized chess set and directions for what to do next. Jian's men will take it from there.

I regret everything—the ancestors know that I do!

My first day in Washington Square, after hooking several people on Glass Snow, I come across a new prospect. His head is down; he is studying his board. He wins, collects his money. I sit down opposite him... and I look across the table into your eyes.

An instant, I believe, was all it took for you to feel the conflict in my person. Could it be that you knew me, even then? I do not think it possible. But of two things I was certain: that if you wanted to discover my identity, you would; and that my brother's operation was already in peril.

Fall turns into winter, and we meet in the park often. Arriving at knowledge is never difficult for you. Always with your nose in the newspapers, always observing the chess that is being played in the park, like a man who knows the affairs of his own home. You could never have failed to observe those over-large chess pieces. "Unsightly and not tournament standard at all" is how you once described them to me.

Soon I was convinced that you perceived the dark trade that had settled over your beloved park. I began to fear that you had made even the connection to myself.

It did not come easily to you. In your eyes, I could see the workings of your mind: capturing it, figuring it, fighting it. For although I never gave you the tainted coffee, I had given you something. I had given you my love. You knew it, and you returned it.

At first, we go exclusively to your apartment. Although I long to, I cannot take you to the studio. I cannot risk you discovering the darkness in my family. In me. Safe in your rooms, away from Jian's schemes, I share myself with you. Sometimes before, sometimes after, we play chess.

Once—was it an accident?—there comes a sudden movement of your hand. Instinctively, my arm slashes upward in a block. My knowledge of the martial arts is revealed. We sit on your couch, and I tell you the secret of my identity. Little do I speak of the genesis of my affections for you. Yet, with you, how little is yet too much?

The next time we see one another, upon your insistence and against my judgment, you come to the studio. Grandfather is there. The meeting of master and student is sweet. Grandfather pontificates and pronounces his benedictions. With your ears you listen, but your eyes observe the hoary hands of your master, clutching at his stomach while he attempts to hide his pain.

I show you to my room, but love eludes us. Your attention is drawn to the sword. My katana. You run your hand along the curved length of its black leather scabbard. Then you recline on my bed and reach for a copy of Modern Chess Strategy. You are lost in pawn structures. It is when you replace the book and stand to take your leave that the seams of this frail fabric I have woven begin to unravel.

Jian is yelling for me. He enters my room, demanding to know my movements of the day. Unaware at first of you standing behind the opened door, he unzips his satchel and empties it onto my bed: large, unsightly pieces. Not tournament standard at all. They are filled with money that needs to be counted—my work for the next hour.

When he turned and saw you, the air froze. You left, my love, and not just

from my room. I cannot show my face in the park, and soon, I fear, I will no longer be welcome at home.
 You are never at yours.
 Where are you, my love?

♞ d7 ♟
FAR ABOVE MANHATTAN'S WATERS.
MARTIN, KING OF SCOTCH.

We entered Fort Tryon Park, then over and under arched bridges and past the remains of the old Billings Mansion, which decades ago had burned to the ground. Abandoning the main arteries, we moved into the capillaries of the park, turning here and there until I spotted a deserted area and said to stop.

We stepped out of the van into a small clearing. A blank sky, damp with spring, pressed down on me. A waist-high stone wall edged one side of the clearing. Monika and I held hands and peered over. Far below, the Hudson River was a choppy highway whose churning silver waters drove on toward a distant industrial shore. A drop of perhaps a hundred feet ended in a thicket of squat trees, which gnarled the bank of the river like the webs of a giant spider. To our right, the wall curved away from the Hudson, giving way to a broad escarpment that climbed from the river to about thirty feet below the level of the clearing.

I understood who our driver was now. I had seen him at the Great Wall of China restaurant; he had ogled our notebooks. Later that night it was certainly he—whose short stature had caused me to take him for a kid—who had bumped into me outside the studio. The notebooks turned up later with Shannon, who had obviously been in a fight. She hadn't stolen them from us; she had returned them—at considerable risk to her life. Maybe we were all lucky to have gotten this far.

Monika's hand shivered a little, or maybe it was my own. I stepped away from the wall. Turning my back to the river, I espied a stone edifice set back into the tree line: an octagon, or perhaps a hexagon. Rectangles of empty space were its occasional windows. A shabby lean-to suggesting a tool shed propped itself against one of its walls like an afterthought. A dozen yards off, Feng pointed to this outbuilding and spoke to the driver in hushed tones. The driver nodded and strode away in that direction.

Feng watched him go, then, looking around, nodded in seeming approval of our deserted surroundings. From the back of the van he withdrew a wooden box about the size of a loaf of bread, then beckoned to me and pointed along the length of the curved stone wall. Some way in that direction I saw a picnic table. The three of us walked there and sat down. He opened the box. It was chess. My life, it seemed, had become something out of a Raymond Chandler novel.

Feng took a pawn of each color from the box, shuffled them behind his back, and extended his fists toward me. I pointed to the one on my right. He opened it, and the white pawn that had been inside landed on e2 with a slap.

I looked at Monika. She gave me a shrug, got up and walked around to the other side of the table, then proceeded the dozen or so feet to the stone wall. She leaned up against it, gazed across the Hudson into the far country of New Jersey. Her red hair hung limply, as if weighed down by river water that had risen from below, moistening the lifeless air.

Feng was speaking to me. "I said I'd like us to know one another better, Martin. Agree?"

"Naturally," I said. What was his game?

Feng's thin smile was lost in the heavy flesh of his face. "I propose that we make a little game of this ... chess business."

Chess business? "What did you have in mind?" I asked.

"If one of us captures the other's piece, he gets to ask a question. If the other wishes to re-capture, he must first give answer. Agree?"

Apparently this game of chess came with a twist. But what choice did I have? I agreed and pushed my king's pawn forward two squares.

The game was a Scotch, with both my center pawns out. Feng made the right move and captured on d4 with his pawn—which meant he got to ask the first question.

"I hope you don't mind playing with a nonstandard chess set. But then, you might be in possession of a similar set yourself?"

What an odd thing to ask. Then I realized: we were playing with an exact wooden replica of the overly large set of pieces that were this man's stock-in-trade in the park. Could Feng be on White Knight right now? If so, I had no chance. I knew firsthand what being on that drug was like. I searched his demeanor for signs. He was playing straight.

Feng was looking back at me, searching for a clue of his own. The feeling I had, the one you get when you drive off to a remote location with someone you think is a killer, was getting worse. How much did this man already know? Was he asking himself the same about me? He narrowed his eyes and returned his attention to the board, where he awaited my re-capture.

It occurred to me that I needn't re-capture at all. I could refuse to answer! A fine way to get slaughtered. So I took his pawn and said, "Nonstandard sets can have their own charms." Feng narrowed his eyes even farther. Just like his sister had, seconds before she'd brought a chair down on my head.

I focused on the game. Feng's knight, I saw, could trade itself for mine. He would get to ask another question. But if he took, my re-capture would place my queen strongly in the center of the board. On the other hand, if he *didn't* capture, he would allow *me* to initiate the trade. Then I would be the one asking the questions. What was the real game here? To ask questions? Or to play good chess?

Feng grunted and developed his other knight—the right move. Immediately I took on c6, but what to ask? This whole game of take-and-ask was Feng's idea. Likely, he had spent the car trip up working out his questions. I decided to ask what I honestly wished to know:

"Why do you think Shannon came to this place?"

Now it was Feng's turn to decide: answer or lose a piece. He could take my knight with either of two pawns. One choice would allow me to trade queens—and ask another question. The other was a much better move. Feng correctly reached for his b-pawn. But instead of answering, he asked, "You think maybe she's looking for something?"

Dodging!? That was hardly sporting! So I grabbed my knight out of his hand and clapped it back on c6. "You want my knight, you answer my question."

He sat up straight, visibly affronted. Was this it? The time for jumping the table already upon me, my life to end with the first fives moves of a Scotch Game?

But Feng paused, then chuckled—a thick and reluctant puff of an enormous bellows. "I have underestimated you, Martin. Shall we try again?" Then, not waiting for a reply, "She's looking for something that doesn't belong to her. She is dangerous."

I didn't think I was going to get any more. "Let's get back to our game," I said.

Feng was attacking my e4 pawn. Normally I would have advanced it, but I wanted to give this guy every opportunity for bad trades, so I guarded it with my king's bishop. Feng aligned a rook with my b-pawn, which was guarded by my queen's bishop. He was attacking wherever he could, daring my pieces to enter the fight. My bishop ignored this threat and moved anyway, pinning his knight to his queen.

Feng had been playing fast, handling his pieces like weapons, cracking them down on their target squares. Now he paused. He hadn't expected I would leave something unguarded. It was a move he would never have made himself.

Leaving Feng to grunt, I looked away from the board. Monika had her back to us. She was remaining detached, staring up at the arch of heaven, looking at nothing. A sudden motion to my left, off by the van, caught my eye. The rear door, opening. It swung toward me; I couldn't see who was there. Not so many minutes ago, the driver had been sent to investigate the building in the woods. Could he have already returned? My curiosity was curtailed by another sudden movement, this one from the board.

Slowly, craftily, Feng was sliding his queen's pawn into battle against its counterpart on e4. He wanted me to take it. Was practically begging. In defiance of Feng's offer, I pushed my own pawn forward, attacking the pinned black knight.

In a half second, Feng slapped his queen in front of my pawn, pinning it to my king. Had I been tricked? Was this some dumb schoolboy reverse-psychology trick, like he knew I wasn't going to take his pawn because he thought I thought he wanted me to?

When in doubt, castle. (Just another of my grandfather's adages; don't go looking for it in Yusupov or Nimzowitsch.) My pawn was going down, and there was nothing I could do to stop it. So I castled, and I did it like I meant it, only then realizing that in doing so, I had poisoned my pawn. Feng couldn't capture it—his queen and king would be exposed to my rook.

Chapter 7

Feng didn't notice my accidental trap. He grabbed the pawn off the board, earning himself a question.

"What did you take from my trophy case?"

But the question was in vain, for the pawn he had captured had been unguarded. There would be no re-capture and therefore no answer. Instead, using the pinky of my right hand, I slid my rook over one square, where it skewered the black royalty.

As quickly as I had thought to demoralize my opponent with this move, just that quickly did he dash my hopes with a trick of his own. The black queen had moved to save her knight, and now she called upon the knight to return the favor. Feng interposed it between his queen and my rook.

The board was chaos. My bishop could take his knight, my rook could take his knight, his pawn could take my bishop, his queen could take my *other* bishop. Where was a good hit of White Knight when I needed it?

But... wait! I saw the tactic I needed. It was as if a trace of the designer drug still coursed through the synapses of my brain. Feng's king, still uncastled, lingered on its home square. The only thing separating my queen from the king's side, where she would deliver checkmate, were a couple of pieces. What I needed was clearance.

Without further deliberation I snapped off his knight. Would Feng re-capture with the pawn? No, he was too good for that mistake. Mate would follow immediately. And then there was the matter of my other bishop. Yes, he would take that. What was taking him so long?

I looked up to see Feng staring at me. I had completely forgotten—I had taken a piece! He was waiting for me to ask a question. To clear my mind, I looked off toward the wall...

... and what I saw there made no sense. A pair of black-gloved hands were moving one over the other, the fingers hooked over the top of the wall, the body they belonged to hanging out of sight on the other side. I must have stared too long, because Feng lost patience and said, "Well?"

He wanted a question? Fine. I gave him one. I asked about the person who had been on my mind every day for the last three months. "Did Butch take something from you?"

"Butch!" Feng said my friend's name like we were a couple of kids on holiday, just arrived down the shore. "Yes, you would want to know about him." His hand hovered over my poisoned bishop on e4. If he answered this question and took that piece, the game would be over, probably in more ways than one. Instead, he used his queen to capture the *other* bishop: a fresh capture, not a re-capture. I was not going to get an answer. Instead, he got to ask a question.

"Tell me, Martin. When I look at my security footage later tonight, will I see the three of you coming through my front door today? Or did you use a different entrance? A different entrance, I think."

There was nothing for me to re-capture, and it had been a rhetorical question anyway. I took his d-pawn, removing my bishop from the e-file, clearing the way to his king. Check. Time for me to ask a question.

"Did you try to kill Butch?"

Feng blocked the check. I grabbed another pawn, allowing for another question, and this time giving check directly with my bishop.

"Where is Butch?" I asked.

Feng moved his king one square to his left. I had mate in two. All I needed was to sacrifice my queen. I did so. Feng had no choice but to capture it, giving *him* license for one final question:

"What am I going to do with you, Martin?"

I reached for my rook to give mate on e8—the home of the black king. But my rook never made it there.

♞ e7 ♞
YOU GOT ME GOING IN SUCH CIRCLES

Like a gymnast, she vaulted herself up and over the stone wall. I had been thrown by her once before and knew her strength. I was reaching for my rook to deliver checkmate, when the driver, coming from behind me, advanced upon Monika. Before he could lay a hand on her, Shannon was there. She jabbed him in the side, buckling him over. Then it was a round sweep across the grass with a foot, and the driver went down. She picked him up off the ground like he was a sack of dirt and slung him over her shoulder into a fireman's carry. By the time Feng and I stood up, she was holding the guy upside down by the ankles, helpless and writhing, over the drop opposite the stone wall, a hundred feet over a riverbank.

Chapter 7

"Stop right there, Feng," she told her brother. "Gooli's a runt, but I can't hold him forever."

"What do you want, Xiang?" said Feng.

Instead of answering, she called to me. "Martin! Get the van. The keys are in the ignition."

"Where did you come from?"

"Martin!" said Monika, exasperated. "The van! Questions later."

So I ran across the lawn, helped by a slight downgrade I hadn't noticed during our walk to the picnic table. I looked back only once to see what looked like cardboard cutouts suspended in mid-action, props on a stage. Even Gooli (*Gooli?* I truly hoped it was a nickname) was motionless as he hung in space, looking up to look down toward the ground far below. It must have been terrifying.

I got to the van and climbed in. The keys indeed hung from the ignition. I started it up, wheeled it around, and drove back to the merry band. As I approached, Monika made a circling motion with her arms, then waved them back and forth in parallel like an airport ground crew guiding a 737 into a gate. I inferred that I was meant to back the van up close to Shannon. Feng stood where I had left him—silent, watching for an opening. Monika opened the back door, then came around and climbed into the passenger's seat.

"Closer," she said, "just get right up to her. The instant Gooli's out of danger, Feng is coming."

"Why doesn't she just make him back farther away?" I asked.

"It's a stalemate between siblings, Martin. Leave it at that."

I still didn't see why she didn't just make him back up. I rolled the van until the open door nearly touched the stone wall, interposed between Shannon and her brother.

"Get ready, Martin." Monika and I watched as Gooli appeared above the wall, then got himself flung into the van, landing with a thump. "Go!"

I went. Shannon ran for it, leaping into the back as we hit five miles per hour. Feng had already sprung toward us, but Shannon shut the door, and the shakedown began.

"All right, you little shit," she said, turning to Gooli, "what did you find in there?" She meant the outbuilding.

"I didn't find anything. It wasn't in there."

"Why would I believe you?"

"The shed is filled with tools and stuff," Gooli whined. "It would take hours to look through it all."

"Then how do you know it isn't there? You miserable little cockroach, you found it, didn't you!"

"I didn't!"

She started patting him down, hands and accusations everywhere. Meanwhile, I had been driving across the lawn toward the dirt road we had come in on.

"Martin!" said Shannon. "Where do you think you're going?"

"Out of the park?" I didn't understand some of the recent moves and wasn't privy to her strategy.

"No, no, no. Turn around. If I don't find anything on this weasel, you and Monika and I are going to have to take apart that shed."

I checked the rearview mirror. "Your brother is still running after us. What do we do about him?"

"Just... keep out of range."

I wasn't sure exactly what that meant, but for the next few minutes I drove in circles and figure eights, carving muddy ruts into the rich, early spring grass, baiting Feng, alternately letting him close in as I made my turns, then creating some distance on the straightaways. Monika's hand would tighten on my shoulder with each swerve, then relax again as we straightened out. Meanwhile, Shannon was going after Gooli with increasing aggressiveness.

"May I at least ask what we are looking for?" I yelled to the back of the van.

"Flash drive," said Shannon, invading Gooli's pockets.

While I executed a particularly wide arc (Feng chugging along behind me, cutting across the swerve of my trajectory; me cutting back, foiling his interception, all the while wondering just what, exactly, he thought he would do if he caught up with us), Monika and I shared a brief, calculating glance. The facts were finally adding up. Butch the amateur sleuth had taken something of Feng's and hidden it; Feng is running a drug ring; Shannon is looking for a flash drive. If one and one and one still made three, the conclusion seemed straightforward.

Calling back to Shannon (finishing off a curve, moving into a

Chapter 7

straightaway, Monika releasing her grip on my shoulder), I yelled, "Are you telling us that Butch broke into the studio and downloaded a bunch of information about your drug operation onto a flash drive and hid it; then, just in case anything happened to him, he left behind an elaborate hunt that would allow me to recover it?"

"It's not *my* operation! Don't you go putting that on me!" Not much of an answer, but then again, it was. So there we had it, friends—the answer to the mystery. Something still bothered me, though, and I said to Monika, "Why wouldn't Butch have just handed this all over to the police?"

"Shannon" was her one-word response.

Of course. Butch would have wanted to handle this in his own way, without implicating his lover. I thought some more and asked, "But why hide it? Why not just keep it safe in his apartment?"

My girlfriend sometimes enjoys an economy of words. "You see his apartment this morning?"

"Right," I said.

"You know," Monika yelled back to Shannon, "someone once told me that *gool* in Jersey Italian means 'ass.' Gooli could have found the flash drive in that shed and hid it up his ass."

"Is that it, Gooli?" said Shannon, rounding on him. "Did you put it up your ass?"

"What?" Poor Gooli. "No!"

I looked in the (heh, heh) rearview mirror to catch a glimpse of the unfortunate man whose name means "ass" in Jersey Italian. He was busy denying that anything, ever, at any time, now, before, or in the future, had ever, ever been up his ass. I said, "Hey, Shannon, what do you say we believe him on this one?"

Shannon shook Gooli anew. "Martin here thinks we should believe you. Is he right?" Several very sincere nods from the man in her grip. "Am I going to need to personally check your ass?" Very sincere shakes of the head. Shannon yelled up to me, "You got a Plan B, Martin?"

For the second time that day I did, and the sweet thing about it, or so I thought, was that it didn't involve searching anyone's ass. But first we needed to jettison our extra. I slowed down and told Shannon to open the back door. Understanding me perfectly, she improvised the rest. Feng, the fastest man I've ever known, was still tailing us. The next time he got within a few feet of us, he caught his lieutenant in the chest.

I turned the van around one last time and found the dirt road leading out. Intending to drive back to Harlem, I started to explain Plan B.

I didn't get far.

♞ f7 ♞
LIBERATED. BEEF, PORK, CHICKEN, FISH. A NEW START.

I was explaining how I didn't believe Butch had hidden the flash drive at Fort Tryon Park at all and how what we needed to do was return to Butch's apartment to recalibrate our search, when a black SUV came out from under the Henry Hudson Parkway, driving toward us. I didn't take any notice, and I didn't notice, either, when it passed us and made a quick turn-around. In fact, my first impression that anything was wrong at all came when Shannon yelled, "Fuck, that's a gun! Martin, get us out of here!"

I looked in the rearview mirror to see the black SUV rapidly gaining on us. It was coming around to my right, and a gun was emerging from the driver's window. Before I could react, the SUV was almost even with us. Two things happened then. Shannon yelled, "Cut right! Into the beam!" I saw it. Ahead, the underpass hooked to the left—if I slanted to the right, into the SUV, it would have nowhere to go but into a support beam that held up the Parkway. The other thing that happened was Monika yelling at me to stop.

The second yell of "Stop!" came with another word: "Father!" and that's probably what I reacted to. I slammed the brakes. The SUV skated past us, turned around, and pulled up to me, driver to driver. It was Tomas.

"Jesus Christ!" yelled Shannon.

"Shit!" hissed Monika, already out the passenger's side.

"Cavalry's here!" said Tomas from his window. "Looks like you managed without me."

Monika was already there, between us, berating her father. A gun? What did he think he was doing? He'd liberated it (his exact words) from the Delmonicos (neighbors, apparently). Kept it at the ready, just in case we were in trouble. Would he put it away? Of course he'd put it away, don't even mention it. The Chevy Suburban? Also liberated. From the same people, nice folks so willing to help a guy. He was coming to pick us up, didn't we remember? We didn't think we'd've all fit into his Alfa Romeo, did we?

The questioning lasted about a minute, and he emerged mostly unscathed. We were all standing outside now, having moved the vehicles onto a patch of grass beneath a tree. Monika caught Tomas up with events and (Shannon being right there) carefully worded revelations.

"Look," he said, "ditch the van. You're not going to want to be seen driving around in that. Let's all get into the Suburban and take a ride. I've got sandwiches for everybody. Martin!" He chucked me the keys. "You were doing a fine job driving just now. How about you take the wheel?"

We left the studio's van there under the tree, but we kept the keys. Feng would get back, but there was no point in helping. We also remembered to fetch our phones from the KFC bucket. Then we piled into the Suburban.

"I've got pastrami on rye, here," Tomas said, climbing in next to Shannon. "The chicken parm's got extra sauce, and the porchetta's the kind with the skin still on. Who wants the tuna salad?" He distributed the sandwiches. I was just about to put the SUV into drive when he startled me with, "Let's all bow our heads in grace."

Taken unawares and responding to deeply buried habits, I began to bow my head. I caught myself and looked around. Shannon was confused, Monika was rolling her eyes, the shadow of a grin lightly dimpling her cheeks. Tomas lifted his hands to the heavens (or at any rate, to the roof of the Suburban) and spoke in a quick, sing-song meter:

Burning snowballs, flying pigs,
Beer is best with nuts and figs.
Last call!

"Last call," echoed Monika. She shrugged and mumbled to me, "It's just a thing he does." I chuckled as we dug into our sandwiches, and we hit the road.

It felt good, driving. A light rain began, lacquering the earth and deepening the colors of the city and the trees. I found the windshield wiper controls; Monika adjusted the heat. We left the park behind us and melded into Saturday traffic. The SUV lofted me above the drifting metal squares of sedan roofs, the extra elevation sharpening my already acute sense of agency.

We used the time to try to clear the air with Shannon. Without any mention of her writer's journal, Monika told her that we understood, if she had been forced to do certain things against her choosing and how, given the circumstances, everything she had done was completely reasonable. The look on Shannon's face downshifted from moderately furious to slightly sullen. It was a beginning. The rest came when that master of diplomacy, Tomas Perfiliev, stepped in.

He ate while he worked, laying a companionable hand on Shannon's shoulder that she remarkably allowed to stay there. "Worried about what happens legal-wise when it all comes down? Doan." Spoken around a big bite of chicken parmesan, this last word apparently was meant to be *don't*. He swallowed and continued, "You're a queen, demoted to a pawn, forced to act against her will. When it comes time, I'll get you good counsel. You just play it straight, cooperate. Most likely end up with a little community service, is all. Not the end of the world." He retracted his hand from her shoulder in order to wipe his mouth, then pointed to Monika. "M-clip, you going to eat the second half of that porchetta?"

"You keep your hands on your own damn sandwich," retorted his daughter.

Tomas shrugged and went back to Shannon. "What was your game, anyway? Use these two," he waved what remained of his sandwich at me and Monika, "figure out where the drive was hidden, then get to it ahead of them? Make off with it?" He looked at Shannon like they were discussing which horse to bet on at the races. "There, there," he said when it became clear he wasn't getting an answer, "you just have your pastrami. It was a fine plan." He finished off the last bite. "It's what I would have done."

We pulled up to Butch's apartment building. I sent Shannon in to retrieve the atlas.

"You sure about that, Martin?" asked Monika when she left. "She could bolt."

"I don't think so. Listen—she doesn't know where to look anymore, and she knows I have a theory."

"A trust test!" said Tomas. "Good thinking, M-doc. Plus, she knows now that we understand her secret and therefore her motivations. She feels we're on her side. Trust me, she's not going anywhere. Now go ahead, M-doc, let's have that theory."

"Okay. When Shannon became convinced that we knew where to look for the flash drive, she made an excuse to take us to the one place she knew she could hold us—her room."

"M-clip," Tomas said, "back when I met you near Fort Tryon Park, didn't you tell me there was a trap door in that room?"

I answered for her. "Shannon would have no reason to suspect I knew about it."

"But you said it was nailed shut?"

"Feng must have done that after watching his security footage."

"All right," he said, "let's have the rest."

"While Monika and I were trapped, Shannon went to Fort Tryon Park. She discovered the lean-to and figured the flash drive was hidden inside. She was looking for it when she heard us approach, and the rest you know."

Monika said, "You're holding out. Where's the flash drive?"

"I don't know where it *is*, but I think I know where to start looking. Butch's apartment is not the home of the black king."

"Well what is, then?"

"Two people at two different times unknowingly pointed to it. The first was Master Lin, during the exhibition. He gave a short speech. Remember?"

Monika thought a bit. "He said something about the studio being a home to his students." Her eyes brightened. "You're saying we should start marking off from the studio? That's the home of the black king?"

"Not exactly. Butch has centered this hunt not around kung fu, but around chess. His 'studio' is—"

Tomas snapped his fingers. "The park! Butch wants the first square to be Washington Square Park! M-doc, I never doubted you for a moment. You're a smart guy, I don't care *what* the people say."

I gave him a sharp look. "Wait, *what*—" I started, but Monika interrupted.

"But who was the second person?" she asked.

"Shannon herself! In her journal, she writes: "… always observing the chess that is being played in the park, like a man who knows the affairs of his own home…"

"You were right about her, Martin." Monika pointed out the window. "Here she comes."

Tomas slid open the side door and Shannon got in. She handed me the atlas.

Before Shannon had a chance to sit, Monika said, "Shannon, we've been talking, and we want to start counting off from Washington Square instead of from Butch's place. We think the Square is what Butch may have meant by the phrase 'the home of the black king.' What do you think?"

Shannon closed her eyes and sighed. I knew the look, like when the game is over, and your opponent shows you the winning move you missed. "Of course," she said. "The *Square*. That is exactly how he would think."

The three of us shared a grin, and I opened the atlas to the now-familiar map of Manhattan. My companions hunched in close while I traced off the moves from Butch's puzzles, this time beginning with the square that enclosed the bulk of Washington Square Park. When my finger finally came to rest, Tomas took a pen from his pocket and drew an X inside the final square.

"Well sonofabitch," he said. "And we just ate, too."

♚ g7 ♝
WWBD. OVER THE TOP. BOTTOM OF THE NINTH.

Chef Tonio was awaiting us inside the wide wooden double doors of The Slipper & the Fez. Tomas had called ahead. "My friends!" the chef wheezed, all quivering jowls and pumping hands. "It has been too long! Please!" He clapped twice; a red-slippered valet appeared. "Park their vehicle!" he commanded, as with clean-shaven arms he collected us into his sanctum.

He led us past the maître d' station, then around a corner softened by tall potted plants. In the main dining room, people lounged on damask cushions and ate with their hands from low tables. Exotic aromas of tagine and sultry spices and colorful stews overlaid one another like Iznik tiles. Neon fish swam in the huge, floor-to-ceiling aquarium I remembered from

Chapter 7

my previous visit. A waiter was covering a long table with white linens and shiny chafing dishes for tomorrow's lunch buffet.

As for the flash drive, it could have been anywhere. There are a thousand places in a restaurant.

Monika pulled Chef Tonio aside and engaged him in hushed conversation. I heard the chef say, "I remember the man of whom you speak, but I know nothing of any hidden treasures…"

Tomas followed the encouraging aromas into the kitchen, leaving me to hunt after my own fashion.

Someone spoke behind me: "He has given up the gods but still believes in his celestial book."

I turned to face Shannon. "Excuse me?"

She nodded to indicate the retreating Tomas. "He is a good man, living in a world that is still good. For people like him, there is a book. There may not be an author, but the story is trusted nonetheless: every moment, there's a belief that all ends well for him and everyone he touches. And so it is left to the agnostics to do the work."

"I see," I said. And the thing was, I actually did see. For the first time, the whole Butch-and-Shannon thing started making sense.

"I see," I repeated. "But for us, there is no book?"

"There is no book."

There was nothing more to say, and for a little while we said it. I wanted to explore, but with everyone gone their own way I felt that I should at least keep Shannon with me. I motioned to the aquarium. We went and stood in front of it, looking at the fish through the glass while we spoke.

I said, "It's true about the flash drive? Butch stole it from your brother?"

She lowered her voice. "Before I gave up living at the studio, I overheard Feng saying that it contains data on the cartel he works for. Names, accounts, transactions. Butch discovered everything, naturally. One night he broke in and copied the files from the office computer. He barely escaped. Feng would have killed him on the spot had Butch been any slower."

"And if we find the drive?"

We stood quite close to the aquarium; the moisture of her breath made pale puffs on the glass. A fish swam by. "The files are encrypted. If we find the drive, I know the access key."

"You would hand yourself in?"

She paused. "Do you think your father-in-law is correct? About the community service?"

My father-in-law. Yes, everyone could see that that was essentially what Tomas had become. "I suppose he knows about such things," I said, remaining as noncommittal as possible.

Her next question took me unawares. "What would Butch do?"

My friend Butch, the self-taught man, living off the disposable concern of strangers, now taken a lover. What *would* Butch say to a lover? It seemed to me that his prescription would not look beyond his own internal logic. I said, "I think Butch would want you to savor the game and look for beauty in the positions that arise organically from its proper execution."

She squinted at me. "What does that even mean?"

"I don't know," I said, "but…"

"But" she sighed and looked back into the aquarium, "it does sound like him."

"Yes. That's odd."

"Don't worry about it, Martin. I really didn't expect an answer."

"No, I don't mean about the question. I meant *that*." I pointed to the bottom of the aquarium, near Shannon's foot. Inside, amid the mossy rocks and coral, was what looked like a perfectly circular rock with a bump in its exact center. I knelt to get a closer look.

It was a sombrero, about three inches across, resting on the head of a plastic man whose red arms were wrapped around his green knees as he took a siesta. Around the rim of the sombrero were the words, SOUTH OF THE BORDER.

"Je-zus," I said, descending to the American idiom. "This has to be it!"

Shannon knelt next to me. "What do you mean?"

"In one of his notebooks, Butch wrote about a tourist who claimed to not have any cash, so he paid Butch with a South of the Border souvenir. South of the Border," I explained, "is a cheesy rest stop off I-95 somewhere in the Carolinas."

"I've heard of it. You think this is our flash drive? Inside the thing?"

"Let's get Chef Tonio," I said.

We found the chef in his kitchen, reciting a stew recipe to Monika and Tomas. Tomas was licking a wooden spoon. He saw me and tried to hand me the spoon. "M-doc, ever eat pigeon? You gotta try this."

Chapter 7

Ignoring the spoon, I explained about the sombrero. Everyone came to look.

"This is what we've been after this whole time?" said Monika, spotting the chintz.

"How did Butch get it in there?" Tomas asked.

"Your friend stopped by on his own, once," said Chef Tonio. His eyes rolled up into his head, searching for lost memory. "This was… mmm… some weeks after he dined here last year with you all. I remembered him when he came: the man with all the questions. I took him back into the kitchen for a tour."

I thought, *I bet getting that tour didn't take too much of an effort.*

Shannon asked, "Is there access to the aquarium?"

"I'll take you," said the chef. "Come, come!"

We went back to the kitchen, then through a walk-in freezer and into a supply room. I easily imagined Butch leading the exuberant restaurateur on, a string of questions at the ready, delving deeper, watching for the right moment and place to deposit his plastic relic.

A black cloth covered one length of the supply room. Chef Tonio pulled it back, and we found ourselves looking through the aquarium into the dining room. The top of the tank was covered by a grate that Tomas was already removing. Before I knew what was happening, the brazen man had pulled off his trousers. Then he handed Monika his shirt, pulled off his socks (kicking them unceremoniously to the side), and there he stood in front of all us, wearing nothing but white briefs.

"Hey, M-Doc, come over here. Can you do this?" He bent at the knee a few inches.

"Do what?" I asked, moving next to my de facto father-in-law and unconsciously mimicking his posture.

"Thanks." He planted a foot on my thigh, grabbed the top of the tank, and with a surprisingly small splash, pulled himself up and over into the aquarium.

"Ma*donna!*" exclaimed the chef, clapping a hand to the side of his head.

Shannon stifled a cry.

The diners on the opposite side of the tank went into a state of pandemonium.

Monika said, "Now *that* was over the top." She turned to Chef Tonio. "Would you happen to have any bath towels?"

Suspended in the middle of the tank, Tomas inverted himself, did a frog kick to reach the bottom, and scooped up the sombrero-wearing tchotchke. Righting himself, he held it out in front of him. Bubbles spewed from the corners of his smile.

"Terrific, Father!" said Monika, when his head came up over the surface of the water. "Now what?"

Sometimes you can spot a shooting star or feel the echo of a memory that taunts you before it slithers away. In precisely this fleeting manner, I witnessed the briefest shadow of embarrassment come and go over Tomas Perfiliev's face. He made a few exploratory attempts at getting out. The problem seemed to be one of purchase.

"I'm fine, everyone," he announced, his head seeming to float there, disembodied, him sounding for all the world like his son. "I just need a good, strong jump... this might be a little... messy—"

"Wait!" Chef Tonio said. He clapped thrice. An employee appeared, was spoken to, disappeared, and soon reappeared with a small stepladder and a stack of neatly folded towels. Tonio handed the stool to Tomas, who planted it in the bed of turquoise rocks that covered the aquarium floor. With somewhat less grace than how he had entered, Tomas bounded off the stool, got half his torso over the edge of the tank, and after a few moments of painful viewing on my part, maneuvered himself out of the tank—along with about two gallons of salt water and one very surprised neon yellow fish.

I took the sombrero man from Tomas.

Chef Tonio began handing towels to Tomas, who dried himself off.

Monika ran out to the dining room to see what she could do about the guests.

Shannon picked up the fish, got a look on her face that made me think she was wondering what it would taste like if properly prepared, and returned it to the tank.

The kitchen helper started drying the floor.

Tomas beamed.

After a while, everything steadied off to what would have to pass for normal for the restaurant that evening. Tomas was doing up the last couple

Chapter 7

buttons on his shirt and advising his friend the chef that he call his aquarium service first thing in the morning to stabilize the tank.

"Perhaps," suggested Chef Tonio, "some baklava before you go? Freshly made! I have mint tea—"

"No!" I said, perhaps more forcefully than was necessary. "Really, thank you. Your restaurant is wonderful. But I'm afraid we must be going."

The chef looked hurt. Masterfully, Tomas managed the situation. An arm around the shoulder, compliments offered and promises made, a fistful of nuts from an open canister. Soon we were out on the dark street, waiting for the red-slippered valet to recover our SUV. If you are ever in New York, I recommend a visit to The Slipper & the Fez. The food is delicious, the staff attentive, and the décor magnificent. And last I checked, the stepstool is still inside the aquarium.

"Now what, M-doc?"

We were back in the Suburban. I was in the driver's seat, the engine idling. I pulled the souvenir from my pocket. "Let's open this thing up."

Everyone leaned in to get a look. The thing, it turned out, was a piggy bank. There was a slot in the back of the sombrero for coins, and a circular rubber plug covered the napping man's gooli. I pulled out the plug and stuck my finger in the hole.

Inside the man's ass was a plastic storage baggie. I pulled that out, unzipped it, and inside of that was another baggie inside of which was a third baggie. Butch had been going for full-fledged waterproof, and I hoped it had worked, because inside the third baggie was our flash drive.

Monika reached over from the passenger's seat and picked up the drive, turning it over in her hands, making sure it was real. "Now what?" She handed it back to me.

"The files are encrypted. Shannon says she can open them. We should get my laptop."

"Is it home?"

"The Ninth."

"This might get a little messy."

Chapter 7

We drove downtown. Twenty minutes later we pulled up to the Bobst. I asked Tomas to stay with the SUV, keep an eye out. The rest of us descended through my underworld of red-glowing space heaters and flickering fluorescent bulbs. We came to L-918. I was about to get out my keys, but the door was already open.

"Well, hey there, Marty!" Postdoc stood up from his desk. His blue jeans were ripped, and his T-shirt said YEAH, I'M THAT GUY. He spotted Shannon. "Chinese! Butch's woman?" He approached with a half-upraised arm, maybe for a high-five. Shannon went into a stance.

I had no intention of calling 911 to come pick another bloody body up off my office floor. I intervened.

"Shannon, this is my colleague, Postdoc. He's mostly harmless. Postdoc, I'd like you to meet Shannon. She's a friend, and, yes, she is with Butch."

Reluctantly, Shannon shook hands. Postdoc's cheeks turned a touch pink, and he sat back down. Monika sat on his desk and engaged him in conversation.

I went to my own desk, turned on my laptop, and inserted the flash drive. A window opened, and a cursor blinked patiently on the screen. I had Shannon take over. She typed in the encryption key. In moments, the window populated with files. Shannon clicked on one; a spreadsheet of names and numbers appeared.

Postdoc's voice came from behind me. "I guess I'm not supposed to ask what that is?"

Shannon ejected the drive and handed it to me. She stood and turned to face Postdoc, and for a moment I thought I was going to need to make that 911 call after all. But whatever she was about to say got interrupted by a text on her phone. She read it, and her face went wan.

"Is everything okay?" asked Monika.

"It's Mi Fan," said Shannon. "At the studio. My grandfather is dying."

She looked up from her phone, and her calculating gaze landed on Postdoc.

"You," she said. "We're going on a trip. You're coming along."

♞ h7 ♟
INTERLOPERS. PLAN D. THE STANDING SIXTH.

Night lit up Manhattan. Five of us were in the Suburban now, driving uptown. When we had returned to the SUV from my office, I had found Tomas sitting in the driver's seat. I handed him the flash drive and shooed him over to the passenger's seat as I got behind the wheel. Monika and Shannon climbed into the seats in the middle row, while Postdoc stretched out on the bench in back.

As we drove, Shannon received further texts from Mi Fan, who gave instructions: Shannon was to arrive as quickly as possible; there was no guarantee of a last good-bye with her grandfather. Clearly, Feng had either returned or had gotten in touch with Mi Fan, because she knew quite a bit, although she thought we still had the van. If Feng had returned—and he probably had—it must have been by some other means. Mi Fan also knew that Monika and I were with Shannon, and somehow she even guessed about Tomas. We were to pull up to the front. Someone from the studio would park the van. Shannon would be met at the door and led to Master Lin's chamber, while the interlopers ("that's you lot," Shannon clarified) would be taken to the main floor.

Tomas was thrilled. "Sounds like a trap!"

"Plan B," I said for the third time that day, which, unbelievably, had begun at Bellevue Hospital. "We drop Shannon off a block away and wait for her in a pub. Feng tried to kill us up there!"

"If my grandfather is dead," said Shannon, "Butch will not be far behind."

"Butch is somewhere in the studio, then?" I asked.

"I'm almost certain of it. I just don't understand where."

"Okay, Plan C. We call the police. Right now."

Shannon slapped the back of my headrest. "What did I say about that, Martin? You're forgetting already about the cameras all over the place? My brother sees cops, blood flows."

"Okay, what, then?" said Tomas. "There's got to be some way to take advantage of the situation."

Naturally. For in The Gospel According to St. Tomas the

Chapter 7

Never-Doubting, the threat of death is a mere plot device, put in the Celestial Book just to keep everyone interested. I looked in the rearview mirror. My presumptive father-in-law was drumming his fingers on a knee, while with his free hand he was popping a fistful of nuts into his mouth. As he chewed, a crunching seemed to come from his skull, where, forced by the fecundity of his optimism and cajoled by the unimpeachable comfort of food, the gears of his brain wound into overdrive.

"Plan D," he said. "We park a block away, just like you said. But *we* don't go to the door. *You* do."

I was trying to work out the object of Tomas's address, when Postdoc ("Who, what, me?") sat up from where he had been lying on the bench all the way in the back, as if hiding from the rest of us.

Tomas explained. "Yes, you. They don't know you, kid. That's why Shannon here wanted you to come along. Isn't that right, S-curve?"

A hurtling light, pooled from the debauched polychrome of Times Square, set fire to Shannon's eyes. She said, "Don't you *fuckin* call me one of those stupid, fucking, *nick*names!"

Monika gave her father a sidelong look of exasperation, I drove through a light that wasn't yellow anymore, and Postdoc's head rose like a loaf of bread from behind the bench where he had ducked. Tomas ate another fistful of nuts. Moments passed, and the blaze in Shannon's eyes abated. Everyone, including the pedestrian who hadn't bothered to turn around to deliver me his middle finger and accompanying coital suggestion, was safe.

"But basically," said Tomas, "something like that was your idea, right?"

Shannon sighed. "Yeah."

In the end, Plan D amounted to this: We ditch the SUV someplace, slip into the studio basement through the tunnel connecting it to the tailor shop,

(*hope that Feng hasn't changed the entry code on the keypad*),

and position ourselves at the base of the stairs to the main level. Once there, Shannon would text the nearby Postdoc, who would knock on the door, creating a diversion. When we heard Mi Fan go to the door, we would creep upstairs,

(*hope that Feng was elsewhere*),

and Shannon would slip into Master Lin's room, while the rest of us

(*interlopers*)

went to her room and waited for her there.

But wait! I hear you say. The last time Shannon sent "you lot" to her room, didn't she … ?

She did. Oh yeah, she did. But we trust Shannon now. Yes, we do. Don't we?

I needn't have worried about Feng and the keypad code. When we got to the end of the tunnel connecting the tailor shop to the studio basement, we found the door ajar. No—the keypad code turned out to be the very last thing we needed to be concerned with that night.

The basement was lit up blood red, and I was hit with the smell of freshly sawn wood. Many more crates were here than before. Sawdust encircled some of the boxes like sketches left by detectives to outline the bodies of the slain. The close placement of the crates, some covered, some not, bunches of them stacked together here and there in formation, made a labyrinth out of the place.

Tomas came up beside me. The glow from his phone illuminated his face from below, like in *The Blair Witch Project*. "It's a trap, all right!" he said. He pointed to the fluorescents fixed to the plywood ceiling. You could see where red spray paint had been applied to the tubes. We even came across the forklift, its engine compartment warm like it had recently been used. "Oh, yeah," said Tomas. "These fuckers know we're coming." And he grinned. As we made our way across the room, the sheer number of crates and their labyrinthine layout made it difficult to keep track of turns and progress. Tomas and I lost the others several times, and even encountered a few dead ends, but we all understood the general direction we needed to go, and we soon stood at the foot of the stairs.

Shannon sent her text to Postdoc. Presently, we heard a distant *rat-tat-tat* at the door. We waited for the sound of Mi Fan's footsteps above. The rapping repeated. Still, we did not hear Mi Fan. I recalled the soundlessness with which she seemed to float from point to point.

"We're not going to hear anything," I whispered. "She's very quiet. We should just go up."

"What if she's walking to the door the moment we appear?" said Monika.

Nobody had an answer to this. A few moments of silence passed.

"She's at the door already," I said. "If she weren't, Postdoc would still be rapping."

A concert of whispers, everybody had an opinion. Monika was suggesting that she go all the way back outside to see what was happening, when our break came.

"No, sir! That is ridiculous!" Upstairs, Mi Fan was scandalized. "I cannot give you a kung fu demonstration right now!"

Good ol' Postdoc. His next month's supply of Mountain Dew would be on me.

We climbed the stairs and, as quietly as Mi Fan herself, fled down the hall of bedrooms. The second door stood half open. Shannon slipped inside. Beyond her, inside Master Lin's bedroom, I caught sight of the old man as he lay on his deathbed. And was it my imagination, or did a flash of light, in this briefest of visions, twinkle in his eye?

We ran on, and I didn't mention my glimpse of Master Lin to the others as we awkwardly found our places in Shannon's small bedroom. Such thoughts as are found in a dying man's eye are not meant for the consideration of interlopers.

Sooner than I had anticipated, Shannon entered her room. The still-sticky trail that mottled one cheek told what was necessary. She went to Monika and, sitting at the foot of the bed, they embraced.

"It's good that you went," said Monika.

"Yes," Shannon said. Then, cutting her consolation short, she took something from her pocket. "He gave me this." A small block of dark-lacquered wood lay in her hand.

"What is it?" I asked, crowding in.

For answer, she went to the empty katana stand above her bed. I could see at once that the wood of the stand matched that of the block. She searched around the stand, feeling for something. "There." The block sunk into a small hole.

Nothing happened.

Shannon pulled on the stand. Nothing continued to happen.

"Push it," said Tomas.

She grasped the middle of the stand and pushed it toward the wall. A sharp click attended the appearance of a vertical line of light along one column of the shelves. In two steps, Tomas was there. He moved the bed away from the wall, then pushed at the shelves. Nothing.

"Pull it," said Monika.

He did so, and the shelves swung silently inward, revealing a hidden alcove.

The alcove was lit by a window identical to the one in Shannon's room and similarly barred. I recalled standing outside in the alley yesterday in heavy rain, seeing a vague face in this window. Whoever that face belonged to had been standing on this very spot, where a spiral staircase descended into the floor.

A faint light came from below, and with it the unmistakable sound of conversation. Whatever room was below us was occupied. I strained to identify the voices, fearing that one might be Feng's. There were two voices: a man's—distantly familiar and decidedly not Feng's—and the other belonging to a child. A girl, upon closer attending. I was mystified as I descended the tight spiral.

It was a meditation room. In one corner, a Coleman kerosene lantern threw its amber, somnolent glow onto a bamboo floor. A close but safe distance from it lay a sleeping mat. The mystery of the "conversation" was solved: a '60s-era tape recorder was playing a book-on-tape of *To Kill A Mockingbird*. Atticus Finch was admonishing Scout regarding the ways of hard neighbors. All around the recorder, dozens of balls of crumpled paper lent company to a stack of the stuff, perhaps half a ream. A pen lay on top of the paper.

Across the room from all of this, six life-size patinated bronze Chinese warriors stood shoulder-to-shoulder in tight formation. A gong anchored their right-most flank, its heavy, black mallet depending from a leather strap.

One of the standing warriors was watching me with blinking eyes.

"My God!" I exclaimed. "Butch!"

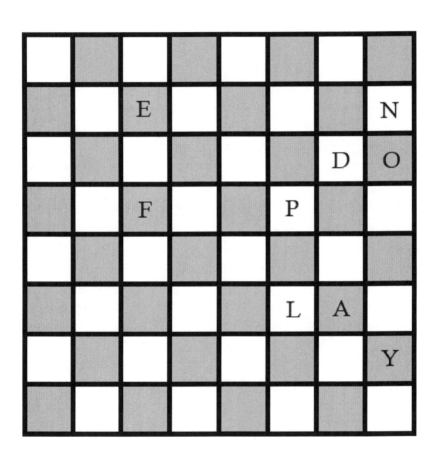

Chapter 8
END OF PLAY

♞ a8 ♞
KING BUTCH THE SAME. ALL THE PIECES.

"JUST BUTCH WILL suffice," he said with a gentle smile.

He stood there, barefoot, still as the statues beside him. His T-shirt, mottled with sweat stains and riddled with small rips and tears, was tucked into a pair of orange and white striped jogging shorts.

I searched his face. I was looking for some sign of spent time, of days effaced in an oubliette of treachery; some calloused-over sense of bewilderment. Lines, perhaps, pressed into his face by the weight of betrayal. I looked, and I saw only Butch.

"It's you," I said stupidly.

"I trust the positions I provided in my notebooks were sound, and that the game developed in a principled and pleasing manner."

"Butch," I said, "we've all nearly been killed!"

"Proving that I was correct to have hidden what I found. May I presume you have recovered it?"

We were standing in a dungeon, probably in a trap, and my friend was talking about a flash drive. "Forget the files, Butch. Are you okay?" I looked him up and down. I saw no apparent injury.

"Naturally. Why wouldn't I be?" As if he were reporting on the condition of a book he had discovered fallen from a shelf, he continued, "Looking you all over from where I stand, I detect no physical injuries on any of you. But the files. They are safe?"

"Well, they're here with us, if that's what you count as—"

I was firmly removed to one side. Shannon took my spot in front of Butch. Butch spread his arms wide in preparation for a hug (or possibly crucifixion) and said her name: "Xiang." As Shannon entered the geometry of his reach, Monika and I found each other's hands, bracing ourselves.

"Everything will play out," Butch said to his lover as she rested her head on his chest.

Whether this was the exact correct thing to say or the exact incorrect thing to say, I don't know, but Shannon then beat his chest repeatedly with the heel of her open hand, and her tears soaked his pitiable shirt. Anybody watching who didn't know better would've seen the ineffectual damsel in distress from a million fairy stories. But if you knew what you were looking at, you'd see a woman who was holding back. Way back.

For what felt like several minutes Butch remained motionless, save for one hand that moved around to cup the back of Shannon's head, tenderly clutching her ebony hair, nearly disappearing into it.

"Say it will be okay?" A whisper amid sobs.

Butch merely repeated himself: "The game will play out as it must."

Shannon replied to this fatalistic remark by kissing Butch's neck, then moving upward toward his face. I regret that I was slow off the mark, waiting until her lips had found Butch's before I took an inordinate interest in a white ceramic urn that sat lonely in a corner of the room. A square of plywood acted as a cover, and from the roll of toilet paper on top I judged the container to be a chamber pot.

"Alrighty, then," said Tomas after a time. "I believe we should be moving along."

Shannon stepped back from her embrace. Butch looked beyond her first to Tomas, then to Monika. He said to Monika, "I'm certain I owe the successful prosecution of your hunt in great part to your considerable skills at the board."

She walked up to him, gave him a quick hug (lightly returned), and said, "It was a team effort. It is so good to see you, Butch."

To Tomas, who remained a few paces behind, Butch said, "Could you tell me, please, the day and the hour?"

Tomas flicked Butch a salute. "It's April thirteenth out there and nighttime, my friend. Twenty-three-oh-seven."

Shannon surveyed the room, her arms akimbo. "I remember this place. I was young. My grandfather wanted a room to train in privately, away from view of the street."

"Did he come here often?" asked Monika.

"At first," said Shannon. "Then the business grew, and it became a storeroom. I assumed it fell into disuse and forgot all about it. The staircase is new. Looks like they wanted a safe room in case they got raided, with access from the main level. I wonder…" She approached one of the walls and started pushing and pulling.

"There is indeed a pocket door in that wall," said Butch. "I detected it soon after being interned. But it's always lock—"

"Got it." The tips of Shannon's fingers disappeared into a crack. She pulled, and a section of the wall slid open, revealing the main part of the basement, still glowing with that bloody red light.

"Wow." Tomas rubbed his hands together eagerly. "This is so definitely a trap."

The five of us exited the hidden room into the basement. Coming from an unfamiliar angle, even Shannon had difficulty gaining her bearings. "Everyone hold hands," she said. "The tunnel should be to our right."

We wound around several crates, piled high and packed close. We got lost a few times and at one point came full circle before Shannon finally found the way.

"Here we are." She opened the tunnel door. Bloody light oozed from behind us and into the black beyond. A figure took shape and emerged from the tunnel.

"Here we are," said Feng.

♞ b8 ♞
THE MANY ARTS OF MARTIAL COMBAT. THE LAST OF THE STANDING BRONZE WARRIORS.

Butch turned his back to Feng to address me. The move struck me as either the height of bravado or the nadir of wisdom. Possibly both, but a show of disrespect either way.

"Martin," he said. "Your strengths do not lie in the many arts of martial combat. I advise that you and Monika go to my cell. Shannon and I will handle this."

This. With a stubby brown forefinger like one of his dirty cigars, he pointed behind him. Didn't even bother to look. From the doorway, Feng growled a growl that remarkably came across as insouciant.

"Butch!—" Monika began.

I grabbed her hand. "Come on."

She made toward the center of the room, back through the jumble of crates. The red miasma.

I pulled her back. "No! We take the long way. Hug the wall."

We moved as if under fire, hunched through the disorienting red, me in the lead, the wall to our left, the concrete cold and screeching against the nylon of my jacket. Behind us, Feng was taunting Butch and Shannon. I heard him clHap twice. Grey-clad instructors leaped from several open crates. They were warriors now, each wielding a staff. We had walked into an ambush.

Monika stopped, bringing me to a jerking halt. "Butch and Shannon! They're not armed!"

I had no time to reply. A grey warrior shot out from behind a crate. He took a swipe at us with his staff as he passed in the direction whence we had come. I ducked and pulled Monika down with me. We were not his main target. He ran on and so did we.

We rounded an inside corner. The meditation room would open to the left along this next wall. I peered ahead, searching for light from the Coleman lantern. From behind us came the smacks of parried blows and the shouts of pursuit. ("She went that way!" "No, over here!") Our friends must have evaded the initial onslaught to dodge about the plywood maze.

My hand found the open doorway, and we nearly fell into the meditation room.

"What are we doing here?" asked Monika.

"Butch said to come here." Then I looked around and felt the cold grip that comes from having forgotten something important take hold of my stomach. "Where's your father?"

Her eyes got big. "Oh, god!" She started to run off. I pulled her back; I had just spotted Shannon passing between two of the crates. A grey warrior followed her—a cat seen through a slatted fence. The hunt was migrating, coming our way.

I saw where a couple of crates had been stacked to within a few feet of the ceiling. It gave me an idea. I said, "Stay here," and went over there. I reached up and felt for the cover on the upper box. It was firmly in place. If we got up there, we could see the lay of the land.

I turned to get Monika. She was right there, splaying her hands out like where the hell did I think I was going. I had her cup her hands, give me a boost up. I pulled her after me just as a grey warrior came around the corner, shouting and swinging his staff.

We were on all fours, keeping the stack stable. From our perch we caught shadows and scraps of the dodge-and-parry going on around us. With no weapons, Butch and Shannon seemed reluctant to engage. I had hoped by now they'd've been able to disarm a couple guys, but the opposition was too good. The battle closed in. Soon the prey would be encircled. The warriors filled the gaps in the perimeter. Swirling staffs, hoots, shuffling feet—the formation tightened. Probably attempting to grab my hand, Monika jabbed her arm out and bopped me good in the face.

I thought maybe drop to the ground, attack them. But even Butch and Shannon weren't attacking. Then I thought maybe get behind one of them. Startle them, make a disruption. I crawled to the side of the box. I had just swung one foot over when, across the embattled circle, I spotted Tomas rising above a crate behind two of the warriors.

His skin was tinged ruby by the red fluorescents, and his grin shone crazy and white beneath his cap of fiery hair. He couldn't've been having a better time. Spreading his arms, he grabbed the two warriors' heads and bashed them together. His laugh mingled with the clatter of their staves as they hit the floor.

In an instant Butch and Shannon each grabbed a staff, and the hunt became a melee. They went back-to-back, fending off attackers as they came, some singly, others in pairs or groups. But this was no kung fu demonstration, the toughs throwing themselves one by one into a choreographed routine designed to thrill an audience. No, they played it smart. They kept their perimeter intact, preventing escape. The game was a grind, and the longer it went on, the more it would favor the grey warriors, who were all catching their breath between attacks.

Chapter 8

I whispered to Monika, "They need a way to break out so they can fight piecemeal."

She said, "Stay here."

She crawled backward and dropped over the edge, touching down with a soft clap. Soon I heard a gentle grunt and saw something white lurching up over the top of the crate. I grabbed it. It was the chamber pot, for gods' sakes, its square wooden lid shifting unsettlingly.

I pulled her up. "What are you doing with that?"

"It's full of shit and piss. I'm going to throw it at them."

"Aw, Monika, what the hell?" But I had no better idea, and we returned to our watch. The fight was still a fluid stalemate.

She took the lid off. God, the fumes. "You do it," she said. "You can throw farther."

I took one glance inside and wished to Jove I hadn't. "But, Monika—"

"You're going to need to clear that crate in front of us."

"Yeah, thanks." Like I hadn't figured that out.

She bobbed her head toward the horrid slurry in the pot. "Well?"

I imagined the wise words of Sun Tzu: "Render your opponent motionless by soaking him with pee. Break through his defenses with flying poo." Feeling quite certain that tossing excrement did *not* count as one of the many arts of martial combat (but then, I had been told that such things were not my strength), I grabbed the urn and launched the contents of Butch's chamber pot toward his captors. The stuff slapped itself mostly onto one man's back and spattered several others.

It just isn't the sort of thing one trains for, and the effect was disconcerting and immediate. The sodden warrior looked up, shocked as a blood-drenched prom queen. Unlike Carrie White, however, this man's work was finished for the night.

Butch and Shannon didn't strike right away. With a spirited leap, they cleared the derailed warrior first, *then* turned on him. Their blows landed simultaneously: their first casualty of the night. I made a mental note to add a line or two to my marginalia in my copy of *The Art of War*.

The scene reverted to what it had been before, with everyone running about. But this time it wasn't clear who was supposed to be hunting whom. Butch and Shannon, now armed, mostly kept together, and no one was a match for their spinning staves. One by one the warriors went down.

Our friends were standing over the last of those they'd felled, the poor blighter moaning and clutching at nothing, when something pushed up against my side, opposite from where Monika crouched.

It was Tomas. "Isn't this fantastic, M-doc? Nice work with the feces." He pointed. "Look!"

From behind a crate, Feng was entering the crimson arena. He clapped slowly. "Nicely done, nicely done," he said. "But I believe you have one more opponent to face." As he spoke, he looked up to where the three of us lay—just to show he knew we were alive. For now.

He approached one of the felled warriors and crouched beside him. The man was whimpering pathetically. I thought Feng was going for the man's staff. Instead he yelled, "Shut up!" and then stood and kicked him in the face. The man shut up.

"What is wrong with you?" said Shannon.

Feng shrugged. "Violence makes me angry. And anger helps me… fight!"

Empty-handed, Feng rushed for a middle point between Butch and Shannon. They separated, whipping around their staves, connecting with nothing but air. He had gone low, tucking into a somersault. He jumped at a crate, twisting in mid-leap, planting the heels of his hands on the top. He pulled his legs up and out, like a gymnast on a pommel horse, just as Butch's staff slammed into the crate. He lunged for Shannon. She dodged left and brought her staff down on the spot where she had stood, finding only floor. Feng had flipped himself over her and landed in front of Butch. Butch's staff slashed this way and that, each time slicing at a space recently deserted as Feng deftly dodged each cut and thrust. But now Shannon had come up behind Feng. Sensing her, he pivoted, twisting the entire engagement as if on an invisible axis. Thus far, Feng had not attempted to strike. It was as if he were working out which of the two made the weaker target. Then, I supposed, he would pick up one of the many weapons that littered the ground and attack in earnest.

Perhaps Butch was thinking the same, for I noticed that he had begun a strategy (or what I *hoped* was a strategy) of gradually giving some ground. Each time the combatants came to a position of equilibrium, the engagement would shift slightly in his direction. He was baiting Feng.

As the lethal dance progressed, it shifted first toward the crates that

Chapter 8

Monika, Tomas, and I lay on, then around them toward the meditation room. About fifteen feet in that direction a staff lay on the floor. Each seemed to know that the others saw it. As if by agreement, the three fighters drifted in that direction. To pick it up, Feng would have to bend over, making himself vulnerable. To my surprise, Feng held out a parlaying hand, and Butch and Shannon paused their attacks, perhaps out of some respect for the many arts of martial combat.

Feng picked up the staff. For a time, the man was a little boy, spinning a new toy in his hands, trying it out, discovering the tricks of a long-desired possession. From where I lay at about ten yards, I could hear the whipping of the air as Feng spun an invisible net about him. Then the whirring stopped. Feng glanced from one adversary to the other… and he lunged toward Butch.

Click and clack, whir and crack! Feng and Butch worked their staves. Shannon repeatedly approached from Feng's rear only to encounter a spare motion from his staff or a backward kick of a bare foot. With each fresh offensive by Feng, Butch gave ground (involuntarily, it now seemed) toward the open maw of the meditation room.

They were near now. The swing of Butch's staff was crossing the plane of the doorway. Feng twisted the axis again. Not understanding his position, Butch cracked his staff against the side of the pocket door, and the staff flew from his grasp.

A howl of victory rose from Feng, set against a shriek of dismay from Shannon. He raised his staff for a finishing blow; Shannon charged from behind. Feng brought his staff down toward Butch but then pivoted on his heel… and the downstroke became a thrust. Like an arrow, his staff shot through the diminishing space between himself and his sister. It struck her in the solar plexus.

Shannon gasped. Her face froze and vomit spewed from her mouth. Feng ran to finish her, and Butch pursued. Feng got to her first. He picked up her paralyzed body and, demonstrating the same strength with which Shannon had vaulted over a stone wall earlier that day, threw her at Butch. His aim was off by a few degrees, Butch's attempt to correct for it too slow, and Shannon careened onto the floor, a motionless doll.

Unimpeded by any weapon, Butch met his foe in full hand-to-hand combat.

Instantly, Monika was on the ground, one hand cradling Shannon's head as she rolled her on her side, keeping her from choking on vomit, the other hand checking her neck for a pulse.

Tomas and I leaped down to help.

"Get Shannon into the meditation room," I said. "There's a sleeping mat you can lay her on."

Tomas looked at Monika. "Does she need a mat?"

"She's alive, if that's what you mean."

They carried Shannon in.

I considered calling the police. Shannon's fear had been that blood would flow if we did that. Well, it was flowing. As for worrying that the law would discover the family business behind the family business, I figured we were past that. Shannon had played her game as best she could. It was time to end that game, and end it right now, while something resembling a draw could still be managed. I got out my phone to call 911.

No signal.

God damn the less-documented chastisements of the Underworld.

I was at the staircase, seeking a signal, when Feng and Butch approached. They were trading kicks, punches, all manner of swirling blocks and parries. I was amazed that Butch had lasted this long under such towering menace. He had not wasted his incarceration. I considered the room before me. It was a space where one could train the mind and body apart from worldly fetter. The scene tugged at my memory, pulling me toward someplace I had recently visited. Some empty place. The gong, punctuated by its heavy mallet like an exclamation mark: it screamed at me. And those five metal warriors, how solidly they stood—inert yet implying energy… frozen, captured, stored…

Butch and Feng fought just outside the doorway. I abandoned the stairs to join the others. Monika and Tomas had rolled out the mat for Shannon. She was sitting up on it, thank goodness, her head between her knees. She was sucking in deep breaths, wiping the back of her hand across her mouth. She stopped in mid-wipe to turn her head and vomit again. It was turning out to be one hell of a night.

The combatants entered the room. The three of us stood, forming a protective wall around Shannon. But the fight pitched the other way, toward the standing statues. Feng swung a roundhouse kick. Butch leaned back, allowing the kick to go over his head. As it cleared he grabbed Feng's leg with both hands and twisted, sending him to the ground. Butch swept in over Feng's prone body to deliver a strike, but Feng's arms came up in an X, blocking the punch. As Butch withdrew his fist, Feng grabbed the retreating wrist. He cranked it, probably hoping to break it. But he was lying down, and Butch was able to get in an awkward kick to Feng's forearm, freeing himself. With a swift roll, Feng was back on his feet.

Off-balance from his kick, Butch lurched forward, arms extended blindly, seeking stability. His hands found the closest statue. He turned around toward where Feng had lain—but he was gone. Confused, Butch looked around.

I saw where Feng had gone—slipped in behind the statues. I started to cry out, but too late. From around the wall of warriors Feng came onto Butch from behind, and with one arm, he wrested him into a vicious headlock.

Behind me, Shannon gasped. She had gained her feet and was now watching in woozy horror as Butch pushed backward, driving the tangled mess of the two of them toward the line of statues. He twisted, pressing Feng against the bronze warrior that stood at the end of the line opposite the gong and its heavy mallet. But Feng's grip was secure. Butch would soon run out of oxygen.

And this was when I found the image that had been teasing my memory. It was the day I had gone with Postdoc to the King's Corner Hotel. It was Melvin's empty office and the Newton's cradle that sat clicking on his desk. And it was Melvin himself: "The pulse of energy continues through many points until it comes to a terminus, and suddenly, there is motion where none previously existed."

In an instant, I saw the whole thing. I'd run and get that mallet, swing it with all my might into the last of the standing bronze warriors. The energy would travel through the line and out the other end. Feng would jolt forward. Butch, freed for one golden instant, would pivot on his heel and land a fist into his adversary's gut. Feng would double over. A second strike from Butch, this one to the back of Feng's head, would lay him out.

Then I realized: The warriors were hollow. The whole idea was shit. It would never work.

So I forgot all about that mallet, and I ran headlong into that first standing warrior; tackled him full on. What was supposed to be a life-size Newton's cradle became the world's shortest (but heaviest) line of crashing dominoes. And the rest of my vision? It played out just like I had pictured.

"Ho, yes!" yelled Tomas. He walked over and gave Butch a bear hug, then turned to me. "And M-doc with the *physics*! Where did you learn a thing like that?" Looking around for some kind of metaphorical football to spike in the end zone, he grabbed the mallet, brandished it in his hand for a moment, then swung it at the gong—a great reckoning in a little room. The idea that someone had just died upstairs, I believe, simply never entered his mind.

The reverberations subsided, and he walked over to Shannon, who had sat back down on the mat. "How you feel, sweetheart?" he asked, leaning down, placing a hand on her shoulder.

She gave him a look that could have put out the Chicago Fire of 1871.

"*Shannon*," Tomas quickly corrected. "How are you feeling, Shannon?"

"Hungry," she said.

"Hungry? That's a *great* sign!"

He went back to Butch, who was leaning against the wall, catching his breath, blood dripping from everywhere. "And Butch! I never doubted you for a second. You know what we should do? We should all go out for a nice dinner. Maybe wait for tomorrow. I mean, what could be more exhilarating than to be shot at and missed? We'll get the files to the cops, and our friend here will be off to prison. Butch! How does it feel to capture the man who tried to kill you?"

Butch looked at him. "You mean the one who stabbed me in the park? That wasn't Feng."

"*What?*"

Tomas, Monika, and I all said it together. We looked at each other in confusion. Then we saw Shannon. She and Butch were holding each other in a wary gaze, and we all heard Shannon say:

"It wasn't Feng. It was me."

Chapter 8

♟ c8 ♞
WEEKEND HELP

Monika was first to speak. "Shannon, what are you saying? It couldn't have been you—"

"No, not *me*," said Shannon. "*Mi*. Mi Fan. She's the kingpin of the whole operation. Feng, here," she pointed to her unconscious brother, "is her top lieutenant."

"Oh, what a relief," I said, recovering from the shock. "The way things were going just now, I thought we were going to have more trouble. I don't think I could bear any more—"

"Oh, we're going to have trouble, Martin."

Shannon gestured to the pocket doorway. Standing there, holding Shannon's katana and dressed in black from her loose blouse to her slippered feet, was Mi Fan, a.k.a. Ninja Cat Lady, a.k.a. the kingpin of the White Knight drug operation in Manhattan. Unsheathing the sword, she said, "You're not giving those files to any cops. You're giving them to me."

Shannon rose. "You're old and slow, Mi Fan. You think you're going to take me out with my own sword? I won it from you fair and square, you know."

If Mi Fan was daunted by this, it didn't show. A grin creased her face as from behind her there arose the sudden rumble of people galumphing down the stairs, another batch of grey-clad staff-wielders, eight of them filling in to either side of her.

Shannon's own grin widened as she took in the newcomers. "Ah... had to call in the weekend crew, huh? What's the matter? First-stringers all laid out on the floor?"

Shannon was not making hollow taunts—this new group of fighters were trading nervous glances; uneasy hands fidgeted on wobbling staves. The fellow all the way to my left looked particularly ill at ease. Like a mouse. I recognized him as the instructor who had helped Stan when he got hurt at the exhibition. I doubted very much that he wanted to be here.

Shannon strutted back and forth, tossing jibes at Mi Fan and occasionally going after an instructor by name. The longer Shannon went on, the madder Mi Fan looked. A hand fell on my shoulder. Startled, I turned to see Butch. He gathered Monika, Tomas, and me into a huddle.

"Listen," he whispered to the three of us while Shannon continued to bait Mi Fan, "Mi wants those files, of course. But there's a lot of bad blood between her and Xiang."

"Bad blood, eh?" said Tomas. "What's that all about?"

"It all goes back to that sword. It's a terrific story. The year was 1984, maybe '85. The place was Outer Mongolia. Mi Fan was—"

Monika broke in. "Butch. Maybe now isn't the time?"

He snapped back. "Right. As I was saying, we can use the bad blood between Shannon and Mi Fan to advantage. Martin, I want you to sneak up behind Xiang and grab her staff." (*Oh, Jesus*, I was already thinking.) "Throw it to me. Give her no time to object. The moment she is unarmed, Mi will come after her. Then I'll jump in and intercept Mi, throw her off her stride. Meanwhile, the rest of you cover the B Team over there. Don't worry, they aren't part of the cartel. They are not motivated to fight. And Xiang will have your back, since I'll be the one taking on Mi."

"Won't Shannon need a weapon?" asked Monika.

Butch looked at the line of fighters. "Nah. Just help her out a bit, go to work on those fellas one at a time. And Tomas? I want you and Shannon to have mercy on them. Everybody clear?"

I was thinking this was a pretty fucking reckless plan when Tomas replied, "Clear as mud!"

The fight situation began not necessarily to our advantage. When I went to grab Shannon's staff, she instantly struck me in the face with the heel of her hand. A howl from Mi Fan told me she had found her opening, and as I careened backward into a wall, I saw Butch run directly into her path, sans weapon. Moments later, as I sat on the floor, tilting my head up to stem the flow of blood from my nose, I saw Butch fighting Mi with Shannon's staff. Shannon had evidently thrown it to him, while she herself, as Butch had predicted, was doing quite fine empty-handed against the B team—although she was soon armed by Tomas. He had rushed Mouse Man, who immediately dropped his staff and fled up the stairs before Tomas even got close. After picking up the discarded staff and trying to fight with it for a little while, Tomas tossed it to Shannon and devised a different strategy: he would take a blow or two from someone's staff, then close in and make use of his fists. Two punches was the most it took (zero, the least) to send an adversary on his way: up the stairs, see ya around town, write if you get work.

Monika, meanwhile, instead of joining the fray, rushed to me in furtherance of her life's calling, which is apparently to minister to bleeding morons.

Everything seemed to be going well with Tomas and Shannon, so I turned my attention to the fight between Mi and Butch. Here, an asymmetrical kind of warfare had developed. On one side, a once-expert, now-greying swordswoman, having been enraged by Shannon, now seemed intent on nothing but attacking her—which meant leaving the room. On the other side, an also-greying yet surprisingly spritely man with a staff perpetually maneuvered to keep his adversary at bay.

The two weaved about the room, occasionally stepping over Feng's unconscious body or around the Coleman lantern that burned next to the pile of papers I'd noticed earlier. (Had Butch kept a journal while imprisoned? It would be just like him.) Strategically on defense, striving only to keep Mi from escaping into the other room, Butch was *tactically* on offense, using the long reach of his staff to maintain a safe distance from that sword. It was a dynamic sort of equilibrium, but one that seemed to favor our side. In minutes, the Shannon-Tomas duo outside would vanquish the last of the weekend warriors and come to Butch's aid. I returned my attention to that arena.

I had been watching for less than a minute (I was in time to see Shannon and Tomas round the same pile of crates from opposite directions and nearly attack one another) when a cry of alarm came from the meditation room. I turned to see many things happening at once.

Butch was throwing himself into the air. Mi Fan was running. The Coleman lantern had upended. There was a fire.

Butch landed on the burning papers; flames shot up from underneath him.

Freed, Mi ran cackling out of the meditation room. Monika and I yelled a warning to Shannon—but too late. Mi swept in behind her, bringing the katana up and around in a victorious arc and holding it fast to Shannon's throat.

"You have lost!"

Chapter 8

"You have lost!" Mi cried. "Now bring me those files!"

I tried to remember who had handled the flash drive last, and I realized it was Tomas. He was looking back and forth between Monika and me. Throughout the entire adventure, this was the moment that scared me most. After all the sacrifices, pins, forks, skewers, and discovered attacks, this was checkmate—and I had no idea how Tomas was going to take it. With a sword held to Shannon's throat, his options were limited, but I simply couldn't imagine the man doing anything against his will. My attitude toward *deus ex machina* is well-known to my colleagues. But if Tomas indeed had access to some celestial book, I felt now was the time for the author to produce a miracle.

Soft, unhurried footsteps perforated the tension. Someone was coming down the stairs. A mere silhouette at first, the figure resolved into a wiry man. He stepped into the red light.

"Hey, everybody! I thought you could use some help."

"Postdoc!" cried Monika. "What are you doing?"

"I got tired of waiting up there for you guys. Then I heard the commotion and did what you told me to do the last time you lot were in a jam."

"What is that?" I asked.

"I called 911."

On cue, a crowd of blue uniforms crashed down the stairs. Cops flooded the room, guns out and pointing.

"NYPD—freeze!" barked an officer.

Then a final set of footsteps sounded on the stairs. Anne Schnapp entered the room, her blonde shoulder-length hair jouncing with each measured step. She placed her hands on her hips and took in the surroundings.

"We have been fighting," she observed in her thick Brooklyn accent. Her right nostril gave a single, stoic flare, but whether in reaction to the feces and urine that smeared the ground, or to the acrid pool of vomit or the cupric stab of blood that pierced the air or the reek of singed flesh and burning paper, or whether it was a mere twitch, apropos of nothing, I could not say.

♞ d8 ♟
CHAIRS AND FLOWERS. THE GREEN FAIRY. A NEW FAMILY.

Master Lin's body was cremated at noon that Thursday.

The earlier gathering at the studio that morning had felt evocative but empty. White sashes over doorways. Floor plants relocated to bookend the open coffin. The air heavy with incense and flowering Osmanthus. Guests in shades of white and subdued pink. Master Lin laid out in white, his hands crossed in a waxy X.

Monika, Butch, Tomas, Lisa, Stanislav, and I had set up folding chairs. Three rows of them, brought up noisily from the basement. Even these were too many; the family itself had died with Master Lin. An efficient officer, Anne Schnapp had made numerous arrests over the previous four days. Xiang (she would no longer answer to *Shannon*, she informed Tomas when he posted her bail) had been able to locate only a few cousins who were undeterred by either distance or shame.

The late and innocent Master Lin had been a man adept at practicing tradition's forms without the clutter of attendant beliefs. The service, if it could be called that, was devoid of priestcraft. Soon, the seven of us were in the Suburban (borrowed once more from the good neighbors), following the hearse to the crematory. There, too, proceedings had been brief. Xiang had picked out a simple, pewter urn… and we were back on the road.

Monika rested a hand on Xiang's forearm. "Can we take you somewhere? Get you something to eat?"

"I hate the city," was her nonsequential response.

Butch reached for a duffel bag that wasn't there. He instead found Xiang's hand and clasped it. A wicked gouge like the dry cut of a Martian canal crossed his left cheek—the only visible sign that he had recently engaged in mortal combat and required hospitalization. He'd only yesterday been released.

Tomas, in the driver's seat, said, "I need to know where to go."

Monika leaned forward to consult with her father. He nodded, and we pulled out into the street.

"What's the deal?" I asked her.

"We're going to Ossining." She looked at Xiang. "If that's okay?"

Chapter 8

Xiang nodded—the slightest of gestures—and put her head on Butch's shoulder. By the time we turned onto Broadway, the poor, exhausted thing was snoring.

Tomas pulled into his driveway. Stan's eyes lit up. "Can we turn on the water?"

Lisa grabbed the bag of deli sandwiches we had picked up along the way and got out of the SUV. "We'll see, sweetie. The adults are going to talk." The kid jumped out and disappeared around the porch to the back.

Dry fountains. Still, glassy pools that reflected a pallid midday sun. Unlit strings of party lights slicing the sky into turquoise wedges. It was Tomas's world chastened, placed in time-out. We sat at a picnic table, eating, watching Stan splash in the hot tub. Lisa had turned it on after bringing out a pitcher of water and a tray of glasses. It churned and steamed away, a concession to the unburdened bliss of childhood.

They say old wine won't stay long in new wineskins. It'll either ooze out or burst out. Neither does the chastened form suit Tomas. He poured an absinthe, a trickle of water over a cube of sugar into a thimble of green at the bottom of a cone-shaped glass.

"Hey," he said. He lifted his drink. "Butch."

Butch, who hadn't been eating, brought himself back from wherever. "Yes, Tomas?"

"I've got to hand it to you, friend. Those notebooks. The chess puzzles. The way you handled yourself with those martial artists. The whole bust, very impressive." The absinthe disappeared down Tomas's throat, and he prepared another.

Monika smiled and gave Butch a quick rub on the back.

"And the way you channeled those authors," I added. "The arcane murk of Lovecraft, the tenacity of Borges, the whimsy of Lewis Carroll—"

Monika said, "Oh, I loved your Lewis Carroll, Butch. How did you do it all?"

Butch ground an invisible cigar between the fractured brown lines of his teeth. "Merely a product of analysis. I applied myself assiduously to various manuals on the craft of writing: Strunk and White, Zinsser, King—"

"King," I interrupted. "It's too bad you never wrote a king notebook, Butch. You had one for each of the other five chess pieces."

"It wouldn't have worked, Martin," said Monika. "The notebooks featured a piece that was captured as bait. You can't capture the king."

"I know that. I was just saying."

"Nonsense." Tomas slid the bottle of absinthe, the water pitcher, a box of Domino sugar cubes, and a glass toward Butch. "He *did* write a king notebook. Didn't you, Butch? Or at least another one of your author pieces?"

"What is he going on about?" Monika said. She took the absinthe for herself and made a drink.

Butch licked his lips, searching again for his missing cigar. "I will tell you everything from the beginning," he pointed to Monika's glass, "if you make me one of those."

"Absolutely." She grabbed a couple of glasses and lifted one toward me. "Martin?"

"I'm game."

"Xiang? Lisa?"

"Why not."

"Sure."

Butch held his drink to his face and sniffed at it.

"Oh, drink it already," said Tomas.

Butch took a sip. Apparently satisfied, he made his explanations. Much of what he had to say regarding White Knight and how it was traded in the open, I had personally experienced, and I found my thoughts drifting to various places as he spoke. I perked up when he described the attack in the park.

"It was late. The chess circle had emptied, save for one game. Gooli was playing. He offered a coffee to his opponent and brought out one of those grotesque sets with the six-inch king. I was watching from several tables away, contemplating a possible ambush, when I heard Xiang cry out in alarm. I spun to see Mi Fan. She had a knife and was about to stab me in the back. I retreated a step, a move that surely saved my life. The knife went in, but not far enough. I made as straight a line as I could for the street, hoping for safety in the open. Before Mi Fan could pursue, I heard Xiang's approach. Mi Fan must have run."

"Ran from me like a chicken-shit bitch," said Xiang. "Tried to get her, but she had too much of a head start." It was the first substantive thing she had said since the crematorium.

Chapter 8

Butch continued. "I needed to press hard against my wound and couldn't maintain a proper hold on my duffel. Somewhere along the way to your office, Martin, I must have dropped it."

"I found it in the park," I said, "halfway between the benches and the street."

"They're going to close it for a while, you know," said Tomas. "I have it from Anne Schnapp."

"Close Washington Square Park? Oh, that's terrible!" cried Monika. She cast Butch a troubled look.

"Not so terrible," said Xiang under her breath.

"What do you mean?" Monika asked.

Xiang looked up from the table as if unaware that her comment had been audible. "My grandfather always meant to leave his business to me, and now he has. But I can't run it by myself." She looked steadily at Butch. Her face held meaning and hope… and yet something else. A kind of despondency. I recalled her words to me that day in the kitchen when she drugged me, and then again in the SUV that very morning: "I hate the city."

Monika beamed. "Oh, Butch! What do you say? You can work at Master Lin's Kung Fu Studio! You can be a kung fu master!"

Butch steepled his fingers together in thought. "I shall consider this move."

"Oh, come *on*," Tomas said. "This'll be a dream come true! When stuff like this comes around, you gotta *pounce*, B-bop! Pounce, pounce, pounce!"

A dream come true? My thoughts drifted again, but this time to an extremely specific place. A place that had been on my mind quite a lot lately. I had received a letter from my grandfather, telling me about Sophie, his home companion. She had moved on. I'd answered that letter, of course. We had even shared a rare phone call a few days ago, during which he mentioned her again. Talked about her almost like he would a child who had moved away. I asked him then about my idea—an idea that had been brewing in my mind for probably much longer than I had consciously realized. He had agreed to it immediately. Since that conversation, I suppose I had been waiting for things to settle. For the correct time to bring it up.

"You can have a whole life together!" Monika was saying to Shannon and Butch. "Aww…" She looked dreamily at me for a moment before returning her attention to her friends.

While Monika planned her friends' lives, I watched Xiang closely and made my decision.

"Would you like to wait a little, Xiang?" I said. "I mean, before taking on the business?"

"What do you mean?" she asked, and the look on her face melted my heart.

"Well," I said, "I have a grandfather. He lives at a place called Margaret-on-the Sea. It's… well, it's in England.…"

I described Gramps's country home, its simplicity, its isolation. I spoke of the ocean. I assured her and Butch that my grandfather was a lonely and kindly man who would relish their company while yet respecting their privacy. I spoke of the library and of the many books there and then, finally, of the games. It was the games that did it. One game in particular—xiangqi. Chinese chess. The symbols corresponding to the pieces came sharply to my mind, and I remembered the piece called the palace guard. The palace guards are not allowed to leave the small section of the board designed to represent the emperor's palace. The guard's symbol resembled a hanzi-style plus-minus sign—the symbol that even now Xiang wore in her ears. That guard had done her duty. She had stayed by the emperor's side, guarding the dignity of his house as best she could, risking her life to do so. But the emperor was now gone, and the guard was free to go.

As I spoke I watched Xiang's face transform, and when, after a short discussion, she and Butch accepted my offer, I felt that this chapter of their story had finally come to a fitting end.

Monika said, "Someone will need to watch the studio for them while they're gone, Martin."

"Aren't you going to need something to do, with Washington Square being closed?" Xiang asked her. "And when we're back, we could use help at the front desk. You could work."

"Work." Monika spoke the word to herself, testing it. "Work."

Tomas said, "This is all fantastic! But tell us the rest, Butch. We left off with you bleeding half to death on Martin's office floor."

Butch continued his story.

"At this point my memory becomes fuzzy. I recall that Feng took me from the hospital. I was in no state to fight him. The doctor had me all but prepped to go home. Go home!? My mind was a cloud! I can only conclude that, after the little testing the hospital gave me, Feng somehow slipped me a sedative, probably in my cup of water. When he took me, I walked as if in a dream. I gained full consciousness in the room where you all discovered me. The room was as you saw it, but lacking everything save the lantern, the bedpan, and the statues and gong. I had access to the spiral staircase, but it led only to a dead end and a barred window. The view of the alley was at least sufficient to inform me where I was. The stairs eventually afforded me, as I became able, a level of exercise and the re-training of my body.

"The days went by. Feng did not show himself, but it was clear from what transpired that he was my self-appointed warden. Only the fragile threads that bound Master Lin to this life spared me my own. He knew, somehow, that I was there."

At the mention of Master Lin, Butch paused and looked steadily at Xiang, as if seeking absolution for uttering her grandfather's name in such close connection to death. After a time Xiang looked around the table. Her eyes came to rest on Monika. Monika moved next to her and gave her hand a squeeze.

"You have us all," she said. Something unspoken passed between them, then, and from that point forward Xiang was part of the family.

Butch resumed his story.

"They brought me food, of course. Usually one of the help. Through them I would relay messages to Master Lin. From time to time I would petition for some object of relief from the interminable blank of inactivity."

"At some point," interrupted Monika, "you must have been strong enough to have taken these guys on. Why didn't you kick their asses?"

"Naturally, my superior kung fu skills and intellect would have allowed me to either outsmart or overpower my adversaries"—here, Monika and I shared an amused grin; it was so nice having our pompous and fatalistic friend back in our lives—"but I saw no reason to place others in danger when I could simply wait for the natural outcome of the pieces and movements I had set in motion.

"My first prize," Butch continued with his narrative, "was a sleeping mat. This at least granted creature comfort, albeit nothing for the mind.

Then came some tapes and a player, mostly music at first, then eventually some audiobooks."

As Butch spoke, I recalled sitting in Xiang's bedroom, distantly hearing Captain & Tennille. Butch is more of a Coltrane man. How horrifying it all must have been.

He went on.

"My greatest acquisition, guaranteeing my happiness for whatever days remained to Master Lin and therefore to me (or so my adversaries would have had me believe), was a stack of printer paper and a pen. I had been pained all along, of course, by the absence of a king notebook. Six unique chess pieces, and only five notebooks!"

Monika and I shared another glance, amused at the sensibilities of a man who, held in captivity and daily facing the specter of death, expressed as his sole horror a trivial numerical disparity.

"It didn't take me long to settle on the author whose voice must be tapped to fill the pages of the king. I set to work at once and had just finished on the morning of the day you showed up."

All at once I understood. "Those burning papers you threw yourself on during your fight with Mi Fan. That was your writing?"

"Precisely. I believe I saved them from destruction. Fire takes longer than you probably think to consume a stack of paper. But then, the police. It all happened so fast."

"Not too fast for me!" said Tomas. "Your manuscript is saved. I've got it right here in my house."

"You have it?" exclaimed Butch. Rarely have I seen him in such a state of pure joy. He made a motion as if to stand, then sat down again, realizing of course that he had no idea where he was going.

"Absolutely. L-word!" Tomas pointed to Lisa, then to his house. "Could you?"

Pie-eyed on her second absinthe, Lisa, whose low tolerance for alcohol is not well suited to marriage to a Czech, said, "You want shumthin', ya go get it yershelf."

Tomas appealed to Monika, who just laughed. Then Tomas started explaining to Xiang where in the house he kept it—the attempt thereby cementing Xiang's status as family. Monika rested an elbow on her new

Chapter 8

sister's shoulder, as if to say that she wasn't going anywhere. Scandalized, Tomas rose, disappeared into the house, and returned with a stack of papers.

"Here you are," he said to Butch.

Butch rifled through the singed papers greedily, seeing to it that everything was there.

"May I?" I extended a hand.

It was a play. As for the author Butch had chosen to emulate, I approved. We doled out roles, and under the gloaming sky and the capricious influence of Butch's pen and the green fairy, we played our parts.

THE END

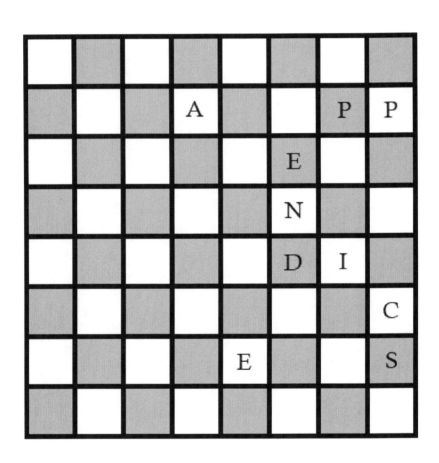

APPENDIX 1

♞ e8 ♝

MARTIN v. THE BISHOP OF 4TH STREET

THE FOLLOWING IS a transcription of Martin's final game against his nemesis, the Bishop of 4th Street, played in Washington Square Park on the 23rd of April, 2010. Under the influence of the street drug White Knight, Martin's play was inventive, forceful, and mostly sound.[23]

1 e4 c5 2 Nf3 d6 3 d4 cxd4 4 Nxd4 Nf6 5 Nc3 a6 6 Be3

> *Martin chooses to face the Najdorf with the English Attack. Very appropriate.* —Monika

6... e6 7 f4

> *But with an unusual continuation.* —Butch

7... b5 8 Bd3 Bb7 9 O-O Nbd7 10 Qf3 b4 11 Nce2 Nc5 12 Ng3 h5 13 a3

> *Fearless.* —B

---

[23] The game bears an uncanny resemblance to L. Christiansen v. S. Reshevsky, 1977 US Championships, Round 9. —Butch

Appendix 1

13... h4 14 Nge2 Nfxe4 15 Nxe6

So inventive! —M
Unsound, I'm afraid. —B
And yet so perfect for the park! —M

15... fxe6 16 axb4 Ng3 17 Bg6+ Kd7 18 Qg4 Nxe2+

Why didn't Black go for Martin's rook? —M
Martin's brazen confidence spooked his opponent.
This is the lifeblood of chess hustling. —B

19 Qxe2 Ne4 20 Bd4 Nf6 21 Rfe1 e5

What was Black thinking? —M
Outrageous. Never allow your opponent to
open lines against your king. —B

22 fxe5 dxe5 23 Bxe5 Qb6+ 24 Kh1 Bd6 25 Rad1 Nd5 26 Be4 Rhe8

All of Martin's pieces are in position. He now
destroys his opponent's defenses. —B

27 Bxd5 Kc7 28 Qc4+ 1 – 0

A crushing finish. If Black had tried 27... Rxe5, White
would have continued with Qg4+ and Qxg7, breaking
into Black's house with devastating effect. —M
A brilliant game throughout. —B

APPENDIX 2

♚ f8 ♞

MARTIN v. FENG

THE FOLLOWING IS a transcription of Martin's game against Feng, played at Fort Tryon Park on the 24th of April, 2010. Note the pronounced lack of quality from both players, as compared to the game in Appendix 1. Feng is clearly a novice player, whereas Martin seems to benefit from the cognitively freeing influence of psychotropic substances.[24,25]

1 e4 e5 2 Nf3 Nc6 3 d4 exd4 4 Nxd4 Nf6 5 Nxc6 bxc6 6 Bd3

Insipid. —Butch.
Perhaps Martin wanted to castle quickly? —Monika

6... Rb8

So Neanderthal, and so typical of Feng. —B

7 Bg5

I like how Martin simply ignores Feng's idle threat to the b-pawn. —M
7 e5 would have been better. —B

---

24 I'm sure with time and training, Martin will be able to reach his peak chess ability sans chemicals. —Monika
25 This time, the game harkens to Shoup v. Marshall, Sioux City, 1906. —Butch

7... d5 8 e5 Qe7 9 O-O

The proper way to handle a fidgety queen. Good work, Martin! —M

Yes, from here in, Martin plays excellently. —B

9... Qxe5 10 Re1 Ne4 11 Bxe4 Qxg5 12 Bxd5+ Be7 13 Bxc6+ Kf8 14 Qd8+ Bxd8 15 Re8# 1 – 0

A beautiful finish. —B

APPENDIX 3

♞ g8 ♞

"THE BACK OF THE NOTEBOOK"

(SOLUTIONS TO PUZZLES)

THIS SECTION CONTAINS the solutions to the swindle puzzles in the main portion of this book. Within each notebook, Butch arranged the puzzles in ascending order of difficulty. The diagrams in this section show what the position from each associated problem would look like after the swindled piece is offered and accepted.

After each solution is given, explaining how accepting the swindle leads to Butch's hoped-for draw, a correct line of play is provided as an improvement to accepting the bait. For an extra challenge, the reader may want to work out these preferred lines of play before consulting the solutions. Because the improved lines refer back to the original problem positions, the reader may find it convenient to keep the relevant page available when reviewing this portion of each solution.

Solution #1–A sleight of mind

After Butch's **1… Qa3**, he had hoped for **2 bxa3?**.

Black to move

Now **2… Bxa3+** gives Black the draw by perpetual check: **3 Kb1 Rb8+ 4 Ka1 Bb2+**, etc.

In the original position, after the key (1… Qa3), 2 Kb1, rather than 2 bxa3?, would preserve White's advantage.

Solution #2—Offsides

After **1 Rh3** by Butch, he had anticipated **1... Qxf7**.

White to move

Now **2 Bf5+ Qh5** (2... Kg8 3 Bh7+ leads nowhere) **3 Rxh5+ Kg8 4 Bh7+ Kh8** (not 4 ... Kf7?? 5 Ng5+ Kf6 6 Nce4#) results in perpetual check.

After 1 Rh3, Black wins with 1... Qe3+!, followed by capturing on h3.

APPENDIX 3

Solution #3—A game between rivals

After Butch played **1... Qxh2+!**, White (large) got greedy and took the queen with **2 Kxh2**.

Black (small) to move

Black now draws with **2... Nf3+! 3 Kh3** (not 3 Kh1? Rh6#) **3... Rh6+ 4 Kg4 Nh2+ 5 Kg5** (not 5 Kf5? Rh5#) **5... Be7+ 6 Kf4** (not 6 Kf5? Rh5+ 7 Kf4 Bd6#) **6... Bd6+ 7 Kg5**, and a three-fold repetition to follow.

After 1... Qxh2+, White should calmly slip out with 2 Kf1, when his extra material would sustain a winning advantage.

Solution #4—Take my queen, please

Butch played **1 Neg5**, hoping for **1... Rxe2**.

White to move

Now **2 Bxd5** leaves Black no good way to avoid the draw after Nh6+ and Nf7+. For example, 2... Bb7 3 Nh6+ Kh8 4 Nhf7+ Qxf7 (to avoid perpetual) 5 Nxf7+ Kg8 6 Bxb7 Rce8 7 Ne5! Rxh2 8 Nxg6, and White is actually winning.

Noteworthy is what happens should Black try to escape perpetual check with 2... Be7?, when 3 Nxd6+! Kh8 (3... Kf8?? 4 Nh7#) 4 Ndf7+ Kg8 5 Ne5+ Kf8 (5... Kh8?? 6 Nxg6#) 6 Ne6+ Ke8 7 Nxg7+ Kd8 (or 7... Kf8 is the same) 8 Ne6+ Ke8 9 Nxc7+ Rxc7 10 Kxe2 gives White a winning game.

After 1 Neg5, best for Black is likely 1... Bb7, supporting the knight on d5 and retaining a material and positional advantage.

Solution #5–Right of second refusal

Butch played **1… Qxf7** as a prelude to a *double* swindle. If White had taken the *first* bait with 2 Qxf7, Butch would have given perpetual check beginning with 2… Rh3+. Instead, White tried the strong **2 Rd7**, whereupon Butch attempted a second swindle with **2… Qxf6** (2 … Qxe6? 4 Rh7#). This time White accepted with **3 Qxf6?**.

Black to move

Black now counters White's aggressions with the stunning **3… Rh2+! 4 Kxh2 Rg2+ 5 Kh1 Rg1+**, after which White may either continue the perpetual checks or take the stalemate with **6 Rxg1**.

Best for White after 1… Qxf7 2 Rd7 Qxf6 is likely 3 Rh7+, giving away the rook and only then capturing the queen on f6. By employing this move order, White's queen guards f3, forfending perpetual check.

Solution #6—Live bait

Butch's **1... Rxf2** was a double bait, and White went for the queen with **2 gxh4?**.

Black to move

2... Rg2+ 3 Kh1 Rh2+, etc., now forces a draw by three-fold repetition.

Rather than 2 gxh4, White could have gone for the rook with **2 Kxf2**. Then it's **2 ... Bxg3+ 3 Nxg3 Qf4+ 4 Ke2 Qg4+ 5 Kf2**, etc., and another draw by three-fold repetition.

After 1... Rxf2, White's only winning move is the difficult-to-find 2 Qf7+!, when after 2 ... Rxf7 3 gxh4, White has a commanding lead in material.

Solution #7–A quiet sacrifice

With his **1... Nb4**, Butch had hoped for **2 Bxe5?**.

Black to move

Black now has **2... Rxc2+ 3 Kb1 Re2+! 4 Rd3** (4 Ka1 Nc2+ is perpetual check) **4... Bxd3+ 5 Kc1 Rc2+ 6 Kd1 Bxf1 7 Rxf1** (all other moves give Black a material advantage) **7... dxe5**, with the idea of... Rd8 and... Rc1+. For example, after **8 Rf2 Rd8+ 9 Ke1 Rc1+ 10 Ke2 Nc2 11 Rg2 Nd4+**, White must play very carefully to avoid a loss. A three-fold repetition of position arises after **12 Kd2 Rc5 13 Ke1 Rc1+ 14 Ke2**.

After 1... Nb4, correct for White is 2 Qxe5, holding on to the slim advantage of the extra pawn. Play might continue 2... Na2+ 3 Kd2.

Solution #8—Old dogs, dirty tricks

With his seemingly laconic **1... Ne4**, Butch tempted Melvin into **2 c8(Q)?** (2 Nxe4? Qxc4; 2 Qxe4? Qxc3 trades knights to no advantage).

Black to move

Black now forces a perpetual check: **2... Nf2+ 3 Kg1 Nh3+! 4 gxh3 Qf2+ 5 Kh1 Qf3+**, etc.

After 1... Ne4, winning for White is 2 h3 Qxc3 3 Qxc3 Nxc3 4 Rc1.

APPENDIX 3

Solution #9–Trash talkin'

In this complex position, Butch played **1... Nxg4**, hoping for any move by White other than 2 Rg8+!, winning:

    2... Kxg8 3 c8(Q)+, etc.
    2... Kf7 3 Be6+, etc.
    2... Kh6 3 Rxg6+, etc.

Happily, White accepted the offered queen with **2 Nxh4?**, and Butch drew.

Black to move

2... Rh2+ 3 Kg1 Rhg2+! 4 Nxg2 Rxg2+ 5 Kh1 (not 5 Kf1? Nh2#) **5... Rh2+** gives a three-fold repetition.

Solution #10—A sinister plan

Butch's **1... Qf4** wasn't much of a *queen* swindle, since 2 Qxf4? Bc6+ would have soon been mate. Butch probably hadn't held out much hope for that. The real question is: what had Butch planned to do, had White taken the *rook* with **2 Qxa8**?

Black to move

2... c6!! now forces a draw by perpetual check: **3 Bxa7** (White must give his king a flee square on g1) **3... Qf3+ 4 Kg1 Qg4+ 5 Kf1 Qf4+ 6 Bf2 Bh3+! 7 Ke1 Qe4+ 8 Kd2 Qd5+ 9 Bd4** (not 9 Kc2 Bf5#) **9... Qg2+ 10 Ke3 Qg5+ 11 Ke4 Qf5+**, etc.

Of the various winning moves for White after 1... Qf4, 2 Qg2 is probably strongest.

Solution #11—A meagre offering

After Butch's **1... Rxg2**, White really should have smelled a rat and not continued with **2 Kxg2**.

Black to move

Black now has **2... Qg4+ 3 Kh1 Qf3+**, with a draw by perpetual check.

After 2 Rfe1, Black is losing, with no way to hold on to all his hanging pieces.

Solution #12—A loss of the right rook

Butch's desperate **1 f5!?** had hoped for **1... Bxe3?**.

White to move

2 Rg7+ Kh6 3 Rh7+ Kxh7 is stalemate.

After 1 f5, Black need only avoid 1... d5?, when 2 Rc3 puts White in the driver's seat.

Solution #13—Law and order

With **1... Rf3!?** Butch threatened 2... Rxh3+ 3 gxh3 Qxh3#, so 2 d8(Q) was out of the question for his opponent. But then he fell for **2 gxf3?**.

Black to move

Black now has **2... Qxf3+**, with perpetual check after **3 Rg2** (not 3 Kh2? Be5+) **3... Qf1+**.

White's correct refutation to Black's offer of a rook is tricky to find. The answer is 2 Qg8+! Kxg8 3 d8(Q)+! (but not 3 e8(Q)+ Rf8, when White has nothing).

Solution #14—Hanging out the rook to dry

Butch attempted **1 Rd1!?** (1 cxb5+ is too soon, when Black has 1... Ka7! [1... Kxb5 2 Qxb7+ leads to perpetual] 2 b6+ Ka6 3 Qc4+ Ka5, and Butch is out of checks.) Then came the hoped-for **1... Qxd1?**.

White to move

Here, finally, **2 cxb5+** works! After **2... Ka7**, White has **3 Qa5+ Kb8 4 Qd8+**, with a perpetual. If instead Black tries **2... Kxb5**, then it's **3 Qc4+**, and Black may choose between a stalemate with 3... Kxc4 or a perpetual following moves like 3... Kb6 4 Qb5+!, etc.

After 1 Rd1!?, Black's clearest path to victory is 1... Rxb2+ 2 Kxb2 Rh2+ 3 Kc1 Qc3+ 4 Kb1 Qb2#.

APPENDIX 3

Solution #15—In a "tale-spin"

With Butch's **1... Rf2!?**, he had hoped for **2 Nxa8?**.

Black to move

After **2... Na4**, White cannot avoid perpetual check on b2, a2, and c2. Trying for more with a move like 3 Rdg2, getting the rook out of the way of the king, would lose: 3... Rxb2+ 4 Kc1 (4 Ka1 Nc3 and mates) 4... Rc2+ 5 Kd1 (5 Kc1 Nc3+ and mates) 5... Nc3+ 6 Ke1 b2 and mates on or soon after promotion.

After 1...Rf2, 2 Rxd5! wins nicely for White.

Solution #16—A matter of relocation

Down a full queen, Butch nefariously swindled away a rook as well with **1... Rc7!? 2 Qxc7**.

Black to move

Now **2... Rd1+ 3 Kf2 Rd2+ 3 Ke3 Rd3+ 4 Kf4 Bg5+ 5 Ke5 Bf6+ 6 Kf4** gives Black the draw by perpetual check.

Instead of taking the rook bait, the simple 2 Nxf3 removes all chance for counterplay.

Solution #17—Under construction

A tough-to-find swindle, Butch's **1 Rxf7!?** had hoped for **1... Qxf7**.

White to move

After **2 Qa3**, Black is now unable to avoid the three-fold repetition of checks starting with **2 ... Kc8 3 Qh3+ Kb8 4 Qa3**. It is worth nothing that inserting 2... Ba4 3 Qxa4 Kc8 4 Qg4+, etc. doesn't help matters, and that after 1... Qxd2, Black is outright losing: 2 Ra8+! Kxa8 3 Qa3+ Kb8 4 Qa7+ Kc8 5 Qa8#.

Correct, however, after 1 Rxf7 is 1... Qd4+, with a dominating position.

Solution #18–Hanging by a thread

Butch used **1... Rf3!?** to lure White into **2 Nxf3?**.

Black to move

Now **2... Nc3!!** draws, as **3 bxc3 b3! 4 cxb3 Qxc3+! 5 Kb1 Rxb3+! 6 axb3 Qxb3+** leads to perpetual check.

After 1... Rf3, strongest for White is 2 Nb3.

Solution #19—Searching for Bobby Fischer

In a truly tumultuous position, Butch[26] tried to gift Black a poisoned rook with **1 a4!?**. After the hoped-for **1... Qxa1+?**, Butch barely walked away with his life.

White to move

After **2 Kg2!**, White is planning Bh2+, threatening both Black's queen and a perpetual check. Black cannot address both. For example: **2... Qb2** (saving the queen) **3 Bh2+ Kc5 4 Bg1+** is perpetual. Or **2... Kxc7** (preventing perpetual) **3 Bh2+ Bd6 4 Rxa1** loses the queen, giving a relatively equal position.

Alternatively, **2... Kd7** tries but fails to escape the drawing net: **3 Nd4+ Kc8 4 Ba6+** with perpetual (not 4... Kxc7? 5 Bh2+, winning).

After 1 a4, correct for Black is 1... Qf6+ followed by... Kxc7 with advantage.

---

26 Braga v. Timman —Monika

Solution #20—Dogfight in the park

Butch shocked White with the insane **1... Raf6!?**, to which his opponent responded greedily with **2 gxf6?**.

Black to move

Now after **2... Rh3!**, all roads led to Drawville: **3 Rxh3 b4! 4 Rd2** (the threat is... h1(Q)+, forcing a stalemate; White is trying to give Black moves) **4... cxd2!** (not 4... h1(Q)+ 5 Raxh1 cxd5 6 c4, when White wins) **5 Bg4** (only move, but now Black throws it all to the wind and gets his stalemate after all) **5... d1(Q)+ 6 Bxd1 h1(Q)+ 7 Rxh1**—stalemate!

The safest path to a White victory after 1... Raf6 is 2 Re1.

Solution #21–A weighty decision

Butch baited his nemesis[27] with **1... Bd4** and drew after **2 Qxd4?**.

Black to move

2... Rxh2+ 3 Kxh2 Qh4+ 3 Kg2 Qg3+ 4 Kh1 Qh3+, etc., is a perpetual.

After 1... Bd4, 2 Qg2 would have preserved White's edge.

---

27 See the titanic Karpov vs. Kasparov 1990 WC match. —Monika

Solution #22—Working it out

Butch's desperate **1... Bc5+!?** had hoped for **2 Nxc5?**.

Black to move

Now it's **2... Rf7+!**, and after **3 Kxf7 Qg6+**, White can choose either a perpetual check or a stalemate, e.g., **4 Ke7 Qf7+ 5 Kd6 Qxd5+ 6 Kc7 Qc6+ Kxc6** or **3 Ke8 Rf8+ 4 Kxf8 Qf1+**, with the same outcome.

Correct for White after 1... Bc5+ is 2 Ke8. Black is left with no good checks, and White's extra material will tell.

Solution #23—A holiday hoodwink

A delicate and well-thought-out swindle transpired after Butch played **1... Bxf2+**, hoping for **2 Kxf2**.

Black to move

The point is that after **2... Rf1+**, White cannot avoid either a perpetual check or putting Black into stalemate. *With the white pawn on c3 instead of b2*, the following sequence wins: **3 Kg3 Rf3+ 4 Kh4 Rh3+** (not 4... Rf4+ 5 Rg4) **5 Kg4 Rh4+ 6 Kf3 Rf4+** (not 6... Rh3+ 7 Rg3) **7 Ke2 Re4+ 8 Kd2 Rd4+ 9 Kc2**, and the king is hidden.

But *with the pawn on b2*, the continuation of the trick doesn't work: **9... Rc4+ 10 Kb1 Rc1+ 11 Ka2 Ra1+ 12 Kb3 Rxa6 13 Rh2** (the h6 pawn was threatened) **13... Rg6!! 14 Ka2 Rg2! 15 Rh1 Rg1!**, etc.

Correct after 1... Bxf2+ is the simple 2 Kf3, when Black would be unable to hold on to his material.

Solution #24—Posing a threat

Butch got Black to fall for the very swindle-y **1 Bg5!? Rg3+ 2 Kh1 Rxg5?**.

White to move

And now it's a draw: **3 R1f7+** (the other rook would also work) **3... Rxf7** (3... Kh6?! is an interesting try, but after 4 Rxc7, White should be fine) **4 Rxf7+** with a draw by either stalemate (4... Kh6 5 Rxh7+) or perpetual check.

There was nothing wrong with 1... Rg3+, but after 2 Kh1 Black needs to play something like 2... Rg4.

Solution #25—Nothing changes on New Year's Day

Butch threw out **14. Bc6+!?** hoping for **1... Kxc6?**.

White to move

White obtains perpetual check with **2 Qc5+ Kxb7 3 Qb5+**, etc.

Winning for Black, after 14 Bc6+, is 1... Kc7 or 1... Kc8.

Solution #26–Subtle is the game

Butch tried **1... Bd7!?**, when White fell into **2 Rxd7?**.

Black to move

Black now has **2... Qg7+! 3 Rxg7** (3 Qg4!? Qxd7 and Black is okay) **3... Rxh3+!** with stalemate after White's next move!

Instead of 2 Rxd7, almost any other second move for White wins; 2 Qd5 is an example.

Solution #27–Divertissement

1 Bf5!? was a fun move for Butch to show his young pupil, pointing out that after **1 ... Qxf5?** ...

White to move

...White can bang out **2 Qxe7+! Nxe7 3 Rg7+ Kh8 4 Rg6+!**, and all lines draw for White, or better. (4... Rf6?! 5 Bxf6+ Qxf6 6 Rxf6 should be winning for White.)

After the key, Black does well to ignore the bait and go into a line like 1... Rc6 2 Bxe6 Rxc5 3 bxc5 Nxe6, when his extra pawns will tell.

Solution #28–Rodeo ruse

Butch's best swindle also happened to be his best chance, and **1... Bf6!? 2 exf6?** (not 2 Rxg8?? Qh4#) was followed by a draw.

Black to move

On **2... Rxg3+ 3 Qxg3 Qh1+**, White has no escape from perpetual check: **4 Kg4 Qxe4+ 5 Qf4 Qg2+ 6 Kh4 Qh1+ 7 Kg3 Qg1+ 8 Kf3 Qf1+ 9 Ke4 Qc4+**, etc.

After the key, White is winning with 2 Rg4!, when after 2... Rxg4 3 Kxg4!, there is no perpetual.

Solution #29–A game between friends

Butch[28] struck back in a losing position with **1 Bc7!!?**, setting Monika a tidy little task: all moves draw (or worse) but one, which, had Monika found it, would have put Butch in a much worse situation than he was before. Monika erred, however, with **1... Rxc7?** (not 1... Qxc7?? 2 Qf8#), giving Butch the draw.

White to move

A perpetual check now obtains after **2 Qd8+! Kg7 3 Qf6+ Kh6 4 Qh4+**, etc.

After 1 Bc7, only the move 1... Nf3!!, breaking up White's Q-R battery, gives Black the full point:

2 Qxf3 Qh5+ 3 Qxh5 gxh5 4 Rb1 Rxc7;

2 Rxf3 b1(Q)+, winning trivially;

2 Qd8+, and Black will be able to interpose her queen (thanks to her trusty knight on f3): 2... Qf8 3 Qxf8+ Kxf8 4 Bd6+ Kg8 5 gxf3 b1(Q)+ 6 Rxb1 Rxb1+ 7 Kg2 Rb3 and wins.

---

28 Kasparov v. Tukmakov —Monika

Solution #30—Playing up

After Butch's tricky **1... b6!?**, there was only one winning move for White, 2 Qe7!, allowing White to interpose a rook on e2 after... Qxc2+. But to make that move, White must first decline the free bishop on c6, menaced by both the rook and the queen. Butch's opponent instead played **2 Qxc6**, and the following draw ensued:

Black to move

2... Ne3+! 3 Rxe3 (if 3 Kf2 Ng4+ 4 Kg2 is perpetual; all other third moves lose for White) **3 ... Qf1+ 4 Kh2 Qh1+ 5 Kxh1**, and draw by stalemate.

Had White captured the poison bishop with the rook, the draw is similar: 2 Rxc6 Ne3+ 3 Kf2 (all other moves lose) 3... Ng4+ (not 3... Qd2+? 4 Kf3, and White is winning) 4 Kg2, with perpetual.

Appendix 3

Solution #31–Candidate moves

Butch's **1 a5!?** should not have been met with **1...Qxa5?**.

White to move

2 Rf5+ forces stalemate.

Almost any other response by Black would be winning.

Solution #32–The most scariest game

With **1... h3!**, Butch had hoped for **2 gxh3??**

Black to move

Now **2... Bc6+! 3 Qxc6 Rg1+ 4 Kxg1** is stalemate.

White is winning with almost any other response.

Solution #33—My craft and art

Butch's **1... e4!?** was worth the try—especially after White played **2 Bxe4?**.

Black to move

Black is stalemated after **2... Qe5+ 3 Qxe5**.

After 1... e4, correct for White is 2 Qf4+.

Solution #34—X marks the spot

With **1... d5!?**, Butch had hoped for **2 Qxd5?**.

Black to move

After the dizzying **2... Rxg3+!**, Black has the following array of draws:

3 Kxg3 Qxf4+, etc., with stalemate whenever White finally grabs the black queen.

3 fxg3 Qb2+ 4 Kh3 Qh2+, and like above.

3 Kf1 Qa1+! 4 Ke2 Re3+, and same as above after the capture of the rook.

To 1... d5, the orderly response 2 Rh5 is one of many winning paths for White.

Appendix 3

Solution #35—One for the birds

Butch[29] tried **1... g4!?**, looking for **2 hxg3?**.

Black to move

Now **2... Qg2+ 3 Ke3 Nd5+!** leads to **4 Bxd5 Qd2+ 5 Ke4 Qe3+** and stalemate. Alternatively, **4 Kd4 Qf2+ 5 Kxd5 Qd4+ 6 Ke6 Qf6+**, etc. results in stalemate or a perpetual.

After 1... g4, White wins with 2 Kg3, avoiding the check traps.

---

29 Jakovenko v. Gelfand —Monika

Solution #36—End-times prediction

Black provided a double bait with **1... b6!?**, after first making sure that either capture by White was wrong. 2 Qxa6 would have lost the game outright for White after 2... Nxd4+. But although Butch could not hope for his opponent to fall for *that* trick, he did succeed in baiting White into **2 Qxb6?**.

Black to move

Black has the following draw: **2... Qc1+ 3 Kd3** (not 3 Kb3? Qc3+ 4 Ka2 Qxd2+, etc.) **3 ... Nf4+ 4 Ke3 Ng2+ 5 Ke2 Nf4+**, etc.

Instead of capturing either pawn, 2 Qd5+ is probably the easiest path to the full point for White.

Appendix 3

Solution #37–Turning the tables

In a particularly exciting swindle, Butch's [30] **1 h4!?** provoked **1... Qxg3?**.

White to move

Here, **2 Qg8+! Kxg8** (all other moves end in mate) **3 Rxg7+! Kf8** (capturing the rook is stalemate) **4 Rf7+ Ke8 5 Re7+**, etc., secures a draw for White by perpetual check.

After 1 h4, Black is winning after either 1... Qg6 or 1... Re1+.

---

30 Evans v. Reshevsky —Monika

Solution #38—When the rook is in the seventh rank, and check aligns with pawns

Butch got Mercury to align with Mars with **1... Rg8!? 2 Rxb7??**.

Black to move

2... Rb8! forces **3 Rxb8** and a draw by stalemate.

With any reasonable second move, White is winning.

APPENDIX 3

Solution #39—These aren't the draws you're looking for

Butch's tricky **1 d4!?** hoped for, and got, **1... exd4?**.

White to move

The amazing **2 Bh6!!** draws, or better!:

2... gxh6? 3 Rg3+ Kf8 4 Qe5, and Black is losing, as the rook is trapped due to the looming threat of Rf3 (4... Rg8?? 5 Qf6+ Qf7 6 Qd8+ Qe8 7 Rf3+ Kg7 8 Qf6#).

2... Qe7 (the only saving move) **3 Rg3 Kf8** (3...g6? 4 Rxg6+ with mate to follow) **4 Rf3+** (there are other moves here as well) **4... Kf8 5 Rg3**, with a draw by three-fold repetition of position.

Multiple responses to 1 d4 would have worked for Black, 1... e4 being the easiest.

Solution #40–An imperfect storm

In desperation, Butch found **1... d2!?**, played in the hopes of **2 Qxd2?**.

Black to move

Now **2... Ne4+ 3 Kb6** (3 Rxe4 is stalemate) **3... Nxd2** leads to a draw: **4 Kxa6 Nc4 5 Kb5 Nxa5 6 Kxa5 Kg5**, with a hard-earned half-point for Black after the h-pawn gets traded for White's g-pawn and White eventually captures Black's remaining pawn with his rook.

After 1...d2, 2 Rh1+ Nh2 3 Rd1! gives White a winning position.

Solution #41—Dark Knight: a self-reflection in black and white

Butch[31] had no reason not to try **1... Nh6!**. The knight is poisoned, because after the unfortunate **2 gxh6?**, White's KB is on the wrong color!

Black to move

Black now easily draws with **2... Kh8**. His king cannot be ousted from the critical queening square by the impotent white bishop, which runs on the wrong color of squares.

It is noteworthy that, like the black knight on h6, the white pawn, too, is poisoned. If, after 2 gxh6?, Black errs with 2... Kxh6?, White can win despite his ill-colored bishop: 3 Kf6 Kh5 4 Bf5 Kh6 5 h3! (5 h4?? Kh5 and the pawn is lost) 5... Kh5 6 Kg7 Kg5 7 Bg4 Kh4 8 Kh6, driving the black king away, and running with the h-pawn to the finish line.

Rather than taking the knight, White can engineer a careful win with 2 h4. For example, 2... Nf7 3 Kf5 Nh6+ 4 Kf4 (getting the king out of check's way) 4... Nf7 5 Bd5 (covering the f7 and g8 squares) 5... Nh6 6 h5 Kh8 7 g6 Kg7 8 Kg5 Kh8 9 Ba2 (losing a tempo to end on e6 at the right time, covering the f5 and g4 squares; all knight moves will now be guarded, and the white king can advance) 9... Kg7 10 Be6 Kh8 11 Kf6, and the knight goes down.

---

31 Polgar v. ? —Monika

Solution #42–A well-suited end

After Butch's **1... Nf3+!?**, he had hoped for **2 Nxf3?**.

Black to move

Now **2... Qg1+! 3 Kh6** (3 Kh5 Qxh2+ 4 Kg5 Qh4+) **3... Qg5+!!** produces stalemate.

After 1... Nf3+, White mates quickly after 2 Kh6.

Solution #43—Catch as catch can

Butch's fiendish **1 Nf3!?** set up **1... gxf3?**.

White to move

After **2 Bh6**, Black is unable ever to make progress,[32] and the countdown to the fifty-move rule soon begins!

After 1 Nf3, winning for Black is, for example, 1... h5.

---

[32] It will take a computer engine a long time to realize this. —Monika

Solution #44—Skating on thin ice

With **1 Nf5!?**, Butch had hoped for **1... Rxf5?**.

White to move

Here, **2 Qe8+ Rf8 3 Rxg6+ hxg6 4 Qxg6+** brings a draw by three-fold repetition.

After 1 Nf5, Black should simplify: 1... Rxd6 2 Nxd6 Qxd7, etc.

Solution #45–By dawn's early light

Butch had offered his knight with **1 Na3!?** in the hopes of **1... bxa3?**.

White to move

Now comes **2 Qa6!**, and Black cannot escape the draw: **2... Kg7** (the greedy 2... Qxb3? 3 Qxg6+ is a perpetual) **3 Qxa7+ Rf7** (3... Kh6 4 Qe7 Ra8 5 h4!) **4 Rb7 Rxb7 5 Qxb7+ Kh6 6 Qb8**, and the queen comes to f8 for the perpetual.

Instead of capturing the poisoned knight, 1... fxe4 is crushing.

Solution #46–Shades of the past

The ridiculous looking **1... Re7!?** hoped to trick White into taking a free knight: **2 Rxd5?**.

Black to move

Black now has **2... Re1+ 3 Kf2 Qf4+! 4 Kxe1 Qc1+ 5 Ke2 Qxb2+! 6 Kd3 Qb1+ 7 Kc4 Qa2+**, etc., with a perpetual check.

After the key, White wins by various means, the easiest probably being 3 g3, leaving Black's knight truly *en prise*.

Solution #47—A pretty situation

After **1 Nxb5!?**, Butch's knight was poisoned, and Black bit: **1... cxb5?**

White to move

Now White has **2 Rc8+! Bxc8 3 Bc6+ Kf8** (3... Qxc6?? 4 Qd8#) **4 Be7+ Kg7** (4... Kxe7?? 5 Qd7#) **5 Qg4+ Kh6 6 Bf8+ Rxf8 7 Qh3+ Kg5 8 Qxg2+ Kf5 9 Qe4+ Kg5 10 Qg2+**, and a draw by perpetual.

After 1 Nxb5, almost any other move wins for Black.

Solution #48—Sonic warfare

With **1 Nxd3!** (the swindle was the best try), Butch tried to set up a fortress, if only Black would be so kind as to capture the knight with **1... Qxd3**. Black did so.

White to move

Now, not 2 Rxd3?? Kxd3, when of course Black wins. Instead, after 1... Qxd3?, White astonishes with **2 Rxa4+! Kd5 3 Rxh4**. The rook then goes to h3, creating a position that is impenetrable so long as White plays carefully, moving his king back and forth between h2 and g2 and his rook between h3, g3, f3, and e3. A draw by fifty-move rule is inevitable.

On the other hand, after 1 Nxd3, Black needs to find 1... h3+!. The pawn cannot be accepted: 2 Kxh3? Qxd3+, etc. White's best try is 2 Kh2, hoping Black doesn't find 2... Kb5!!, placing White in zugzwang. White must move the king. But if 3 Kxh3, Black has 3... Qc8+! 4 [any] Qf8!, when any rook move will be met with an appropriate check on the g-file. The rook is lost.

Solution #49—The thing in yellow

1... Nxa4!? was an ingenious piece of bait set by Butch, meant to provoke **2 Rxa4?**.

Black to move

After **2... Rxa4! 3 Kxa4 g4!!**, all continuations draw. For example, **4 fxg4 fxg4 5 Kb4 h5 6 Kc3** (not 6 Kc4?? h4 and Black wins!: 7 Kd4 g3 8 hxg3 h3!, etc.) **6... h4 7 Bb5** (forced, as there is no way to hold d5 without Black queening as before) and now **7... Kxd5**, closing in on White's last pawn: **8 Bf1 Ke4 9 Bg2+ Ke3 10 Bc6 Kf2 11 Kd3 Kg1 12 Bd7** and draws.

Alternatively, had White played 4 Kb4 gxf3 5 Kc3 f2 6 Bb5 Kxd5 7 Kd2, etc., White would have retained the rook pawn to no avail, as its queening square does not match the color orientation of the bishop!

After 1...Nxa4, White's strongest continuation is likely 2 Rd8+, leaving Black worse off than before the key move.

Solution #50—Existence precedes essence

After **1 Nf4!?** from Butch, perhaps his opponent was absurdly afraid of 2 Qh8+ Ke7 3 Nxg6+ and mates. But there was no cause for fear. He could simply have played 1... Kg5, with a triple fork of Butch's pieces. Instead, Black chose **1... Qxf4?**.

White to move

Here, **2 Qd8+ Re7** (2... Kg7?? 3 Qh8#) **3 Qh8+ Kg5 4 Rh5+! gxh5 5 Qxh5+ Kf6 6 Qh8+** is a perpetual. (Or, if the reader prefers, eternal recurrence.)

"Butch rifled through the papers greedily."

APPENDIX 4

♞ h8 ♞

KING BUTCH AND THE BARD

BUTCH WROTE THE following play while being held against his will in the basement of Master Lin's Kung Fu Studio. It was performed for the first time in Tomas Perfiliev's back yard. Tomas played the role of Borachenko, Lisa was Natalie, Monika was Elijah the black king and Andre the black pawn, Martin was Elmer the white king and Albert the white pawn, Xiang was the Chorus and Rochambeau. Butch portrayed himself.

APPENDIX 4

THE HUSTLER OF GREENWICH

DRAMATIS PERSONAE

CHORUS, *a group of onlookers and tourists*
ELMER, *the white king*
ELIJAH, *the black king*
ALBERT, *a white pawn*
ANDRE, *a black pawn*
ROCHAMBEAU, *a chess hustler*
BUTCH, *a chess hustler, himself*
BORACHENKO, *an opponent*
NATALIE, *his wife*

Scene: *Winter, Washington Square Park*

Enter CHORUS, *standing in a huddle*

CHORUS

> If swindles be the move of kings, play on!
> Lend us delight in dubious devices,
> In sleights of mind and slick artifices,
> The footwork of wood and knackish contraption.
> Give us excess of it that, surfeiting,
> We may sustain as is befitting,
> The grey repute of these poor,
> These clever poor, these street magicians, or,
> With due dose of our privileged contrition,
> We may to warmth and roasted nutrition.
> At last make some rare move, and for a lark,
> For 'tis bitter cold, and we are long at park.

Enter ELMER, ELIJAH, ALBERT, ANDRE, *and assorted chessmen*

ELMER (*to* ELIJAH)

>   Our crowns be blessed, rum friend, the time returns!
>   And ever as anon, to me shall move
>   Sweet victory!

ELIJAH
>   Thy moves are like to wind
>   From old men's beans. The vict'ry shall be mine!

ALBERT (*aside*)
>   'Tis good to be as kings, that knoweth how
>   Each color is to fall, ere the pieces
>   Take their stand.

ANDRE
>   Or e'en before the players
>   Be at hand!

ALBERT
>   Aye, 'tis good to be the king.

ANDRE
>   But soft! The carnal kings are coming.

Enter ROCHAMBEAU *and* BUTCH, *sitting down at their chess tables*

ROCHAMBEAU
>   Another day, another dollar.
>   How urge thee to the flock, dear Butch?
>   What wide word to wag the wit?

BUTCH
>   O, love a throng!
>   Regard with me in apt representation
>   How to one word, *moon*, two moons give answer:
>   One, subject behold'n to beholder's eye,

Round like wheel, driving day's silver gloaming
Into night's cold pitch, draining poet's ink,
And filling lover's het up eyes with star-spun light.
Two, akin to One as fire to Plato's Shadow,
An object of mass and extension,
By astronomer's sharp compass dropped,
Fallen through force of logic's gravity
From heav'n to Copernicus's notebook.
Round as rich man's paunch, his power tasted
In measure by which he turns to back-turned face
Those black acts he will, and heaves to orbit
About a planet of men those bright deeds
He wills his world to view. Sooth, I would as lief
My urban lily planted in this downtown field
Toil in pastimes and spin for daily bread,
Than cast to silent space a mite of my days.
Nay, who amongst high rank wouldst give dispute?

ROCHAMBEAU

As Black must follow White, by my game
Thou speakst aright.

CHORUS

Sing the city, which has to us confirmed
All answers to our pre-ordained petitions!
Look good courtesy upon these poor friends,
Denizens all, most base and Ethiop,
Five to ten on substances quite illicit.
What faith be flattered, that we should find here
Such fine industry for legal tender
And excess tenderness! Which shall engage?

Enter BORACHENKO *and* NATALIE, *stepping forward*

BORACHENKO

Marry, shall I so. An my Slavic blood give me no small favor over one of chance circumstance, I on an oath must grow pale, and as one who is green to the world verily eat this hat and walk myself to school. Sweet Natalie, do for a beat lay off the selfies.

NATALIE

'Slid! And as well on our long-designed venture to the apple of this new world's eye! Mark me, man, before the sun benights our return and those of easy friendship grey our stoop, wilt thou praise me for taking such sweet memories. Know thee how thine eyes do love to feast upon thyself near as much as to me.

BORACHENKO

The less thy cloth, the more thy frame than mine.

NATALIE

Prithee, turn off and lay on.

BORACHENKO

(*Aside*) Forsooth shall I play, an once I gain certain assurances from yon dark-brooding fellow.
(*To* BUTCH) Pray, what be thy terms of engagement?

BUTCH

So please thee, sir, five dollars.
(*Aside*) And now will this loving tourist treat of me with interrogations most offensive. Such will I bear under, the chief hardship of this my profession, coming short of freezing in winter, baking in summer, and soaking whene'er grey skies rip open.

BORACHENKO

If me thou best, the buck to thee shall pass. But what oath can now thee,
That should the score be mine, the buck shall pass to me?

BUTCH

Methinks these words befit one darkly favored,

Nor would be put to one less darkly flavored.

BORACHENKO
Thy words bite air.

BUTCH
Come, let us measure kings. As surely turns
Our game, so by my word shall flow the dough.

CHORUS
By our patience, something to watch! In hope,
The game be not so dreadful as the parley.

A game of chess begins between BUTCH *and* BORACHENKO

ELMER (to ELIJAH)
I pass my water in thy castles' moats
And physic thy horses on sweet purgatives!
The white pieces shall prevail!

ELIJAH
                    Nay, the black!

ALBERT
Mewonders to whom which color shall go?

ANDRE
'Twas wisely read in heav'n when gods did grant
Our speech to pierce no fleshly ear, else such speech
Would red'n my face, could wood turn fleshly here.

ALBERT
By same heav'n's will, what fools these mortals be!

ELMER
To the mate! Now see thee, dog, the high hand

Of the white cav'lry!

ELIJAH
All thou sayst is false
For thee and true for me!

ALBERT
By my troth,
I would, i' faith, put odds on Black.

ANDRE
b2 or not b2? That is the question.

ALBERT
Taken all in all, I have seen better moves.

NATALIE
Though board and bard be Greek to me, many pictures shall bring many friends to see. To Facebook shall I with these. Sayst cheese!

BORACHENKO
Nay, nay, sweet Natalie. 'Tis a tradition more honored in the breach than in the observance. Prithee, stand off.

BORACHENKO *attempts to swindle* **BUTCH** *by adjusting a piece onto an incorrect square*

BUTCH (*aside*)
Swift send a runner: does the Bishop of Rome
Yet practice Sunday mass, while Monday's bear
Take leave of his woods to find his relief?
If so and if not, on what day falling
Ere Wednesday's dawn and past Tuesday's dusk
Will such a one as this tourist teach to me
The tread and turn of this my toilsome trade?
The knave's knight from f3 now on g3 sits,

And I am willed to whistle 'neath this elm
And throw elderly comment to the breeze?
Such greenery shall not be so greenly returned,
Nor an eye paid for eye, but as the whip
Multiplies the trick of the groundward wrist,
E'en to break of sound, so shall I extend
My master stroke, and with no less sharp crack
Than found at rope's end.

ANDRE
                      O cankerous scab!

Pox and contagion! My earlier words
That blessed the myst'ry of our wooden speech
I would now rescind, and with ample voice
Sound alert to our imperiled master!

ALBERT
    Alas, that we are but pawns, mere players
In a world too wide for our lean means
To bear effect!

ANDRE
                      All the board's a stage
And all the kings and pieces merely players.
They have their advances and their retreats,
And one pawn in his time plays many parts,
His acts being seven stages. At first, the dead wood,
Groaning and bumping in the satchel's cloth,
Then the hopeful youth, with his hastened cut
At game's bright morning, charging like cheetah
Unerringly to center. Then the lever,
Passing like neighbor with a kindly rumor
Made to slow the enemy's plans. Then foot soldier,
Full of honor, working for least wages,
Born defender, sudden and quick to expand,

Awakening the men in the rear,
E'en by the cannon's mouth. Then lusty summer,
The criminal, to be kept under lock and key,
Unappealing to those of higher rank,
Yet a candidate worth his due respect.
And so he plays his part. The sixth age shifts
Into the lean and studied endgame,
With kings at his side, and rook behind,
His youthful pose well-kept, a board too brief
For his storming surge and passing swagger,
Rushing once more toward far ebon shore, luff
And plundered file in his wake. Last scene of all,
That ends this strange eventful history,
Is second birth and queenly metamorphosis,
With rank, with file, with slope, with everything.

ALBERT
    A speech most moving. Let us to the din.

BUTCH *swindles* BORACHENKO *by capturing the adjusted piece from its correct square*

BORACHENKO
    What giveth?

BUTCH
    That only which thou prior minute gave.

BORACHENKO
    Annul thy move, for thou canst nothing prove.

BUTCH
    Mayhap the camera's eye shall our matter
    Settle? Shall we consult sweet Natalie?

BORACHENKO

APPENDIX 4

    The game and the purse are yours. They are as nothing to me.

Exit BORACHENKO

CHORUS
    Nothing comes from nothing. Our excess
    We have had. To Starbucks, we!

Exit CHORUS

NATALIE (*to audience*)
    And thus with end of game comes end of play.
    Betwixt ourselves, I shall to road repair
    With for company one bruisèd husband's
    Ego; and to you, audience fair, remit
    Your lives with one less hour to claim for it.
    As all good games comprise good moves, so must
    Good plays comprise good words. What sorrow, ours,
    That these masters of their crafts have swindled us
    From hope of both. But let us now leave blame,
    And oft to park to play the royal game.

Exeunt

King Butch And The Bard

WRITING BLACK TO MOVE AND DRAW

The morning after Thanksgiving, 2015, I woke up laughing, and that's how *Black to Move and Draw* got its start. I had just published *Public & Private Space*, so maybe not having *that* weight on my shoulders anymore had put me in a particularly capricious mood. I was at my sister- and brother-in-law's place—"down the shore," as they like to say in Jersey—and there's always something about being next to open water that inspires me. So maybe that was it. One way or another, I woke up thinking about a story my brother had told me years before.

Alan's a decent chess player—perhaps on par with the narrator of the book you've just read—and one day he (my brother, not my main character) calls me up to tell me about a game he had recently played. He had been losing badly, in the kind of situation where you're getting ready to topple your king and ask for another game. He describes the position to me a little; then, he says, he noticed he could "throw his rook out there." Just some dumb square, no reason for the move—but no reason his opponent should bother with the rook, either. In fact, if his opponent *does* take it, well, it's mate next move. And that's indeed what happened—the guy took the rook. My brother swindled him, pure and simple. What we're basically talking about here, dear Reader, is the chess equivalent of Curly from the Three Stooges (*nyuk! nyuk! nyuk!*) going up to a boxer in the ring, pointing at something over his shoulder ("Hey! What's *that*?"), and then sucker-punching the guy when he looks.

I got a chuckle out of the story and stored it away.

Years later, the only slight modification I made to my brother's story, in order to adapt it for use by my chess-hustling protagonist, Butch, was to replace the opponent's accidental and abrupt loss with a *draw*. I don't remember anymore why, exactly, I did this, other than that the puzzles I started working on came out more interesting that way.

If you're wondering about those puzzles, by the way, many of them are derivative of positions I found in various Fred Reinfeld manuals, while others spun from games I came across in databases. A third source of material was simply the kind of ad hoc discovery that a chess lover naturally encounters while futzing around on the board.

If you've already read *White to Move and Lose*, you've seen me do this before—wrap a story around a set of chess puzzles. This time, however, I wanted to produce a novel-length story. (*White*, at roughly thirty-five thousand words, classifies as a novella.) The effort took me nearly five years, during which time I also wrote a large chunk of a nonfiction book on chess parenting that I intend to publish in the next couple years, as well as the first half of a short story collection, also pending. But most of my writing efforts have been spent on this book.

It turns out I'm mostly a seat-of-the-pants kind of writer. Little of what you've just read was plotted or outlined. (Although bear in mind the magic of backfilling.) Stephen King's *On Writing* is my go-to manual regarding everything related to the craft, so it makes sense I should write this way, in his unplotted style. Therefore, if you came across something in this book that was well-thought-out, and which generally conveyed a sense of order and reason, the person you'll want to thank for that is my brilliant and patient editor, Nicole Klungle. Other places, you'll know you were looking at something where I ignored her advice.

My daughter, Mallory, made herself constantly available as I ramblingly developed the story, and she also alpha-read my first draft. My wife, Laura, read closer to the other end of the pipeline. All my love belongs to both of you.

Every inch along that same pipeline, my Writers' Circle has been there, cheering me on—so thank you, Amanda, Amber, Bill, Cel, Daniel and Rosie, Dave, Dawn, Eric, Erin, Janet, Jennifer, John, Karla, Magda, Nick, Phil, Roopa, and Taylor. You guys are the best.

The novel centers around drugs and would never have gotten off the ground without Ali Thompson, who helped me understand various information regarding effects and side effects. The book also has a thing or two to say about chess hustlers, so a thank-you goes out to a certain player who maybe told me a thing or two about drug use and the chess scene in New York City parks.

When my characters needed to precisely navigate around town on buses and subways, my friend Mark Abramowitz was there to help. My sister-in-law "down the shore," Michele Pierro, gave me frank insights into seasonal changes in the big city, while Michael, my brother-in-law, assisted with fire escapes and emergency responder protocols. I hope I got it right.

In the realm of professional production, I want to thank David Craig for the awesome illustrations, as well as Chrissie from Damonza, who went back and forth with me nineteen times to get that front cover just right.

Finally, thank you, Alan, for throwing your rook out there.

Kevin Stokker
Home, under Covid-19 shelter-in-place orders
Memorial Day, 2020